Y0-BCM-165

Soviet and Kosher

ANNA SHTERNSHIS

Soviet and Kosher

Jewish Popular Culture in the Soviet Union, 1923–1939

INDIANA UNIVERSITY PRESS

Bloomington and Indianapolis

This book is a publication of

Indiana University Press
601 North Morton Street
Bloomington, IN 47404-3797 USA

http://iupress.indiana.edu

Telephone orders 800-842-6796
Fax orders 812-855-7931
Orders by e-mail iuporder@indiana.edu

© 2006 by Anna Shternshis

All rights reserved

No part of this book may be reproduced or utilized in any form or by any means, electronic or mechanical, including photocopying and recording, or by any information storage and retrieval system, without permission in writing from the publisher. The Association of American University Presses' Resolution on Permissions constitutes the only exception to this prohibition.

The paper used in this publication meets the minimum requirements of American National Standard for Information Sciences—Permanence of Paper for Printed Library Materials, ANSI Z39.48–1984.

Manufactured in the United States of America

Library of Congress Cataloging-in-Publication Data

Shternshis, Anna.
    Soviet and kosher : Jewish popular culture in the Soviet Union, 1923–1939 / Anna Shternshis.
        p. cm.
    Includes bibliographical references and index.
    ISBN 0-253-34726-2 (cloth : alk. paper) — ISBN 0-253-21841-1 (pbk. : alk. paper)
    1. Jews—Soviet Union—History. 2. Jewish communists—Soviet Union. 3. Jews—Identity—Soviet Union.
4. Jews—Soviet Union—Social conditions. 5. Jews—Soviet Union—Intellectual life. 6. Popular culture—Soviet
Union. 7. Yiddish literature—Soviet Union—History and criticism. I. Title.
    DS135.R9S5227 2006
    305.892′404709042—dc22

                                                                                            2005026653

1 2 3 4 5   11 10 09 08 07 06

To my grandparents: Faina Hromaya, Isaac Zimmerman,
Charna and Zus Shternshis

Contents

Acknowledgments

My grandparents, Faina Hromaya and Isaac Zimmerman, met in Lenskorun, Ukraine, at a village gathering, where Isaac's family was condemned for being kulaks (rich men). Like everyone else at the meeting, my grandmother voted to exclude Isaac from the Komsomol. The next month she followed him to Moscow, where they married. Decades later, when she rocked my sister and me to sleep, she would sing us Yiddish songs that she had learned in her youth; her favorite one was about a beautiful girl named Beyle, who left her husband because he was not a Communist. My father's parents, Charna and Zus Shternshis, also spoke Yiddish and observed some Jewish traditions and holidays at home. Zus's five siblings were able to leave the Soviet Union in the mid-1920s to settle in Palestine. Yet these aspects of the family history were kept secret, and, on the outside, my father's parents looked like average Soviet citizens.

My interest in Soviet Jewish culture was inspired by my grandparents, even though as a child I could not understand Yiddish and had no idea that the special dinner they served every spring was a version of the Passover seder. Nor did I know that when my grandmother kissed the upper corner of the door three times when entering and leaving the house she was acknowledging the nonexistent mezuzah.

Only several years after my grandparents passed away, it became possible to openly study Jewish culture, history, and tradition in Russia. I thank Professor David Fishman for organizing and maintaining Project Judaica, a joint undergraduate program between the Jewish Theological Seminary, the YIVO Institute for Jewish Research, and the Russian State University of Humanities in Moscow during the turbulent year of 1991. I was fortunate to be among the first graduates of this unique program, which brought professors of Jewish studies from the United States, France, England, and Israel to Russia. The wonderful, devoted instructors opened a world of Jewish history, culture, and language for some twenty undergraduate Russian students, and inspired many of us to continue into graduate programs in the field of Jewish studies. I was especially inspired by the lectures of Zvi Gitelman and Mordekhai Altshuler. Peysakh Fiszman, Dov Ber Kerler, Sheva Zucker, Gennady Estraikh, David Roskies, Mikhail Krutikov, and the late Shimon Sandler made me fall in love with Yiddish language and literature.

I thank Gennady Estraikh and Mikhail Krutikov for encouraging me to start working on a serious research project on Jewish popular culture in the Soviet Union. I thank Gerald Stanton Smith for supporting me at all stages of my research, for his patience, advice, and guidance, and for his belief in me. His deep understanding of Russian culture helped me to think in depth about the context of Jewish popular culture in the Soviet Union. Without Gerry, this book would never have been written. Zvi Gitelman helped in many more ways than he will ever acknowledge, including sharing his tremendous knowledge of Soviet Jewish history and culture, introducing me to the method of oral history, helping me to crystallize my arguments, and even arranging a match with my future husband!

Yoav Alon, Helen Beer, Sholem Berger, Joel Berkowitz, Motya Chlenov, Barbara Henry, Gennady Estraikh, Zvi Gitelman, Anat Helman, Catriona Kelly, Mikhail Krutikov, Nathan Lulov, Ezra Mendelsohn, Alice Stone Nakhimovsky, Edna Nakhshon, David Rechter, Robert Rothstein, David Shneer, Michael Steinlauf, Jeffrey Veidlinger, and an anonymous reviewer from Indiana University Press read different parts of this book in various stages. I thank them for their comments, constructive criticism, and advice. I thank Kalman Weiser for his advice about some Yiddish translations. Of course, any mistakes and problems in this book are solely my responsibility.

The Rabbi Israel Miller Fund for Shoah Research, Documentation and Education of the Conference on Jewish Material Claims Against Germany, Inc., generously funded the oral history research for this book. Igor Akselrod, Dmitrii Morgulis, Ella Shakhnikova (Berlin), Vladimir Oks (Potsdam), and Leonid Essen (Moscow) facilitated the project. Yoseph Wisse helped to conduct group and street interviews in New York. I thank Lara and Oleg Troyanovsky for hosting me in New York in August 1999, and for helping me to find respondents. Oleg's grandmother Sofiya Lipkina introduced me to many informants, and also fed me between interviews! I thank Svetlana Brodetskaya, Julia Shternshis, and Bella Shternshis for transcribing the oral history interviews. Bella Shternshis also helped to categorize and systematize the data.

On the financial side, many institutions supported this research. The Ian Karten Charitable Trust awarded me the first grant. I was also a recipient of the Wingate Scholarship, the AVI Fellowship, Anglo-Jewish Association grants, Jewish Widows and Students grants, the British Federation of Women Graduates grants, St. Antony's College bursaries, and the Kennan Institute for Advanced Russian Studies fellowship, travel grants from the Modern Languages Faculty at Oxford University, St. Antony's College, the Tell Scholarship awarded by the Jewish Research Institute (YIVO) fellowship (U.S.), the Ian Karten Charitable Trust, travel grants by the Joint Initiative of DAAD and the University of Toronto, the Dean's Travel Fund at University of Toronto, the Department of Germanic Languages and Literatures travel grant, and the generous assistance of Neil Kummer (Israel).

I thank the Center for Advanced Judaic Studies at the University of Pennsylvania for awarding me a fellowship in 2000/2001. The weekly seminars conducted by the Center were extremely enriching, and I thank Charles Dellheim, Anat Helman, Kathryn Hellerstein, Jon Karp, Barbara Kirshenblatt Gimblett, Mark Kligman, Ezra Mendelsohn, Benjamin Nathans, David Ruderman, David Stern, Judith Tissen, Nina Warnke, and Carol Zemel for stimulating discussions and for their help in situating Soviet Jewish culture in the context of the general relationship between modern Jewry and Arts. I wish to express sincere gratitude to David Ruderman for creating and running this intellectual forum.

For facilitating this research I thank the Russian State Archive (GARF), the Russian State Archive of Socio-Political History (RGASPI), the Russian State Library (formerly Lenin's Library), The Vernadsky National Library of Ukraine (especially Mila Sholokhova), the YIVO Institute for Jewish Research (in particular, Lisa Epstein), the New York Public Library, and the African and Middle Eastern Division of the Library of Congress.

The Department of Germanic Languages and Literatures at the University of Toronto has hosted me since 2001, and I thank all my colleagues there for their interest in this book, especially James Retallack, John Noyes, and John Zilcosky. I also thank Jacques Kornberg, Andrea Most, David Novak, and Derek Penslar of the Jewish Studies Program; and Susan Solomon and Peter Solomon of the Center for European, Russian, and Eurasian Studies for their support and encouragement.

Some earlier parts of chapters 1 and 2 appeared in *East European Jewish Affairs* as the following: "From the Eradication of Illiteracy to Workers' Correspondents: Yiddish-Language Mass Movements in the Soviet Union," *East European Jewish Affairs* 33, no. 1 (2002): 120–37; and "Passover in the Soviet Union, 1917–41," *East European Jewish Affairs* 31, no. 1 (summer 2001): 61–76. I thank Howard Spiro for permission to reprint that material here.

I thank Janet Rabinowitch at Indiana University Press for believing in this book and supporting it all the way. I also thank Rebecca Tolen and Dawn Ollila of Indiana University Press for their professionalism and patience while working on this project. I thank Rita Bernhard and Janet Hyer for editing the manuscript.

My husband, Dan Rosenberg, not only painstakingly edited the book before it was sent to the press, but he also made writing it fun. Our children, Isaac and Shana, born during the latter stages of the book, deserve credit for helping me to focus and to put everything into perspective. I thank my parents, Bella and Arkady Shternshis, and my sister, Julia, for giving me the courage to start and to finish this work. Their help ranged from finding books and documents in Moscow, and then urgently e-mailing me the scanned copies, to moral support and encouragement. The book is an attempt to understand my grandparents' culture and identity. It is also a tribute to their memory and therefore is dedicated to them.

Introduction: Sara F.'s Kosher Pork

"This is how to cook kosher pork; it is really quite easy," remarks Sara F., an eighty-two-year-old resident of Brooklyn. Sara was born in Derzazhnya, a small town in Ukraine. She explains that Jewish religious laws (which prohibit the consumption of pork) do not matter to her, "because only a Jewish soul can make food kosher."[1] Sara has never been inside a synagogue and does not celebrate any Jewish holidays. She cannot recite a single Jewish prayer. Every year she commemorates the anniversary of the October Revolution (November 7), New Year's Eve, and May Day. Yet three decades ago Sara insisted that her three children marry Jews, and now she is extremely concerned about the love life of her grandson. "God forbid, he will go out with a *shikse* [somewhat derogatory term for a non-Jewish girl]," she says about her twenty-five-year-old grandson.

Sara speaks fluent Yiddish (with an authentic Ukrainian dialect), loves to read short stories by the famous Yiddish writer Sholem Aleichem, and enjoys singing Yiddish folk songs, especially the sentimental "Papirosn" (Cigarettes).[2] She was especially happy when her son took her to see a new production at Folksbine, the only Yiddish-language theater in New York. Sara evaluates all contemporary world events by considering, "Is it good or bad for the Jews?"

Sara's Jewish identity is full of apparent contradictions. On the one hand, she is almost militantly negative toward Jewish religious traditions, and yet she is extremely attached to Yiddish language, Yiddish songs, and especially Yiddish theater. Why did Sara mention the word "kosher" when describing her pork? Why would the notion of kosher even come up in the conversation? Why does she want her grandson to marry a Jew, while at the same time, strongly oppose his Jewish education in a New York yeshiva (which she considers "fanatical")? What is it about Sara's Jewishness that makes her so different from Jews of her generation from any other part of the world? And what precisely makes her "Jewish"?

Zvi Gitelman asserts that post-Soviet Jews maintain a "thin" culture, and thus their Jewishness is based on feelings, memories, and shared experiences without the "thick culture" of language, religion, customs, food, dress, music, and ethnic neighborhoods.[3] The transformation of the Russian Jewish identity of the 1920s from a "thick" to a "thin" culture took only one generation. Sara belongs to the "transitional" generation, whose parents largely led a traditional Jewish way of life, and whose children were "fully-formed," "thin-cultured" Jews, usually without any knowledge of Jewish languages and traditions. Post-Soviet Jews, including Sara's children and grandchildren, completely disassociate Jewishness from Judaism. A recent sociological survey conducted in the late 1990s revealed that less than 1 percent of post-Soviet Jews think that knowledge of Judaism, observance of the Sabbath and kashrut (Jewish dietary laws), and circumcision are relevant to being "a good Jew."[4]

Rapid industrialization, urbanization, and change of occupations were perhaps the most important factors in this transformation. Still, the Soviet cultural programs directed at Jews reached their targeted audiences and helped to develop a positive ethnic identity associated with the Soviet regime. This identity, though short-lived, was almost universal among Soviet Jews of the interwar period, and played an important role in how Jewish consciousness has been transmitted to subsequent generations. The examination of its features reveals implications of Soviet policies toward nationalities during the interwar period and of Soviet society in general.

The study of Soviet Jewish identity of the interwar period also opens new dimensions in our understanding of Jewish culture around the world. The question of whether Jews can exist without Judaism is mainly relevant in twenty-first-century Russia, as well as in countries in Western Europe and North America. Attempts to create a secular Jewish society did not start and end in the Soviet Union. East End London Jewish radicals conducted Yom Kippur balls in the late nineteenth century, and the New York Workmen's circle hosted a "humanistic" nonreligious Passover Seder in 2004. Moreover, secular identity dominates modern Western Jewish communities, even though no other country in the world has ever created a government apparatus devoted to secularizing its Jews. The difference between "natural" and "forced" secularization is the resulting nature of this new secular identity. For example, a significant number of modern North American Jews, just like their Russian counterparts, refuse to think of the ultra-Orthodox as model co-religionists, yet many Americans (unlike Russians) celebrate Passover and Rosh Hashanah, and attend synagogues on Yom Kippur.[5] While many American Jews do not strictly observe the laws of kashrut, most know that pork is not kosher, whether prepared by a Jew or not. Yet, in the vocabulary of the Soviet Jews who lived through the government policies of the 1920s and 1930s, the word "kosher" means something that "Jews do" (this applies to secular, religious, and even antireligious activities). If a Jew prepares pork, and eats it in a company of Jews, it is "kosher pork." The word "kosher" in the title of the book refers to this unorthodox definition of kashrut.

Arnold Eisen and Steven Cohen concluded that American Jewish identity is a matter of picking and choosing rituals and practices that seem suitable for various individuals.[6] Ironically Soviet Jews did not consciously choose their Jewish practices. They had to deal with the fact that their ethnicity was recorded in their internal passports, which became mandatory identification documents for all Soviet citizens starting in 1932. The much discussed "fifth point" (nationality) in the Soviet passport probably played the most important role (comparable only to popular antisemitism) in maintaining a conscious ethnic identity among Jews during the entire Soviet period. However, Soviet cultural policies directed toward Jews, conducted in the 1920s and 1930s, largely shaped the content of this identity.

Soviet Yiddish Culture in 1921–1939

In 1917 the majority of Russia's Jews lived in the cities and shtetlach (small Jewish towns or villages) of the former Pale of Settlement, and over 90 percent spoke Yiddish on a daily basis.[7] In 1918, soon after the Bolsheviks came to power, organizations designed to "Sovietize" the Jews economically and culturally were established. These were the Jewish sections (*Evsektsii*) of the Communist Party, which functioned until 1930,[8] and the more short-lived Jewish Commissariat (*Evkom*), which operated until 1924. Their leaders saw the Yiddish language as the only medium with which to reach out to the Jewish masses and encouraged Jewish intellectuals to compose popular works in Yiddish.[9] The Yiddish language itself was reformed several times during the Soviet period, initially with the goal of systematizing the spelling, including phonetic spelling of words of Hebrew origin, and later of purging the language of Hebraic elements that were seen as "bourgeois and clerical." Yiddish popular culture was used as a tool to manipulate Jewish public opinion. The values of Soviet ideology filled short stories, theatrical performances, Yiddish songs, and even new holidays. These cultural products were designed to speed up the modernization and Sovietization of the Jewish population.[10]

In 1924 the Communist Party began a campaign of "nativization" (*korenizatsiia*) among Soviet national minorities, including Jews. This program strived to establish cultural and political institutions in the national republics in native languages.[11] Because Jews did not have their own national territory, Party activists suggested creating such regions. The civil war left many Jewish shtetlach economically devastated. According to the government's vision, Jewish resettlement to new lands could provide jobs and sources of income for the impoverished residents. The Committee for the Rural Resettlement of the Jews (KOMZET in Russian or Gezerd in Yiddish) was established in 1924. It aimed to create several agricultural colonies in Crimea and Ukraine, and to relocate thousands of Jews there. By 1928 there were already 220,000 Jewish farmers in these settlements. In the late 1920s Jews were also encouraged to settle in Birobidzhan, a territory in the Soviet Far East. Even though the Birobidzhan project turned out largely unsuccessful (in 1933 the Jewish population reached only about 8,200), the area was declared a Jewish autonomous region in 1934.[12]

These agricultural settlements and Birobidzhan were supposed to become the centers of new Jewish mass culture with Yiddish as an official language, along with Russian.[13] The government helped to establish Yiddish courts, schools, Party cells, clubs, and theaters in all regions where large populations of Yiddish-speaking Jews lived.[14] By 1930, 169 Jewish councils, 57 trade unions, and 1,100 schools functioned in Yiddish, but by 1939 most of these organizations began to function in Russian or disappeared, as, officially, the Sovietization of Soviet Jewry was seen as complete.[15] After the annexation of Eastern Poland, the Baltic states, and eastern Romania in 1939 and 1940, Sovietization efforts directed at local Jews were renewed. Once again Yiddish councils, schools, trade unions, theaters, and clubs were established but only in the newly acquired territories, whereas those that functioned in the 1920s and early 1930s were not reopened.[16] Subsequently the Holocaust destroyed the majority of the Yiddish-speaking community of the Soviet Union, and most Yiddish cultural institutions were never restored.

Thus the question remains as to whether these institutions were initially designed to survive after the Sovietization of the Jews had been completed. Even though some activists claimed that they had worked on creating a long-term Jewish proletarian culture, with its basis in the Jewish settlements in Ukraine, Byelorussia, and Birobidzhan,[17] many others admitted that they found the question of the future of Jewish culture "irrelevant."[18] The resolution of the first All-Union meeting of Jewish cultural workers in Moscow in 1924 stated the purposes of Jewish cultural programs in the Soviet Union in the following terms:

> Our goal is to create a culture, one that is not nationalist or spiritual, Hebrew or Yiddish, not even Jewish, but our own culture that is harmonized with the needs of the current moment, the everyday life of the Jewish proletariat. When the Jewish proletariat internationalizes, our culture will have fulfilled its mission.[19]

Indeed, the culture created by Jewish activists during the prewar period included a great number of intentionally "transitional" institutions and products. Yiddish schools existed only at the elementary level, and there were no possibilities for higher or professional education in Yiddish (with the exception of a few vocational schools). As a result, in the mid-1930s, most of these schools were shut down. Similarly Yiddish trade unions and Party cells began to conduct their activities in Russian and Ukrainian. "Transitional" works of literature, theatrical performances, songs, and newspapers incorporated parodies and criticism of the traditional Jewish way of life. These products were meant to break the connection between the Jews and Judaism, and to prepare their audience for original Yiddish works with purely Soviet content. But in the 1930s, as noted above, the Soviet government considered the Sovietization of the Jewish masses to be complete and saw no need to develop Soviet Jewish culture further. Thus, ironically, the "transitional" works of the 1920s attracted much larger audiences than their "original" equivalents of the 1930s (such as Yiddish songs about Stalin that lacked catchy melodies and Yiddish local theater productions that often featured pale copies of Russian performances). But were the Jews indeed Sovietized by the end of the 1930s? And what exactly did "Sovietization" mean?

Dusty Archives, Oral History, and the Department of "Rarely Requested Literature": Sources and Methodology

This book examines how the methods the government used to control and shape Jewish culture and identity from 1923 to 1939 were understood and accepted by the "Jewish masses," the targets of statewide propaganda. In order to study the reception of these methods, I analyze the leisure activities of Soviet Jews, the books and newspapers they read, the songs they sang, the music they listened to, the holidays they celebrated, and the theatrical performances and movies they watched over and over again. Thus this book also explores the popular culture of the Jews who lived in Russia, Ukraine, and Byelorussia.[20]

Studies of popular culture and identity are hard to separate. After all, popular culture is leisure, and use of leisure is an attribute of one's identity.[21] An examination of how people spent their free time in the early Soviet years reveals that despite the limitations imposed by totalitarian policies, the Russian Jewish public had the possibility of maintaining (to some extent) their choices of entertainment. Further, even politically approved artistic and literary expressions were often viewed in ways that the government did not expect. In analyzing Western popular culture, scholars now see consumers as active interpreters of the cultural commodities that are fed to them.[22] In Soviet society the opportunities for political protest against government policies were extremely limited, and, at times, dangerous. Therefore the public developed the ability to "read between the lines," that is, to look for hidden meanings in all forms of official publications.[23] Thus the study of popular reception in the Soviet context also opens a window to a better understanding of state indoctrination and "silent resistance" on the individual level.

Research on Soviet popular culture, especially during the Stalinist period, has flourished in the past two decades. Works by Richard Stites, Peter Kenez, and James von Geldern looked at entertainment options during the Soviet period. These were followed by important studies of popular literature, songs, youth culture, religion, press, theater, and other aspects of Soviet popular culture. While there is still room for further study on this subject, our knowledge of everyday life in Stalinist Russia is now much more complex and multifaceted than it was two decades ago.[24]

However, if we turn our attention away from the analysis of Russian majority culture, Richard Stites's concern is still valid that "most works on Russian culture deal exclusively with high culture, including dissident or underground masterpieces that had little or no popular resonance."[25] The scholarship examining the culture of the Jewish minority (perhaps the most studied ethnic group in the Soviet Union) still revolves around the official status of Jewish religion, language policy, the development of Soviet Yiddish theaters, press, and literature, Russian-language Jewish literature, Jewish education, and scholarship—in other words, the culture of the Jewish elite. While these studies are certainly important, they present an incomplete and one-sided understanding of the lives of ordinary Soviet Jews. This book attempts to look at the "other" side of Russian Jewish culture. It is not centered on belles lettres, Russian Jewish literature, Soviet Yiddish poetry, the Moscow Yiddish Theater, or Yiddish literary journals. The only works of the "elite of Jewish culture" discussed are those that achieved widespread popular reception. I hope to present the cultural world of average

Jews during the Stalinist period and to show how this identity was influenced by Soviet popular culture.[26]

The study of popular culture during the Stalinist period of Soviet history has been complicated historically by a lack of reliable sources, and the Jewish community is no exception.[27] Press, popular literature, published songs, and scripts of theatrical performances certainly help to re-create what was available to Jewish consumers of that era. Archival records of the Evsektsii often provide accurate information and describe local events in greater detail, and many of these scripts and texts of lectures are still available. It is important to remember that all of these documents were created under state control. Therefore one cannot rely on them for a complete understanding of how this material was actually perceived.[28]

Oral history is an important resource in approaching this problem, as it often reveals facts and tendencies that are simply unavailable from other sources.[29] It has certain disadvantages, however, such as the unreliability of memory, occasional oversimplifications, repetition of published sources, limitations of the interviewer, unrepresentative samples, biased questioning, and, of course, interpretative errors.[30] But the benefits of this method outweigh these concerns, as it is perhaps the only way to establish how Jewish popular culture developed in the Soviet Union in the 1920s and 1930s. Cross-examination of testimonies with archival and published data gives us the fullest picture to date of the daily lives of Soviet Jews during this period.

Oral history sources for this study come from 225 in-depth interviews that I conducted with Jews who were born between 1906 and 1930 in Russia and the Soviet Union, and who grew up there. Informants were interviewed in New York, Philadelphia, Minneapolis, Berlin, and Moscow. The two criteria of eligibility were age (one had to be born in the Soviet Union no later than 1930) and ethnicity (both parents of a respondent had to be Jewish). I tried to collect a broad range of testimonies, including men and women, residents of the bigger cities and smaller shtetlach, and Yiddish speakers and non-Yiddish speakers. Some responded to a letter published by New York Russian-language newspapers, which invited former residents of prewar Jewish shtetlach to share their life stories. Others were encouraged to participate in the study via Jewish adult day care centers for Russian-speaking seniors and clubs of Jewish war veterans. As a result, this is a self-selected group of men and women who thought that their life stories could contribute to the project "Recovering Jewish Daily Life in Stalinist Russia."[31]

Nearly two-thirds of the respondents were raised in Yiddish-speaking environments. The ability to speak Yiddish indicates that the respondent was able (at least theoretically) to understand the Yiddish-language publications and entertainment in which the Soviets packaged their propaganda messages. I also interviewed people who grew up in strictly Russian-speaking environments (and consequently knew very little or no Yiddish at all). Their testimonies provide invaluable insights into the understanding of Russian-language Jewish popular culture. Each conversation, which lasted from one to four hours, was structured as a life-story interview. The interviews were conducted in Russian, Yiddish, or a combination of both languages. The choice of questions varied among respondents; questions covered personal milestones, in general, and, more specifically, concentrated on family relations, customs, work, places and sources of recreation and entertainment, and knowledge of Yiddish and Yiddish literature, songs, and theater.[32] All respondents signed release forms, giving permission to be quoted; some signed with their full names, others anonymously. I have chosen not to use respondents' full names in this book in order to maintain their privacy. The transcripts of all interviews, however, will be available in 2007 at the Frankel Center for Judaic Studies at the University of Michigan.

The Structure of the Book

The first four chapters analyze various aspects of Soviet Yiddish popular culture: religion, mass periodicals, amateur theater, and songs. Chapter 1 describes the methods used to destroy Jewish religious beliefs and to establish new traditions. These methods included the distribution of popular brochures explaining the harmful essence of religion and the organization of Red Passover ceremonies, Yom Kippur dinners, and antireligious performances in schools. These programs were all created by Jewish activists and spread through the network of Communist institutions, such as clubs, libraries, and houses of culture that were established in the 1920s in almost every shtetl. I also examine testimonies both of contemporaries who participated in these antireligious events as well as those who have never heard of them. Although only parts of the population adopted the state's negative attitude toward religion in the 1920s and 1930s, the effects of these antireligious campaigns eventually led to the popular opinion that observing religious traditions was not the primary way to express Jewish identity.

The second chapter describes the methods and techniques employed by the Soviet government to influence the reading tastes of Jews. These included the establishment of Yiddish literacy courses, the Jewish worker correspondent movement,[33] and the institution of wall newspapers. Oral history demonstrates that some young people saw writing as a way to advance in society. These (typically amateur) writers used harsh criticism of "anti-Soviet" deeds in order to be noticed, often overlooking the consequences for the objects of their criticism (which at times included friends and family members). Others wrote pro-Soviet letters in order to deflect suspicions and give the appearance of loyalty to the state. The Yiddish periodicals where worker correspondent materials appeared included professional journals, children's magazines, and newspapers. In the second part of this chapter I analyze how the audience reacted to the propaganda messages in these periodicals. I demonstrate that the Yiddish-reading public developed numerous ways to understand, interpret, and enjoy the propagandistic writing in the Yiddish press.

The development of propaganda via the spoken word and the establishment of local theater is the subject of the third chapter. While the activities of the

Moscow Yiddish Theater and some central Ukrainian and Byelorussian theaters have been studied, this is the first analysis of rural and small-town stage productions. Yiddish plays were organized on a wide variety of subjects, including theatrical trials condemning Jewish practices and historical figures, oral newspapers, and buffooneries mocking traditional ways of life, in addition to dramatic productions. The government promoted Jewish theater for propagandistic purposes. Still, these plays became very popular among Jews even though the subject matter was in stark contrast to their traditional upbringing. Oral history reveals that, for Jews, attending Yiddish performances became the expression of their ethnic sentiments and a key part of the new Soviet Jewish identity.

Music and folk songs played an important role in Soviet society in general, and especially among Jews. Officially published songs created in the early 1920s campaigned against religion and encouraged Jews to engage in agricultural work. In the 1930s some songs glorified the achievements of the government, and others aimed to distract people from the struggles of daily life. Soviet Yiddish songs mirror the cultural policies of the state toward the Jews. Chapter 4 looks at the texts and melodies of officially sponsored Yiddish songs about Stalin, the Communist Party, and the Red Army, and analyzes how propaganda messages were inserted into them. Sometimes old Yiddish songs were altered; at other times officially promoted songs became popular for different reasons than the government expected. For example, a song entitled "Birobidzhan" was intended to encourage Jews to settle in this Far Eastern province for which the song is named. Oral history, however, demonstrates that people used to sing this song as a parody of the failed settlement. The popularity of these songs, in general, also emerges from the oral testimonies.

The second layer of material in chapter 4 consists of songs that have gone unpublished until now (for example, songs from ethnographic expeditions from the 1920s and 1930s) plus recollections by my respondents. I compare both bodies of material and analyze how and why some Soviet notions, such as frequent references to agricultural labor and images of Soviet leaders, entered genuinely popular songs, some of which were also officially sponsored, and others that were clearly anti-Soviet. For example, officially published Yiddish songs often painted a picture of life in Jewish agricultural settlements as a virtual paradise. However, the archives contained another Yiddish song, also titled "Birobidzhan," about a homesick Jewish collective farm worker who was miserable with his new lifestyle, which consisted of sleeping in a tent and being eaten alive by mosquitoes. The existence of such songs demonstrates that people often found ways to express themselves, even within the permitted ideological framework.

In the 1920s and 1930s Jews were rapidly assimilating into mainstream Soviet society, in large part a result of government policies as well as the processes of internal modernization. Although many changed their everyday language to Russian, they did not abandon their ethnic sentiments.[34] Jewish artists, composers, writers, and theater directors took an active part in creating mainstream Russian culture but occasionally incorporated some elements of Yiddish culture.

Russian-speaking Jewish audiences learned to recognize these elements and saw them as expressions of Russian Jewish culture. In addition, the Soviet government published brochures and pamphlets in the 1920s and 1930s that were designed to combat popular antisemitism. These works also gained popular reception among Jewish audiences. Paradoxically the ideological statements in these works also impacted the way Russian Jews understood their own culture and identity. Therefore Jewish culture in the Soviet Union existed in two realms: one for Yiddish-speaking Jews, and the other for Russian speakers, which was primarily intended for a non-Jewish audience. The latter was initially created to present Jews to the Russian-speaking public via the press, literature, and the arts. These included popular brochures designed to discourage antisemitism, Russian translations of Yiddish literature, theater performances about the role of Jews in the Russian civil war, and movies about Soviet Jewish settlements.

As Jews became more assimilated in the 1930s, Russian became their primary language, and they developed into attentive recipients of literature and arts created in Russian that dealt with Jewish culture. Because Russian-speaking Jews were deprived of any official channels through which to exhibit their Jewish identity, some unconventional ways to assert ethnic identity appeared. Chapter 5 analyzes the difference in how Jews were described to the non-Jewish Soviet audience compared to their depiction in the Yiddish press. The chapter also discusses the role of Russian-language works that mentioned Jews in the creation of a Soviet Jewish "non–Yiddish-speaking" identity. It looks at the Jewish elements in Soviet mainstream culture and discusses which of these elements were recognized by the Jewish audience.

The book concludes with a discussion of the expressions of Jewish identity in modern Russia that are the direct results of the Soviet cultural engineering programs that were aimed at Jews in the 1920s and 1930s. These policies helped to shape generations of Soviet Jews, a group that does not observe traditional religious beliefs and yet has a distinct Jewish identity, marked by a love for Yiddish songs and theater, as well as pride in Jewish achievements in Russian society.

Note on Transliteration

For Russian, I have used the Library of Congress system. The names of famous personalities are spelled as they are customarily spelled in English (e.g., Maxim Gorky, rather than Gorkii).

For Yiddish, I have generally used the YIVO system of transliteration. When citing Yiddish works published in the Soviet Union, however, I have used phonetic transliteration, to reflect the original spelling. Yiddish words in oral testimonies are transcribed phonetically as well (as respondents pronounced them) in order to keep the dialects intact. For example, if a respondent said "*olef*" in the Ukrainian dialect of Yiddish, I transcribed it as "*olef*," and not "*alef*," as YIVO transcription rules would require. Famous personalities, such as Sholem Aleichem, are spelled as they are usually spelled in English, without references to the rules of YIVO transliterations. For poetry, I started each line with a capital letter for elegance. Personal names are also capitalized in Yiddish transliteration.

Yiddish words mentioned frequently in the text, such as *kheyder, loshn koydesh, melamed,* etc., are italicized and translated the first time the word is used.

The word "Hagaddah" (the Passover story) is written in its most popular English form and is not italicized. Similarly I use the word "Sabbath," not *shabes,* since the English-speaking reader is more familiar with this term.

Respondents' names are transcribed as they are pronounced in Russian.

Soviet and Kosher

1 Antireligious Propaganda and the Transformation of Jewish Institutions and Traditions

"You should try some of our food, it is all kosher," explains Gary, the manager of an old-age home in Berlin, as he leads me to the cafeteria. Every day its residents, most of whom are Jews from the former Soviet Union, gather here for lunch. On this particular day, they are served chicken and vegetables.

I sit next to an elderly gentleman wearing a baseball cap, Grigorii P. (b. 1920, in Ukraine). He looks at me, at the chicken, and at the manager, and says, "When I was a little boy, I ate real kosher meat, not like this. It was tasty, it was greasy, and it was great."

"What kind of meat was it?" I ask.

"It was pork," replies Grigorii. "There are special butchers for pigs. Otherwise their meat is not kosher. Ordinary butchers cannot slaughter pigs."

"That is right," says Lyubov B. (b. 1928, in Ukraine), who is sitting at the end of the table. "I heard about it," she adds. "One also needs special butchers for rabbits. I like rabbit meat. I ate it a lot during the war, and it was very good. But there are no butchers in Germany who can slaughter them right. Because this place is kosher, they cannot serve us non-kosher pork and rabbits."

"Why are you listening to them?" shouts Yehuda K. (b. 1910), as he joins the conversation. "These Russian Jews do not know anything about Jewish culture. They are not really Jewish," he interjects. "I was born in Lithuania, and I know that there is no way you can make pork Kosher."

The heated argument lasts for about fifteen minutes and eventually engulfs almost everyone in the dining room. In the end, all sides leave the cafeteria dissatisfied, more confident than ever in their opinions about what indeed is kosher meat.

Most Western Jews would probably agree with Yehuda's interpretation of Jewish dietary laws. How can pork be kosher? What about Yehuda's opinion that Lyubov and Grigorii are "not real Jews" because of their nontraditional views of religious traditions? The answers to these questions are far from simple. Lyubov and Grigorii speak fluent Yiddish. They both wanted their children to marry Jews. Lyubov still likes to play matchmaker, regularly introducing her younger single acquaintances to one another, explaining that she does so, "only if they are Jewish, of course." Lyubov never cooks or cleans on Saturdays. She thinks that it is a bad omen. She knows how to bake matzo for Passover and *kulich* (Easter bread) for Russian Easter. Lyubov does not like going to the synagogue, but she has been to church several times. "There is a God, of course," she explains, "but does one have to go somewhere to pray? If you are a good person, He will surely reward you," she adds confidently.[1]

Grigorii does not go to synagogue or believe in God. However, when we speak privately about the "kosher pork" incident in the dining room, Grigorii says:

> What right do they have to call us non-Jews? We suffered so much because of our nationality. My son did not study at the university that he wanted to, my wife was harassed at work, and I was not promoted. It was all because we were Jewish. Yet I never hid the fact that I was Jewish. And who has the right to tell me that I am not a Jew?[2]

Indeed, Grigorii, Lyubov, and thousands of other Soviet Jews are caught in this dilemma: they see themselves as Jewish, while many members of the Western Jewish communities recognize them as Jews in name only. In Germany (where Grigorii currently lives), and in the United States and other Western countries, religion, in the broadest sense of the word, is a key part of Jewish identity, as Jews are largely considered a religious minority rather than an ethnicity.[3] Soviet Jews who were born in the 1920s saw their Jewishness in a radically different way, even though their parents usually defined themselves as Jews based on the observance of Judaism.

Many factors, including increased social mobility and assimilation, contributed to this radical transformation. These processes certainly took place in other countries as well during the same period, including the United States and Poland. The key difference between these developments was that only in the Soviet Union was Judaism (along with other religions) officially attacked in statewide propaganda, which aimed, among other things, to separate Jews from Judaism. I argue that, although antireligious propaganda failed to persuade Soviet citizens of the negative nature of religion, it did succeed in convincing many Jews that religion was not an essential part of their culture and identity.[4]

Antireligious programs began soon after the establishment of the Soviet state. First, the decree of January 23, 1918, separated church and state, and consequently forbade religious instruction in schools where general subjects were taught.[5] Three years later, in August 1921, the Communist Party Central Committee began its ideological campaign against religion and called for the publication of atheist pamphlets, books, and newspaper articles. Later that year the Tenth Party Congress adopted a resolution calling for antireligious agitation and propaganda using mass media, films, lectures, and other methods. The resolution acknowledged the need to combat not only the Russian Orthodox Church but also other religions.[6] In the late 1920s new laws were created that restricted the roles of churches and other houses of worship in Soviet society. Several laws forbade members of the clergy from joining collective farms, restricted their choice of housing, and deprived them of social security rights.[7] These laws severely affected the Jewish community as well. For example, in 1926–27 nearly a third of the Jews in all Ukraine were ineligible to vote.[8]

In 1928 the sale of Easter food and Christmas trees was prohibited, and

Christmas decorations were banned from shop windows, replaced by mountains of special anti-Christmas literature. During this time antireligious education campaigns were mounted in schools and mobile theaters, and showed antireligious films in church buildings. After these screenings, resolutions were usually passed to close church buildings and to secularize them.[9]

A six-day week was introduced on September 24, 1929, making it difficult for believers to observe the Sabbath.[10] In November 1932 a single day's absence from work without authorization was decreed punishable by confiscation of food and ration cards, which made it impossible to skip work during non-Soviet (i.e., religious) holidays.

During the mid-1930s antireligious agitation and propaganda were decentralized. Local public and voluntary organizations—the Komsomol (Communist Youth League), the Young Pioneers, workers' clubs, and the League of the Militant Godless (an organization designed to combat religion at the grass roots) were encouraged to undertake a whole range of antireligious initiatives.[11] In 1936 the Soviet Constitution ended the disenfranchisement of priests and all other "nonworkers." Also, sales of Christmas trees (named New Year's trees) resumed, and *kulich* was once again sold openly.[12] In 1937, however, purges of priests and clerics of all religions led to further weakening of religious institutions in the USSR, and by the end of 1939 visible religious life had been virtually destroyed.

Zvi Gitelman points out that the Jewish connection between religion and nationality is quite strong, since Judaism is a "tribal religion" rather than a universal one. For the most part, the only national group that practices Judaism is Jews. Therefore Soviet policies that affected the Jewish religion ipso facto affected the Jews, and vice versa, despite the fact that not all Jews practiced their religion.[13] On the other hand, as Igor Krupnik reminds us, Jews were probably the only group within the Soviet population that actually benefited from the revolution, as all tsarist restrictions (education, employment, and places of residence) were no longer valid.[14] This was true for all Jews, including observant ones. Therefore antireligious campaigns directed against Judaism were often seen by Jews as "part of the deal," where Jews were able to obtain all civil rights but had to abandon some of their religious sentiments. Besides, all the antireligious campaigns directed against Jews were often organized by the same people who directed the campaigns to fight popular antisemitism. Oral history testimonies strongly suggest that the Jewish public's appreciation of these efforts was generally far greater than the disappointment regarding the antireligious battles.

Rituals connected with the Jewish way of life, such as those for food consumption or wedding ceremonies, were subjected to massive attacks. According to Jewish religious law, animals permitted for consumption must be slaughtered in a specified manner by a man licensed to do so, a *shoykhet*. The *shokhtim* were included by Soviet authorities in the category of *lishentsy* (persons deprived of civil rights). Thus they were harassed, jailed, and deported. There was never an official prohibition of kosher slaughter itself in the Soviet Union, but its practice was made difficult. The Soviet authorities also tried to close the *mikves* (Jewish ritual baths). Rather than explicitly objecting on religious grounds, they closed the bathhouses under the guise of new sanitary and hygienic restrictions. Still, an unspecified number of *mikves* remained in the Soviet Union through the 1930s.[15]

New antireligious campaigns designed to decimate the clergy and to reduce the number of believers to a bare minimum among Jews began in 1927–28. Hundreds of rabbis and other clergymen were arrested or deported to remote provinces.[16] These physical attacks, which have been widely reported by numerous historians, were accompanied by a massive propagandistic assault. The specific messages of the antireligious propaganda against Judaism have not been comprehensively studied. In this chapter I attempt to fill this gap. Analysis of the texts used to attack Jewish tradition and rituals helps us to understand how Soviet propaganda was organized, how it promoted its ideas, and how its messages were consumed by individuals. We shall see that this antireligious propaganda sometimes actually helped to foster Jewish national identity and pride.

Laying the Groundwork: Soviet Arguments against Traditional Jewish Education and the Postulates of Judaism

In 1922 the Eleventh Party Congress resolved to turn the state publishing house Glavpolitprosvet (the Main Political Enlightenment Board) into a center for popular Marxist and antireligious literature. In accordance with this resolution, a number of specialized antireligious periodicals appeared. *Nauka i religiia* (Science and religion), edited by Mikhail Galkin, a former priest, came out in December 1922 and was soon replaced by the weekly *Bezbozhnik* (The godless), edited by Emel'ian Iaroslavsky, the secretary of the Party's disciplinary Central Control Commission.[17] These publications were designed to deliver clear, entertaining, and educational antireligious messages to the Russian-speaking masses. State-organized antireligious publishing in Yiddish started a few years later, but anti-Judaist diatribes were found throughout all types of Soviet Yiddish publications, from newspapers to scholarly discourses. At least seventy-four titles of specifically antireligious Yiddish literature were issued between 1917 and 1941.[18] The Yiddish Communist newspaper, *Der emes* (The truth), became a leading forum for antireligious writing. The most intensive period of publishing antireligious literature was from 1927 to 1935. A special Yiddish-language periodical, *Der apikoyres* (The godless) was published from 1931 to 1935 by the League of the Militant Godless.

The first book about the harm caused by the *khaydorim* (Jewish primary schools) appeared in 1922.[19] The book presents a series of arguments about why these schools should be closed. Here are a few examples. First, the authors imply, *kheyder* teachers are not competent:

> Very old teachers work in khaydorim. Some of them have difficulties speaking and hearing. Many are only part-time teachers. . . . During the rest of the day they help their wives in the market, and serve in synagogues and houses of study.[20]

The publications also attack the teaching methods of these schools:

> In almost all khaydorim the teachers terrorize their students. They often beat them up. Sometimes they force children to kneel as a form of punishment. The pedagogical goal of these teachers is that children should "sit still like a wall." . . . In the majority of khaydorim one can observe the old methods of teaching.[21]

The sanitary conditions are characterized as follows:

> The sanitary conditions of khaydorim are very poor. Most khaydorim are filthy and look like a pigsty. In some khaydorim there are not even any chairs, and the children are all forced to sit together on a bed. In addition, most schools do not have separate rooms and are located inside synagogues.[22]

According to the authors, the poor sanitary conditions lead to an increase in diseases among Jewish children. They also target the curriculum itself, arguing that it does not include useful subjects, focusing too heavily on the study of religious texts:

> Khaydorim teach children things that are part of the old, prerevolutionary worlds. They have very little connection with modern life. The old education, not relevant either in form or in content, is a remnant of the past, which molds the minds and bodies of our children.[23]

The authors conclude that the best solution is to close all khaydorim and force the pupils to attend Soviet secular schools.

Stylistically similar brochures "explained" the essence of Sabbath and the Torah.[24] Hilel Lurye, the author of many of those brochures, including *Sabbath: What One Says about It and Where It Indeed Came From,* emphasizes that the Sabbath is not specifically a Jewish holiday but rather existed in ancient Assyria and other countries long before Judaism appeared. Therefore, he insists, since this holiday was not exclusively Jewish, Jews were not the "chosen people." Moreover, Lurye asserts that Jews suffered many consequences through the observance of the Sabbath. He claims that Jews lost many wars since they were not able to fight on the Sabbath, and enemies used this to their own advantage.[25]

The motif of bourgeois exploitation in the name of religion is prevalent in Soviet propaganda. Another brochure portrays religion as follows:

> Religion prevents workers from struggling for a better life. Where are the roots of religion? Lenin says: "The working energy of the working masses . . . is struggling against the blind and cruel power of capitalism. The only possible way for them to make the working class do what it does not want is through religion. . . . The new socialist society we build does not need religion, as it is based on different principles." Socialism will destroy the religious roots, and the Communist Party will lead the Soviet people according to Lenin's commandment.[26]

The anonymous author of the brochure suggests that Lenin's commandments replace their religious equivalents as the ideological basis of modern life. The Communist Party assumes the role traditionally played by priests and rabbis, and traditional religion has no place here. The author presents negative

ה. לוריע

שאבעס

וואס מען זאגט וועגן אים און פון וואנען ער האט זיך
אין דער עמעסן גענומען

———

אלאוקראינישער מעלוכע־פארלאג
ייד שע סעקציע פון ארעסער אפט־ילונג
1922

Hilel Lurye, *Shabes: vos men zogt vegn im un fun vanen er hot zikh in der emesn genu-men* (Sabbath: What one says about it and where it indeed came from), title page of the brochure, Odessa, 1922.

counterarguments for virtually every aspect of Jewish tradition. The brochure, *What Every Militant Godless Should Know,* offers historical, geological, and archaeological explanations for ancient customs and rituals, and emphasizes the harmful social impacts of these on the poorest levels of the Jewish masses. The text represents a typical example of the style of at least forty such brochures that were centrally published between 1927 and 1932.[27]

In the late 1920s publications began to include concrete practical instructions for local organizations on antireligious propaganda. They consisted of plans to organize antireligious rooms in local clubs and libraries, instructions on how to stage protests if the co-op of a shtetl made an attempt to sell kosher meat, and explanations on how to convince friends not to observe Jewish rituals such as eating matzo during Passover and resting on the Sabbath. Such works primarily addressed antireligious activists, who in turn often altered, and at times reinterpreted, the propagandistic messages of the brochures. However, these publications constituted the ideological basis and provided official justification for closing synagogues, Jewish religious schools, kosher butchers, and *mikves.*

Transformation of Public Space: Synagogues, Clubs, and Schools

Synagogues into Clubs: The Same Jews in the Same Buildings?

For centuries Jewish life in Eastern Europe revolved around the synagogue. Most communal activities and institutions, such as the ritual slaughterhouse, the ritual bathhouse, and the hostelry were, as a rule, centered in close proximity to the synagogue. With the development of the Jewish enlightenment and secularism in the nineteenth century, the synagogue no longer retained such an important status but was still quite powerful, especially in smaller towns.

The mass closings of traditional Jewish houses of worship began in 1921. Between the revolution and 1929, 646 synagogues were shut down. More closures followed in 1937–38, when the campaign against Judaism and other religions was carried out under the banner of the struggle against fascist espionage. By 1939 only about 200 synagogues remained in the Soviet Union. The larger houses of worship were transformed into secular buildings, typically into clublike settings, and their property nationalized. This process led to a curious situation: the former synagogue buildings still served Jewish audiences, but now these transformed structures were used to deliver entirely different messages.

Often believers, led by rabbis or on their own initiative, protested against the closing of large synagogues.[28] These protests were especially visible in bigger cities, where they attracted the attention of the central press. Therefore these cases are widely described in the scholarly literature about Jews in the Soviet Union and are often seen as the only story regarding the reception of antireligious propaganda against Jews. In reality, the process of how Jewish houses of worship were closed was politically less severe than the closing of the Ortho-

Kharkov, Ukraine Jewish workmen's club, formerly the Jewish Synagogue, c. 1925.
Photograph courtesy of the Joint Distribution Committee Photo Archives.

dox churches, partly because many synagogues were impossible to use for other purposes (Jewish houses of prayer were often old, small, and dark, and thus could not serve the immediate needs of the Soviet government).[29] In fact, many synagogues were closed in order to demonstrate that the Jewish religion was no different from any other religion and that Jews did not have any special privileges.[30]

The Komsomol was entrusted with the responsibility for conducting antireligious campaigns, including the closing of synagogues. Often young Jewish activists were the major force in the expropriation of synagogues; according to official Soviet sources, these actions were dictated by the wishes of the "toiling masses," who wanted to transform their religious backwardness into a modern culture.[31] Official sources, such as the reports of local Evsektsii, report that these actions were conducted within the framework of centrally organized campaigns. The leaders were specially trained activists who rallied school students and young Komsomol members. Thus, according to these sources, the Jewish community was divided into two parts. The first—small, old, and backward—opposed the Soviet government's measures. The second, which constituted the majority, fully approved the official actions. The latter community was the ideal shtetl, as portrayed in the official press and documents.[32] Western historiography, on the other hand, emphasizes only the cases of protest against such campaigns. For example, David Fishman analyzes the efforts of the Lubavicher Rebbe in Russia to support the network of Jewish religious schools, despite the new government's prohibitions.[33] Mikhail Beizer offers a comprehensive overview of attempts to preserve some religious life in Leningrad, where believers managed to preserve their synagogue until 1938.[34] In other words, the history of the believers and synagogues in the Soviet Union is portrayed as the history of resistance and survival, and not as a story of adjustments and compromises.

The realities of daily life for Soviet Jews and their attitude toward religious observance during this period were more complex. Indeed, for the majority of the middle-aged Jews of the 1920s and even the 1930s, the destruction of synagogues meant the obliteration of their traditional lifestyle. Even more painful for these believers, those who attacked Judaism were young Jews, often their own children or grandchildren, which rendered the older generation incapable of resisting. The testimony of Ian D. serves to illustrate this:

> I remember how the Jewish Communists closed the Jewish synagogue in Berdichev in 1929 or 1930. There was a synagogue near the sewage works. There were many synagogues in Berdichev, more than 130. There was a tailor's synagogue. Some old Jews used to go there; they prayed *minkhe* and *mayrev*.[35] It was a small synagogue.
>
> Some younger children and I were walking around there. Suddenly, we saw many young people marching in the street. They were playing musical instruments. It was a small band. For us children, it was a big deal at that time, so we all followed them. They were lined up in columns. They were wearing beautiful clothes, some green and blue, white shirts. At that time,

the *komyugistn* [Young Communist League members] used to wear uniforms. They were approaching the synagogue. They came to the synagogue, and they stopped and played. After playing, they set up a platform and a table, and we, all children, were there, because we loved the band. One of them took out a paper and read aloud that religion was not good, and that the synagogue is evil, too. "We, the members of the Young Communist League, voted that the synagogue disturbed our work and was harmful to youth so it had to be closed." So, some people went into the synagogue and they kicked out the old Jews who were praying there. The old Jews went out; they said they were not able to fight with Jews. All these young men were Jewish. After that, the *komyugistn* took a board, a hammer and some nails, and shut the door and put a notice on the front of the synagogue that it was closed by resolution of the Communist Youth Organization of the clothing factory. That was it. From that moment on, the synagogue did not exist any more.[36]

Stories like Ian's are not rare. Many respondents explain that although many believers felt unhappy about the closing of synagogues, cases of active confrontation were infrequent. At the same time scholarly literature emphasizes numerous protests, based on memoirs published abroad, contemporary publications in the Western press, and even some archival documents that contain letters of believers with requests to allow the synagogues to remain open. How can one explain such contradictions? Are all the memoirs portraying life in the Soviet Union as dominated by persecution biased? Or are the respondents in this project honest in presenting their past as deprived of contradictions, resistance, and other unpleasant moments? Actually, to some extent, both views are true. However, another reason for this wide disparity is that these two kinds of sources refer to different groups of people. Information available in the West primarily came from émigrés and refugees who managed to escape the Soviet Union in the 1920s and early 1930s. Their views of Soviet policies were entirely negative: they saw the reaction to the implementation of government projects as resistance, and the entire Soviet Jewish history as a history of oppression. The availability of these sources even led some historians to conclude that the resistance to Soviet policies among Jews was stronger than among non-Jews, and that campaigns against Jewish religion were harsher than those against Christianity.[37] Another reason for the creation and development of the model "story of oppression" in analyzing Soviet Jewish history originates from the general tendency to see history as a story of the elite. Many émigrés who left in the 1920s came from more privileged backgrounds. However, the majority of Jews stayed in the Soviet Union after the revolution, and many took advantage of numerous professional and social opportunities offered by the new regime. Thus, to write a broader cultural history of Russian Jewry during the early Soviet years, one needs to utilize additional sources such as oral histories that reflect the perspective of the majority.

Most of my respondents left Russia or the Soviet Union in the late 1980s and

early 1990s. During the 1930s they were teenagers committed to the Soviet regime, to its ideology and ideals. Their perspective is that of the majority of the
Soviet Jews who remained in Soviet Russia at the time. Ninety-five percent of
my respondents finished high school, about 60 percent have higher education,
and the rest had received some other professional schooling (e.g., at a *tekhni-*
kum, or training college). Their testimonies, therefore, also represent the views
of the more educated segment of the Jewish public. Most important, all remained in the Soviet Union at least until the late 1980s, and therefore have a
more "Soviet" perspective on events.

The testimonies confirm that the difference of opinions among Jews regarding Soviet antireligious policies was tremendous. The Jewish religious elite (such
as rabbis) saw the Russian Revolution as a threat to religious tradition and the
religious way of life. Unlike many priests of the Russian Orthodox Church, only
eight Jewish rabbis (out of more than a thousand) tried to combine Jewish religious doctrine and Soviet ideology or tried to attack religion itself.[38] However,
when one looks at other social classes, such as workers, craftsmen, and intelligentsia, the lack of active resistance to antireligious propaganda seems to be a
key difference between the Jewish case and its Russian equivalent. Jews significantly benefited from the revolution, as noted above, since it gave them new
opportunities in education and, for the first time in the region, equal civil rights.
Antireligious propaganda was seen as a price they had to pay in exchange for all
the benefits given by the new regime. Moreover, the internal processes of secularization started in the Russian Jewish community before the revolution, and
were catalyzed by the abolition of all previous restrictions on Jewish places of
residence, education, and employment.

My respondents confirm that many Jews considered it more important to be
able to enter institutions of higher learning and to move to bigger cities than to
object to the destruction of their synagogues. In other words, they saw the antireligious campaigns of the Soviet government as unavoidable and preferred to
keep the status quo rather than cause more problems by actively resisting. Second, some respondents speak about a profound fear that fighting Jews who performed anti-Jewish activities against their own families would create "more reasons for antisemites to hate the Jews." Finally, the lack of significant resistance
stemmed from the youth's relationship to the Komsomol, to which they were
initially attracted by the organization's various external manifestations, such as
uniforms, orchestras, and interesting and unusual activities, as we have seen in
Ian's testimony above. Besides, teenagers joined the Komsomol not only for its
ideology but also because of the perception that the Komsomol was a means of
social mobility. Sometimes the religious parents helped their children to perform antireligious and even violent actions in public, while the same families
observed traditional religious rituals together at home. This is demonstrated by
the testimony of Sara Fr.:

> My grandmother and mother told me I had to become a Young Pioneer.
> They were very happy to hear all my stories about the Pioneer activities in

school and various Pioneer actions (including the stories about the campaigns against observing Yom Kippur, the wall newspaper, and playing various games). They encouraged me to be active in these deeds as they thought it would help me to have a better life. At home, though, I had to keep kosher and celebrate all traditional Jewish holidays, learn to cook Jewish food, and I would not dare say I would marry a non-Jewish boy.[39]

Like Sara, many Jewish children were raised in families full of apparent double standards. Torn between family and school values, many still chose not to notice these contradictions because of the separate functions that school and family performed in their lives.

Even those who expressed less conformist attitudes often avoided active confrontation. Viktor Kh. was born into a religiously observant family in the Ukrainian shtetl of Pilyava in 1919. His mother refused to immigrate to the United States (when she had this possibility in 1909), because she thought it would be impossible to retain a Jewish lifestyle there and because she considered America to be a "*treyf land*" (non-kosher country). In the 1920s, when her sons were forced to work in collective farms in order to support their family, she did not want to compromise her religious beliefs with economic necessities:

I was thirteen, and he [my brother] was seventeen when we were enrolled to work in the collective farm. During the Sabbath, however, my mother was praying. The [Jewish] chairman of the collective farm would come to our home and would wait until she finished her prayer. Then he would tell her: "Madam Kh., please, I beg you, let your boys work. There is so much work, we need them." She would answer: "Mr. Kogan, my boys do not work on the Sabbath. They are not Komsomol members or Pioneers, and they are not going to work." She said they would never become Pioneers or Komsomol members.[40]

Although Viktor's mother prohibited her children from working on the Sabbath, she did, unlike many Ukrainian and Russian peasant parents, permit them to labor on a collective farm during the week and to study in a Soviet school where they were exposed to antireligious propaganda. Some parents expressed their protest by encouraging their children to stay away from antireligious campaigns. Manya L. (b. 1918) recalls a story about the closing of a synagogue in her shtetl in 1929, when she was eleven years old. Her father, who was a rabbi at the synagogue, generally did not involve himself in the children's activities in school. But when Manya told him that their class (in a Soviet Jewish school) was given a task to go to a synagogue on a Saturday, find the scrolls of the Torah, and burn them in a schoolyard, he asked her to find the Torah, which belonged to their family, hide it under her clothes, and bring it home—an act with serious risks, including her permanent expulsion from school and her father's possible arrest. Manya followed her father's instructions, and today, seventy years later, the scroll is one of her family's most precious possessions.[41]

Still, an overwhelming majority of respondents do not speak of active (or

Sofiya Lipkina, Bronx, New York. Photograph by Lara Troyanovsky.

any) resistance to the closing of synagogue buildings. Even in the case that Manya described, we can see that the majority of children who took part in the action were not told to rescue Torah scrolls. According to Manya, a tremendous fire erupted when scrolls were burned the same evening, and the synagogue was closed forever. Its building was then used as a Communist club. Manya had a different perspective, because she was from a rabbinical family. The majority of other children, however, did not dare to object to school activities.

Many testimonies indicated that, although many of the closed synagogues were transformed into Soviet clubs, schools, and theaters, they functioned as Jewish community centers of one sort or another (in the places where Jews constituted the majority of the population). The content of their activities changed dramatically, but the people who attended events in the former synagogues remained the same. In fact, reconstructed as a club, the former synagogue attracted more people than ever, as youngsters were involved in various workshops and adults came to watch amateur theater performances, concerts (by local or visiting artists), and movies. These activities are examined in other sections of this book, yet here it is important to point out that the community often saw the transformation of synagogues into clubs as an expression of government support of Jewish culture and not as an act of state antisemitism. Paradoxically other government policies toward Jews, such as the establishment of Soviet Jewish schools with instruction in Yiddish, provoked more mixed reactions than closures of synagogues.

Soviet Jewish Schools versus Jewish Traditional Schools

In 1918 the Evsektsii began to take steps against the traditional Jewish educational system, against khaydorim and yeshivas, and against the Jewish religion itself.[42] In July 1919 most non-Communist Jewish organizations, from yeshivas to sports clubs, were ordered closed.[43] In 1922–23 committees for the "Liquidation of the Khaydorim" were organized in towns and hamlets where Jews resided. By the end of the 1920s the Soviet press proudly reported that all khaydorim had been shut down, but, in fact, many were simply driven underground. David Fishman believes that "kheyder and yeshiva actually underwent a process of consolidation and growth during the mid- and late 1920s."[44] The agency primarily responsible for this underground resurgence was the Vaad Rabbanei SSSR (Committee of Rabbis of the USSR), a clandestine organization founded and headed by the Lubavicher Rebbe Joseph Isaac Schneerson, which existed from late 1922 until the spring of 1930.[45] There is no comprehensive statistical information on the size of the committee's religious educational network between 1925 and 1927; retrospective reports by Schneerson and Y. L. Zevin describe these years as a period of growth and expansion. This is corroborated by figures from Minsk, which report 273 children in committee-supported khaydorim in 1926, and 324 children in 1928. Shneerson estimated at the time that there were at least 20,000 Jewish children in the USSR whose parents were eager to give them a religious education, a figure that represents slightly less than 5 percent of Jewish school-age children in the USSR in 1928.[46] According to Fishman, khaydorim existed until approximately 1930, when massive arrests of rabbis and *melamdim* (instructors at khaydorim) prevented them from teaching.

Oral history testimonies confirm that khaydorim continued to be quite popular in Ukraine and Byelorussia during the 1920s and early 1930s. One line from a Yiddish song popular in the 1930s read: *Ikh vil nit geyn in kheyder ober di shul iz erger* (I do not want to go to kheyder, but the [Soviet] school is worse). Respondents name various reasons why parents sent their children to kheyder or to a private teacher. First, children had been attending kheyder for generations. Second, Soviet schools (including Jewish, Ukrainian, and Byelorussian) only enrolled pupils from the age of seven and sometimes not until the age of eight. Khaydorim usually accepted students from the age of three or four; so before children went to Soviet school, they attended kheyder, which fulfilled the role of a day-care facility. Fira T., a former pupil of such a kheyder, explains:

> When I was four my parents sent me to kheyder. I do not remember it well. I just remember the rebbe telling us the legend about the beautiful Joseph. . . . I also remember the benches were extremely hard, so my mother would tie a pillow to my back, so that it should be nice and soft for me to sit on. My parents worked very hard. My mother and my father owned a small business. I was the youngest in the family, so when I went to kheyder, it was much easier for my mother to keep her eye on the business.[47]

When children grew older they often attended kheyder after school. Fira goes on:

> When I was seven I went to the Soviet Jewish school. The teachers were wonderful there. Sometimes they were young and we called them *khaver lerer* [comrade teacher]. If they were from the old gymnasium, we would call them by their first name and patronymic. We all studied very hard. It was not like today, when girls think only about stupid things, such as nail polish, hair, and nose rings. . . . I liked to study a lot. I wanted the teacher to tell me I was good. We did homework all the time. We were all so busy. After school I would go home, have my lunch, and then I would go to kheyder. In kheyder we studied to read Hebrew. I was so busy all the time, I did not have time to help my mother in the shop.[48]

In 1928, during massive antireligious campaigns, the government strengthened its persecution of kheyder teachers. Khaydorim began to operate as underground schools. Classes took place in private houses, mostly in those of melamdim. Ian D. recalls:

> When I was five years old [in 1928], my parents sent me to an "underground" kheyder. It was run by a *melamed*. This was all forbidden. But the teacher still did that. He took fifteen to twenty children to his home and taught them. What did he teach us? What he was able to teach. . . . Some

aleph-beys [abc's, reading]. He was very scared that the authorities would find out about him. He was always telling us to keep quiet. It was very cold that time. . . . He was telling us not to come near the windows, so we would not be seen from outside. If someone told him that he saw an inspector or something, someone who had a briefcase, he would always tell us: "Children, sit down on the floor!" Then one day someone wrote a report on him, so we only got to study for a few months. The teacher was sent away.[49]

Massive arrests of the melamdim in the late 1920s radically decreased the number of existing khaydorim and damaged the quality of kheyder education. Only devoted teachers continued to run the remaining underground schools. Jewish clubs and extracurricular activities in Soviet Jewish schools replaced the recreational needs originally served by the khaydorim. By the 1930s only rare cases of attending khaydorim were reported (and those parents who sent their children to kheyder had fewer practical reasons). By the mid-1930s many children did not even know what the word *kheyder* meant, but the duality between public education and family upbringing still remained, as the values children were taught at home often differed radically from what they learned in school.

A great number of Soviet Jewish schools were established in the mid-1920s. In theory, these schools were designed for children who spoke Yiddish as their native language. Jewish parents often preferred Russian schools because they felt that such an education would give their children more opportunities in the future. But government officials insisted that Jewish children attend Soviet-run Yiddish-language schools, as many ideologues believed that children would learn Soviet values better if they were taught in their mother tongue. Special committees to enforce attendance at these schools were established. These committees conducted preliminary examinations to see who spoke Yiddish in order to determine which children were eligible to attend these schools. If a child was eligible, he or she had no other option but to enroll in Soviet Yiddish schools.

Ida V. (b. 1923) told me the following story about how she ended up in a Jewish school in Odessa in 1930:

My parents did not speak Yiddish to me or my sister. They wanted us to speak Russian. But they spoke Yiddish between themselves, so we understood and learned it. Also, I spoke Yiddish with my grandmother, who did not speak Russian. When I was seven I was supposed to go to school and was very excited about it. My mother wanted me to go to the Russian school. One day she took me to the director of the school. Then she told me to say that I did not speak Yiddish. I was very surprised, because this was the first time my mother asked me to lie. I said: "Mother, you used to say it is not good to lie!" She answered then: "This time, it is better for you not to say the truth. Do not reveal to them that you know Yiddish."

When we arrived there were three men in the room. I entered with my mother. They asked me in Russian my name, my age, and then they asked if I knew any Yiddish. I said I did not know Yiddish. Then one of the men told me [in Yiddish]: "*Meydele, gey farmakh di dir!*" [Girl, go close the door!] I went to close the door. That was how they enlisted me in a Jewish school.[50]

In addition to pragmatic concerns, some parents had other reasons not to send their children to Yiddish schools. Religious Jews preferred sending their children to schools with instruction in Russian, Ukrainian, or Byelorussian because the antireligious propaganda in these schools was not aimed specifically at the Jewish religion, unlike in the Yiddish schools.[51] However, despite a significant number of Jewish parents opposed to sending their children to Soviet Yiddish schools, these institutions rapidly expanded from 366 in 1923 24 to 775 in 1926–27 and then to 1,100 in 1929–30.[52]

From the perspective of the Soviet government, Yiddish-language schools were designed to become an effective alternative to traditional religious-based education and to raise a generation of devoted Soviet citizens. Soviet Yiddish schools were required to provide the necessary range of practical information for Jewish children, which included ideological training as well as general education. The specifically Jewish element in the curriculum was used simply as a tool to convert the Yiddish-speaking population into a Soviet-thinking one. Therefore attending kheyder was supposed to be the opposite of attending a Soviet Jewish school. Indeed, some respondents report that children were forced to stop attending kheyder once they began studying in Soviet schools. For example, Semyon Sh. (b. 1918) describes how and why he stopped attending kheyder:

> I did not go to study with the rebbe, because my parents thought that rebbes were not knowledgeable enough to teach. . . . They could only teach the alphabet [*olef-beys*][53] and how to open a prayer book [*sider*]. My parents decided to pay for my private lessons with an educated yeshiva student [*yeshiva bukher*]. His name was Leib Green. He was very smart. He knew lots of Jewish history. I do not know exactly how he came to Kupel. You never know. Some Zionists from Leningrad lived in Kupel. Maybe he was one of them. . . .
>
> In my first and second class, there was a woman named Lyuba. I remembered her last name . . . she was a pioneer leader. I think she was Polish. She was very kind and nice. But she was a Komsomol member. Jewish Komsomol members gave her instructions on how to conduct Komsomol work. When I was walking home, she met me. I was alone and she was alone. She asked me: "Syunya, do you go to a Jewish tutor?" I was a child. I answered: "Yes, I do." She said: "Stop it. Otherwise they are going to expel you from school." It was in 1928. I listened and then told my parents, but I continued to study with the tutor.
>
> Later, some time passed. Lyuba met me again in the street and asked me: "Are you still studying there?" Everything was known, even among children. She said that I was going to get into trouble. I told my parents, and after that they stopped my private lessons.[54]

The Transformation of Jewish Institutions and Traditions 17

This testimony shows how Semyon's parents tried to find a balance between Soviet and traditional Jewish education, and made an effort to negotiate the demands of the new system. The respondent's parents apparently took religious education quite seriously, since they had not simply hired a *melamed* who they thought could provide an adequate but insufficient training in Jewish matters. Yet, it was the parents who made the decision not to send their child to study with the *yeshiva bukher* perhaps to provide a better future for their son. There were cases, however, when similar stories were told from a different perspective. Here is a story of how another student, Semyon K. (b. 1918), explains his decision on which school to attend:

> Although my parents were very poor, they still managed to pay a teacher to teach me Hebrew and little bit of the Torah. I was in the fourth grade. Then suddenly, someone in the shtetl found out I was studying and they said this in school. The director called me and said that if I continued to study, I would be expelled from the school. Immediately after that, I came home and threw away everything I had from these classes with that teacher: my notes, my book. . . . I wanted an education more than anything. . . . That is why I do not know Hebrew (*loshn koydesh*) now.[55]

According to this respondent, as a ten-year-old boy he had convinced his parents to stop providing a Jewish education for him. It is hard to say whether this testimony is factually accurate or whether the respondent prefers to present himself as a "decision maker," even at such a young age (as many other respondents do). Yet if he did indeed convince his parents, his behavior was what the government expected of young children. Soviet schools encouraged youngsters to educate their older family members in new government policies and, in the Jewish case, also to conduct propaganda against the traditional Jewish way of life, which included Jewish education. Semyon portrayed himself as the "perfect Soviet Jewish pioneer," who trusted the school more than he trusted his parents. This transformation was an important goal of Soviet education, but very few testimonies suggest that this goal had been successfully accomplished. Testimonies like Semyon's are quite rare. More often people speak about the dualities that penetrated their daily lives. And the duality between the ideology in schools and family values is one of the most significant, a subject we will return to when we analyze antireligious propaganda. Here, I would like to draw attention to the constructive role that Yiddish schools played in building Soviet Jewish culture.

In the early 1930s the schools were becoming centers of public expressions of Jewish identity and culture. The original aim of these schools was to introduce a Soviet upbringing to Jewish children in their mother tongue, Yiddish. That Jewish culture was largely inappropriate because of its religious beliefs and Hebraic roots could not but affect the curriculum of Jewish schools, which differed from general schools mostly in form but not in substance. For example, Jewish history was studied only in the context of the general struggle of Jewish artisans against capitalist exploiters.[56] Similarly Communist criteria played the decisive role in the selection of Yiddish literary works for the required course on Yiddish literature. Jewish classics, works by such authors as Sholem Aleichem and Mendele Moykher Sforim, were studied in order to contrast their satirical descriptions of the ghetto community with the achievements of Soviet society.[57] The creators of the Jewish content of the curriculum probably did not intend to aid in the development of Jewish identity but rather wanted to explain the benefits of the Soviet lifestyle to Jewish children in Yiddish. However, the very fact that Jewish children were studying with Jewish teachers in Yiddish as the language of instruction was significant in the formation of their identity. Pupils of these schools, therefore, did not perceive themselves as simply Yiddish-speaking children who learned the values of Soviet society in Yiddish because they did not speak another language; rather, they understood themselves to be Jews studying in their own language in a state-sponsored school. A clear example of this relationship can be seen in interschool competitions (both in curricular subjects and extracurricular activities) that became widespread in the 1930s. Jewish schools often competed with neighboring Ukrainian or Russian schools in mathematics, football, chess, and other activities. When a Jewish school won, both Jews and non-Jews considered it a victory of one ethnic group over another, not as a victory of one Soviet school over another Soviet school, as the state had intended. Thus, these activities unintentionally helped to develop a national Jewish pride. This phenomenon is illustrated in the testimony of Tsirl B.:

> I remember how we prepared for an all-subjects competition with a Ukrainian school. It was in 1933. I was in the seventh grade. We had to prepare representatives for all sections of the competition: mathematics, physics, history. . . . The greatest attention was paid to sports. I remember we spent all our free time jumping, running. . . . The boys lifted weights, the girls practiced gymnastics. We had to be the best. We wanted to show that the Jews were not worse in sports than non-Jews (*goyim*). Our teachers were very worried that the boys would not win, so they trained them as much as they could. My father was a blacksmith, so he was very strong. He trained the boys in our school. . . . He said they had to win. We were all very enthusiastic. . . .
>
> On the day of the competition, we all came with our parents and were very nervous. I took part in the theater performance and in gymnastics. The girls won the gymnastic competition, and the boys won the sprinting and many other sports. I do not remember all of them. However, we lost in mathematics and chess. The director of our school said that it was Soviet Power that had transformed the weak Jewish child into a strong Soviet citizen. We were very happy.[58]

The Jewish elements of the curriculum played a key role in the formation of a positive Jewish identity. Children who read the stories of Sholem Aleichem did not think of these stories as representative of an old lifestyle. In fact, as many of the oral testimonies reveal, pupils saw more similarities with their own lives than with the hardships faced by previous generations. Parallel to that, the works of the new Soviet proletarian Jewish poets enjoyed a significant popularity. Children studied these poems about Lenin and other Soviet heroes in Jewish schools and performed them in Yiddish at private celebrations for Passover and Rosh Hashanah. These recitations became part of the ritual in the observance of traditional holidays. This phenomenon, like many others described below, was part of the joint existence of Jewish and Soviet in the same shtetl, in the same school, and within the same person.

Alternative Jewish Holidays and Rituals

The period of the New Economic Policy (NEP)—from 1921 to 1928—was seen by the Bolsheviks as an ideal setting for social and cultural experimentation. The very atmosphere of peace and normality, of relative tolerance and pluralism, created a sympathetic environment for leisurely culture building. In October 1923, following an intense period of public discussion on the subject, the Party issued a circular recommending Communist public festivals and private rituals. Emel'ian Iaroslavsky, secretary of the Central Control Commission, promoted sober and joyous ceremonies, processions with revolutionary songs and music, lectures and reports, and dignified games. These festivals, supplementing the already established holidays of the revolutionary calendar, were not to eschew mockery and insult but were intended instead to offer fun as well as enlightenment.[59] Komsomol members organized anti-Easter and anti-Christmas demonstrations, celebrations, and concerts. The carnivals included parodies of religious rituals, antireligious songs, and small theatrical performances. In June 1923 official holidays were transferred to the so-called New Calendar so that Church holidays became working days and could no longer be celebrated.[60]

Similarly Soviet ideologists saw a clear need to create viable alternatives to established rituals and holidays for Jews. They considered that, during the transition period, these rituals had to be based on Jewish traditions and then gradually lead to the establishment of completely new Soviet holidays. In the 1920s these holidays were used both as propaganda against the old religion and promotion of the new political system and ideology. The most notable attempt was the organization of alternative Passover and Yom Kippur celebrations.

Struggle with the Celebrations of Rosh Hashanah and Yom Kippur

In 1923 the Rosh Hashanah and Yom Kippur holidays marked some of the earliest celebrations against which direct antireligious campaigns were mounted. A massive number of articles, special supplements to newspapers, flyers, and slogans appeared in the press. Evsektsii published the first anti–Yom Kippur brochure in 1923, which, in quasi-academic terms, explains the devastating economic effects of the holiday, including harvest losses and reductions in productivity. In addition, the brochure argues that such holidays foster hostility between Jews and non-Jews by creating misunderstandings. The article further claims that these holidays help the Jewish "bourgeoisie" and "clericals" to become richer (since rabbis and kosher butchers gain economically through this observance).[61] A special supplement to the periodical *Der apikoyres* was published in August 1923 as part of this campaign.[62] Copiously illustrated with caricatures, this magazine offers a popular interpretation of the most solemn day of the Jewish year. An editorial, "Far vos zaynen komunistn kegn religye" (Why Communists are against religion), and an article, "Fun vanen shtampt roshashane un yomkiper" (The origins of Rosh Hashanah and Yom Kippur), both by I. Yakhin, argue that Judaism specifically uses the fall holidays to exploit poor.[63] Caricatures and skits, which parodied Jewish holy books and traditions, supplemented these theoretical explanations. The point was driven home by labeling books, songs, and even prayers as "capitalist." For example, the thirteen principles of the Jewish faith (*ani maamin*) were called "Der kapitalistisher ani maamin" (The capitalist principles of belief) in an article written by P. Lafarg in *Der apikoyres*.[64] The introduction of negative ideas expressed via familiar forms associated with religion were supposed to create a negative association with the original (this principle was widely used throughout Soviet antireligious propaganda). "Der kapitalistisher ani maamin" predictably replaces God with money:

1. I believe that capitalism rules over body and over soul.
2. I believe in spirit (the capitalist child) and in credit (that originates from it).
3. I believe in gold and silver, from which an altar is made in order to breathe a soul into paper money.[65]

In the first statement the mockery is structured as a direct parody of the thirteen principles of belief. (The original ani maamin states: "The Creator creates and controls everything.")[66] To balance the seriousness of these statements, the author of "Der kapitalistisher ani maamin" adds some details intended to show the reader the absurdity of both the capitalist way of thinking and traditional religious form:

4. I believe in a 5 percent rent increase and also in a 4.3 percent inflation of paper money.[67]

It is worth noting that, while the form and structure of this sketch parody familiar Jewish text, it does not relate to the Jewish experience (or use common negative stereotypes, such as Jewish capitalists) but rather emphasizes general issues of exploitation, including that the "rich rule over the poor." The publications aim to clarify the ideological approach of the Soviet regime toward the capitalist system as well as to ridicule a traditional religious text.

In addition to the general descriptions of the low moral values of capitalism, the parody explains how the old system harms average working people:

"Der kapitalistisher ani maamin" (The capitalist principles of faith). *Der apikoyres*, special fall edition. Kiev, Ukraine, 1923.

9. I believe in extending the working day.
10. I believe in a constant decrease in salary.
11. I believe in fooling the public and falsifying products.[68]

The summary of the entire conception is expressed in the final, thirteenth statement:

13. I believe in the eternal principles of our holy faith, the official political economy.[69]

"Der kapitalistisher ani maamin" expresses the essence of Soviet arguments against capitalism in a form familiar to traditional Jews. Ironically this form derives from the text that summarizes the essence of Judaism. Yet the new *ani maamin* is not offered as a surrogate replacement for the religious text. Rather, it works as an aid to the transition from religion to atheism, capitalism to socialism, and "backwardness" to "modernism." Once these goals are achieved, texts like this one will not be needed.

A similar principle is used in rewritten popular short stories, jokes, articles, theatrical performances, and songs, which are parodied in order to convey a new Soviet message. An example is a remake of the Yiddish song "Zol ikh zayn a rov" (Let me be a rabbi). Here is the original song:

> Zol ikh zayn a rov,
> Ken ikh nit keyn toyre!
> Zol ikh zayn a soykher,
> Hob ikh nit keyn *skhoyre.*
> Vil ikh zayn a shoykhet,
> Hob ikh nit keyn khalef,
> Vil ikh zayn a melamed,
> Ken ikh nit keyn alef.[70]

> Let me be a rabbi,
> I don't know the Torah!
> Let me be a merchant,
> I don't possess goods.
> I want to be a shoykhet,
> I don't have a ritual knife.
> I want to be a melamed,
> I don't know the alphabet.[71]

The published Soviet parody reverses the meaning of the old song:

> Zol ikh zayn a rov,
> Keyner darf mayn toyre!
> Mitsves un maysim toyvim
> Iz gor a knape skhoyre!
> Keyner efnt nit mayn tir,
> Nit keyn khupe, nit keyn get,
> S'bageyt zikh shoyn on mir![72]

Let me be a rabbi,
Nobody needs my Torah!
The commandments and good deeds
Are now useless goods!
Nobody opens my door,
No wedding, no divorce,
People get along without me!

Later in the song the rabbi wants to be a *melamed*, but he cannot because all the children attend the Soviet school; he wants to be a *khazn* (cantor), and he cannot since his entire audience went to the philharmonic society. Finally, he decides to become a *nepman* (businessman) and goes to prison for not being honest. The song clearly emphasizes that all the duties of religious authority figures are obsolete. It introduced new alternatives to the traditional Jewish way of life and forced changes in the professions. The song incorporates humor and is full of Jewish folk associations: *toyre* (Torah) rhymes with *skhoyre* (goods), which evokes the old Jewish proverb "Toyre is di beste skhoyre" (Learning [Torah] is the best merchandise). However, the song changed "best" into "useless" in reference to the Torah and thus inverted its message.

As in the case of "Der kapitalistisher ani maamin," the new song is not meant to become the new Soviet anthem. Instead, it serves as a parody of prerevolutionary values. Once these values lose their popularity, such songs will have fulfilled their mission and will no longer be needed.

Excerpts from *Der apikoyres* were recited during antireligious meetings, concerts, and stage performances organized in shtetlach in the mid-1920s. These concerts often followed *Yom-Kipernik* (state-organized voluntary work on Yom Kippur), which were conducted in various regions in 1923 and 1924, when young members of the Evsektsii marched in front of synagogues full of worshipers and sang revolutionary songs.[73] Sometimes they came into the synagogues and ate bread in front of the congregation against the rules of observance of Yom Kippur, and even organized antireligious feasts during the holiday.[74] Yom Kippur feasts made very strong impressions on those who witnessed or participated in them. Yakov M. (b. 1908) provides an exceptionally detailed recollection of this event:

On Rosh Hashanah 1923, the youth groups of Romanov gathered together for several meetings. I was a member of two groups: the young Zionists and the young Communists. The leader of the Communist group announced that the plan was to listen to a lecture on international relations and then have some dancing. He said that those who would attend synagogue for the service would be expelled from the Communist group. I fancied a girl there. I can't remember her name now. She said that her mother would kill her if she did not join her family for the synagogue service. I told her: "Look, go to the synagogue and then sneak out when no one is looking." I really wanted her to come dancing, you see. . . .

Der apikoyres, special fall edition, Kiev, 1923. The text reads: "The Torah is the best merchandise."

I myself also had different plans. . . . The Zionists organized a singing evening, and my best friend was a leader of the group. So, first I went there and then convinced the rest to come for the dancing organized by the Communist group. That girl was also there. . . .

A week later the Communist group announced that we were going to have a march and a demonstration around the synagogue during Yom Kippur. They said that praying and fasting were only for old people, and young people should realize that God did not exist. I did not care, as my parents went to another synagogue, but that girl said that she would not take part in the action, because she did not want her parents to see her do this. Later that evening a group of us marched to the synagogue, and I saw her. . . . We were busy shouting and screaming, when the rabbi came out and said he would tell our parents. Then one boy took out a piece of bread and ate it in front of the rabbi, and then said: "I ate on Yom Kippur, why did God not punish me?" The rabbi replied: "Dogs also eat *treyf* [non-kosher food] and do not die." We all started laughing. . . . But then I was afraid that somebody would tell my dad, and I ran home and stayed with the family all day. Later I found out that the group proceeded to the other synagogue, where my dad was praying. I was glad I had left.[75]

The testimony demonstrates that this respondent participated in the events not primarily because of his antireligious convictions but rather because he saw it as a way to socialize with other young people. His membership in both Zionist and Communist groups illustrates that political views did not play the decisive role in his choice of social activities. It is also noteworthy that, although Yakov took part in actions he knew his family would disapprove of, he and some of his friends wanted to avoid open confrontations with their parents. Finding a balance between family, social life, and politics was a central problem faced by many young Jews, like Yakov, and the events staged during these Jewish holidays mirrored various contradictions that existed in the Soviet Jewish community in the mid-1920s. Like everywhere in Eastern Europe, young Soviet Jews were becoming more politically involved than their parents. But in the Soviet Union political involvement often meant attacking the essence of the parents' way of life.

The events organized by Jewish Komsomol members during Rosh Hashanah and Yom Kippur signified more than just a "Jewish" parallel to other antireligious campaigns. Unlike many other Jewish holidays, these fall celebrations did not coincide with similar Russian Orthodox or Muslim counterparts. Therefore the propaganda messages usually explained that, although these Jewish holidays were different from those of other religions, the Jews who followed these customs were victims of exploitation by Jewish "capitalists." Still, mounting these campaigns against uniquely Jewish holidays meant that only Jews, and no other national minorities, were affected by them. Thus, when organizing these programs, the government was mindful not to foster antisemitism. Consequently far fewer fall holidays were targeted compared to Jewish holidays that had parallels with other religions. For example, the government staged mass anti-Passover campaigns (this holiday corresponds to Easter) and, in fact, mounted five times the number of programs designed to target Passover compared to those that focused specifically on the Jewish holidays of Yom Kippur and Rosh Hashanah.[76]

Alternative Passover

The celebration of Passover is traditionally associated with the spirit of freedom and independence. The seder ceremony features a special menu, the reading of the Haggadah (the retelling of the story of Exodus), songs, and even games. Passover is also the only Jewish celebration whose ritual requires dialogue between children and parents. All this creates an ideal basis for the introduction of new concepts in a popular, well-known format. By the end of the nineteenth century Jewish radicals in Poland, the United States, and Canada were employing the Passover seder for the promotion of political views as well as a way to criticize their opponents. Various political movements organized political seders in interwar Poland.[77]

Soviet Jewish activists, too, did not miss the opportunity to use Passover as a propaganda tool. In 1921 the Central Bureau of the Bolshevik Party's Evsektsii sent instructions to all local branches to organize "Red Passovers." Popular brochures that came to be known as "Red Haggadahs" were published, specifying how to conduct the alternative celebrations. Many were written by local activists following a series of centrally directed patterns. One of these was the *Komsomolishe Haggadah* (Komsomol Haggadah), published in Moscow in 1923 by Moyshe Altshuler.[78] Traditionally the start of Passover (an eight-day holiday during which the consumption of bread or leavened products and yeast is forbidden) is marked with the *Bdikas khometz*—a search for all remaining traces of leavened food, followed by its burning. In Altshuler's *Komsomolishe Haggadah,* this ceremony was transformed as follows:

> Ten years ago the working class of Russia with the help of peasants searched for *khometz* (leaven) in our land.[79] They cleaned away all the traces of landowners and bourgeois bosses in the country and took power in their own hands. They took the land from the landowners, plants and factories from the capitalists; they fought the enemies of the workers on all fronts. In the fire of the great socialist revolution, the workers and peasants burned Kochak, Yudenich, Vrangel, Denikin, Pilsudskii, Petlyura, Chernov, Khots, Dan, Martov, and Abramovich. They recited the blessing: "All landowners, bourgeois and their helpers—Mensheviks, Esers, Kadets, Bundists, Zionists, Esesovtses, Eesovtses, Poaley Zionists, Tsaarey-tsienikes, and all other counterrevolutionaries should be burned in the flame of revolution.[80] Those who are burned should not ever survive, and the rest should be given to us and we shall transfer them to the hands of the GPU.[81]

The Komsomol Haggadah combines all enemies of the Soviet regime as *khometz,* and recommends burning them. Equating antagonists who were notori-

הַגָּדָה שֶׁל פֶּסַח

אַף אַיוורע־טײַטש.

בדקת חמץ

Bdikas khomets (Search for leaven). Illustration from the first
edition of *Hagadah far gloybers un apikorsim* (Passover story for
believers and atheists). Kharkov, 1923.

ously anti-Jewish, such as the commander of the White Army Alexei Denikin,
to Jewish Soviet opponents, such as Bundists or Zionists, was a popular method
of Soviet propaganda. It was not important why or how but simply that they
were portrayed as being equally obnoxious.

Every seder ritual was transformed in the Soviet Haggadah. The traditional
hand-washing and blessing before the meal became a political statement:

Wash off all the bourgeois mud, wash off the mold of generations, and do not say a blessing, say a curse. Devastation must come upon all the old rabbinical laws and customs, yeshivas and khaydorim, that becloud and enslave the people.[82]

These rituals prepared the participants of the Komsomol seder for the reception of new information, and, indeed, the principal segments follow. In the traditional Haggadah the youngest child of the family asks four questions about the meaning of the festival. The father tells the story of the Jews' exodus from Egypt with God's help, emphasizing that their liberation is the symbol of freedom, that Jews should strive for freedom, and that every Passover is a reminder of the power of God.

The Komsomol Haggadah at times altered the order of activities. Its style also differed from the traditional Haggadah, as the Soviet publication was geared for a different audience, a meeting of friends rather than family. The following provocative questions are modeled after the four questions in the original Haggadah:

Why is Passover not a true festival of the Jewish people if all Jews celebrate their release from slavery? Is it not harmful for young workers to refuse to celebrate it? You always teach us to hate slavery and show how necessary it is to struggle for freedom. You have festivals like May Day and the [anniversary of the] October Revolution, and all the workers go to demonstrations, so why can't we celebrate the liberation from Egypt and regard this as the national day of Jewish freedom?[83]

Indeed, some Soviet Haggadah texts provide more moderate explanations. They simply replace "God" with the "October Revolution":

We were slaves of capital until October came and led us out of the land of exploitation with a strong hand, and if it were not for October, we and our children would still be slaves.[84]

The Komsomol Haggadah, however, provides another answer. It explains the appearance of the ancient holiday of spring and how it was transformed into Passover for the benefit of priests and, later, rabbis. It introduces historical and ethnographical "facts" to show that a similar festival existed among some "Arab tribes" and that the custom emerged entirely because of illiteracy. It provides "logical" explanations for every detail of the story. Thus the fire on Mount Sinai is not a reflection of the divine appearance but rather an eruption of an old volcano; the matzo are flat because this is a traditional spring bread; the exodus is the wandering of a nomadic tribe; and so on. The final exclamation of the seder, "Next year in Jerusalem," symbolizing the connection of the Jewish people to the Promised Land and the hope that the Messiah will come, is substituted by "This year a revolution here; next year—a world revolution!"[85] The Komsomol Haggadah argues that Passover is not a celebration of real freedom but rather of spiritual slavery, because the holiday comes only from heaven. In contrast, genuine freedom is in the hands of the proletariat, and therefore one must celebrate May Day.

According to the Komsomol Haggadah, Passover deals with only Jewish mat-

קאָרבן-פּעסאָך

The sacrifice of Pesakh. Illustration from the second edition of
Hagadah far gloybers un apikorsim (Passover story for believers
and atheists). Moscow, 1927. Drawing by A. Tyshler.

ters, whereas May Day is an international holiday meaningful to all. Therefore
Altshuler also internationalized the Haggadah:

> Instead of the story of how the sea was divided, we speak about the brave heroes
> of the Red Army near Perekop.[86] Instead of the groaning of the Jews in Egypt and
> God's miracles, we speak about the real sufferings of the proletariat and peasants
> in their resistance against their exploiters and their heroic struggle.

The final part of the Komsomol Haggadah instructs followers to cast away "the
mold of generations"—the clergy and nationalist festivals—and praise the revolution and workers' holidays.

In 1927 Altshuler's *Haggadah* was reprinted with minor changes. The second

קוירצך

עפּנט אויף, כאַװיירים, די כוירערן פון דער פּראַלעטאָאוישער מעלוכע און
װייַזט אַלע אַרבעטסער און פּויערים פון דער גאַנצער װעלט, װאָס גע וגעַן זיך
נאָך אונטערן יאָך פון קאַפּיטאַל, װי מיר האָבן פֿאַר אונזער כרייַהייַס גע=
קעמ=ט, און װי מיר האָבן די מאַכט אין אונזערע אייגענע הענט גענומען.
רופט צו אַלע אַרבעטער פון דער גאַנצער װעלט: שטייט אוף קעגן

18

Koyrekh (The ritual of matsa and bitter herbs sandwich). The Red Army soldier eats a
sandwich "made" of Yulii Martov (the former leader of the Menshevik movement),
Raymond Poincar, and Neville Chamberlain. Illustration from the first edition of
Hagadah far gloybers and apikorsim (Passover story for believers and atheists).
Kharkov, 1923.

Haggadah shel pesakh (Story of Passover), cover from the second edition.
Drawing by Alexander Tyshler. Moscow, 1927.

דאַיינו

ווען באָלשעוויקעס וואָלטן קומען
און וואָלטן גאָרנישט צוגענומען
וואָלטס געווען, אַז ווי צו אונז גאָר...דאַיינו

ווען זיי וואָלטן יאָ גענומען
נאָר זיי האָלטן לאָזן האַנדלען,
וואָלטן מיר אַלץ צוריק באַקומען
און ס'וואָלט געווען ... דאַיינו

בײַ רעם אומגליק'לעכן האַנדל,
ווען ס'וואָלט ניט געווען קיין טינאָסטײעל,
וואָלטן מיר פון זיי געמאַכט אַ טעל
און ס'וואָלט געווען ... דאַיינו

ווען ס'איז דאַ סינאָטדיעל,
נאָר די גע־פּע־אוי וואָלט אויסגעריטן,
וואָלטס מען אָן אַיצע שוין געסיטן
און ס'האָלט געווען ... דאַיינו

Dayenu (Enough), a page from a special Passover edition of
Der apikoyres. Moscow, 1929.

edition featured a new illustrator—Alexander Tyshler (1898–1980), who worked
for the Moscow State Yiddish Theater—but retained the mood and the essence
of the first publication. Rabbis were portrayed as old, angry, and frightening
individuals, the antithesis of the proletariat which was shown as young, cheerful, and healthy. Compared to the first edition, which featured Hebrew words,
ridiculed Orthodox Jewish dress, and caricatured traditional Haggadah covers,
the second edition was more universal. Although it still mocked traditional Judaism, the pictures were milder and included more positive images of Jewish
workers and soldiers. Instead of ridiculing religious traditions alone, the second
edition incorporated other "hostile" elements, such as Zionists, bourgeois Jews,
and even Soviet bureaucrats. Judaism was now seen not just as a religion but
rather as a banner under which all Soviet enemies were united. In other words,

from an anti-Judaic piece of propaganda, the Red Haggadah eventually became anti-Jewish in general.

In later years additional variations of the Red Haggadah appeared as supplements to the Moscow Yiddish monthly *Der apikoyres*. They are predominantly in verse form and stray further from the traditional version than Altshuler's rendition. The Red Haggadah of the 1930s consists of new stories of the Exodus connected with Soviet reality, which were to be accompanied by the singing of the *Internationale* and the eating of bread (strictly forbidden during Passover). Some traditional motifs, however, are retained, including the popular seder song "Dayenu" which recites all the benefits the Jews have received from God. After each verse the refrain says: "If You [God] had done only this for us, it would have been enough!" The Red seder presents this song as being sung by counter-revolutionaries. It explains, in popular form, the reasons for the interruption of the NEP campaign and shows that "capitalist elements" will survive if they are given the slightest opportunity:

> Ven bolshevikes voltn kumen,
> Un voltn gornit tsugenumen
> Volt geven, az vey tsu undz gor . . . dayenu.

> Ven zey voltn yo genumen,
> Nor zey voltn lozm handlen,
> Voltn mir alts tsurik bakumen,
> Un s'volt geven . . . dayenu.

> Bay dem umgliklekhn handl,
> Ven s'volt nit geven keyn finotdiel,
> Voltn mir fun zey gemakht a tel,
> Un s'volt geven . . . dayenu![87]

> If the Bolsheviks just came,
> And did not take anything
> It would be for us quite . . . enough.

> Even if they took something,
> But only let us trade,
> We would get everything back
> And this would be . . . enough.

> We would trade unsuccessfully,
> And if there were no financial [e.g., taxation] department,
> We would do away with them,
> And for us it would be . . . enough!

In the parody dishonest entrepreneurs criticized the Soviet regime, incidentally revealed the flaws in its economic system, and plotted its destruction. In this way the authors of the parody attempted to convey that opponents of the Soviet regime used religion and religious songs to mask their intentions. Thus religion and religious observance are subtly equaled with economic sabotage. Generally this is how religious songs are parodied in Soviet propaganda texts. Yet a notable exception is a version of the four questions in the same Haggadah in which a positive character transforms the four questions into an accusation: the son blames his father for observing the "dark" tradition and not struggling with the rabbis:

> Kh'freg dikh tate, ma nishtane,
> Bist oysvaksn gor gevorn
> Host keyn deye un di meye
> Iz oykh nit vi in yene yorn![88]

> I ask you, father: "How does it differ?"
> You are completely grown up,
> But you don't have any standing, and your business
> Is also not like it used to be.

Following his speech, the son does not wait for a response but begins telling the story of the Red Exodus. The action takes place in Soviet Russia. Those who are expelled are "evil," whereas, ironically, the heroes are identified with the Egyptians, signifying that, during the Exodus, Jews did not deserve to stay in Egypt and were therefore discarded. The villains in this Haggadah are "Rabbi Denikin" and "Rabbi Kolchak," who are attempting to ruin the lives of the proletariat. By equating White Army generals such as Denikin and Kolchak, who were known antisemites, with rabbis, the Red Haggadah tries to demonstrate that both groups are dangerous enemies. Kolchak and Denikin continued to be represented as enemies in Soviet ideology many decades after the Red Haggadah and Red seders were discarded and forgotten. Yet the principles used in the construction of Red seders, such as across-the-board negation, played an important role in the formulation of Soviet propaganda messages.

Alternative seders were conducted through the mid-1930s. Gradually these activities moved to Jewish schools and aimed to attract children rather than to convince adults. New Soviet holidays such as May Day and the anniversary of the October Revolution finally replaced modified versions of Jewish holidays in the mid-1930s. Some families continued to celebrate the Passover seder, often in its modified form (without prayers), and although red seders disappeared from public memory, their message still lived in the minds of many of those who witnessed them.

The New Religion: Soviet and Kosher

It is very difficult to find out how people actually incorporated these new rituals into their daily lives. One source is contemporary Yiddish journals and periodicals. However, they have one significant disadvantage regarding their objectivity. The sociological surveys that appeared in these publications were conducted in the late 1920s as part of the preparation for the mass antireligious campaigns. Their main purpose, therefore, was not to reveal the state of religion in the Jewish shtetlach but to show that certain measures were needed to "improve" the situation. As a result, the articles may have exaggerated the level of religious observance among Jews or emphasized elements that would justify further antireligious propaganda.

Thus, in 1928, the Kharkov-based magazine *Di royte velt* (The red world) published an article by I. Veitsblit entitled "Toward a Monographic Description of One Shtetl," in which much attention is paid to the state of religion in the Ukrainian shtetl of Darevke.[89] In his case study Veitsblit emphasized, inter alia, that Soviet councils ignored the charity and aid functions that religious activists organized for "dark purposes," namely, to promote religion. According to the report, the rabbi became an even more powerful figure after the revolution. Veitsblit goes on to say that before the revolution the inhabitants were not very religious: they traveled on the Sabbath, women did not light candles on Friday nights, and many ate pork in secret. By the late 1920s the situation had changed. Because the local authorities did not speak Yiddish and could not assist people in their daily lives, the rabbi became the most authoritative figure in the shtetl; new houses of prayer opened; the charitable institutions existed only in the religious communities; local inhabitants spent a great deal of money to sustain the kosher bakery and to support kosher meat production; they paid the synagogue cantor; and so on. The report also states that it was impossible to find money to pay the teacher in the Soviet Yiddish school and to convert a synagogue into a club. The women started lighting candles, the men returned to the synagogues, and the antireligious propaganda was dull.[90] Similar observations are found in reports of the Evsektsii from various regions of Byelorussia in the early 1920s, emphasizing that the people often did not attend antireligious lectures or clubs and libraries but went to synagogues instead.[91] The details vary, but the majority of the authors agree: religion was gaining strength, and the main reason for this was the lack of effective propaganda materials.[92]

Another source of information is sociological surveys conducted in Soviet Yiddish-language schools. Children were asked which traditions their families observed, what they talked about at home, and what their parents' opinion was of the Soviet government's policy toward the Jewish religion. One such survey was published in the Byelorussian Yiddish magazine *Shtern* (Star) in 1931 and another in the Ukrainian Yiddish magazine *Ratnbildung* (Soviet education) in 1930.[93] The author of the *Shtern* articles, K. Khadoshevich, analyzed the results of the research conducted in Byelorussia, where 1,560 children from larger towns and shtetlach were questioned about religious practices.[94] The questions in this survey were the following:

Who is religious in your family?
What do your parents think about antireligious education in school?
What do your parents think about the transformation of synagogues into clubs?

What do your parents say about the fact that kosher meat is not sold anymore? Do your parents punish you because you don't believe in God?[95]

The article analyzes the children's answers and compares the differences between cities and shtetlach, the social status of parents, the authority of teachers in particular schools, and other factors that might have influenced attitudes toward religion. The children were even offered three possible responses—negative, positive, and neutral. The interviewers feared that children would protect their parents with answers such as "my parents are very positive toward Soviet policies."[96] Generally the survey asked for detailed explanations, for example, "My father says that closing the synagogue is good because the club is better, or be cause there is a place for meetings now."[97] The article's conclusions are presented in tables displaying the percentages of believers and nonbelievers among rural and urban inhabitants and the percentages of workers, *kustars* (handicraftsmen), men, and women. The survey concludes that cities were less religious than shtetlach, that women observed traditions more than men, and that practically everyone fasted on Yom Kippur and ate matzo during Passover.[98]

The results of another survey, published in *Ratnbildung,* demonstrate that most of the children knew how to celebrate Passover and did so every year; the families obtained American matzo and saw Passover as the only festival of Jewish national solidarity. The inhabitants liked the festival much more than May Day because during Passover they received gifts, the entire family gathered at home, and they ate delicious food. May Day, on the other hand, was a day full of boring meetings and lectures. Typical responses included: "My father was angry because he had to attend the official gatherings"; "My mother was angry, too, because Father was not at home"; "The children were not in a festive mood, especially since they did not fully understood why it was a holiday."[99]

In 1999–2003 I asked similar questions to people who grew up in the same towns. While many respondents' memories were not perfect, and some later events may have altered their perceptions, their responses provide interesting insights that at times balance and supplement biased reports found in the Soviet press.

All respondents in my study note that Jewish festivals were normally celebrated in smaller shtetlach in the 1920s and 1930s. Many remember Purim, Hanukkah, Yom Kippur, Rosh Hashanah, and, most of all, Passover. They also remember the alternative Red seders that were conducted in Jewish clubs. These activities were very well attended and generated much enthusiasm. The form of the Red seder celebrations is hard to reconstruct, but there is some evidence about their content. For example, Efim G. remembers a song of the Red seder conducted in his shtetl of Parichi:

Mi asapru, mi adabru,
Hey, hey, lomche dreydl,
Ver ken visn, ver ken tseyln
Vos dos eynts batayt, vos dos eynts batayt

Eyner iz Karl Marx, un Marx iz eyner,
Un mer nit keyner.
. . .
Vos dos tsvey batayt, vos dos tsvey batayt
Tsvey iz Lenin-Trotsky
Un eyner iz der Karl Marx,
Un Marx iz eyner, un mer nit keyner.
. . .
Vos dos dray batayt, vos dos dray batayt
Dray iz internatsional, tsvey iz Lenin Trotsky,
Eynts iz Karl Marx, un Marx iz keyner, un mer nit keyner.

Who will tell me, who will say
Hey, hey, turn the dreidel
Who can know, who can count
What does one mean, what does one mean?
One is Karl Marx, Marx is one
There is no one else.
. . .
What does two mean, what does two mean?
Two is Lenin-Trotsky
One is Karl Marx,
Marx is one, and there is no one else.
. . .
What does three mean, what does three mean?
Three means Internationals, two means Lenin-Trotsky,
One is Karl Marx, and there is not one more.[100]

This song is a parody of a traditional Passover song. The original words say: "One is God, two are two scrolls of Torah, given to the Jews on the mount of Zion, and three are the number of the Jewish fathers [Abraham, Isaac, and Jacob]." Efim G. actually thought that this was a Soviet Jewish song. He did not know that this was an adaptation of a much older Jewish song until he came to the United States in 1989, where he was invited to a traditional Passover dinner.

The structure of this "Red Passover" song differs markedly from that of officially published antireligious songs. Official songs retain old melodies and commonly substitute religious themes with negative images, such as in the "Red Dayenu," which portrays NEPmen, or capitalists, as enemies. Consequently songs adapted from religious sources were designed to satirize those people who were still observant (and who were also presumed to be anti-Soviet). Here, the content of the Soviet Passover "counting" song clearly reflects the popular, even subconscious understanding of Soviet ideology that replaced old sacred symbols with the new gods (positive images of Soviet leaders). In the 1920s this type of substitution occurred only in unpublished songs. The government did not want to "replace gods"; rather, it wanted to attack religion through the creation of negative associations. It was not until the mid-1930s that Stalin replaced God in many officially published Yiddish folksongs.

Despite the antireligious content of the Red seders, they were distinctly Jewish events, organized for Jews, by Jews, and, equally important, they were conducted in Yiddish. Even the building in which the event took place was frequently a former synagogue. Most Jews did not perceive these activities as anti-Jewish. They saw them as Soviet Jewish events, created for their entertainment, and also as traditional holidays. Even after the most successful Red seders, which were attended by large audiences, the majority would go home and celebrate traditional Passover seders. Furthermore, those who conducted the Red seder often hurried to conclude the event since their families were waiting for them at home to celebrate the traditional seder. This was described by participants at such events. Velvl K., for example, was one of the organizers of the Red seders:

> While I was at the Yiddish teachers' training college [*tekhnikum*], my fellow students and I were sent to the shtetlach in the Ukraine to help organize anti-Passover campaigns. We prepared long lectures and discussion meetings. Sometimes even khometz food (such as bread) was provided for distribution. Many people came to join us. People in the shtetlach liked to see us, educated young men and women, who came to their shtetlach from Kiev. They were extremely friendly. I remember that, by the second day after our arrival, each of us had several invitations to private Passover seders in different houses. . . . We enjoyed the holiday just as everyone else did after the official part of the day was over.[101]

It is important to note the different generational perspectives on these antireligious events. Naturally children and young people were more involved in antireligious activities, but this was not necessarily connected to rebellions against their own parents, who retained a traditional lifestyle. It was more complex. Etya G., a devoted young Pioneer of the 1930s, explains:

> It was like two different worlds. My parents went to the synagogue and kept the Sabbath. I had my own obligations in school. During Passover they would go to the synagogue and I would go to school for rehearsals of the antireligious performance. In the evening they came to see me starring in the antireligious play. They were proud I was selected to sing in the performance. It meant I had a good voice and was better than the other children.[102]

Because traditional public institutions such as synagogues and Jewish religious schools were closed, the family became the center of Jewish tradition and education. At times their families may have seemed "backward" to my respondents, but their homes were still a place for holidays such as Passover, a celebration that fascinated children. At the same time the Soviet school and the new Soviet holidays were associated with a modern, exciting life. My respondents celebrated parades on May Day, the anniversary of the Great October Socialist Revolution, International Women's Day, and so on. Children lived in two parallel worlds that rarely touched each other directly: the world of the family and the world of school. Ian D. asserts:

> I remember Soviet holidays very well. There were parades. There was a holiday called MYUD [*Mezhdunarodnyi iunosheskii den'*, International Day of Youth]. On that day all schoolchildren went to parades. I remember that all these holidays were widely celebrated in schools.
>
> My parents did not really celebrate these Soviet holidays. It was good for my parents, because they had the day off, but they did not make any celebrations (*keyn simkhes hot men nit gemakht*) out of it. We had a Jewish house. . . . We had many Jewish things at home. We had an eastern wall in our house, *mizrekh vant*. We had a painting of the Temple hanging on this wall. It was in a bedroom. In another room there was a picture depicting the torture of the Jews at the time of the Spanish Inquisition. . . . We also had some Jewish things from my grandfather that were in our home. . . .
>
> At home everything was Jewish and in Yiddish. We celebrated all the Jewish holidays. My mother was a pious person; she was keeping *Yidish-kayt* [Jewish way of life]. She had a woman's prayer book (*tkhine*). She used to pray on *Shabes* [the Sabbath] and on *Yontev* [each holiday]. She used to pray that the children would be healthy. I remember all the Jewish holidays very well.
>
> There was no Jewish holiday that we did not celebrate. I remember *Simkhes Toyre*. I was given a small flag, and on the top of it there was an apple. We danced a lot in the synagogue there. I was also given a small *Toyre*, a *Toyrele* [The Scroll of the Torah]. We danced with the *Toyre*.[103] My father often went to the synagogue. I used to go to the synagogue even when I grew older.[104]

The children often did not see any contradiction between their religious upbringing at home and antireligious propaganda in school. They thought that the family followed certain rules, and society followed others. Ian D. further explains:

> My family was traditional. My father used to go to the synagogue. She [my mother] kept a good kosher house. Everything was kosher at home. We lived a Soviet way of life [*sovetish shteyger*], but it was all kosher.[105]

Compare this testimony to that of a representative of the younger generation, Philip G. (born ten years later than Ian D.), who felt embarrassed about his parents' religious background:

> Jewish holidays were sacred. All these holidays were celebrated in our family. We even did the Sabbath evening prayers. My grandmother and her generation took it more seriously. People of her age would gather for collective prayer, and so on. In an ordinary family it was all done at home. But it did take place. I remember candles. . . .
>
> The situation with the Soviet holidays was different. My father was not

a member of a collective farm. He was very independent. But we children loved Soviet holidays. We celebrated them in school. My father loved to watch us, but he did not celebrate. This bothered me as a child. I respected him so much, and I understood that it was much more serious than his ideological backwardness. He was tolerant toward me. I loved wearing my red tie, white shirt; I was happy. He did not say anything negative about this, but he did not share my happiness about the matter either. . . . My father did not forbid anything, but he was trying to distract me from that. For example, he bought me pigeons. I used to take care of them. . . . There were so many things about pigeons. You have to feed them properly to take good care of them. It was such a pleasure to watch them. . . . When they fell in love with each other, they would hover high in the air for hours. I loved watching them. . . . That was how he distracted me.[106]

For children of Philip's generation, being Jewish meant being Jewish at home and being an "ordinary human being" (i.e., non-Jew) out in the street. They thought that Jewish holidays were part of a family tradition. The Soviet holidays had a more universal character for him. Children observed both Soviet and Jewish holidays; they were Soviet in the outside world and Jewish at home.[107]

Sometimes children were forced to perform antireligious actions in school that were organized in the form of a game. Many respondents reported that the idea of Passover was connected with various unconventional activities. Samuil G., who took part in these events in a shtetl in the Ukraine, remembers:

As a child I loved Passover very much. I loved the kugel [baked pudding, as of potatoes or noodles] that my mother baked for the holiday. She made it in a very special way that I have never tasted since. I loved how everything went crazy in the house as we were changing dishes for Passover and my grandmother was cleaning the house ferociously. The atmosphere at the [Yiddish] school was different, too. Of course, we didn't have the day off or anything like that. Still, we had many interesting activities taking place in school. First, older children, the *komyugistn* [Komsomol members] would come to conduct some activities for us. They explained how religion oppressed the masses in other countries. We played many interesting games together. For example, on the first day of Passover, they would gather us together and give each of us ten pieces of bread. We were given the task of going to Jewish houses and throwing a piece into the window of ten different houses. The one who was the fastest would receive a prize. We enjoyed the game very much, especially when the old, angry women came out of their houses and ran after us screaming "*Apikorsim!*" ["Heretics!"]. We felt like heroes of the revolution and were very proud. But in the evening we would all go home and celebrate the traditional seder with all the necessary rituals.[108]

Children were not the only ones who faced the complexities of this dual existence. Adults, too, had to make compromises between their traditional ways of life, modern changes in society, and, perhaps most important, their possible sources of income. Here is the testimony of a former Byelorussian resident, Efim G.:

> My father could do any job. He was a jack-of-all-trades. He was a tailor, a barber, and a baker. After the revolution he became a professional atheist and the chairman of the working committee. Then he became a chairman of the shtetl council. My father had an especially good income during the time of Passover, when he worked as a *zetser* [matzo bakery assistant]. The fact that he was also a professional atheist didn't prevent him from carrying out his job. It was a very good source of income because all our neighbors were believers. We didn't even think there were any contradictions in this.[109]

On a cultural level, Passover and May Day were viewed not as contradictory but as fulfilling different functions. Passover was a family holiday, with specific rituals and traditions that celebrated national freedom from slavery. May Day, similarly, signified deliverance from servitude but on a class level. Yurii B. asserts:

> Passover was only for the Jews and it was celebrated at home, whereas May Day was celebrated at the club. There were people of different nationalities there. There were Ukrainian, Polish, and Czech villages around us, so inhabitants of these villages would come to the club to celebrate the holiday. The club was a cultural center for them, too. Because it was situated in a Jewish shtetl [Romanov], it united Jews with all other nations. May Day was the perfect opportunity to celebrate something together with other nationalities.[110]

The coexistence of Soviet and Jewish holidays created mutual influences on the rituals associated with these celebrations. Many of the traditional Jewish holiday ceremonies changed in the Soviet Union because they received an infusion of new elements of Soviet culture. Sometimes traditional Jewish rituals were mixed with Russian Orthodox traditions. This occurred frequently in larger cities, and, as a result of large migrations in the 1920s, Galina K., a former Muscovite, recalls the following story:

> Two families shared our communal apartment. Our family was Jewish, the other was not. We celebrated both *Paskha* every spring.[111] We had a common table: one side of it was Jewish, the other side was Christian. We had matzo, they had *kulich* [Easter bread]. They had their guests, we had ours. After a couple of glasses of wine, however, we all shared food and sang Russian songs with them. Sometimes my parents sang in Yiddish, and the neighbors would repeat the refrain. It was all very friendly.[112]

Galina's testimony exemplifies the radical changes taking place at that time, as religious customs and traditions were being molded, combined, and reshaped. Her assertions also fit into the observations made by the historian William

Husband who has stated that the "critical mass" of Soviet citizens stood somewhere between active believers and antireligious activists. According to his analysis, this popular worldview often incorporated both Soviet and religious notions, and, "in combination with the collective inertia, could and did overwhelm religious and antireligious proselytizing alike."[113] Instead, Soviet and church notions (which did not always contradict each other) were combined; the result can be referred to as Soviet popular religion. Similar to any popular religion, it included its postulates, values, holy texts, and rituals that did not always correspond to a "higher doctrine" but nevertheless did not lack meaning for its followers.[114]

David Fishman has noted that the combined forces of emancipation, on the one hand, and state persecution of Judaism, on the other, generated a pace of secularization, acculturation, and alienation from Jewish traditions unparalleled in modern Jewish history.[115] I argue, however, that what occurred was not an "alienation" from Jewish tradition but rather an appearance of a new system of beliefs and values. To rephrase Husband, a new Jewish popular religion emerged in the 1920s and 1930s with some elements inherited from old Jewish traditions and others reflecting developments of Soviet culture. This is the religion that can be roughly referred to as "Soviet and kosher," the basis on which Soviet Jewish secular culture was built.

2 From Illiteracy to Worker Correspondents: Soviet Yiddish Amateur Writing

In 2001 Fira Abramovna S. was living in a small communal apartment in central Moscow. She had recently turned 102 and was residing with her 83-year-old roommate, Vasilii Alekseevich. "Fira Abramovna is very excited to have a visitor," explains Vasilii, as he opens the door for me. "But please be brief," he adds. "Don't take more than half an hour of her time, and don't ask her too many questions. She cannot hear very well anymore. Just listen to what she has to say. It will make the old woman very happy."

Fira greets me with a smile and speaks quietly but clearly and intelligently, in a Yiddish that is heavily laden with Russian. She does not get up from her bed and asks Vasilii to bring her a green folder. ("It is hard for me to move," she explains.) Fira takes out a small piece of paper and hands it to me. The ink has almost dissolved from the yellowish piece of stationery but still reveals an old handwritten letter in Yiddish:

Dear Comrade S [. . .],
   Thank you for your insightful note about my poem "Yatn" (Guys). I will think about your comments, and will take them into account in my future work.
With comradely greetings,
Itsik Fefer

"I am sorry I cannot give this to you," says Fira, as I start copying the text of the letter into my notebook. "This letter is very important to me. It was written by a very famous Soviet Yiddish poet, Itsik Fefer. He was killed by Stalin, but he was a wonderful poet. And he liked my comments—you saw it for yourself!"

Fira then embarks on a daylong monologue in which she talks about Jews, her life, and everything she feels that I need to know in order to write a book on "Jewish culture." Fira was born in the small Ukrainian town of Monastyrschina in May 1899. She describes her family as extremely poor: "They did not own a house but rented two rooms from a Jewish landlord," she explains. Her father was a striving shoemaker; her mother died young, when Fira was just ten years old. Fira never went to school and began to help her father at work at the age of twelve. Her father remarried shortly thereafter, and Fira was forced to look for ways to support herself. "At the time, no one wanted to marry me," she explains, "because I was from a poor family with no *yihes* [pedigree]." During the pogroms of 1918, she lost her father and virtually everyone she knew. Her landlord and his family were also killed. With no one to turn to, she took up various residences as a live-in maid.

In 1919 Fira's life changed completely. She remembers how soldiers with Red flags marched to Monastyrschina. The large synagogue became a Soviet town hall. She says that people regularly gathered in the streets and discussed what the new government was doing. Fira overheard various conversations and decided to go to the council to ask if the Soviet regime could help her to get a room. The first official she talked to, a young Jewish man named Itsik S., invited her to live temporarily in his little apartment. "Times were different," she sighs. "People were nicer." The young man later helped Fira to get her own room. After that he convinced her to enroll in the new literacy courses that were held in the building, a former synagogue. It turned out that this was the first time Fira went inside this synagogue. During the four-month course she learned how to read and write both in Yiddish and Russian. As a result, she was able to get a job as a clerk in a local office. A year later Fira and Itsik married and eventually brought up three children.

Reading and writing opened a new world for Fira. She began to devour newspapers, magazines, and books that were available in the new Yiddish library. She eagerly attended literary events, was active at local Soviet council meetings in her town, and even played an old witch in a local theater workshop. She said, "What we liked most, however, was when 'real' artists from bigger cities, such as Kiev or Odessa, came to Monastyrschina and recited poetry dealing with the civil war, about new people, women and children killed in the pogroms, and anything in general with Soviet characters." She was so inspired by a poem at one such event that she wrote a letter to its author, Itsik Fefer:

> I told him all about my life, my poor mother, the pogroms, and about what the Soviet regime gave me. I wanted him to write more about people like me, people who would have been dead if the Bolsheviks did not save us. I also asked him whether he could write some novels, as I liked them best. I said that I wanted him to write a book that would teach me and my children how to be real Soviet women: honest, proud, and hardworking.[1]

Fira mailed the letter, and three months later, in November 1935, she received a reply. That letter from Itsik Fefer became one of Fira's most precious possessions. It survived her evacuation to Frunze during World War II, and she managed to bring it with her every time she moved in Ukraine and Russia. She arrived in Moscow in the late 1950s, when her husband was offered a new job there. During most of her postwar life Fira wrote and read predominantly in Russian. However, this did not affect her attitude toward reading in Yiddish. For example, she devotedly subscribed to *Sovetish Heymland* (Soviet homeland), the only Yiddish language periodical that appeared in Russia after de-Stalinization. "I did not read all of it, but I liked to think that I supported Yiddish literature," she explained.

Fira would be surprised if she were told that she represented the embodiment of the ideal Soviet Jewish reader as imagined by state ideologues. She learned to read Yiddish because the Soviet regime gave her an opportunity to do so; her political and ideological views were formed under the influence of the propaganda integrated into the newspapers and magazines used in the literacy course, and her previously absent literary tastes were developed through reading works by Soviet Yiddish poets and writers. Fira would be even more surprised if she found out that these literary tastes might have indeed played some role in the development of Soviet Yiddish literature. Soviet writers were encouraged to read the feedback from their readers, analyze it, and incorporate it into their work. Fira's life is an example of successful attempts to use the Yiddish printed word as a way to influence the Soviet Jewish public.

This chapter tells the story of how the infrastructure designed to deliver propaganda to Jews was received in revolutionary Russia, Ukraine, and Byelorussia.[2] From the outset the Bolsheviks favored the close supervision of reading, and by the late 1920s the process of reading had been transformed from an individual action to a state-controlled activity. David Shneer has demonstrated that Jewish activists saw the printed word as the dominant means of agitation and propaganda in the Soviet Union, and that the development of the Yiddish print culture became the basis of the new Soviet secular Jewish polysystem.[3] The goal to achieve 100 percent literacy led to the establishment of government institutions dedicated to promoting literacy among Jews: Yiddish writers and journalists were instructed to incorporate Soviet messages into their writing, and state-sponsored libraries organized programs to encourage people to read these works. This chapter first takes a close look at the pattern of development of Soviet Yiddish culture in print and then analyzes the major strategies of its distribution, organization of literary evenings, and the wide-reaching propagandization of the process of reading in general.

The second part of the chapter examines grassroots movements that appeared as a result of government campaigns, such as amateur letter writing to the press. In letters people often expressed their criticism and praise of the Soviet regime. The government learned to manipulate these letters as propaganda, a process that evolved into the worker correspondents movement. Worker correspondents became a mechanism through which the authorities were able to receive information on the perception of state policies "from below." Yiddish amateur correspondents influenced not only the social and cultural policies of the regime but also had a huge impact on the formation of styles and genres of the new Soviet Yiddish literature. They were often also seen as the future face of Soviet literature, even if some of these new correspondents had only recently learned to read and write. In the words of Haim Gildin (1894–1944), a Yiddish poet and literary critic of the 1920s, "it was easier to teach illiterates to write new interesting novels then to make our Yiddish literature proletarian."[4]

Down with Illiteracy!

The Russian intelligentsia, political groups, and government ideologues had long believed that reading was the key to the education and cultural transformation of the public. Revolutionary democrats in the 1860s, *narodniks* (popu-lists) in the 1870s and 1880s, the liberal intelligentsia of the late nineteenth cen-tury (including the famous Russian writer Leo Tolstoy), and the tsarist Ministry of Education each had its own views on the desirability of various types of popular reading material.[5] These groups often disagreed on the fundamental question of what the reader wanted or needed to read or both, but they all agreed that reading choices should not be left to the masses alone. These choices should be controlled, supervised, and directed.[6] When the Soviets took power, they embarked on a program of social engineering and mass propaganda at a level never seen before. Rather than simply censor the "final product," they set out to completely reshape the printed word. This included telling writers not only what they should write about, but also "how" they should write. Mass lit-eracy programs were launched, as were regional and national periodicals. The Bolsheviks also understood that manipulating the distribution of existing lit-erary works could help bring Soviet values to the masses.

On the eve of the October Revolution, approximately three-quarters of Rus-sian citizens were illiterate. One of the first goals of Bolshevik cultural policy was the establishment of literacy courses. The prerevolutionary intelligentsia's urge to enlighten became more dogmatic and politically charged in its Soviet successors. From the very beginning of the revolution, even under the truly catastrophic conditions of the civil war, the Bolsheviks attached great impor-tance to publishing cheap editions of imaginative literature. Just like their Rus-sian counterparts, Jewish readers were believed to require supervision and di-rection, though for slightly different reasons. Because of their long tradition of learning, about 87 percent of Jewish men were literate in Yiddish on the eve of the revolution. Thirty-one percent of Jewish men and 16 percent of Jewish women had a reading knowledge of Russian in 1897.[7] (Only 21 percent of the Russian population was literate in 1897.)[8] By 1926, 85 percent of all Jews were literate in Russian.[9] Still, the eradication of illiteracy was one of the first cultural campaigns directed at Jews to be undertaken by the Soviet regime. An analysis of the organizational process of the literacy campaign (among people already predominantly literate) reveals that Soviets had other goals in addition to teach-ing people simply how to read. They wanted to teach them to read the "right" literature in the "right" languages in order to acquire Soviet values.

In 1918 sporadic programs designed to eradicate illiteracy among Jews were organized in Gomel, Berdichev, Druz, Polotsk, and other towns and villages in the former Pale of Settlement. In January 1921 the Section for National Minori-ties of the All-Russian State Commission for the Eradication of Illiteracy issued the following resolution:

> The primary goal of [the Commission's] local organizations is to change the men-tality of the Jewish working masses so that they should work for the needs of the Soviet Republic. Local organizations must organize campaigns of a specifically Jew-ish character, such as campaigns against kheyder, Jewish evening schools, emigra-tion, and Zionism. New methods should now be actively incorporated, especially Jewish theater, Jewish posters, special Jewish exhibitions, and movies.[10]

To carry out the plan the authorities had to decide which language to use. According to an earlier resolution regarding the organization of literacy courses in the Russian Federation, national minorities were supposed to be taught the grammar of their mother tongue.[11] Therefore Jews were to be educated in Yiddish. Although a majority of the male Jewish population already could read and write in Yiddish, they often did not consider Yiddish to be the appropriate language for education. In the early 1920s many Jewish sections reported that Jewish workers preferred literacy courses in Russian, stating that they felt Russian was essential for their full integration into the new society.[12] Another report concluded, "it was impossible to establish literacy courses in Yiddish, as no one wanted to attend these classes."[13] In some places two classes were organized: one in Yiddish and the other in Russian.[14]

At the same time functionaries of the Evsektsii collected sufficient evidence to show that, despite their desire to study in Russian, Jews usually spoke Yiddish much better than Russian. One of the meetings of the local Evsektsii in Odessa in 1921 reported:

> Even if a Jewish worker knows some Russian, he is still not able to express himself fully in the language and remains mentally retarded when he speaks Russian. Real conversation or propaganda is possible only in Yiddish.[15]

Another Evsektsii report about the situation in the Jewish shtetl, written three years later, recorded the following observation:

> Many Ukrainian factories have large proportions of Jewish workers. Most of the meetings were conducted in Russian or Ukrainian. It seemed that Jewish workers understood Russian pretty well, but during Russian meetings they usually kept silent. When a meeting was conducted in Yiddish, the situation was completely different: Jewish workers spoke freely and expressed their ideas without any embarrassment.[16]

A second major problem faced by the literary campaign was a distinct lack of teachers. As a result, the government organized Yiddish teacher training courses for Jewish Communists.[17] In the mid-1920s former kheyder teachers constituted the majority of the staff for the literacy courses. Nonetheless, the curriculum differed greatly from that of a traditional Jewish education. Study of the Torah, Talmud, and Hebrew was replaced by learning Yiddish and Marxism. The methods of teaching changed from lectures to discussions. However, the most important part of the campaign was to teach people the primary postulates of the new regime. The Yiddish word *ameratses* (ignorance) was adopted as a general term for illiteracy, although its subcontext implied unfamiliarity with important Soviet texts. The campaign was called *Oys ameratses!* (Away with illiteracy!).

As part of this campaign, the Soviet government extensively published elementary grammar books for adults. Teachers used books that featured clear and easy-to-learn slogans to illustrate the rules of basic grammar. It is worth noting that these Jewish grammar texts had significantly fewer pictures and were printed in smaller fonts than their Russian-language equivalents. This was because most Jews already knew how to read and just needed to be taught the new Soviet "catechism." At the same time the authorities faced a lack of sufficient funding for the publication of new textbooks. Therefore the government looked for additional resources to use in Yiddish classrooms for adults. They turned to Yiddish periodicals, which regularly included educational sections. (This approach had the added benefit of raising the number of subscribers to these magazines and newspapers, and thus helped to cultivate the habit of reading periodicals.)

In October 1924 an official Soviet directive was issued that ordered the use of the magazines *Yungvald* (Young forest) and *Pioner* (Pioneer) as the primary texts for the Jewish literacy campaign.[18] These magazines described Soviet ideas about the social structure for the new country in simple terms, such as the relationships between classes and nationalities, and the equality of men and women. The texts emphasized that Jews were not given opportunities to study or to farm before the revolution and, more important, were oppressed by the tsarist regime.

Educational materials often included poetry, short stories, and skits. These poems were frequently parodies of Yiddish folksongs. The following is an example of a poem based on the traditional Jewish ABCs:

> "Komets alef—o?"
> "O!"
> "Komets beys—bo?"
> "Bo!"
> "A got iz do?"
> "Nito!"
> "A kremer iz do?"
> "Nito!"
> "A porits iz do?"
> "Nito!"[19]
>
> "Is 'komets' and 'alef' o?"
> "O!"
> "Is 'komets' and 'beys' 'bo'?"
> "Bo!"
> "Is there God?"
> "There is not!"
> "Is there a shop owner?"
> "There is not!"
> "Is there a landowner?"
> "There is not!"

The primitive level of sophistication in both the political content and teaching methods used in this poem is striking. Specific notions are emphasized exclusively for the Jewish audience, such as the line "Is there a shop owner?" Owning a small shop was a common Jewish occupation in shtetlach before and after the revolution. Soviet ideology directly opposed a merchant class and actively tried to shift this population to work in collective farms.

One of the most important genres that appear in Yiddish popular magazines is educational short stories. Most deal with tales describing how individuals successfully adapt to their new roles in Soviet society. A typical example is *Dodke der leninets* (Dodke the Leninist), a story about how a Jewish boy rose from being a beggar to become a respectable member of society, a Young Communist.[20] The lead character, Dodke, is a ten-year-old boy from a poor family who cannot attend school because he has to help his mother earn a living. However, when an American Jewish society helps the boy's mother by sending financial aid, Dodke is able to go to school, where he becomes a member of the children's Communist organization the Young Pioneers. His mother is afraid that his activities will provoke antisemitism, and she fears that her son will get too involved politically. Still, despite all prejudices, Dodke becomes the chairman of the Young Communist club. This story includes several major ideological lines: it describes the poor life of the Jewish workers before the revolution, the Soviet campaign against antisemitism, and the "progressiveness" of Soviet Jewish schools. Such stories created a model of the ideal Soviet hero. They were designed to build the impression that readers would enjoy ideal lives if they emulated the behavior of these characters.

Almost all the stories published for use in literacy courses deal with the promotion of Soviet campaigns, but their primary focus is on the mechanism of personal transformation. Such pieces are often built as moral fables: a hero sins, then repents, and then, with the help of a peer, becomes a devoted Communist or a Komsomol member. The role of the savior can be played by a colleague, a teacher, and, most often, by a person of the opposite sex. Men are described as "progressive" in stories about women's transformation, and women are portrayed as more enlightened when they have to convince men. Most of these stories are written in the first-person narrative. A typical tale of male transformation is "A mayse mit Shmerlen, velkher ruft zikh Zhak, un a komyugistke Rivechke Faynbak" (A story with Shmerl, who calls himself Zhak, and of a Komsomol member Rivechke Faynbak) by P. Birman, published in *Yungvald* in 1925. The story depicts a young man, Shmerl, who does not like any Komsomol activities. He prefers to wander the streets and pick up girls, and impress them by introducing himself by the foreign name "Zhak" (which symbolizes Shmerl's adoration of Western values and popular culture, as well as his remoteness from his Soviet and Jewish roots). Shmerl keeps a diary of his affairs, where he records not only the number of kisses he enjoyed with each of the girls, but also lurid details that he knows "could not be printed in this magazine because of censorship." Shmerl eventually finds his way to a Soviet club, where he is initially bored with activities such as choirs and workshops about Leninism. Then he meets a Komsomol girl who is responsible for his transformation:

> She laughs. He laughs. He smiles. She smiles. He kisses. She kisses, they both kiss.
> From that moment on they start a secret love affair. Shmerl is always at the club.
> He enrolls in a drama workshop. After that, he finds out that Rivke is a member of
> a Leninism workshop, so he enrolls in that as well. She reads Ester,[21] he reads Buk-

דאָדקע דער לעניניעץ

Dodke the Leninist. The cover story of the third issue of *Pioner* (Pioneer), a Yiddish magazine for children. Moscow, April 1925.

harin.[22] He does not want to be behind. What's next? She says all the time "capitalism, materialism, materialism, capitalism," and Shmerl does not want to be left out! Will he look at that like a blind horse in darkness? Shmerl is not such a person. He will not be backward![23]

Eventually Shmerl becomes more politically aware, joins the Komsomol, proposes marriage to Rivechke, and she happily accepts.

It is noteworthy that Shmerl is attracted to Rivechke primarily because of her appearance—her looks are what brings him to Communism. The reader even picked up hints of this from the heroine's last name "Faynbak," which means Pretty Cheek. While "immoral behavior" is condemned at the beginning of the story, it is flirting that eventually brings the hero to "salvation." The gender roles are pronounced even in the choice of literature: even though Rivechke is more advanced in Soviet matters, she still reads Communist works by Ester Frumkin (a popular writer who wrote in Yiddish), whereas Shmerl prefers more serious and mainstream Russian works such as those by Bukharin. This pattern is reminiscent of the nineteenth-century comedies by the Yiddish Maskilic writers Israel Axenfeld (1787–1866) and Solomon Ettinger (1803–1856), in which progressive female characters speak only Yiddish whereas positive male characters also speak German or Russian or both.

Here, the Soviet short stories play on emotions and instincts as opposed to rationality in order to try to transform both male and female readers. These stories typically follow a pattern: the lead male character (either a son or a husband) tries to convince a woman about the benefits of the Soviet regime. In the story "*In undzer otryad*" (In our detachment) by L. Zelik, the man has a great social life as a result of his activities in a Communist club. His mother wants to be a part of it, and so she, too, enrolls.[24] In other stories women become jealous when their husbands spend all their time talking about politics and Leninism.[25] The women resolve the problem by becoming more politically aware.

Communist doctrine replaces religion for what is considered acceptable courtship behavior. Traditionally church and family frowned upon the idea of marriage outside their group (which was defined along ethnic and religious lines). In these stories it is considered socially unacceptable to go out with a member of the opposite sex who is not a Communist. For example, the worker correspondent B. Shlosberg ridicules a man who married a non-Komsomol woman just because he thought she would make a good housewife (*baleboste*).[26] It is worth noting, however, that in virtually all Yiddish stories characters marry (or date) Jewish members of the opposite sex as long as they are Communists. Very few stories in Yiddish during this period promote intermarriage. This is not accidental. Assimilation was not the primary target of propaganda directed at Jews. Rather, because of the competing influence of Zionists and Bundists, the government promoted the development of a new Soviet Jewish culture that was socialist in content but national in form. Assimilation was seen as a possible next step, after Jews fully understood the values of Soviet society. That is why the Yiddish press paid so much attention to personal stories of transformation of the poorest inhabitants of the Jewish Pale.

Many magazines published articles with titles like "How I Became a Young Communist" or "How I Became a Red Army Soldier." These stories typically chronicle how Jewish characters endure pogroms and restrictions on their freedom before the revolution. They describe how the characters search for ways to improve their condition and ultimately realize that the best route is to join the

ע. מעשטשינסקי

ווי אזוי דארף א פיאנער איינטיילן זיין טאג

א פיאנער דארף קענען גוט איינשטעלן די צייט און
ארגאניזירן פארטיילן דעם טאג.

דעם טאג-רעזשים דארף מען ארגאניזירן אזוי, אז מע זאל
קענען א סאך אויסטאן, ניט פארשטרעבנדיק קיין סאך קויכעס. בא
א רעכטיק רעגולערן רעזשים ווערט אפגעהיטן דאס געזונט, די
שטימונג איז שטענדיק א מונטערע.

דער איקער איז די ארדענונג, אין וועלכער מע דארף פאר-
ברענגען דעם טאג: ווען און וויפל שלאפן, לערנען זיך, ארבעטן,
שפּאצירן א. א. וו.

דאך לייג אין אייך מער א מוסטער-פלאן, ווי אזוי
איינטיילן דעם טאג.

עס איז זייער א ווינשנסווערטס, יעדער פיאנער זאל אים
אויספירן, דאס וועט זיין ניט שווער.

מער א פיאנער, וועלכער דארף זיין מער אלע איבעריקע
כעורעם פון ארדענונג, פינקטלעכקייט און דיסציפּלין.
איז דאס לעבן צו ליב א פלאן אומבאראינגעס נומעריק.

מאטאק און מערני.

פלאן פון טאג

7½ ביז 9 אזייגער - אינ-
דערפרי. שנעל
אנגעטאן זיך. מאך דעם אינדער-
פריאיקן טואלעט.

קע.מאך עטלעכע פיזקולטוריש איבונגען,
וואש זיך גוט אויס, ווינשטסועטערס דעם
גאנצן קערפער, קלייב אויף די בעטסנ-
וואנט, טרימל אויס אסן הויף די קאל.
דרע מיט מיטל לימעלף און ריין אויס דעם
מאן, דערנאך עס אפ א פרישטיק, וואש
אויס וי צייַן, קלימב צונויף די לערנביכער און גיי שוועק אין שול.

פון 9 ביז 1 אזייגער
לימודים אין שול.

1. אין שול גיב אכטונג אויף דער
אלגעמיינער רייניקייט און פיר דער שטענ-
דיקן קאמפ מיט יענער כעורע, וואס
זיימען ארום זיך שמוץ.

2. אף דער שול-באנק זיץ גלייך, מיט רוקן צום וואנטל,
ניט איינגעבויגענערהייט, מיט דער ברוסט שפאר זיך
ניט אן אן ברעג טיש.

3. אף דער באנק זעץ דיך אזוי, אז זי זאל וויין נאך דיין
וואוקס, די פיס זאלן זיך ניט אראפההענגען, נאר מעסט זיך בארירן
אן די אדער אן דעם אונטערשטן ברעטל.

4. אין שול דארפן די בענק שטיין אזוי, אז די פענסטער
אן די שיין זאלן זיין פון דער לינקער זייט.

5. די שיין פארשטעלן ניט פון זיך מיט דיין האנט אדער
מיט א בוך.

6. אויב די זון-שטראלן פאלן גלייך אפן העפט אדער
ביכל, מער מען צו אזעלכע באדינגונגען ניט ליינען און ניט
שרייבן, די פענסטער זיך פארשטארן די ארגן.

7. דורכן סאנקאס הויב אויף אויף די פראגע ווען איבערשטעלן
די בענק אזוי, אז די שיין זאל זיין פון דער לינקער זייט.

8. זיץ אזוי, אז צווישן ביך אדער העפט און די ארגן זאל
זיין א מערקאט פון 25 סאנטימעטער.

פון 1 ביז 2 אזייגער
באטאג קער זיך
אום פון שול אהיים.
עס מיטאג.

1. קומענדיק אהיים, וואש אויף
די הענט און דעם פּנים.
2. עס ביסלאך, ניט איילנדיק זיך.
3. צעקיי גוט דאס עסן. בעצאיסן
עסן זאלסטו ניט ליענען.
4. דעם וטשריומפעם דארף מען עסן ניט זייער הייס
און ניט צופיל קיין קאלטן.
5. היס אפ, דער מאן זאל ארבעטן ריכטיק און רעגולער:
גערוויין זיך צו אים אויסצייינייק אין אין אין דערועלבער צייט.
6. אויב דו באמערקסט א הארטן אדער א שלאפן מאַגן,
בארעכן זיך מיט אן דאקטאר און פארלאז אן עס צום אווי.

פון 2 ביז 3 רוען.
עס איז ניט געווען נאכן מיטאג שלאפן, נאך ערגער איז
נאך מיטאג גיך גיין, לויפן אדער שפּרינגען.

אין דער צייט דארף מען מאכן א קלייני
צייג אין א רואיקן אָרט.
נעם גרינגן שפּאציר אין דערנאך אביסל.

פון 3 ביז 5 ליינען.
אדער צוגרייטן די
לימודים.

1. ביכער צום ליינען קלייב
אויס געדרוקטע מיט גרויסע דייטלעכע
אויסיעס.
2. דאס פאפיר וואס דארף זיין ווייסע.
3. ליינען צו לינגדיקערהייט אדער גיימענדיק.
4. די באסטע זאך איז א בעם ליינען זיצן אף א ארט.
5. זיץ ניט די גאנצע צייט בא איין און דערזעלבער אַר-
בעט: פיל די גנעטשטאנוי אינעם מאָן די געשטאנוי אינעם
אזא צווישן — דאס לייענען אפ שרייבן, ארטמעטישע אויס-
גאבן אף צייכענען א. א. וו.
6. די לימודים מאכי ניט אף לאנג. זאלסט ניט
ווערן איינגעמודעט.
7. עס איז אויך זייער גוט צו פאר מאל פאר דער צייט
אויסשטעטין פון ארט, זיך דורך-גייין א פאר מינוט און ווידער
זעצן זיך צו דער ארבעט.

8. שרייב ניט מיט קליינע אויסיעלעך, מאך דייטלעכע בוכשטאבן.
9. באנוץ זיך שטענדיק מיט ווייכע סעדערס. בלייערס
דארף מען אויך האבן ווייכע און ניט קיין הארטע.
10. אין דער צייט פון הויף אטעמען ניט פריש לופט.
נעם אן אקסטיאון אנסטעל אין פארשיידענע אטאגצרלעכע שפּילן, וועלכע
דו מוזט אליין ארגאנזירן.
11. אין די שול-צימערן זאל מען ניט ליומן און שפּילן,
ווייל דאס הויבט אויף א סאך שטויב.

No 4
צעלעם. האלטם: שלאפעם זיך. שיסם זיך.
מאכם אונ מערני שטעגעל מיט...
דער משטאסמאונטעשיקל אין הויסם.

No 5
לוימם כעורע בעם הויף
אנטשקעגן זיי אין א טומל בים ליומם.
אינגם א צוויי און עטט וזאר
צאיל כעורע פאר.

How a Pioneer Should Organize His Day. An article in the issue of *Pioner* (Pioneer), a Yiddish magazine for children. Moscow, September 1926.

Red Army or to become a Communist. These types of stories constitute the core of the course curriculum. The grammar and vocabulary of these literary pieces were simplified and, in effect, secondary.

Both literacy workshops and Yiddish elementary schools taught students not only how to read but also how to develop a respectful attitude toward the very process of reading. By the mid-1920s Yiddish magazines began to publish instructions for children and adults on how to read "correctly." For example, a proper Soviet Pioneer is instructed to observe certain rituals while reading and writing:

> [Every Pioneer must] read between 3:00 and 5:00 P.M.
> 1. Choose books with big clear letters.
> 2. Write notes on white paper.
> 3. Do not read while lying down or while eating.
> 4. While reading, it is best thing to sit still.[27]

The following list of reading guidelines was published in 1927:

> 1. When you take a book, look at the cover.
> 2. Keep proper body posture.
> 3. Whenever you don't understand something, be sure to use questions and exclamation marks to note what you need to ask about later.
> 4. Underline difficult words.
> 5. Try to retell yourself what you just read.
> 6. Read out loud.
> 7. Read together with friends.[28]

Associations with praying are unavoidable here. Not only are readers encouraged to have a respectful attitude toward books and the printed word, but they are also instructed to "behave" in the presence of books. Just like prayer books, Soviet equivalents were to be handled in certain ways and read at certain times. These instructions present reading as a serious (as opposed to recreational) activity. The references to "difficult" words are also not accidental. Jews, just like many newly literate Russians, often had troubles understanding new Soviet newspapers: the language, style, and choice of themes.[29] Contemporary observers noted that many Yiddish periodicals, such as the central Yiddish daily *Der emes,* were regarded as quality newspapers, but, ironically, the language of the periodicals was difficult for most readers, sometimes even more difficult than the Russian in *Pravda.*[30]

Literacy courses were part of a huge propaganda campaign. Graduates of these courses were supposed to become the "ideal readers," representing the "new workers and peasants" who had triumphed over illiteracy as well as superstition and religion.[31] Students of literacy courses were taught to respect the press and other official publications. In turn, the government ensured that Yiddish readers had access to ideologically correct literature as a source of entertainment.

The Yiddish Worker Correspondents Movement: Organization and Development

The Soviet government encouraged people, even those who had just learned to write, to send letters to the periodicals that they read. The government promised that every letter would either be published or at least read carefully, and official reaction would follow in either case. The grassroots letter writers were called "worker correspondents" (*arbeter korespondent,* or *arbkor* in Yiddish) and "village correspondents" (*dorf-korespondent,* or *dorfkor* in Yiddish).[32] The government hoped that the worker correspondents movement would help to encourage people to keep an eye on local events, inform the central press of various developments in the implementation of Soviet policies, help newspapers to receive materials for publication, and create a loyal readership of the Soviet press.

The First Congress of Russian Worker and Village Correspondents was held in November 1923 in Moscow. Forty-two delegates from seventeen newspapers attended the meeting. By the end of 1924, 100,000 people considered themselves members of the worker correspondents movement. Their numbers increased to 125,000 by March 1926, and to more than half a million in 1928. State support for village correspondents began in 1924, and by 1926 the number of village correspondents exceeded the total number of worker correspondents.[33]

The Jewish worker correspondents movement was launched by the Kiev Yiddish daily *Komunistishe fon* (Communist flag) in 1922. Shortly thereafter, every Yiddish newspaper had its *arbkorn, dorfkorn, kustkorn* (artisan correspondents), and *kindkorn* (youth correspondents).[34] There are no exact statistics on how many people were involved in the Yiddish worker correspondents movement. In the mid-1920s a significant number of new Yiddish magazines and periodicals appeared and immediately began encouraging their readers to become contributors. Some of them were trade union publications such as the Minsk-based tailors' monthly journal *Dos royte nodl* (The red needle), which primarily concentrated on the affairs of the workers of the industry concerned. Regional newspapers, including *Odeser arbeter* (Odessa worker, 1927–37) and *Vitebsker arbeter* (Vitebsk worker, 1925–28), consist almost entirely of worker correspondence materials.

By the early 1930s the government began to focus its attention on peasant correspondents. The most important of the periodicals targeting Yiddish village dwellers was *Kolvirtishe shtern* (Collective farm star, 1931–35). This newspaper was published in Kharkov (Ukraine) and most of its readers resided in the Jewish national districts in Ukraine and Crimea. During the first three months of its existence *Kolvirtishe shtern* received more than eight hundred letters from 320 village correspondents, and printed as many as twenty-five of them in each issue. More than a third of these letter writers were women.[35]

Publications that targeted young readers, such as the monthlies *Yungvald*

(1923–28), *Pioner* (1925–28), *Yunger leninets* (The young Leninist, 1929–37) and the newspaper *Zay greyt!* (Be ready!, 1928–37), feature sketches and letters that are predominantly from students and young worker correspondents. In the 1930s two Ukrainian cities, Kremenchug and Vinnitsa, launched their own Yiddish papers, *Kremenchuger arbeter* (Kremenchug worker, 1932–35) and *Proletarisher emes* (Proletarian truth, 1935–37). Similarly many factories, building organizations, and collective farms with large numbers of Yiddish-speaking workers published their own Yiddish newspapers.[36] Jewish professionals were encouraged to write for the Yiddish press. For example, the teachers magazine *Af di vegn tsu der nayer shul* (On the road to the new school) published a call to its readers to become *pedkorn* (pedagogical correspondents) in order to "share their work experiences." The representatives of *pedkorn* met each month to discuss how to write their correspondence letters as well as how to become better teachers and help build the Soviet nation.[37]

The subject matter covered in these periodicals does not differ much from the general press of that time: glorification of the achievements of the Soviet regime, sorrow about Lenin's death, concern about the low involvement of women in Soviet work, and complaints about bureaucracy. The Jewish worker correspondents also tended more often to cover specifically Jewish subjects and themes such as agricultural labor among Jews, the organization of antireligious propaganda, and the struggle with the Zionist movement. This allowed Yiddish worker correspondents to maintain a closer connection between the periodicals and their readers, as well as to increase the impact of state-promoted ideas on the targeted audience. Below I analyze some typical examples of Yiddish amateur writing.

The campaign to resettle Soviet Jews from shtetlach to agricultural colonies was an important topic in the correspondents movement. Amateur writers developed their subjects in one of several patterns. One model is that of a younger correspondent himself offering a description of successful propaganda. V. Markin's "Kolektivchikes" (Small collectives) is illustrative of this pattern. The sketch pictures a poor observant Jewish family. The father in the story is not interested in moving to pursue agricultural work, but his fifteen-year-old son convinces him that if he went to the Society for the Settlement of Jewish Toilers (Obschestvo po zemleustroistvu trudiashchikhsia evreev, or OZET) and took the family to work on a farm in the Crimea, they would be much happier. After they receive financial help for the move, the father, excited with this news, goes to a meeting in a Jewish club to encourage others to follow his lead and switch to agricultural work. The meeting is even held on Saturday (a deliberate antireligious move), but the formerly religious man does not mind attending, as he is now more interested in this new opportunity than in religion. The conclusion is that the right economic policy, along with the behavior of the son, changed not only this family's wealth but also the religious views of the father.[38] This story summarizes key aspects of propaganda toward Jews as expressed in Yiddish periodicals of that time: encouragement to move to Jewish collective farms, a break with religious traditions, and education about the benefits of the new Soviet regime.

Yiddish correspondents focused on reports of successful activities, including how they organized Yiddish clubs and mobilized their friends to work extra time in the fields, and especially about the break with religious tradition. The antireligious campaign gave letter writers the difficult task of illustrating both the campaigning enthusiasm of some people and the skepticism or open hostility of others. The magazines had to monitor the proportions of the "positive" and "negative" publications: too much criticism meant that the propaganda was not effective, but the absence of negative information signaled that "enemies" were being overlooked. In describing the enthusiasm and unmasking enemies, the correspondents created a new genre of personal transformation stories. Letter writers described how they overcame their old prejudices and became devoted Soviet citizens. In every issue the antireligious magazine *Der apikoyres* (The godless) published a "pattern story," which described the process of transition from a traditional to an antireligious way of life. The magazine announced a competition for the best "How I Became an Atheist" story. The winners were promised yearlong subscriptions to *Der apikoyres*. Former kheyder teachers, rabbis, ritual slaughterers, and "ordinary" citizens testified how their lives had changed without God, stating that they used to be fooled by religion. A typical example was a letter from Rita Gvirtsman, a fifty-eight-year-old resident of a Jewish shtetl:[39]

> During the tsarist regime the lives of working women were extremely difficult, because they were under the double exploitation of economy and religion. I remember it was especially tough before the holidays, such as Passover and Yom Kippur. We had to work really hard. . . . From early childhood on, we were encouraged to look at ourselves as the worst people.
>
> I remember that once, before the revolution, I had an argument with a ritual slaughterer about whether the meat he gave me was indeed kosher. He told me my words were not valid because I was a woman. I went to ask for the advice of a rabbi. He said he was going to discuss the matter with the ritual slaughterer, but he did not, since the slaughterer had helped him financially. Furthermore the rabbi said he needed to save money because he had daughters that he needed to marry off and could not risk a rift with the slaughterer. I was left stranded. Gradually I was becoming an atheist.
>
> When the Soviet regime came, my beliefs were validated. I read the books by Comrade Stalin and was convinced that I was right, because he wrote that women have rights and were equal to men. This was the most important thing for me. Also, it was very good that Comrade Stalin said that one could not laugh at women any more, because that stopped men from treating us badly. All that helps us to be more productive women and to help build socialism in the Soviet land.[40]

This type of story combined several important ideological themes of the time: the struggle with the traditional way of life, "the backwardness of clerics," and women's liberation. The path of female transformation started with the woman's realization of injustices and then her instincts to learn more about alternatives to religion. The conclusion of the story demonstrates that traditional Jewish values were no longer valid for the heroine after they were replaced by Soviet ones.

The editors of Yiddish periodicals encouraged amateur correspondents to write not only about their personal transformations but also to include information about how the Jewish community was adjusting to the new Soviet way of life. Periodicals used these reports to direct young people's activities. The program worked as follows: worker correspondents described state-sponsored community activities; the editors then selected some of these letters for publication; the editors also added their own comments and recommendations, and invited further correspondence on the subject. This method was especially pronounced in many editions of the magazine *Pioner*. Here is an example of how the editors encouraged their reader-correspondents in a campaign against traditional Jewish schools, including khaydorim. In 1928 the magazine published the following letter by Sholem Zelikson from the shtetl of Kulbich (in the Polotsk region of Byelorussia):

> There are still several khaydorim in our shtetl, with twenty-five or twenty-six students. Even though the children go to kheyder, they still come to the meetings of our Pioneer organization. They say what they think, they play with everybody, and they take part in the general meetings of the Pioneer organization. In short, children do not only partake in the meeting, but they fully know the entire work of our Pioneer detachment.[41]

The editors provided the following comment to this letter:

> It is good that the detachment attracts children who study in kheyder and involves them in their activities. However, we also want to know the kind of influence the detachment has on those children. Do they know what a kheyder really is, and what a rebbe is, and after learning this do they still want to stay in kheyder? What does the Pioneer detachment do to explain the role of the new Soviet schools? What sort of success did the Pioneer detachment have in trying to convince those children to leave the kheyder?[42]

These editorial comments not only encourage more correspondence on the subject but directly instruct the readers and writers on how to proceed further, and suggest the framework for follow-up letters from other correspondents. The comments also clearly elaborate the "proper" position that children should adopt toward those who continued to study in kheyder: "be friendly but try to convert 'the lost souls' into the Soviet way of thinking."[43] The primary mission of the Soviet Yiddish press was to create a new Soviet Jew, and it used every opportunity to direct and instruct its readers on how to become Soviet (i.e., better) persons.

Worker correspondents often reported how government "cultural" campaigns were received locally. When the Soviet government conducted a public health awareness campaign to promote good hygiene, many letters dealt with the poor sanitary conditions of the shtetlach. For example, one letter described life in

Lenskorun (Kamenets-Podolsk region), where no one washed their hair and feet during the summer. The author stated that girls only washed their hair on Fridays, and boys virtually never did so.[44] By the mid-1920s editors of Yiddish periodicals started to encourage their readers not only to report successes but also failures of Sovietization. The editors emphasized that it was important for correspondents to express their concerns and to report the mistakes made by local councils, failures in the organization of Pioneer activities, and critiques of local leadership. *Yungvald, Kremenchuger arbeter, Pioner, Yunge gvardye,* and other periodicals each established a special section called "Undzere khesroynes" (Our failures). Correspondents reported on topics such as low enrollment in their clubs and a general lack of interest in Soviet activities among the older generation. Editors encouraged these correspondents to write about the problems they encountered at work, in clubs, and in local institutions of authority. Here is an example of a typical set of directives given to amateur contributors in 1924:

> The time has come for worker correspondents not only to write critiques of obvious facts that scream to be written about, they need to pay much more attention. They have to search for enemies at the workplace, and describe them without mercy, and explain how these enemies hurt working people.
>
> What kinds of problems should a worker correspondent look out for? Here are some of the results of enemy behavior: low productivity, irrational organization of labor, inefficient use of machinery. Plus, at every workplace, there are many little things, such as people who do not work hard. These things decrease productivity of all workers and thus need to be reported.[45]

Similar sets of instructions were issued by many Yiddish periodicals, stressing that, in the end, letters critical of backward workplaces would help to improve the quality of life in the countryside (these letters were also used to increase workplace safety and to fire "unproductive" workers).[46] Editors also wrote about specifically Jewish problems that would interest worker correspondents, such as the state of the Zionist movement, the perception of antireligious propaganda among Jews, the influence of Hassidic rabbis, and the observance of religious holidays.[47] Notably issues relating to Soviet antisemitism, widely discussed by worker correspondents in the Russian press, were not included in this list and, in fact, were rarely discussed in the Yiddish press at all.

Some of the topics young correspondents dealt with were the lack of enthusiasm in Pioneer work, "boring" activities in school, and the lack of sufficient entertainment in their shtetl. Older writers regularly complained about unproductive Communist party meetings, abusive bosses, "backward" spouses (who abused alcohol or did not pay enough attention to political education), and, again, the lack of entertainment. The content of these Yiddish letters was virtually identical to that published in the Russian or Ukrainian press.

A key aspect of these letters is the specific problems that were discussed. The problems people faced during this period, such as harsh working conditions, a severe lack of food, low salaries, and the struggle to adapt to a new environment (many Jews moved from shtetlach to bigger cities in the 1920s and 1930s) were never mentioned in these periodicals. According to the "official press," these problems simply did not exist. Other hardships faced by Soviet Jews during this period, including the change of traditional professions, new kinship patterns, and the struggle to learn new languages, were also ignored.

One explanation for this discrepancy has to do with the concept of Potemkin culture developed by the historian Sheila Fitzpatrick regarding the Russian village. She defines it as follows:

> If the typical Russian village of the 1930s was hungry, drab, depopulated, and demoralized, there was another village, happy and prosperous, bustling with people, and enlivened by the cheerful sounds of the accordion and balalaika, that existed in the imagination. . . . Potemkin villages existed for the benefit of the educated Soviet public—even to some degree for the benefit of peasants. Like other socialist-realist representations of the Stalin period, the image of the New Soviet villages lovingly created in newspapers, movies, political speeches and official statistics was not life as it was, but life as good Soviet citizens hoped it was becoming. The Potemkin village was a preview of the coming attractions of socialism.[48]

The Yiddish press followed this model and successfully created an image of a Soviet Jewish community that had little to do with reality. The press featured the perfect Soviet shtetlach and Jews that did not exist. The perfect Jewish community portrayed by the journalists of the Yiddish press consisted of devoted Communists and Komsomol members whose Jewish identity, if they had any, was only expressed by the fact that they spoke Yiddish. These ideal Jews existed in a family of other friendly nationalities and ethnic groups of the Soviet Union, and they never experienced antisemitism because in this ideal society intolerance did not exist. If one followed the rules of writing about "real events" while looking through "Soviet glasses," even a story of disloyalty to the Soviet regime could be turned into a lesson on exemplary behavior. Comparative analysis of the stories published in the press against oral testimonies of "what really happened" provide noteworthy answers on how the ideal Soviet shtetl was created in the Yiddish press.

One example of this phenomenon is the appearance of the genre of family *denunciations*. In the 1930s correspondents, especially younger ones, were encouraged to write personalized critical materials about "backward" family members. A typical example is the piece below, originally published in 1932 by the local Yiddish newspaper *Kremenchuger arbeter*:

> I grew up in a family of exploiters and clerical bourgeoisie. My father slaughtered animals, and he charged ordinary workers a higher fee for his services than he did for the rabbi and family members. He had a Russian maid, who was treated terribly because she was not Jewish. She went home hungry because her wages were not sufficient to cover her food. She also wore the same clothes for more than a year, as she could not afford to buy them. . . .
>
> Now, fifteen years after the Great October Socialist Revolution, a time of technological progress and new possibilities for all peoples of the Soviet Union, independent of their nationalities, my father still dreams of times gone by, when he was able to do what he wanted and make poor people suffer. I refuse to be part of

this family any longer. I feel that my real father is the Komsomol, who taught me the important things in life. My real mother is our motherland; the Union of Soviet Socialist Republics and the people of the USSR are my family now.[49]

The impression the reader drew from the above segment was that the writer clearly rejected his ties with his family, resented the negative attitude toward non-Jews, and fully accepted the new Soviet antireligious and social values. There were other reasons behind writing such pieces, however, and these motivations did not always derive from the ideology. Writing a public rejection of a religious or rich parent opened doors to institutions of higher education and provided other means of social mobility otherwise inaccessible to children of *lishentsy;* included in this category were persons deprived of civil rights, many rabbis, ritual slaughterers, synagogue servants, as well as shop owners.

One would expect that a public rejection of parents would morally destroy families, but oral history once again provides an unexpected dimension to this phenomenon. I was fortunate during my research to meet the sister of the author of the paragraph quoted above from *Kremenchuger arbeter.* The testimonies of my respondents reveal concrete reasons for these public betrayals. Many respondents agreed to talk about the subject only when I promised to keep their anonymity. Here is what Sofia G. recalls:

> I loved my father and mother very much. So did my brothers. During the war my father saved my life when he helped me escape from a cart filled with Jews that the Germans were about to deport. He was a ritual slaughterer and we had a very traditional household. At the same time I was a Pioneer, and my older brother was preparing to become a Young Communist League member. When I was fourteen, my father called me and my brother into a room, and he explained that his lifestyle was not appropriate for modern life. He did not want us to repeat his mistakes, such as observing Jewish religious traditions. . . . He said we had to go to the editor of a school wall newspaper and announce there that we were now living a new life and that we did not want to have anything in common with the religious past of our father. My father simply made us do this. He said it meant nothing to him, but he thought this action would open up a brighter future for us.[50]

One can interpret the situation differently. The initial impression is that parents sometimes sacrificed their social standing out of love of their children. Further, this testimony demonstrates that real-life circumstances changed the act of public betrayal into almost a technicality. According to some respondents, such denunciations began to be considered appropriate reactions to the situation and not serious acts of betrayal toward parents. One might argue, however, that these respondents were trying to justify their actions decades after the event. Moreover, most people cried when they recalled these incidents, which means that the "peaceful" solution was more traumatic than they were trying to present. Still, the denunciation usually did not create a stigma around the person.

Frequently the authors were teenagers who were about to leave their place of residence to go to a bigger city to enroll in school or start a new job. They continued to visit their families during summer vacations, even though they had publicly denounced them. Saul M. explains how he handled the situation:

> I considered that my parents were quite well off [financially] for that time. We had three cows and a dozen chickens. When the "golden nights"[51] began in 1929, they [the members of the City Council] came to ask for gold. My parents had a box where they hid their coins, but the authorities didn't find it. When I went to school the next morning, the teacher told me: "Your father should give away what he has, otherwise you can not come to school." I was really scared and told my parents. The next day they came to arrest my father. I was thirteen at the time. Later, my mother brought that box of gold to the authorities, and my father was released and came home. They also confiscated our cows and chickens, and the teacher said I could not come to school, because the school was not the place for the "enemy element." I was so mad at my father that he did not give away that box, so I went to school and asked to be put in an orphanage because, I said, I did not want to be an enemy of the Soviet regime.
>
> The teacher said that I should write how I feel and submit my note to the school newspaper. After that I was allowed to go back to school and not sent to an orphanage. My parents never spoke about what happened, and then, a year later, I went to Kiev to study, and that incident was gradually forgotten. I came to visit them during the summer, to get some sun, swim, and eat fruits and vegetables.[52]

Saul's denunciation was published in his school's newspaper. He included, "exploiting workers, greed, and collaboration with the rabbi" in his list of "major crimes" committed by his family. In this case the initiative to denounce the family came from Saul himself, not from his father. Saul's conflict was much more pronounced, but it did not result in the total disintegration of his family.

The public rejection of parents is probably one of the most controversial subjects of articles by young worker correspondents. This phenomenon represents the clearest manifestation of the differences between the *real* and the *ideal* Soviet Jew. The perfect Soviet Jew rejected his or her parents because of their ideological views, whereas the real Jew did so to acquire means of social mobility. The perfect Soviet Jew denounced his or her family entirely and, in so doing, cut off all contacts with them. The real Jew tried to disguise the official rejection by remaining in rather close touch with his or her family. In some ways such behavior was an expression of silent resistance: people did not actively protest against the rules but neither did they follow them precisely, and sometimes they even used them against the system. And, as oral history reveals, many youngsters were still convinced that the benefits of being accepted into Soviet society were worth sacrificing the manifestations of public respect for their parents. In this sense, the state's cultural policy succeeded in promoting Soviet values among the Jewish youth.

Impact of the Yiddish Worker Correspondents Movement

The significance of the worker correspondents movement was far-reaching. First, it was designed to train a new generation of literary cadres, one that would eventually create the body of Soviet literature. This indeed happened; many Soviet writers started as nonprofessional correspondents. Aron Vergelis (1918–1998), a famous Yiddish journalist and writer, began his career as a worker correspondent for the local Yiddish newspaper *Birobidzhaner shtern* (Birobidzhan star) in the 1930s. Second, the movement trained potential writers in the art of seeing reality through "special Soviet glasses." It encouraged them to describe things not as they actually were but as they were supposed to be. In a sense it marked the beginning of socialist realism in Soviet Yiddish literature.

Third, and most important in the minds of Soviet leaders, the movement taught people to observe negative events. Without this, the correspondents would have had nothing to write about. Everyone who wanted to be published had to keep track of events in their town or village. What may seem to have been simple journalistic practice was organized, in this case, into a mass movement. Everyone was encouraged to follow one another around and act as the eyes and ears for the state, a process that created millions of correspondent spies. Often, as a result of these letters, special investigations were initiated and people lost their jobs; some were even tried and punished. Several years later this lesson was applied in the writing of denunciations, which also became a mass phenomenon. However, these denunciations were never published in the press; instead, they were sent directly to the local Party cell or People's Commissariat for Internal Affairs (NKVD). Correspondents provided information about unproductive workplaces, inattentive supervisors, lazy workers, and the "backwardness" of the Jewish masses who still failed to "appreciate" Soviet cultural achievements. Correspondents were also responsible for reporting on potential threats against the Soviet regime. Many correspondents feared retaliation for their reports, so the government promised them protection:

> A great deal of the worker correspondent materials tends to be critical. Protest letters describe the mistakes of various organizations and individuals. This is natural and useful. The Russian worker correspondent can be sure that, in every case, his discoveries and protests, if they were valid, will be dealt with. They can be confident that the people who are criticized will be aware that they cannot avoid punishment. . . . For the Jewish correspondent, it is not so easy. He often doubts that his findings will be heard and taken into account by the people and organizations criticized, that they will not attract the attention of the Party Committee, inspectors and attorneys, because they understand that all these people do not read Yiddish. But we promise that all valid correspondent letters of complaint will be dealt with promptly.[53]

The fourth reason for the success of the movement was that it attracted talented young people to work in favor of the Soviet regime, diverting them from involvement in independent Jewish movements. For instance, a secret report to the Evsektsii in Ukraine in 1925 explained that the popularity of the Zionist movement in the region was a result of the lack of alternative "interesting and entertaining events." The same report encouraged the creation of "non–Communist Party" Jewish organizations, consisting of teachers, artisans, and students, and designed to become the medium through which the Party could influence the Jewish masses.[54] The report underscored: "We should especially encourage participation in the worker correspondents movement by those young people whom we cannot accept as members of the Young Communist League."[55] Soviet Yiddish periodicals published letters from former Zionists and active Communists who attempted to fight the Zionist movement locally. Just as with antireligious propaganda, editors provided their comments on how to make the struggle more efficient. Below is an example of three activists who wrote a story about how the "Zionist problem" was solved in Bykovo, a shtetl in the Mogilev region of Ukraine:

> First, we young activists decided to introduce the Jewish youth to the ideas of Jewish nationalism and internationalism. We organized a meeting for Jewish youth, during which we explained why the entire network of Jewish organizations, such as Poyley Tsien,[56] Khaluts,[57] and others were against the revolution. Many members of these groups who came to the meeting were convinced by the event, and asked if they could join the Komsomol.[58]

Many worker correspondents not only reported about local events, such as the activities of Jewish clubs, drama workshops, and Communist gatherings but also helped to organize them. Their correspondence often described how an activist had conducted successful events. In fact, many of these activists organized events in order to be able to write about their own work. By reporting an event to a periodical, and getting it published, young worker correspondents saw themselves (and were often seen by others) as elite members of society.

The social and psychological reason for the enormous success of the movement was that it enabled anyone to become a "celebrity." This was a realization of an important theme in Soviet propaganda, the idea of the equal opportunities offered by the new regime. In this way the worker correspondents movement influenced not only the worker correspondents themselves but also the readers of the amateur letters. The very existence of the movement proved that if a former illiterate was able to become a journalist, then, indeed, in the words of Vladimir Lenin, "a cook can now rule the state."

Popular Attitudes toward the Yiddish Press

The worker correspondents campaigns attracted new readers to the Yiddish press, although at a level significantly lower than the Soviet Jewish functionaries had expected. In the 1920s the government conducted several surveys designed to analyze what people actually read. The pollsters noted that, among Jews, the Russian press was significantly more popular than the Yiddish press. Their survey in the Ukrainian shtetl of Darevke found that out of its eighteen thousand inhabitants, approximately five to six hundred people read newspapers (in either Yiddish or Russian). In 1926 the majority of readers in Darevke preferred the Russian-language Moscow dailies *Pravda* (107 subscribers) and *Izvestiia* (53 subscribers) and only 7 subscribed to the Moscow Yiddish daily *Der emes* and 3 to Kharkov's *Der shtern*. The Ukrainian newspapers were not popular in the shtetl and had no subscribers during this period.[59] Similar survey results were seen in Byelorussian towns with significant Yiddish-speaking populations.[60] Many readers often explained that they held a higher regard for *Pravda*, even though its language was too difficult for them, preventing them from reading many of the newspaper's longer articles. Still, they thought it was better to read Russian newspapers, which published serious articles, than Yiddish papers, which they considered primitive and secondary, and therefore untrustworthy.

The aim of these surveys was to prove that the existing Yiddish press and literature needed to be changed (to make it more appealing to the Jewish masses), and therefore the extent it could be trusted was unclear. Further, these studies were conducted only in the 1920s and not in the 1930s. Oral history serves as an additional (not necessarily objective) source of information. The majority (137 of 180) of the Yiddish-speaking respondents from larger towns within the former Pale of Settlement (such as Berdichev, Bobruisk, Minsk, and Zhitomir) mentioned that their parents were subscribers to central Yiddish newspapers. They usually remembered the dailies such as *Der emes, Shtern,* or *Oktyaber.* However, those who lived in smaller shtetlach within the former Pale, as well as many of the non-Yiddish speakers from Moscow, Leningrad, and Kiev, did not recall ever seeing a Yiddish periodical. The dwellers of shtetlach did not know of the Yiddish press, since it did not reach them, and those who lived in bigger cities gradually lost interest in the Yiddish printed word because of rapid assimilation. Thus, surprisingly, oral history demonstrated that in the territory of the former Pale of Settlement, reading Yiddish newspapers and periodicals was more popular among the Jews in the 1930s than the Soviet surveys indicated. The reason for this discrepancy is that the Soviet official sources of the mid-1920s were written with the agenda of justifying *korenizatsiia,* or "nativization," of the Jews so as to prove that the quality of Soviet Yiddish periodicals needed to be improved and Soviet propaganda work among Yiddish speakers strengthened. Similarly, to justify the furious antireligious propaganda, the surveys suggested that inhabitants of the shtetlach were more religious than they actually were.

Attitudes toward Yiddish newspapers or mass media in general varied among families. Some respondents noted that the feelings of the older generation differed from those of the younger set. Many interviewees told me that their parents did not forbid them to read newspapers but were always saying that they should not totally trust the publications. One respondent remembers:

We had Yiddish newspapers at home, including the newspaper *Shtern.* I remember my brothers read these papers all the time. My father used to say,

"Me makht a bibliteke" [It's like a library]. My brothers were always sitting and reading the papers. My father did not like it and constantly repeated that one cannot believe newspapers, especially Yiddish ones.[61]

Trust in the Soviet Yiddish newspapers was a serious concern of the government. People often did not believe what was printed in newspapers, recognizing that it was propaganda rather than a reflection of reality. One respondent told me that his father always said: "If a paper says that the living conditions are prosperous in Ukraine, it means that people are starving there."[62] Among some respondents this attitude remained consistent for many decades of Soviet history. For example, in the late 1930s Jews often did not believe Soviet information published in the press about Nazi Germany. As a result, they did not want to evacuate during the war when the Germans began invading Russia in 1941. The consequences were fatal.

Some Jewish families were more tolerant toward the Soviet press. Ian D. emphasizes:

We subscribed to many newspapers. There was *Der emes, Der shtern.*
There was also a newspaper called *Zay greyt!* [Be ready!]. It was a Pioneer newspaper. We respected and loved these newspapers, and our parents did, too. They felt they had to support them because this was a part of our Jewish culture.[63]

Another respondent, Yakov T., recalls that his mother used to repeat to him: "The new times have come. Read papers and you will be able to advance in society."[64]

When I asked interviewees about their attitudes toward the press in general, almost all of them, independent of age or place of residence, talked apologetically at first, explaining that they were "young and naïve," and therefore believed "everything written in the papers." Only when we talked about the nuances of the meanings of the words "everything" and "believed" was I able to distinguish between various attitudes, which depended on age, place of residence, and the language of the periodical. Negative or skeptical attitudes toward the Soviet press developed later, in the years following World War II and, in the Jewish case, following the 1967 Six-Day War in Israel. In the 1930s, however, many Yiddish-speaking Jews thought of themselves as loyal readers of the Soviet press, both in Yiddish and Russian.

Popular Attitudes toward Yiddish Literature

When the ethnographer I. Veitsblit visited the Ukrainian shtetl of Darevke in 1924, he observed that there were no Yiddish books there and that people primarily read Russian translations of American authors, such as Jack London and O. Henry.[65] The historian Ivan Pulner confirmed that "no one read Yiddish books in Gomel (a town in Byelorussia), except children in 1925."[66] Both researchers noticed that children read Yiddish books because they were required by the curriculum.

Oral history gives a slightly different perspective on the understanding of popular Yiddish reading. It reveals that even in the 1930s, the time of the acknowledged change in nature of Jewish culture, reading in Yiddish was more popular than the surveys of the 1920s assert. According to many respondents, both children and adults enjoyed works by Sholem Aleichem, Mendele Moykher Sforim, and Itskhok Leybush Perets. Some respondents told me that the secret to the popularity of Sholem Aleichem was that his novels could be enjoyed from many different perspectives: as a critique of the contemporary situation, a nostalgic tribute, or simply leisure reading. Sometimes the shared reading of Sholem Aleichem solved ideological conflicts within a family. Ian D. described his family's literary preferences:

> We had Jewish books at home. We loved to read. I remember there was a book called *Yidisher deklamator*.[67] There were many poems and songs there. My brother used to read to me out loud from this book. I also read. . . . My mother, however, was a pious person; she was keeping *Yidishkayt*. She had a woman's prayer book [*tkhine*]. For Sabbath, after she lit the candles, we read Sholem Aleichem stories together.[68]

Popular attitudes toward new Soviet Yiddish writers and poets were more complicated. In the larger "Jewish" towns, these writers were usually accepted by the public. The promotional activities of libraries and clubs often stimulated interest in new Soviet literature. According to oral history testimonies, the majority of the readers of these materials were schoolchildren (as opposed to their parents). As pupils in Yiddish schools, these students read the poetry of Itsik Fefer, Perets Markish, Izi Kharik, and Dovid Hofshteyn. During my interviews some were also able to name Dovid Bergelson as a popular Yiddish writer, but many later confessed that they actually read his works in Russian. It is also noteworthy that when I asked respondents who liked Yiddish poetry, they often selected Yiddish verses with heavy ideological content, such as those about pioneers, the civil war, and the October Revolution. For example, Grigorii B. recited the following verse as one of his favorite Yiddish pieces:

> Gekoyft hot mame Shimelen
> A shterndl a roytn,
> Hot Shimele es ongeton
> Un hot zikh shtark gefreyt.
>
> Zogt di mame Shimelen:
> Kum Shimele aher!
> Bavayz nor mit di fiselekh
> Vi geyt a pioneer![69]
>
> Mother bought for Shimele
> A little red star,

Shimele put it on,
And became very happy.

Mother tells Shimele,
Come, Shimele, here!
Show me with your feet,
How a Pioneer walks!

This poem, written by L. Rosenblum, appeared in the January 1926 issue of *Pioner*.[70] Strikingly Grigorii's recitation did not stray from the published text. He says he remembers the poem because he read it as part of a stage performance in a local theater workshop at a Jewish orphanage in Leningrad in 1929. Grigorii explains that the poem reflects the "spirit of that era." When I asked him about other poems he liked during the time, he replied:

We liked Russian classical poetry, like Pushkin and Lermontov. We also liked Yiddish poems like "Shimele," as well as some of Itsik Fefer's works. These were things of a high cultural level.

Almost none of the Yiddish-speaking respondents mentioned enjoying Soviet Yiddish prose works, despite the efforts of social engineers to shift popular reading patterns away from poetry.[71] Further, subjects such as tractors and Pioneers were not as memorable to readers when they appeared in prosaic descriptions as opposed to poetic forms. Some respondents remember the Yiddish prose works that they had read in school. However, most of those works were not original Yiddish works but rather Yiddish translations of Russian and foreign writers. Efim G. gives the following examples:

I read *Kolne greber* [The coal miners] by Emile Zola in Yiddish.[72] I read Victor Hugo in Yiddish as well. I know Gorky's "Stormy Petrel." I do not know who translated these into Yiddish. I know there are Russian versions, but I only know the Yiddish translations.[73]

Efim G. was able to recite the Yiddish version of Gorky's "Stormy Petrel" by memory. This gives one reason to believe that he actually learned it in the 1930s, when he was a pupil in a Jewish school. He also claimed, however, that he read the works of the Polish-American Yiddish writer Sholem Asch in Yiddish before the Second World War. But this writer was never published in the Soviet Union in Yiddish, only in Russian translation. Obviously, after more than seventy years, it is possible that this respondent could not remember all these details. Still, this pattern emerged in many other interviews, which demonstrates that Yiddish originals found an audience.

Passion for reading was common among respondents, who came from a wide range of backgrounds—religious or secular, Yiddish- or Russian-speaking, white- or blue-collar. All respondents stated that they loved to read. When I asked about their choice of literature, most answered just like Ioan K. (b. 1908, in Parichi):

I read everything that I saw. I read books about love, about work, about technological progress, about animals, books in Yiddish, in Russian. . . . I read like an addicted person [*zapoyem*]. I wanted to know everything.[74]

"Addiction to reading" was described by Evgenii Dobrenko as a typical feature of the youth culture of the 1920s. Literacy, and therefore the ability to read, was popularly seen as a key to success in the Soviet way of life. Young people were convinced that reading would help them become "cultured" and bring them closer to the fulfillment of their career ambitions. It is worth noting that the majority of my respondents pointed out that their parents did not own many Yiddish books—or Hebrew or Russian books. Ioan, for example, stated that his father only had a *Siddur,* but there was no other book in the house. Despite the popular self-definition of Jews as "people of the book," Soviet Jews born in the 1920s and earlier usually said that they were the first generation in their families that read for leisure. Many saw this development as a direct result of Soviet cultural policies toward Jews, and even as a benefit that Jews received from the Soviet regime.

Conclusions

In the 1920s the Soviet Jewish population was, for the most part, literate in Yiddish but did not necessarily want to read and write in this language. For many, Yiddish literature and the Yiddish press were not as authoritative as their Russian equivalents. When the policy of *korenizatsiia* started, Jews were almost forced to return to the Yiddish press and literature, sometimes against their will. Yet the creation of local Yiddish wall newspapers and the growth of the Yiddish-language worker correspondents movement stimulated the development of literary works inspired by Soviet ideology. The worker correspondents movement created a new population of writers, who at times became the eyes and ears of the state.

According to oral histories, the real problems Jews faced during Soviet times, such as difficulties with assimilation and relocation, were typically not discussed in the contemporary press and literature since these problems did not seem to belong to the imaginary Potemkin culture promoted and developed by the Soviet press. Worker correspondents' letters are an extreme example of this: these letter writers often paid more attention to what the government wanted to see than to what the public craved to read. Therefore adults often preferred reading prerevolutionary writers. For young people, however, the new Soviet literature was less alien; it described their potential future and allowed them to hope for a better life. And this was precisely what the government wanted: to make people change their dreams in order to fit into Soviet reality.

3 Amateur Local Yiddish Theaters

In 2000 Moisey and Mila Sh. (b. 1910 and 1911, respectively) celebrated their seventieth wedding anniversary in Brooklyn, New York. When I interviewed them at their cozy apartment located near Brighton Beach, I began by asking Mila how she and Moisey met. Mila replied: "We first saw each other in 1929, at an amateur Yiddish theater production in the Ukrainian shtetl of Kopaigorod." And Moisey added: "The performance was about the revolution, army, and spies. That is all I remember."

"Of course, what else would you remember?" Mila interrupted. "You were looking at me during the entire play!" The couple grew up in Kopaigorod and never missed the weekly productions at the local Yiddish amateur theater. "I especially liked when they staged Sholem Aleichem's works because they included so many nice songs," Mila pointed out. "I had a nice voice and used to sing the songs I learned from these performances at home."

The elderly couple was quite excited to talk about every detail regarding Kopaigorod's local theater. Moisey explained:

> When the synagogue in Kopaigorod was closed in 1927, the theater was the only place where Jews met regularly. Furthermore, because there was something going on in the club every Saturday, a dance night, a play, or even a lecture, people went there all the time. But theatrical performances were the most popular events, especially when professional actors came from Kharkov. The dramas were often about Jewish collective farms and against religion. Once we had a theatrical trial about a kosher butcher who cheated his customers, and we, the audience, had to judge whether he was innocent or guilty. I do not remember how it ended. I just remember that the theater was packed and everyone had an opinion.

Mila added:

> If there was no Yiddish theater in Kopaigorod, our life would have been very rough. We worked twelve hours a day and did not have much to eat. The theater was the only place where we could relax. We left Kopaigorod [for Moscow] in 1932, and we heard that the theater was closed in 1939, when there were no more young people left in the shtetl. When we got to Moscow, we continued going to the [Yiddish] theater all the time, but there we never felt such a sense of connection with the other members of the audience and the actors as we did in that small Jewish club in Kopaigorod.

And Moisey concluded: "We did not go to synagogue, rarely celebrated Jewish holidays, but we went to the Yiddish theater. I guess this is what made us feel Jewish."[1]

The couple's attitude toward the theater is, in fact, quite common for Soviet Jews of their generation. Yiddish amateur theaters not only provided Yiddish speakers with a source of entertainment but also became, de facto, Jewish community centers, often filling the void left when synagogues were closed. Although the couple attended plays regularly, they were both unable to remember many details of the performances. This can be explained not only by the loss of memory of events that took place more than seventy years ago but also because the content of these productions was less important to spectators than the theater's role as a communal Jewish gathering place. Still, Moisey and Mila were influenced by the repertoire of the amateur theaters more than they acknowledge. For example, that Mila sang the songs she heard during performances at home meant that she sometimes involuntarily helped to spread the Soviet propaganda messages that were often included in these works.

Although Jews attended Yiddish theater to express and affirm their Jewish identity, Jewish activists saw the theater as a useful tool for disseminating propaganda.[2] Not surprisingly, given the generally high level of Bolshevik interest in all forms of theatrical performance, the state had a special interest in the development of stage productions in all the languages spoken in the USSR. Both Yiddish and Hebrew theaters appeared immediately following the revolution.[3] Their establishment did not mean that these theaters immediately operated as weapons of propaganda, especially because Hebrew was not seen as a language suitable for the ideological indoctrination of the Jewish masses. Even the ideological content of the early productions of the Moscow Yiddish Theater (established in 1918) was quite elitist and did not carry much direct Soviet messages. The first productions of the Moscow Yiddish Theater were *Les aveugles* (The blind) by the Belgian symbolist Maurice Maeterlinck and *Der zindiker* (The sinner) by the Polish-American Yiddish writer Sholem Asch (1880–1957). Alexander Granovsky (1890–1937), the director of the theater, hoped that the productions featuring these works would prove that fine art could be expressed in the Yiddish language.[4]

Seven years after its establishment, the Moscow Yiddish Theater began to include more direct ideological messages in its performances. For example, in 1925, an adaptation of Yitzhok Leybush Perets's *Bay nakht afn altn mark* (Night in the old market) was performed. The play was a full-fledged attack on traditional shtetl life, in tune with the Party campaign of the *korenizatsiia* (nativization). The plot, about a graveyard wedding of the dead, symbolized the belief that a new beginning cannot occur in a dead world. In 1928 Alexander Granovsky defected to the West. When Solomon Mikhoels (1890–1948) replaced him as director, the theater became even more "Soviet" in spirit. Mikhoels staged adaptations of works by Soviet Yiddish writers such as Perets Markish, Shmuel Halkin, and David Bergelson. By the late 1930s the theater became a forum of the Jewish intelligentsia and the most recognized body of Yiddish cultural activity in the Soviet Union.[5]

Similar developments took place in Ukraine, where local Yiddish theaters appeared in the early 1920s. These included Kiev's Experimental Theater and Kunstvinkl (Art corner). The state did not establish an "official" Yiddish theater in Ukraine until 1925, when Efraim Loyter (1889–1963) founded one in Kharkov. The plays staged in Kharkov featured works by Soviet Jewish writers, including Aron Kushnirov, Lipe Reznik, Boris Orshansky, Itsik Fefer, and Ezra Finninberg. The following year a Soviet Yiddish theater was launched in Minsk, Byelorussia, where Mikhail Rafal'skii (1889–1937) organized a repertoire similar to the one in Ukraine. By 1934 there were eighteen professional Yiddish theaters in the Soviet Union: four in the Russian Republic, two in Byelorussia, and twelve in Ukraine.[6]

Like most professional Soviet theater companies, the Yiddish theater troupes organized tours to the provinces during the summer. Jeffrey Veidlinger asserts that the Moscow Yiddish Theater was more popular in the provinces than in Moscow.[7] Indeed, audiences from the "provinces" (i.e., towns and cities with large Yiddish-speaking populations) were more capable of appreciating the repertoire of Yiddish theater than residents of Moscow or Kiev, who were rapidly assimilating into the mainstream culture. Yet, while visits by a central theater were seen as a significant event for shtetl residents, they did not constitute the main form of theatrical entertainment available to provincial Yiddish speakers.

The typical Yiddish speakers were very likely to have seen one or two professional Yiddish theater performances during their lifetimes and at least ten amateur local Yiddish productions a year. Although this amateur repertoire was strongly influenced by professional Yiddish theaters, it did not mirror them precisely. That everyone in the audience knew one another (and the actors as well) helped to create a special atmosphere in amateur productions, where everything that took place was understood in a local context.

The first Jewish (Hebrew and Yiddish) amateur drama theaters were organized by Jewish political parties. Zionists and Jewish cultural organizations, such as the Kiev-based Kultur lige ([Jewish] Culture League), hoped that the development of amateur theater would bring Jews closer to modernization and promote Jewish political movements.[8] Leaders of the Evsektsii hoped to create a Communist alternative that would attract the less-educated (and often politically unaffiliated) youth, targeting especially those who were not able to join Zionist groups (usually because of a lack of knowledge of Hebrew or Russian). "Such youth," asserted Sonya Fray, an Evsektsii activist, "will become a reliable group that will develop into the Jewish proletarian vanguard."[9] By 1923 most independent amateur theaters were either closed or transformed into Communist theaters. Communist Jewish clubs (or at least Jewish departments of regular clubs) were established in every locality that had a significant Jewish population.[10] Further, no other activity at these Jewish clubs was as popular as theater. Local coordinators of Soviet clubs reported that the most successful events were theatrical performances. One report stated that "there are almost no shtetlach that do not have their own drama workshops."[11] These amateur theaters were organized in factories, clubs, libraries, collective farms, and Yiddish schools.

Many Yiddish amateur theater performances entertained shtetl residents on a weekly basis. Amateur actors lacked theatrical experience, elaborate costumes, and time to prepare for their performances properly, but the enthusiasm of both the actors and spectators helped to overcome technical difficulties. By the end of the 1930s, throughout the Soviet Union, amateur theater workshops were the only places where Jews could hear Yiddish "officially" spoken. Therefore, in addition to being an entertainment institution, amateur theaters also became the primary means for the expression of Jewish identity. That only Jews saw these performances, and acted in them, also helped to establish a special bond between viewers and actors. An analysis of the repertoire of these amateur Yiddish theaters and its audience reception opens up a new perspective on how the Yiddish-speaking community understood new Soviet culture, and how its identity was influenced by it.

Yiddish Classics on the Amateur Stage

Shlomo Rubin, a former resident of the Lithuanian shtetl of Rokiskis, wrote his memoirs as part of the *Yisker bukh* (Book of memory). In his writing he focuses on the activities of the amateur theater that developed in Rokiskis in the early years following the revolution. In describing the repertoire, he asserts:

> We concentrated on plays and dramas by Sholem Aleichem, Yakov Gordin, D. Pinsky, and Yud Leib Perets. It became clear to us that through the medium of the theater we could disseminate Yiddish culture: every performance made a cultural impact on the audience and brought joy to the town. Throughout, we maintained a high standard and our repertoire contained only the best creations of the Yiddish classicists. We never considered literary trash.[12]

Indeed, Jewish intellectuals in Eastern Europe saw Yiddish theater not simply as a focus of cheap entertainment but rather as a medium for the dissemination of "high culture." That is why, in the early 1920s, the most popular Yiddish amateur theatrical productions were adaptations of Yiddish classics. Reports of the Evsektsii noted that the adaptations of Y. L. Perets's works were included in the repertoire of almost every amateur theater in Byelorussia in 1922.[13] Works by the Polish-American Yiddish writer Sholem Asch and the renowned Ukrainian author Sholem Abramovich (commonly known as Mendele Moykher Sforim) were admired among both Jewish and non-Jewish audiences.[14] The plays were typically full of Jewish folklore, music, and imagery. The most common genres in the productions of these local theaters were sentimental love stories and satires (these frequently criticized prerevolutionary traditional Jewish life). Popular plays that fall into this category included *Mirele Efros* by Jacob Gordin; *Di tsvey Kuni Lemlekh* (Two Kuni Lemlekh) and *Kishefmakherin* (The witch) by

Avrom Goldfaden; and *Dos groyse gevins* (The great prize), *Der farkishefter shnayder* (The bewitched tailor), *Menakhem Mendl,* and *Dos meserl* (The knife) by Alexander Rabinowich (better known as Sholem Aleichem). Some sketches written by local authors, their titles self-explanatory, were also successful, including *Farvos hot Itsik nit khasene gehat* (Why Itsik did not get married) and *Di heyse libe* (Passionate love).[15]

The state encouraged adaptations of Yiddish classics, since these works were often critical of the tsarist regime as well as the traditional Jewish way of life before the revolution. Although Jewish activists selected the plays, the actual scripts were prepared, and at times locally altered, by individual instructors and actors, and, as a result, carried the potential for subversion.[16] For example, the portrayal in an amateur production of Sholem Aleichem's character, Menakhem Mendl, as a Jew who became confused by Soviet slogans in a big city provoked disapproval from the local officials in Nahartov, Ukraine, because the comparison presumed similarities between tsarist and Soviet bureaucracies.[17] Even when actors did not consciously alter the content of these plays, audiences often understood the meanings quite differently from what the Soviet ideologists had originally intended. For example, a popular play often staged at amateur theaters was a vaudeville based on Avrom Goldfaden's *Di tsvey Kuni Lemlekh,* a tale about a young woman whose parents betroth her against her will to a bumbling Hasidic Jew. Meanwhile, the woman falls in love with an uneducated commoner. The play tells the story of how these two lovers overcome all obstacles put in their way, and culminates in a happy ending, where the commoner appears at the wedding ceremony disguised as the groom and convinces everybody that he is the bride's choice.[18] Jeffrey Veidlinger points out that critics liked the play because it mocked tradition.[19] Yet oral history demonstrates that the audience liked plays such as this because they provided an escape from reality and even sparked nostalgic feelings about prerevolutionary life. Spectators often saw these performances as a caricature of their contemporary lifestyle rather than as a criticism of the prerevolutionary past. A former participant in these shows, Sonya G. (b. 1920, in Ukraine), explains:

> The plays of Sholem Aleichem, such as *Tsvey Kuni Lemlekh*[20] and *Dos groyse gevins,* were about us, about our life in the shtetl, about our problems and joys. People loved these plays because they recognized themselves and their neighbors on the stage.[21]

The play *Dos groyse gevins,* which was also staged under the title *Two Hundred Thousand,* tells the story of Shimele Soroker, a poor tailor who suddenly wins the lottery. After he obtains his newfound riches, he insists that people should address him more formally in Russian, as Semyon Makarovich, rather than as Shimele, as he was commonly known in Yiddish. He then organizes an engagement between his daughter and a rich man's son (even though she is in love with a poor tailor). By the end of the play Shimele-turned-Semyon-Makarovich loses all his money when he signs a check with too many zeroes on it. When his daughter learns of this blunder, she becomes elated because it allows her to marry the poor tailor. This performance was included as part of the repertoire of the Moscow Yiddish Theater for more than twenty-five years, from 1923 to 1948. *Dos groyse gevins* gained such a large following not only by virtue of its believable characters and melodramatic plot but also because it spoke about the contemporary cultural transformation that many Jews were experiencing. It was common during this period for young Jews to change their names into ones that sounded more Russian, just as Shimele Soroker had done. The song about Shimele-turned-Semyon-Makarovich is still remembered more than half a century later by many theater patrons.

When I ask Efim G. (born in the Byelorussian shtetl of Parichi) what he remembers about Yiddish theater from his childhood, he responds with the song "Shimele" from *Dos groyse gevins:*

> Fun Shimele bin ikh Semyon Makarovich,
> Mayn altn nomen hob ikh farloyrn
> Vayl ikh bin a yid.

> From Shimele I became Semyon Makarovich
> I lost my old name,
> Because I am a Jew.

It is revealing that the version of the song Efim G. remembers is slightly different from the original song performed onstage at the Moscow Yiddish Theater. The original text reads:

> Mayn altn nomen hob ikh farloyrn
> Vayl ikh bin a gvir.[22]

> I lost my old name
> Because I am a rich man.

Efim and many others who saw amateur productions of this play remember this verse differently, as: "I lost my old name because I am a Jew." The viewers and actors added their own interpretation to the original text of the song, because changing Jewish-sounding names was associated with the new Soviet Jewish experience.

Another former Parichi resident, Iona K. (b. 1906), who also saw the same amateur production of *Dos groyse gevins*, remembers the song exactly how Efim had recounted. Iona explains:

When I heard the words about Shimele losing his name and becoming a Russian person, I felt for him. I also altered my name, changing it from Iona to Ivan, so that it would be easier to pronounce. I never thought much about it, but whenever I heard the song, I thought that this play was also about me. . . . While Shimele did not change the place where he lived, I moved. . . . Also, I did not win the lottery but changed my name for different reasons. . . . Still, I really felt for this poor guy.[23]

The identification with characters and themes in ways unintended by the state ideologues occurred in a variety of other plays. Faina (b. 1918), a former resident of Novozlatopol, Ukraine, who played the lead part in an adaptation of Sholem Aleichem's *Dos meserl* in 1934, feels that the plot of this play related to her contemporary experience:

> In the seventh grade we staged a performance called *Dos meserl*. It was about a boy named Motl. I played Motl, a boy from a very poor family. Motl had a friend from a very rich family, and they used to play together. This rich boy had a small knife. The poor boy really wanted this knife so desperately, but no one was able to help him. . . .
>
> I myself felt that I had so much in common with this boy. I was also from a poor family, and sometimes I also wanted things desperately, and no one would ever help me. . . .
>
> The play described a Jewish shtetl, which also provoked nostalgia from people in the audience who worked in our colony. It reminded them of their childhood. When we staged this play, it was a great success, and all the parents were very happy.[24]

Staging Jewish classics meant much more to Soviet Jews than taking part in simple nostalgic exercises. These plays were often seen as a source of national pride, especially when official Soviet culture began to promote Russian writers of the nineteenth century. In the 1930s Jews saw Sholem Aleichem as "their own Chekhov." Semyon (b. 1918), a participant in a Jewish theater workshop at Vinnitsa Medical Institute, shares his observations of that time:

> The repertoire of our workshop consisted almost exclusively of Sholem Aleichem's plays. We staged *Stempeniyu* and *Tevye der milkhiker* [Tevye the dairyman]. Many Ukrainians came to see our performances. Many of them knew Yiddish and understood the content of the plays. But this actually was not so important. The important thing was that the Jews were able to say they had their own classics, which were not worse than the Ukrainian or Russian classics, such as Taras Shevchenko, Pushkin, or Gogol. When we staged Sholem Aleichem's works, we were proud that we were Jewish. It was especially so when we were invited for the all-Ukrainian competition of theatrical workshops, a competition that we won.[25]

Tevye the Dairyman, one of Sholem Aleichem's most beloved works, tells the story of a father and how he deals with the marriages of his five daughters. Each of Tevye's daughters chooses a husband who strays further from the "traditional" Jewish way of life: the first daughter marries a man without her father's permission, the second weds a Communist, the third ties the knot with a non-Jew, and so on. Evsektsii leaders, as well as critics, supported the idea of staging this play because it criticized the prerevolutionary order and the traditional Jewish way of life. Yet spectators saw this play as a reflection of the processes that many Jewish families had experienced. The issues of assimilation, Jewish participation in contemporary politics, and, above all, intermarriage were important to the Jewish public, yet they were rarely discussed honestly in the Soviet Yiddish press. The theater turned out to be one of the few places where one could openly talk about these problems, even though they were disguised as criticism of the old regime.

The popularity (and therefore impact) of these performances among Jewish audiences was much greater than one might have expected. These plays, staged in local clubs, held an almost sacred meaning for a majority of shtetl residents. Their influence was comparable to that previously held by traditional religious authorities. The following testimony of a former resident of a Ukrainian shtetl is representative of the common attitude toward Yiddish theater. Sonya G. (b. 1920) recalls:

> My mother was a traditional woman, very religious and pure. She kept Kosher and lit candles on the Sabbath. She never left her house during the year because she had so much to do at home, to care for her children, and so on. She also said it was inappropriate for a married woman to leave the house. Only twice a year she made an exception to this rule. Once a year she would leave the house to go to the synagogue for Yom Kippur services. The only other time each year was when the district theater would come to show its touring production in the shtetl, which took place approximately once a year. She especially liked the performances that were based on the Sholem Aleichem stories.[26]

The recollections of other respondents were similar. Sonya's mother went to the theater because she did not think it contradicted her traditional way of life. The enormous popularity of amateur cultural activities meant that a large number of locals became involved in these productions. Oral history reveals that even the most Orthodox Jews went to see performances starring a friend or neighbor.[27]

Like all other genres of Soviet-sponsored entertainment, Yiddish amateur theaters were supervised. One of the state's goals was to incorporate ideologically suitable portrayals of the new Soviet reality into the theater scene. From the early 1920s through the late 1930s new genres of theatrical performances called "small forms," such as living newspapers (theatrical presentations related to contemporary politics), theatrical trials (mock trials of famous political or literary figures), buffooneries, and short sketches, came to the Yiddish amateur stage. Although such plays are not as vivid in the memories of contemporaries (an indication of their popularity and effectiveness), they still constituted at least half the repertoire of amateur Yiddish theaters. Oral newspapers were convenient vehicles to discuss current issues of the day, buffooneries were easy to produce for amateur actors, and theatrical trials proved to be as entertaining (if not more so) than staging Jewish classics. Each genre had its admirers and critics, each had its peak and downfall, and each has its own place in the history of Yiddish theater in the Soviet Union.

Oral (Living) Newspapers

"Living newspapers" represent one of the earliest forms of local theatrical performances on the Soviet Yiddish amateur stage.[28] Although the Yiddish term *lebedike tsaytung* (living newspaper) remained unchanged for two decades, its content varied remarkably during the period examined here. The *lebedike tsaytung* began simply as a live reading performance where Soviet activists (not necessarily actors) read the newspaper from the stage. Initially, given the unavailability of the Yiddish press in the shtetlach, many *lebedike tsaytungen* were simply oral translations of Russian newspapers. Such readings were quite successful; they were widely attended and offered audiences opportunities to ask questions about the local implications of Soviet policies for their own lives. The leaders of the Evsektsii in Minsk reported that their living newspaper was the most successful event of the year, attracting more than fifteen hundred people.[29]

The physical condition of the Jewish clubs where these events were staged could be described, at best, as extremely poor. At a Jewish club in the Russian town of Chita, for example, organizers had virtually no supplies: no chairs, no tables, and, of course, no books or newspapers. When one of the activists who had a subscription to a newspaper was able to organize an event, spectators were asked to bring their own chairs.[30] Living newspaper performances were especially popular when the editors themselves came to the club to read their own Yiddish publications. One of the Byelorussian Evsektsii reported that the "oral issue of the Jewish newspaper *Veker* attracted a huge audience."[31]

The state paid serious attention to the timing of these events. Russian-language living newspapers were typically staged during new Soviet holidays (such as May Day and the anniversary of the October Revolution) and during antireligious festivals aimed at holidays such as Easter and Christmas. Similarly Yiddish living newspapers often took place during Jewish religious holidays, such as Passover and Rosh Hashanah. The performances not only included the latest political news but also provided a forum to discuss local issues, including criticism or praise of local authorities or both. The results of these events were occasionally, and amusingly, quite different from what the organizers originally intended. For example, during Passover living newspapers often criticized people who baked matzo and sold it to their neighbors. Such testimony, however, actually helped members of the audience find out where matzo was being baked and how to get it.[32]

By the mid-1920s, when the circulation of printed newspapers increased, there was no longer a need to read newspapers from the stage in order to educate the audience in contemporary politics. However, oral newspapers remained quite popular. Audiences craved theatrical interpretations of current events on the stage. During this period centralized control replaced the relative spontaneity of the early 1920s, and instructions on how to organize and conduct oral newspapers were issued. The instructions usually emphasized that oral newspa-

Children performing in an amateur theatrical play. Children's home #36, Petrograd, Russia. Photograph courtesy of the Joint Distribution Committee Photo Archives.

pers should try to involve as many club activists as possible and not be limited to a few specialized actors:

> Oral newspapers should, of course, reflect the general policy of the Soviet Union, remembering that the primary goal is that all general subjects should be interpreted through concrete examples of local life. . . . In other words, it [the oral newspaper] should play the role of a local newspaper reflecting the interests of the local workers and peasants, and provoking their interest in the current affairs of the State. . . .
>
> Unlike the first years of the revolution, nowadays oral newspapers must be completely theatrical, despite their political content. We should also use as many posters, revolutionary caricatures, and stage performances as possible. . . . It is very important that the order of the materials presented in the living newspaper should keep the audience alert, because attending the performance should be a form of a recreation. The newspaper should contain one serious article, with the remainder consisting of lighter subjects, easier performances, humorous sketches, ditties, and caricatures. Sometimes, it is useful to provoke a discussion in the audience about a certain problem, such as agricultural work among Jews, and then solve the problem onstage.[33]

Despite attempts to attract adults to these performances, most of the "actors" who took part in living newspapers were children and teenagers. Magazines and newspapers regularly published reports on the social impact of amateur theaters and discussed how to accomplish the educational mission without compromising the entertainment value. Evsektsii collected data on who participated in amateur drama workshops. For example, a 1925 survey of the Kharkov theater workshop revealed that 80 percent of the forty-nine participants were members of the Komsomol (and ranged in age from fifteen to twenty years old).[34]

The material in the Soviet Yiddish press gives us a rough impression of the content of oral newspapers. Many scenarios include question- and answer-segments. The actors were directed to quiz audience members. For correct responses people were awarded prizes, such as books, fruit, or subscriptions to Yiddish magazines. In 1927 the Yiddish magazine *Pioner* published a list of questions that were to be asked during a Yiddish oral newspaper performance.[35] The questions mostly draw on a general knowledge of the Soviet Communist movement, history, and geography. Eight questions (out of fifty) are specifically related to the Jewish audience:

- What writer's last name means "hello" [in Yiddish]?
- In what town was Mendele Moykher Sforim born?
- What was Sholem Aleichem's real name?
- Which young character in Sholem Aleichem's stories was not able to pronounce the letter *kuf*?
- When, where, and how did Hirsh Lekert die?
- Who was the "grandfather of Yiddish revolutionary songs"?
- What three writers (two Jewish and one Russian) have "bitter" last names?
- Where did the Yiddish writer Perets die?

These eight questions serve as a vivid demonstration of the spectrum of knowledge of Jewish history and literature that was thought proper for an ideal Jewish child to know. It includes the historic figure of Hirsh Lekert (a Jewish revolutionary from Lithuania), classics of Yiddish literature, and Soviet Jewish writers. The questionnaire illustrates the selection process in the creation of the Jewish "usable past," which was designed to demonstrate that radical ideas existed in Yiddish literature *before* the revolution. This particular knowledge of Jewish literature and episodes of Jewish history were the only elements of Jewish cultural identity sanctioned by the state.

The scripts were usually written by teachers, who typically used materials and followed instructions published in the Yiddish press. Unfortunately only a handful of texts of these local scenarios survived, so it is practically impossible to discuss their content in detail. Many contemporaries remember that oral newspapers were often used as a part of the antireligious campaigns of the Soviet state. Etya G. (b. 1920) took part in the staging of an oral newspaper when she was in school in the Ukrainian shtetl of Kopaigorod in 1928. She describes it as follows:

The most popular of the children's activities in the club was the *zhivaia gazeta* (living newspaper). Each child received his or her own lines to recite. We staged a living newspaper against religion. It was in Yiddish. I even remember the words. . . . I remember we were fighting against Passover, against these Jewish religious ceremonies. We used to sing:

Vi ikh efn a Peysekhdik zekl,
Gefin ikh an apikoyres a brek.

When I open the Passover bag,
I find there a piece of a heretic.

We used to have special costumes. One boy played a rabbi, another played someone else. It was such fun. . . . These performances were hugely successful. The whole shtetl came to see us if they knew the school was putting on a performance.[36]

Etya also remembers that Komsomol members in her shtetl used to throw pieces of bread into the Passover bags that children were given. These pieces of bread (which were forbidden to be eaten during Passover) were called "a piece of a heretic" (*apikoyres a brek*).

The dominance of children as chief participants discouraged authorities. They realized that this had the effect of driving elder workers away from clubs. In addition, they were concerned about the spontaneous and uncontrolled nature of these shows. Criticism came from professional journalists, especially worker correspondents, as well as audience members. Professionals criticized amateur theaters for trying to create "false aesthetics" instead of promoting the revolutionary ideas of the time. These critics suggested the following changes in local productions:

Get rid of national Jewish characters and replace them with class characters, replace performances of ten actors with those involving *massovost'* [mass scenes], change general apolitical content with the important political issues of the day, and include more music and songs.[37]

Worker correspondents who wrote about these living newspapers emphasized that they wanted to see more interesting plots and that they were getting tired of the standardized depictions of cruel bureaucrats, honest workers, fat capitalists, and greedy Zionists. Many argued that the public loved the shows only because they were free.[38]

The mounting criticism of living newspapers led club participants to consider different kinds of works in order to engage a broader range of viewers. Critics encouraged playwrights to develop their story lines and create more sophisticated characters. To facilitate the process, professional writers were encouraged to compose special scenarios for amateur theaters, adapting them to small clubs and the limited acting abilities of performers, and also including the principle of *massovost'*. This broadened and modified the early repertoire of amateur Yiddish theater and eventually led to the appearance of new genres in these theaters, such as buffooneries and humor sketches, described in the next section.

Buffoonery and Humor Sketches

The mass production of Yiddish propaganda plays began in 1925 and reached its peak in 1931. During this period buffooneries (*bufanades*), typically short, one-act comedic plays with political undertones, became a popular genre that was used for propagandistic purposes. At least fourteen books containing scripts of recommended plays were published between 1925 and 1932.[39] The content of these amateur performances often mirrored the subjects of modern buffoonery on Russian and Ukrainian stages, such as support for the draft, the development of electricity, the need for technological progress, and new family relationships. Yiddish performances also attacked Judaism, Jewish political parties (especially Zionists), Trotsky, and kulaks.[40] The plays often promoted policies of the Soviet regime that were directed toward Jews, such as the organization of agricultural settlements. Most of these performances were musicals, consisting of alterations of traditional Yiddish songs, rewritten so as to make them simple to learn and easy to remember.

Many parodies were based on the story of Passover. For example, Avrom Vevyorke (1887–1935) first published the play *In midber* (In the desert) in 1925.[41] This anti-Passover parody revolves around two competing groups of Jews. One group includes members of the Komsomol, and the other brings together their opponents, notably Zionists and Bundists. The head of the second group is Moses, who wants to lead them to Palestine. The Komsomol group, in an effort to convince other people to join them, offers to build a socialist state instead. The Komsomol members use various arguments and methods, including the sexual seduction of Moses by one of the Komsomol members. The play ends with a complete victory for the Komsomol. All the members of the second group repent and go on to build the Socialist Soviet country. Even Moses refuses to go to the "Arab land" and stays to help establish the new Communist state with his new Komsomol girlfriend.

The sharpest conflict of the play is in the area of international politics. The lyrics of the songs used in the performance often incorporate idiomatic Yiddish expressions combined with Soviet ideological messages. For example, the "villains" explain their agenda as follows:

> Mir zaynen sheyne yidn,
> Gehandlt in dem mark,
> Ver a shoykhet, ver a rov,
> Un ver a feter kark—
> Firt undz Moyshe iber yamen
> In Balfurs medine,
> Vet men vayzn dort di tir,
> Geyen mir keyn Khine,
> Marsh, marsh, marsh!
> Oy, Oy, Khine,
> A goldene medine,

Chan Kay Shi un Chan Tsai Li
Tsienistn fun bestn min![42]

We are good Jews,
We were trading in the market place,
Some are ritual slaughterers, some are rabbis,
Some are just fat necks.
Moses leads us across the seas,
To Balfour's country,
If they don't let us in there,
We will go to China,
March, March, March!
Oy, Oy, China,
A golden land,
Chiang Kai Shek and Chiang Tsai Lee
Are the best Zionists!

The Yiddish expression *sheyne yidn* (literally, "beautiful Jews"), which usually refers to "respectable Jews," here applies to market traders, one of the least respected professions according to Soviet ideology. In the next two lines, "the rabbi" and "the butcher" are called "fat necks." In Soviet jargon "fat" meant "bourgeois" or "capitalist," that is, antisocialist. The Yiddish expression *feter kark* (fat neck) also refers to an "insensitive person." Therefore, by calling butchers and rabbis "fat necks," the author of the play created a negative association with these professions and made them an object of satire. In the play Moses, an acknowledged Jewish leader, only assists market traders and "fat necks," not the poor Jews in need of help. This implies that Moses is not a leader of all Jewish people but rather only the rich.

In this song the playwright used a familiar tune and featured Yiddish idioms in order to create the feel of an authentic Yiddish piece.[43] Yet these familiar words and melody were situated in a completely unexpected context and, as a result, provided a comical effect. I would argue that the Freudian theory of laughter as a reaction to talking about forbidden issues explains why the audience thought such parodies were funny. The Jewish listeners were shocked to hear new meanings and interpretations of familiar idioms and taboo subjects (such as calling pious Jews "fat necks") and therefore laughed at it. In the words of the anthropologist Mary Douglas: "The essence of a joke is that something formal is attacked by something informal, something organized and controlled, by something vital, energetic."[44] In the play the Jewish religion was portrayed as something "organized" and "dull," whereas Soviet ideas were spontaneous and energetic. The contrast provoked not only laughter but also sympathy for the new ideology. After the author established a common ground with the listener by using familiar terms, he introduced new notions, such as Soviet policy toward Zionism and China, and attacked them both. The dominant simplistic approach is an example of the type of propaganda that I call "across-the-board negation." This method was widely used in the creation of popular scenarios for local theaters and drama club workshops.

The play *In midber* equated Chinese leaders (who were hostile to the Soviet government at the time) with Zionists, and suggested that both were equally harmful to the Jews. To summarize, Avrom Vevyorke's creation effectively rejected Passover, ridiculed Jewish customs and social structure, and informed the audience about the latest trends in Soviet policies.

Other antireligious performances were constructed in a similar manner. Yekhezkel Dobrushin (1883–1952) wrote the majority of them, while Fayvl Sito (1909–1945), Yoysef Kotlyar (1908–1962), and other Yiddish poets and playwrights also contributed to this campaign.[45] Their plays denigrate traditional Jewish culture and values, and encourage the adoption of the new Soviet way of life. Playwrights were careful in how they dealt with religious matters to ensure that Jews would not see these works as antisemitic propaganda. Consequently the plays always have a "positive" Jewish image, such as a devoted Jewish Communist or Komsomol member.

The play *Mitn ponim tsum khazer* (Turn your face toward the pig), published in 1932 by Yeheskil Dobrushin, is characteristic of this trend. The title mimics the popular slogans of *korenizatsiia* among the Jews: *Mitn ponim tsum shtetl* (Turn your face toward the shtetl) and *Mitn ponim tsum kustar* (Turn your face toward the craftsman). The name of the play implies that the Soviet government freed the Jews from religion so that they could start breeding pigs (prohibited by Jewish law). Actually, however, the expression was commonly understood as ridiculing Soviet slogans and politics. In this play some children decide to pursue the breeding of pigs for a living. Their grandfather protests and argues that Jews are not allowed to raise pigs. At the end, however, the grandfather is convinced that pig breeding is useful because it will provide a good living for the family:

> FEYGE: Father, did you forget that we live in a village?
> SHNEYER LEYB: So, in a village should one forget about *yidishkayt*? It is written in the Gemorah that our wise men forbade us to raise pigs because the tsar Titus took a pig and threw it against the walls of our temple. Then the earth was shaken five hundred miles around this place. Do you understand? You will provoke an earthquake!
> FEYGE: Where was this earthquake?
> . . .
> SHNEYER LEYB: In Jerusalem, in Jerusalem!
> ESTHER [Shneyer Leyb's daughter]: How far is Jerusalem from here?
> SHNEYER LEYB: I do not know. . . . Probably thousands of miles. . . .
> ESTHER: You see, there is no danger . . . the earthquake was only five hundred miles around the place. But do you know all the benefits of a pig?
> ZALMANKE [Feyge's son, Shneyer Leyb's grandson]: Yes, a pig can eat everything. And it can provide twice as much meat as a sheep. You do not know this, Grandfather!
> SHNEYER LEYB: How do you know?
> ZALMANKE: We studied this in school!
> SHNEYER LEYB: What else did you learn?
> ZALMANKE: We learned that if we take very good care of the pigs we will have

one thousand pigs at the end of the year. . . . In 1927 we will have twenty million pigs! Maybe even twenty-one million![46]

This scene criticizes the basics of Jewish religion, glorifies the benefits of the Soviet school system, and demonstrates a potential economic achievement. The play is designed to illustrate that old values are no longer important, because they do not provide the necessary tools to achieve success and well-being in modern times. The knowledge that the grandson acquired in a Soviet school is portrayed as more valuable than his grandfather's traditional Jewish upbringing.

This theme is repeated in the 1926 play *Fun Kaslovich keyn Kherson* (From Kaslovich to Kherson) by I. I. Yafe. The following lines illustrate the trend of replacing Jewish values with Soviet ones:

> Vos iz geven a mol, darf men
> Haynt fargesn, azoy zogn di yevsekn,
> Oys Palestine, oys toyre,
> Haynt iz Kherson un Krym a skhoyre![47]

> We should forget now how it
> Used to be, so say the *yevsekn*[48]
> No more Palestine, no more Torah,
> Kherson and Crimea are the best merchandise now!

In the play Evsektsii members possess knowledge that they consider more powerful and valuable than the traditional Jewish source of wisdom, the Torah. The object of Jewish longing, Palestine, is replaced with the Crimean city of Kherson, where Jewish agricultural colonies and collective farms were established in the 1920s. In fact, the principal propaganda message of the play is to convince Jews to move from Kaslovich (a general name for an old-fashioned shtetl) to Kherson. When the author describes "Crimea" as "the best merchandise," he is creating a play on words based on the famous Yiddish saying "Torah is the best merchandise" ("Toyre is di beste skhoyre"). Again, a known idiom was used as a parody in a new context and, consequently, provoked laughter at the old tradition.

Parodies based on popular folksongs were one of the chief methods of creating buffooneries. One such play, Isaac Verite's (1890–1969) *Fun yener velt* (From the other world), consists entirely of modified Zionist songs and traditional Jewish tunes (*nigunim*). Zionism and Judaism were equal enemies, according to Soviet ideology.

The play focuses on a meeting of rabbis and other religious activists who are conspiring to destroy Soviet life and confuse Jews by encouraging them to pray (and therefore ignore the Soviet regime). The hero of the play, a young Jewish Communist, tries to persuade Jews not to believe these "clerics" and instead to go to and work in an agricultural settlement in the Crimea. By the end of the story he succeeds, and all the poor Jews move to the collective farm.

Unlike the characters of *Mitn ponim tsum kustar,* who use intellectual arguments to persuade people to abandon their traditional Jewish practices in favor of new Soviet policies, those in *Fun yener velt* play on emotions to achieve their aims. At the beginning of Verite's play, the rabbis, synagogue servants, and ritual butchers sing a song to the melody of the Zionist anthem *Hatikvah* (Hope, which later became the national anthem of Israel). While singing, all the characters stand up to demonstrate their respect for the song. The words of the famous anthem, however, are completely changed. The original lyrics, which encouraged national pride, are altered to focus on unattractive features of traditional Jewish life:

> Vu a shlak, un vu a tsore
> Vi a yidene an akore—
> Tsu dem rebn kumen, loyfn,
> A pidyen gebn, a hitl koyfn![49]

> If there is a stroke, and if there is trouble,
> Like a Jewish woman's troubles—
> Come, hurry to the rabbi,
> Give him donations, buy him a coat!

The musical parody is designed to create a negative association related to the song, so when people heard the original version on different occasions (such as an underground meeting of Zionists), they would be reminded of the satire.

According to the author's recommendations, all the characters, including the Communist, were not to move around the stage but rather sit on benches and sing their parts, with melodies borrowed from traditional liturgy (especially Psalms) so as to resemble a synagogue worship. The lyrics consist of modified popular folksongs spiced up with familiar expressions from prayers. The words strongly curse Soviet agricultural policies, which apparently deprived these negative characters of their easy and often dishonest sources of income:

KHAZN:
Veynt, rabonim. veynt, dayonim,
Afn umglik dem groysn—
Di royte tsore iz umetum
In shtub un in droysn.

A DAYEN:
Veynt, kley koydesh, got strapochet,
Rabonim un dayonim.
A sof tsu shuln, batey-medroshim,
Tsu gaboim un khazonim!
. . .
A SPEKULYANT:
Der arbkom numer fir
Farkoyft mir skhoyre durkhn unter tir,
Eyn mol, tsvey mol un tsvelf—
In dopr alemen ayngezetst![50]

CANTOR:
Cry, rabbis! Cry, judges!
Because there is great sadness—
The Red trouble is everywhere,
At home and outside!

A TRUSTEE:
Cry, religious functionaries, God is angry,
Rabbis and rabbis' assistants,
The end is coming to the synagogues,
To synagogue trustees and cantors!

. . .

A SPECULATOR:
The workers' committee number four
Sells merchandise from the back door,
Once, twice, and twelve—
They are all in prison.

The combination of religious and economic concerns expressed through this traditional melody is designed to demonstrate that only rabbis and speculators suffer from the Soviet regime. These characters sing anti-Soviet songs, using tunes from the traditional *nigunim,* because the play implies that religious melodies can easily mask anti-Soviet content. And this content thereby provides a foundation for antireligious propaganda. Yet it was extremely important for the Soviet ideologists to prove that the struggle with religion was based on charges of exploitation rather than on the persecution of religion itself. For this purpose, the amateur plays sometimes portray religious people as positive heroes who are unhappy about the involvement of the bourgeoisie in religion. In the play *Fun yener velt,* an old rabbi laments:

AN ELTERER ROV:
O, leysonim, az vey tsu di oyern,
Vos fun a mokem-koydesh iz gevorn
Anshtot tsu hern dem koyl-Toyre—
Redt men fun handlen un fun skhoyre.[51]

AN OLDER RABBI:
Oh, evil people, it is painful to hear
What became of the Holy God.
Instead of listening to the voice of the Torah
We are speaking about selling and buying.

Here the rabbi himself complains that religious services are just masking commercial operations and have nothing indeed to do with God. Such testimony is meant to demonstrate that religion cheats people instead of helping them. The Soviet state, and its ideology, is presented as an example of the opposite attitude.

The choice of language used by each of the characters in these plays reveals the character's political inclinations. The rabbi's speech is full of Hebrew words, which are considered reactionary. Other negative characters use excessive numbers of Russian words mixed into Yiddish conversation. This was presented as a more serious faux pas because, in the mid-1920s, during the policy of Yiddishization, the pure use of the Yiddish language was strongly promoted by Jewish Communists. The Russian words spoken by the speculator in this play were primarily Soviet jargon commonly found in newspapers, such as *mezhdunarodnoe polozhenie* (international situation), *zasedanie* (a meeting), *sobranie* (a gathering), and *povestka dna* (agenda). The use of Soviet slogans by negative characters such as rabbis and speculators indicates that these people often use Soviet vocabulary (just like traditional Jewish liturgy) to mask their true "evil" intentions:

> Ikh, a nepman, a spekuliant,
> Vislushaite menia:
> Pervym delom vyrabotat'
> Di povestke dnia.

> Ikh, a gabe fun Kharkover khor-shul,
> Trog arayn a *predlozhenie*
> Me zol makhn a *doklad:*
> *Mezhdunarodne polozhenie!*

> Ikh, a Kremenchuger rov,
> Bin ikh nit kin nar—
> Mir muzn makhn fest di "*smychke*"
> Mit horepashnik un kustar'.

> Kukt nit, az ikh bin a melamed,
> Kh'shtam fun inteligentn
> Zorg fun khaydorim un yeshives—
> Far undzere studentn![52]

> I am a NEPman, a speculator,
> Listen to me:
> First, we have to discuss
> Our agenda.

> I, the trustee at the Kharkov choral synagogue,
> Would like to propose
> That first we should listen to a lecture:
> About international affairs!

> I am a rabbi from Kremenchug,
> I am not stupid—
> We have to strongly unite [connect]
> A worker and a craftsman.

> I am just a *melamed,* but
> I come from intelligentsia.
> You should support khaydorim and yeshivas—
> For our students!

The use of Russian words (highlighted above in italic) within the Yiddish body of this text is not accidental. The "Kremenchug Rabbi" reinterprets the Soviet slang word *smychka* (alliance). The Soviets used this word as an indicator of the rapprochement between the interests of workers and peasants. The rabbi, however, uses *smychka* to create the idea that he can take advantage (i.e., unite or connect) all types of Jews, such as a *horepashnik* (toiler) and *kustar* (craftsman). This use of jargon is designed to create the impression that religious leaders used Soviet ideas to hide their true anti-Soviet intentions. The Russian words used in the Yiddish speech are often grammatically incorrect.[53] Thus the character misuses Soviet terms, confuses Yiddish with Russian, and mispronounces Russian words. The rabbi's illiteracy illustrates not only his general ignorance but also his hostility to the literacy programs of the Soviet regime. The message of the play is this: if a person becomes literate, then he or she will be able to understand and fully appreciate Soviet ideology. And a further implication is that a literate person would not be fooled by the use of Soviet jargon in anti-Soviet speech, because he or she would understand the meanings.

The use of Soviet slang also ridicules bureaucrats, a popular theme of the 1920s and 1930s. Many Russian-language stories, plays, and songs blame bureaucrats for economic and social problems, and Yiddish equivalents are not an exception. It is notable that the play *Fun yener velt* mocks both Soviet bureaucracy and Jewish nationalist movements with equal enthusiasm.

Many *bufanades* try to explain that different sectors of the Jewish population benefited economically from the switch to agricultural labor. The propaganda stresses that if people maintain their traditional lifestyles, they will not be able to earn a living because of the competition with state enterprises. This situation is described in the play *Nay broyt* (New bread) by I. Shrayer:

> A SELLER: I have not eaten anything today.
> . . .
> A SHOP OWNER: What will I bring today to my children?
> ANOTHER SELLER: Oh Jews, the cooperative and financial department will destroy us. . . .
> A TAILOR: Do you think it is better for craftsmen?
> . . .
> A SHOEMAKER: The Shveyprom, Kozhetrest, and Skorokhod are around, who would ever need us shoemakers?[54]

The Shveyprom, Kozhetrest, and Skorokhod (the first Soviet corporations that produced clothes, leather, and shoes, respectively) are portrayed as a better alternative to traditional Jewish businesses. Thus the only way for small companies to avoid bankruptcy is to go to Crimea and establish an agricultural colony. The play also asserts that the eradication of traditional occupations will lead to the creation of new Jewish men and women free from the "inferiority complexes" of the older Jews, who grew up in tsarist Russia:

> OLD JEWISH WOMAN [about young Jewish people who work in the collective farm]: They do not look like Jews. They are like *shkotsim* and *shikses*.[55]

GROUP OF YOUNG PEOPLE: Ha-ha-ha! This is true. We are like *shkotsim* and *shikses*. We are proud that we changed from *netrudovoi elementy*[56] to become ordinary peasants. It is fine, now we do not have anything to be embarrassed about in front of the *shkotsim* and *shikses*. We are now as good peasants as they are.[57]

In this play the youth reject old-fashioned values and moralities as well as the stereotypical image of Jews as physically weak people. Moreover, they are proud not to look like Jews but rather to appear like *shkotsim* and *shikses*. In Jewish shtetlach there were certain patterns in the manner in which parents criticized (or even insulted) their children who misbehaved. For example, it was rather common to call a daughter *mamzerte* (bastard) but not a *zoyne* (prostitute). The logic behind this is that a daughter cannot become a bastard but can theoretically become a prostitute. Thus, because Jewish children could not "become" *shkotsim* and *shikses*, they were often called that by their parents for inappropriate behavior.[58] Young people were very familiar with these terms. That the play incorporates these taboo terms and reverses their meaning from negative to positive creates an effective parody that results in laughter ridiculing old traditions and customs.

In some plays the older generation is portrayed as quite "progressive." For example, an old grandmother in I. Yafe's *Fun Khaslovich keyn Kherson* (From Khaslovich to Kherson) accepts Soviet values in the following manner:

> Biz meshiekh vet nokh kumen,
> Vi es shraybt zikh in di tkhines,
> Veys ikh, veys ikh, Soyge Tsiye,
> Ikh, an alte vel oykh esn,
> Vel ikh oykh geyn mit di fonen![59]

> Until the Messiah comes,
> As it is said in the Tkhines,
> I know, I know, I am Soyge Tsiye,
> I am old, but I also shall eat,
> And I shall walk with the flags!

The grandmother's tolerance is based on the economic benefits of socialism (she says that she wants to eat more than she wants to pray) as well as the disappointment in long-term religious commitments. The character refuses to hold on to her old values (such as waiting for the Messiah and reading holy books) to ensure that she will not miss out on the pleasures of the new Soviet lifestyle, such as "walking with flags." Acceptance of the Soviet regime is associated with youth, strength, and happiness. The rejection of the Jewish traditional way of life is portrayed not as an ideological change but rather as a return to the joys of youth. Soyge Tsiye's character embodies the backwardness of the elderly traditional Jewish woman, according to the Soviet perspective. Soyge Tsiye is illiterate; she is not even able to read the core religious books, including *Tkhines*, a Yiddish-language collection of prayers designed for women. Later in the play, the Soviet regime enables Soyge Tsiye to study in a state school for adults and learn the basics of Marxism (to replace her "old-fashioned values").

Antireligious propaganda in this play, therefore, is accompanied by the promotion of Soviet literacy programs.

An important target of criticism of Yiddish buffooneries, in addition to everything associated with religion, was non-Communist Jewish political movements, especially Zionism. Rumpus Zionists were equated with White Army civil war generals, dishonest religious activists, and even Chinese leaders. Yet plays rarely criticized political agendas, concentrating, instead, on the negative personal characteristics of Zionists: their hypocrisy, greed, and absence of moral values. For example, the play *A tuml afn mark* (Noise in the market), by D. Mayerovich, presents a situation in which a Jewish activist disguised as a Communist turns out to be a Zionist. When his comrades decide to do him a favor and send him to Palestine, he is disappointed:

> A SHTETL POLITICIAN (cries and begs, with tears): I don't want that! Jews, do not make a father with little children an unhappy man! I do not want to travel anywhere, I am a local Zionist!
> A SHOEMAKER: What do you mean by a "local" Zionist?
> A SHTETL POLITICIAN: I am local, I am not going anywhere. I am just worrying for Jews in general, they should have a place to go. . . . But I myself am local. . . . I have a wife, children, a Soviet position.[60]

The image of a "Jewish worrier" is often ridiculed in Soviet Yiddish literary works. According to the author of this particular play, the "Jewish worrier" "worries" about Jews only theoretically. When the real possibility appears, he does not want to go to Palestine himself because he does not want to lose the perks associated with his "Soviet position." There are at least two reasons why a Zionist occupies a position in the Soviet local government. First, the general Soviet media, in all languages, spoke about "enemies in our midst." Such propaganda encouraged viewers to look for failures in the activities of people in positions of power. The atmosphere of spying on one another, and especially finding "spies" among government bureaucrats, developed into a predominant feature of Soviet propaganda in the late 1920s. Even in the mid-1920s this theme penetrated many Yiddish plays. Second, by featuring "enemies" in positions of power, the author attempted to convince the audience that all the failings of the Soviet regime come from the misdeeds of personalities within the system rather than the system itself.

The negation of Zionism and Zionists was meant to prove that Jews prospered and thrived under the Soviet system and therefore had no motivation for leaving the Soviet Union. Moreover, numerous plays emphasized that Jews actively participated in the revolutionary movement that created a land of wonderful opportunities, free of tsarist residential restrictions and pogroms. The Soviet Union was represented as the ideal home that many generations longed for:

> Oh, Ratn land, bist tayer,
> Vi farbn shpil baginen.
> Bist yederer a mame,
> A frisher kval a brunem.

S'hot shtetl dir gezukht,
S'hot shtetl dir gefunen![61]

Oh, Soviet land, you are precious,
Your colors are brilliant.
You are a mother to everyone,
You are a fresh source, as well.
The shtetl searched for you,
And the shtetl found you!

I. Yafe, the author of the passage above, asserts a specifically Jewish connection with the physical land of the Soviet Union in order to offer the Jewish public a valid alternative to Zionist rhetoric, whose main claim is that Jews should live in a land to which they have a historical link.

Glorification of the natural beauty of the Soviet Union is a common theme in Soviet Yiddish productions, mostly visible in the songs and plays about Birobidzhan. (Ironically one of the most important reasons for the failure of the Birobidzhan projects was the harsh climate.) When I asked oral history participants about Soviet themes in the plays they saw in the amateur theaters, appreciation of Soviet land made the strongest impression on the viewers from this era. Sofiya B. (b. 1928) explains that she saw numerous amateur Yiddish performances when she was a child because her uncle used to perform in them. Her mother, a teacher in a Jewish school, also used to stage these types of performances. Sofiya explains that she especially liked "patriotic themes":

> We liked our country, and we wanted to protect it against all enemies. Staging such plays meant that we were part of the exciting life of our country, that we were their true citizens![62]

Sofiya's attitude typifies how many people felt about the Soviet themes in these performances. They appreciated the possibility of experiencing a sense of unity with other people in the country and of being regarded as full-fledged citizens. Therefore the concept of protecting Soviet land was described by many as "very popular" (some people, such as Sofiya, were able to reproduce exact verses from these plays).

Other themes, such as encouraging the move to agricultural settlements, antireligious propaganda, criticism of Soviet bureaucracy, and Jewish corruption, also enjoyed some popularity. Many respondents of the oral history project remembered these subjects, but almost no one was able to reproduce the verses or describe the context of these plays. Yet almost everyone spoke of the nice Jewish music that was played during these performances, the interesting costumes, and, most important, the atmosphere of "Jewishness" they had felt. Ian D. (b. 1919, in Berdichev) explains that he liked the performances because they were "full of laughter, tears, and many other emotions, and also because it was in Yiddish."[63]

Yiddish buffooneries that dealt with specifically Jewish issues helped to connect the Jewish audience to various political processes in the country. While the propaganda messages in these plays usually did not result in convincing a vast number of Jews to immediately pack up their possessions to resettle in Crimea, they did help to establish the cultural place of the Jews within the Soviet Union. Buffooneries, oral newspapers, and humor sketches entertained the audiences and in some ways controlled the leisure of the Yiddish speakers.

Yet one additional genre of amateur performances made audiences feel especially significant, and that was theatrical trials. Spectators of these plays not only passively observed the action from the stage but became active participants themselves. No other genre of Soviet Yiddish plays attracted as much attention among Jews, and no other genre was more employed as a propaganda medium (and a tool of audience manipulation), than theatrical trials.

Theatrical Trials in Yiddish

Richard Stites has noted that the trial-as-theater or political mock trial that appeared in the early years of the revolution was a fusion of popular theater and revolutionary tribunal. It was called agit-trial (*agitsud* in Russian, *agitgerikht* in Yiddish) and had a distinctly didactic purpose: to convince the audience of the guilt of the accused (whether person, thing, or concept) by means of vivid acting.[64]

In her recent study of theatrical trials in early Soviet Russia, Elizabeth Wood noted that these trials touched almost every aspect of Soviet life. She distinguishes six types of Russian-language trials, including literary trials of fictional figures, political trials organized around specific historical and current events or political figures, sanitation trials, agricultural trials, antireligious trials, and production trials.[65] Wood suggests that all such trials attempted to draw on topics that organizers hoped would arouse their viewers' passions.[66] Despite general similarity to Russian-language trials, Yiddish equivalents usually incorporated uniquely Jewish notions especially relevant to their audience. Therefore the classification of Yiddish trials is slightly different.

I discern four categories of Yiddish theatrical trials. The first included trials against religious customs or rituals. Trials of Passover, the Sabbath, and Yom Kippur, for example, were extremely popular in the early 1920s. The second category included trials regarding political and religious movements. In the early 1920s many trials took place against yeshivas, khaydorim, synagogues, the Bund, Poalei Zion, and other Jewish political parties, as well as general trials against the bourgeoisie, imperialism, and capitalism. In these the audience was both judge and jury. The third and most serious category were trials that were partly theatrical, partly real, against individuals accused of "crimes" such as performing religious activities, failing to bring their children to Soviet schools, or not attending Soviet clubs. Both the accused and the relevant organization were judged in these trials. For example, those who observed Passover were tried together with the very concept of this religious holiday. These trials often resulted in the transfer of those convicted to city or regional courts for actual prosecution. The fourth category, which appeared in the late 1920s and continued until the mid-1930s, concerned literary works. These trials judged literary heroes and discussed how one should behave if faced with similar circumstances. Also in this category were mock trials of charismatic figures such as Leon Trotsky.

The members of Evsektsii organized every detail of these trials during the 1920s. The Moscow Central Bureau's elaborate instructions dealt with how to maximize audience attention and how to convince them to agree with the verdict (which was obviously decided well before the trial began). The trials were conducted in both Russian and Yiddish. A trial against Jewish religious customs was more likely to be conducted in Yiddish, whereas cases involving Jewish political parties and individuals were often conducted in Russian. We shall examine each category separately to discover what made these trials effective.

Trials concerning Tradition

The theatrical trials against the Sabbath, Passover, and Yom Kippur served both philosophical and practical purposes. In their philosophical function, the trials were supposed to prove the negative effects of religion in general and its influence on Jews in particular. The "evidence" was composed of various antireligious publications that appeared between 1921 and 1923. These "anti-clerical" books and articles explained in pseudo-academic terms the harmful role of Judaism and its traditional customs on the Jewish masses. The specially issued instructions emphasized that the trial should look "real." The participants were not supposed to know where education ended and punishment began. For example, a report about a trial against khaydorim conducted in Polotsk in 1920 emphasized that audience members were scared to send their children to khaydorim after the trial because they did not know that the trial was just an educational performance.[67] The trials also had an important practical function, teaching the audience not only how to deal with religion but also how to behave at Soviet state gatherings. For sometimes members of the audience would be sent to prison simply because they did not behave appropriately during the trial.[68]

During theatrical trials genuine discussions involving a great number of participants would sometimes take place on such topics as the meaning of Jewish religious holidays. In Vitebsk, Byelorussia, for example, the trial of Yom Kippur lasted for three days. During the proceedings the greatest levels of interest were generated by debates about the existence of a human soul and arguments detailing the economic consequences of observing Yom Kippur. The "prosecutors" were not able to convince participants that they were soulless. However, a majority of the audience was persuaded that they were too poor to endure the economic hardships associated with observing Yom Kippur. The Evsektsii in Vitebsk reported that, as a result of the trial, many people, especially youngsters, took part in voluntary community work the following Saturday.[69] Similarly Jewish workers in the Byelorussian town of Gomel were so impressed by a trial that demonstrated the burden that Jewish traditions placed on its practitioners that they conducted a "public funeral of religious traditions and prejudices."[70] At times the trials led to a return of certain pagan customs. For example, as a result of a 1923 trial of Passover in Moldavanka (a working-class area of Odessa) "paper images of gods were burnt," and the trial proclaimed "to announce the day of Passover as a working day, and to transfer all income of the day to charity."[71]

Not all trials were as successful. An Odessa trial of circumcision, staged in 1928, failed to convince an audience of more than three thousand about the harmfulness of the ritual. Respectful Odessa doctors (all Jews) were invited to testify about the harmful impacts of circumcision upon health. An Odessa *moyel* (a circumcision performer), Mr. Bibergal, presented the arguments in defense of the custom. A contemporary, Grigori Kalatun, describes in his memoirs Bibergal's testimony at the event:

> Mr. Bibergal talked to the entire audience [thirty-five hundred people] with his weak voice. "Do you want to know what I think about the issue of our dispute? What can I say? The operation I do is very short—chik, and that's done! I suppose my talk should be no longer than the operation itself. But out of respect to the audience, to all of you who came here, I will say a few words. Look, who is present on our stage. Such stars! Here is Professor Zilberberg. He is a star of medicine, known in Chicago and Philadelphia—these are American cities. I am not talking about banal appendicitis, but if a person needs a serious operation, people come to Odessa from backward America. If you have problems with your heart, you hurry to another doctor, Professor Bukhshtab, who is also present here today. Who is a better cardiologist than him in Odessa? I am saying it not to promote him, he does not need it. Now, if your child is sick, you go to Drs. Tartakovsky and Tartakovsky, the father or the son, who are also present here today. Odessa is proud of them. Our chairman today, his name is Dr. Tsiklis, I will tell you, when both of my grandchildren came down with scarlet fever, I took them to the hospital. Dr. Tsiklis was so attentive toward them, and to all of the other children. I am telling you, he was more attentive than me, their grandfather. . . . So all these respectful people are telling us today that what I do is not good. That this is harmful! Well, if such stars insist, it must be the truth. But just to be just, I have to tell you something. I look at you, my audience, and I see that 90 percent of you are 'my productions!' So I look at you, and I am asking you, and your lady friends. Who feels worse because of that?"
>
> Bibergal looked at the audience, and within a second, thousands of arms went up to the air. They all began to clap, and the entire theater exploded with applause. "Bravo, Bibergal, Bravo! We won, 100 to 0! Hurrah! Bibergal!"[72]

The inability to achieve an audience conviction did not mean that a theatrical trial was a complete failure, since one of the key tasks was to attract people to these sorts of Soviet-organized events. Both successes and failures helped the government ideologues to understand better ways to reach the Jewish audience. Even an unsuccessful trial probably provoked some members of the audience to question long-established values, such as the need for circumcision. In the early 1920s this was a sufficient accomplishment for the authorities. However, in order to achieve better results, the Evsektsii sponsored more elaborate trials complete with professional actors as well as sets and costumes. Zvi Gitelman has documented an interesting example of this type of trial, which took place on Rosh Hashanah (the Jewish New Year) in Kiev in 1921:

> A weird cast of characters appeared before the "judges": a lady dressed in old-fashioned clothes explained that she sent her children to *kheyder* because, she proclaimed haughtily, she was no "low-class tailor or cobbler," but from a "distinguished religious family." This was submitted as evidence that the Jewish religion was a creature of the bourgeoisie. A "rabbi" testified that he taught religion in order to keep the masses ignorant and servile. When someone in the audience accused him of being a "lying ignoramus," "stormy applause" broke out, according to a stenographic report. The interpellator in the audience was immediately arrested. After further testimony by a corpulent "bourgeois" bedecked with glittering gold and diamond rings, the Evsektsii "prosecutor" summarized the "case against the Jewish religion" and asked for a "sentence of death for the Jewish religion."

> Moshe Rozental, a Kiev Hebrew teacher, rose to defend Judaism. . . . He was arrested immediately after completing his speech. The "judges" retired to their chambers and returned with a verdict of death to the Jewish religion.[73]

The practice of adjudicating an idea and judging individuals, taken together, played an important role in the choice of punishment. Those who initiated the trials intended to create the illusion that, compared to the death penalty given to religion, other measures of punishment, such as arrest, was not so frightening.

Trials of Religious Schools, Synagogues, and Jewish Political and Religious Movements

The Jewish club Grosser in Minsk conducted its first successful public event in 1923, a full year after it was opened. It was a trial of *musorniki,* members of the Musar religious movement within Judaism that claimed its members had the highest level of spirituality.[74] Musar was the most popular branch of Judaism in Lithuania and Byelorussia. The Minsk branch of the Evsektsii decided to stage the trial in order to explain to the Jewish population why the Musar yeshivas were closed and why the movement's leaders were being arrested. The goal was to demonstrate that the Musar movement was, in fact, an anti-Soviet organization that harmed the ordinary Jew and that its members were brainwashed. Because the trial was so successful, a stenographic report was sent to all Evsektsii members in Byelorussia, who were encouraged to organize similar events locally.[75] The structure, organization, and outcome of the trial help to reconstruct the methods of audience manipulation that were designed by Soviet ideologues. The Minsk trial started with the following scene:

> STAGE DESCRIPTION: *There are seven stupid, exhausted students of a yeshiva (yeshibotnik) who are seated as "the accused."*
> CHARGES: They created artificial suffering for themselves and tried to redeem their imaginary sins. They were wearing fur coats in summer and not in winter. They conducted agitation and propaganda among the Jewish youth. Because they were always ill, they would transmit their diseases to healthy young people.[76]

Here one can see many significant themes of Soviet ideology. First, young people are not working productively for the sake of the socialist state but rather torture themselves for "nonexistent" ideals. They go without fur coats during the winter because of supposed stupidity, not poverty. The judge refers to the Musar practice of behaving in absurd ways in order to break down pride and arrogance. They were initially Orthodox Jews who proselytized other Jews and were probably seen by Soviet ideologists as particularly dangerous. But the judge draws the audience's attention to the fact that these young lads, who look harmless, are actually dangerous to society because they transmit their diseases to healthy, working young people. The notion of hygiene is raised in almost every Soviet performance. The positive heroes are always clean and healthy, and the negative ones never know the way to the bathhouses.

The deeper message is that the enemy can appear normal and even evoke pity, but he or she is still extremely dangerous to society and needs to be rooted out and exposed to judgment. This idea was confirmed as the proceedings of the same trial continued:

> Fat butchers went up to the stage and sat next to students of the yeshiva. None of the butchers served in the army because of fake illnesses, and now they receive money from abroad and help the development of the rotten movement [Musar]. They also gave money to a rich synagogue servant, while poor Jewish workers received nothing and a Jewish school did not function because of a lack of money.[77]

The kosher butchers are portrayed not only as merchants who forced poor Jews to buy more expensive meat but also as people who take money from poor Jewish children and give it away to rich synagogue trustees. They commit their "crimes" under the mask of a deeply spiritual religious movement that also seduces youngsters. The audience is led to conclude that kosher butchers are at the center of this evil, and religion and religious ideas only serve their dishonest intentions. When the final verdict is issued, however, an important shift suddenly takes place. Two verdicts are proclaimed: one theatrical, the other real.

> The court resolved that the butchers must serve one year of forced labor and must be expelled from Byelorussia for one and a half years. The *yeshibotniks* must go to Soviet schools. The servants of the synagogue must pay the community two hundred rubles. After the verdict was proclaimed, the audience asked for amnesty, and the forced labor was replaced by an additional fine. The verdicts were transferred to the local council court.[78]

At the very end of the trial, the *yeshibotniks* take off their costumes, and everybody sees that they are really Komsomol members. For these participants the trial was a performance, but for others it was painfully real, especially those who were punished for their "incorrect behavior." The mixing of professional actors and amateurs was another invention of these mock trials. Two birds could be killed with one stone: popular religious figures were vilified at the same time that an effective propaganda event was conducted. This was just the beginning, a rehearsal for the forthcoming mass trials where the actors involved would never remove their masks.

Trials against Individuals

The easiest trials to organize were those against particular individuals who had erred in their political behavior. These trials were arranged as spectacles—held in theaters during the evening, with public singing during and after the event. The results of the trials for the defendant, however, were often not so cheerful. A convicted defendant was frequently punished seriously, not just theatrically. People were tried for observing religious traditions and even for being part of a family that did. For example, a Pioneer could be tried for his or her father who still attended synagogue services. Often the accused included *melamdim* (khaydorim instructors), who were charged with disseminating "harmful ideas" to youth. The melamdim were seriously punished. During one such proceeding, three out of the nine defendants were sentenced to three months of forced labor, four were expelled from the town, and the remaining two were found innocent.[79] The audience often protested, as they did not understand why harmless old teachers were being put on trial. Sometimes the authorities had to conduct several meetings after these trials to explain the verdict. In Kremenchug, Ukraine, officials conducted two lecture meetings before and one after the trial against melamdim in October 1922. At the last lecture, entitled "Za chto sudili melamedov" (Why the melamdim were tried), the lecturer explained the theory behind the verdict. Someone in the audience asked about the practical implications of the trial. The lecturer responded: "If you do not send your children to kheyder, there will be no trials against 'innocent' teachers."[80]

The trials of individuals feature several unique characteristics. The "defendants" were real people and their punishments were genuine. In fact, these institutions functioned as actual courts, despite their theatrical embellishments. The Komsomol Evsektsii circulated proposed scenarios for such trials in which statements of accusation and defense were clearly written out.[81]

Trials against youngsters who observed Yom Kippur typically started with a reading of the counts of indictment. These included accusations of low work efficiency, failure to participate in the cultural activities of the Komsomol, and unnecessary "self-torture," which included fasting. Then an expert on religion usually gave a speech in which he (most of the time this was done by a man) explained the importance of observing Yom Kippur for the survival of capitalism and workers' exploitation. His argument included assertions that starvation enabled people to enjoy their inadequate food in the days after Yom Kippur, and observance of the holiday created a false sense of union between rich and poor because all Jews, whatever their status, fasted together. Finally, the same expert concluded with a statement of how Yom Kippur disturbed the proletarian unity of all workers by creating artificial religious contradictions between them. The next speaker tended to be a medical expert who would explain all the negative consequences of observing Yom Kippur in accessible terms. First, starvation was extremely harmful to young bodies. Second, when many people came to the synagogue for long periods, they transmitted diseases to one another, and their bodies were more susceptible to infection because they were weak from hunger. Finally, statistics were presented recounting the number of fatalities occurring on Yom Kippur, such as illnesses resulting from parents not feeding their children and old people dying of hunger. The defendant would usually acknowledge these "sins" and ascribe this unacceptable behavior to the backward heritage of his or her parents, the negative influence of older friends, and to propaganda by a local butcher or rabbi. The trial concluded with a statement by the defendant, who promised that he or she would never observe the holiday again. During sentencing, a lawyer advocated punishing the kosher butchers and other religious activists in the shtetl so that they could not "seduce" more "victims." At the conclusion of the trial, everyone sang the International.[82] The aim of these trials was to show the harm of religion on both public and personal levels. According to Soviet ideologists, this would discourage other youngsters from following the negative example of religiosity. Such trials also had the effect of displaying the consequences of antisocial behavior.

Many trials against individuals aimed to combine several ideological campaigns. For example, in Polotsk, Byelorussia, some members of the Hassidic Lubavich synagogue were put on trial for selling homemade alcohol (*samogon*). However, the trial was not real but theatrical and, as a result, while the "hypocrisy of synagogue-goers" faced public condemnation, the *samogon* makers were not imprisoned.[83] Paradoxically Party officials and Communist activists were tried for "crimes" such as attending synagogues, for celebrating Jewish religious holidays, especially Passover, and for baking matzo more often than regular believers.[84] Sometimes theatrical trials did not go as planned. A politically active worker, a Communist, was once tried for observing the Sabbath. This particular trial did not appoint its regular prosecutors but instead invited people from the audience to express their attitudes toward the Sabbath. The report stated that most workers condemned the idea of resting on the Sabbath, and only one teacher defended the tradition. That teacher, however, happened to convince the rest of the audience that the custom was harmless. Still, the Evsektsii activist optimistically recorded that this trial provoked interest in the "meaning of Sabbath rest."[85]

The "crimes" faced by "defendants" were often quite unusual. In Gaysin, Ukraine, an individual was tried because he brought his son back home (from a Communist boarding school) for the Passover holiday. As a result, the man was "theatrically" convicted and advised to read more antireligious literature.[86]

Some trials acquitted one set of defendants and later convicted (and punished) another group. An example of this is a case involving four workers who did not attend a local workers' club and encouraged others not to do so. This trial took place in 1926 in Shepetovka, a small Jewish town in Ukraine.[87] The charge against each defendant was failure to attend clubs or political meetings after work. First, the judge asked the workers to explain their antisocial behavior. One elderly man said that he was so tired after work that he did not feel like going to the club. Then he confessed that he was also telling others not to go, arguing that there was nothing to do in the club, that there was no place there to meet with his friends, and that he wanted to relax after a hard day of work. After his speech a "witness" stood up and said that the defendant was actually an alcoholic and simply went to the pub after work, where he usually consumed a great deal of vodka and, as a result, had to be carried home. The defendant's wife, who was also present, corroborated this testimony. The accused blushed and acknowledged that he skipped the meetings in order to go drinking. The verdict was to appoint a Komsomol member to follow him around and to make sure that he went directly home or to a required club meeting after work. In addition, the convicted worker lost his right to vote.[88]

The next defendant was a middle-aged man who said that he did not attend clubs because he was not fluent in Russian, and, as a result, he could not understand most of the activities (which were typically in Russian). The verdict was to address this complaint to the club director and to conduct more programs in Yiddish. The director of the club apologized and promised to remedy the situation.

The third defendant was a woman who attended the trial with her infant son. She said she wanted to come to the local club but did not have any free time to socialize since she had to care for her child all the time. The audience supported her, explaining that women had freedom only on paper. The judge pronounced a resolution to establish a local nursery in which local authorities would have jurisdiction. The woman was released and went home to feed her baby.

The last of the accused was an eleven-year-old boy, a Pioneer, whose parents did not allow him to go to the Soviet club until he finished his homework. The verdict was that a Pioneer must not pay so much attention to his parents and that his or her political and social obligations must always have top priority. The task of a Pioneer was to educate his parents, not to obey them.

Trials like this were conducted in every Soviet town or hamlet. In Igumen, Ukraine, a drama workshop in a Jewish workers' club was put on trial for staging "inappropriate" repertoire. The group performed short love stories without a Soviet motif. The verdict stated that the workers (the members of the workshop) "should be more conscious in their choice of the repertoire and not forget their proletarian origin for the sake of cheap romance."[89] The local Komsomol activists did not create the scenario for this trial; a draft of it was published in the Russian-language magazine *Rabochii klub* in February 1924.[90] This publication included all the main features of such trials: the approximate number of participants, the arguments to be used by the judge, and a draft of the verdicts.

The results of such trials were far-reaching, affecting not only the defendants but the public as a whole. In the trial of the Jewish workers' club described above, the director of the club (who was not one of the original defendants) was also convicted. No one could be certain that he or she would escape punishment, even at a semi-theatrical trial. This created an additional element of fear, which would become a dominant feature of Soviet society as a whole in the years to come.

Trials of Literary Heroes

The success of show trials concerning personal and religious matters encouraged the regime to broaden their horizon and use this model to condemn other opponents. From 1924 to 1927 trials were widely employed onstage and even in classrooms. On February 13, 1923, the Central Bureau of Evsektsii in Moscow issued a document entitled "Directions and Methods for Conducting Trials of Literary Works in the Yiddish Language."[91] It describes trials of literary works as "one of the methods to employ literature in our propaganda."[92] The chief criterion in the selection of a literary work was the possibility of extracting heroes (workers, peasants, Communists) and villains (kulaks, rabbis, merchants). The instructions included elaborate trial details, complete with purely technical matters:

> When the trial is conducted in a club, everything should be done to make it feel serious. The trial should look official. There must be a presidium, a dock, a place for a lawyer, and a public prosecutor on the stage. When the judge enters, everybody must stand up, as if it were a real court.[93]

The literary work determined the method used to conduct the trials, and there were three possibilities:

> Sometimes, if a story is powerful enough, the public prosecutor may just read it out loud, and then one can start a debate. If a story is very well written, than one should read only short quotations and openly debate it afterward. Sometimes, for the purpose of clarification, it is necessary to adapt these stories onstage. In this case, first hold a performance and then conduct an actual trial.[94]

When officials organized a small play before the trial, a larger audience was often attracted. Literary trials were conducted quite often during the October celebrations, on May 1, and, when dealing with Jewish subjects, on Saturdays and Jewish holidays.

A popular scenario for trials coinciding with Yom Kippur was a short story by the Yiddish Polish-American writer David Pinsky (1872–1959) called "Erev yom kiper" (Yom Kippur eve). It tells the story of poor religious Jews who come to pray in a synagogue before the Day of Atonement. There they see a very rich merchant. A worker begs him for a kopek for his sick wife. The greedy man refuses, saying that he is "pious and should not be disturbed during prayer." All the worker's friends try to convince the merchant to have pity on the poor man on this holy day but to no avail. The workers are disappointed in the businessman who thinks of himself as pious, and, as a consequence, they condemn the entire idea of Yom Kippur. They realize that on this day the poor are punished and the rich forgiven. This story was adapted for the stage throughout the country, where the workers who did not rebel against the merchant sat as the accused.

The most popular themes, however, were those not directly connected with Soviet Jewish life but with the struggles of workers in America. A story widely adapted for the stage concerned a factory strike. A group of underpaid workers decide to go on strike, but one of them, whose wife is very ill and children lack sufficient food, decides to go to work after being offered twice the rate of pay for this day. The leader of the Communist workers' union tries to convince him not to do this for the sake of their common cause, but the worker does not listen. The union chief, however, feels that he cannot allow anyone to break the strike and kills the worker. The trial was intended to judge the man who killed the strikebreaker. By the end of the trial, the killer was found not guilty because he struggled for common interests. The verdict was meant to show that, if everyone cared only about his or her own family, the socialist revolution would never have been possible.[95] The methods of audience manipulation had been worked out in advance for these mock trials, whose alleged purpose was to encourage the reading of more books. Literary trials were both a very popular form of entertainment and a medium for enlightenment and cultural revolution.

One of the more curious aspects of these literary trials was the tendency to conduct them simultaneously with trials against real people. Verdicts passed in such trials affected both imaginary literary heroes and real human beings. This mixture of the imaginary and the real was instrumental in forming the new Soviet culture. One could argue that the concept of socialist realism is a leading example of this tendency to mingle fiction and reality.[96]

The literary works that were used for theatrical trials were not limited to those with socialist content but rather were predominantly popular stories or novels as well as classics of Yiddish literature, simply because the Jewish audience was familiar with these works. For example, during antireligious campaigns, the most widely attended trials were those based on Perets's *Der shtrayml* (The fur-trimmed hat). A trial such as this once lasted two days.[97] Sholem Aleichem's character, Menakhem Mendl, was put on trial in a variety of places. One oral history respondent, Yakov T. (b. 1908), told me a detailed story of how he, a graduate of Kiev Pedagogical Institute's Faculty of Jewish Culture organized such a trial and how it influenced the cultural life of the shtetl where he worked.

In 1932 Yakov T. began working as a Jewish primary school teacher in the Ukrainian shtetl Novoust'itsa. When he arrived at his new job, he quickly discovered that his duties included more than simply teaching Yiddish and Russian literature. The local council also assigned him the responsibility for establishing "cultural life" in the shtetl. Novoust'itsa already had a Jewish school, a club, and a Yiddish library, but most residents ignored the public events conducted in these institutions. The men preferred to spend their free time in the synagogue, and the women were taking care of their children and doing housework, rarely leaving their homes at all. Yakov (who is now living in Brooklyn, New York) explains how he found a way to alter the situation:

> I had no literature to guide me regarding how to make people interested [in cultural activities], especially Jews. . . . However, I owned a Russian magazine, *Rabochii klub* (Worker's club). In it I read about a theatrical trial based on Gorky's *Mother*. I thought the idea of a mock trial was brilliant, but I had to find something Jewish in order to create a similar event in our shtetl. I decided to organize a theatrical trial against Menakhem Mendl, a character in Sholem Aleichem's famous novel of the same name. In the story Mendl changes his profession from matchmaker to stockbroker and ultimately loses all of his own and his family's money. I instructed the children in my classes to read the book and to tell their parents about the trial. We selected students to play the parts of judge, attorney, Menakhem Mendl, and other characters. We organized the trial on a Saturday night. It was a huge success. All the Jews from the shtetl came to see it. The verdict was quite sympathetic toward Menakhem Mendl, who was found inno-cent.[98] The judge announced that because Menakhem Mendl faced diffi-cult social conditions before the revolution, it was hard for him to become a "conscious proletarian." This trial broke the ice of distrust among the residents of the shtetl toward me as a Jewish activist and toward the Jewish school. After that, people began to come to more and more events.[99]

Yakov explained that the success of the first theatrical trial eventually led to the creation of an amateur theater workshop, which presented new productions every week. The theater became famous among neighboring villages, attracting large audiences, often numbering in the hundreds, of both Jews and non-Jews who enjoyed amateur productions based on works by Yiddish and Russian writ-ers, as well as original scripts (mostly written by schoolteachers). Novoust'itsa's theater remained open until 1939 and, in fact, constituted the largest source of entertainment available to the local population. Moreover, when the last re-maining synagogue was closed in 1933, this theater was the only institution where Yiddish was publicly spoken in Novoust'itsa.

Theatrical trials were successfully used by Soviet authorities, indulging the hidden desire of every person to be a judge. They also satisfied a need for infor-mation, as people often came just to listen to what the "performers" would say about certain issues. They involved entire communities, with one's friends and acquaintances frequently at the center of events. Another important feature of the trials was that they created a pattern of behavior and accustomed the popu-lation to such events. Later, when mass trials (not show or theatrical ones) be-came widespread, the "audience" was already quite used to the concept and, as a result, was easier to manipulate.[100]

Choir singing in Petrograd Orphanage, c. 1921. Photograph courtesy of the Joint Distribution Committee Photo Archives.

Conclusions

Amateur Jewish theaters were organized not only in Jewish shtetlach but virtually in any place where Jews lived or studied. Two of the respondents in my survey, Semyon Sh. (b. 1918) and Isai K. (b. 1917), were students at the Vinnitsa Medical School in the late 1930s. According to their testimonies, about two-thirds of the students at this institute were Jewish. This was not a Jewish school per se, but since most of the students were Jewish, when they organized a drama workshop they conducted it in Yiddish. Its repertoire consisted of Jewish classics.[101] Similar stories were repeated throughout this oral history project. Grigorii Braziler (b. 1922) lived in an orphanage for Jewish children in Leningrad until 1938. He remembered that the language of communication between children and teachers was Russian, even though all the children in the orphanage were Jewish. At the same time the drama workshop staged performances in Yiddish, because this was the language the children spoke best.[102]

For many contemporaries, the content of the performances was less important than the fact of their actual existence. Yiddish amateur theaters were the places where Yiddish was openly spoken, Jewish-related issues were discussed publicly, and, most important, Jews met regularly. Even though the content of the performances was frequently heavily propagandistic and filled with unpopular messages, almost every amateur performance was widely attended. In the words of one respondent, Mariya S. (b. 1919, in Ukraine), "Yiddish theater was considered a respectable place to meet a suitable man for marriage. The fact that a boy went to the Yiddish theater meant that he was a Jew, understood Yiddish, and wanted to meet a Jewish girl."[103] Although young people thought it was important to choose a partner on their own, without a matchmaker (matchmaking and arranged marriages were ridiculed by the Soviet ideology), their parents were at least satisfied that the young people met at a respectable place "where only Jews went."[104] Thus, contrary to the intent of the Soviet organizers who saw Yiddish amateur theater as a vehicle of propaganda, these institutions became the centers where Jews spent time together and where in many ways they asserted their culture and identity. Staging adaptations of Yiddish classics familiarized Jewish audiences with their cultural heritage and helped them to appreciate the value of Jewish national culture.

Yiddish performances had a special significance for the Jewish audience, because these theatrical events remained the only possible way of expressing Jewish identity in the Soviet Union. Jews were attracted to the performances because it was rare for Jewish matters to be discussed publicly. On a cultural level, attending a Yiddish theater performance replaced, in a way, the ritual of attending a synagogue, and was paramount in transforming the cultural identity that influenced Soviet Jews for generations in the postwar and even post-Soviet years.

4 Soviet Yiddish Songs as a Mirror of Jewish Identity

In the late 1980s the Jewish theater Shalom opened in Moscow. One of its first productions was a concert of Yiddish songs. Such events were unusual in Moscow at the time, and, as a result, the theater was packed. That evening I sat next to an elderly lady named Anna K., who was extremely excited to hear old Yiddish tunes. The concert concluded with the beloved hit "Tum Balalayka," which resulted in a series of standing ovations, with the audience demanding that the band repeat the song four more times. At that point Mrs. K. said to herself (rather loudly), "I wonder how many of them know the real words of the song." On the way to the exit, I asked her what she meant by the "real words." She then sang quietly, using the melody of the refrain of "Tum Balalaika":

> Stalin ruft zikh on der mentsh,
> Zol zayn nomen zayn gebentsht.
> Zol zayn nomen, zol zayn nomen,
> Zol zayn nomen zayn gebensht.

> This person's name is Stalin,
> Let his name be blessed.
> Let his name, let his name,
> Let his name be blessed.

Mrs. K. remembered this song from her youth in Bobruisk, Byelorussia. She could not recollect where she first heard it but was confident that both children and adults sang it on various occasions. Only later in life did Mrs. K. discover that there were other versions of this song. That the song still lived in her memory almost sixty years after its creation, rather than simply remaining buried among volumes in the Russian State Library's Department of Rarely Requested Literature, demonstrates the important place that official Yiddish songs occupied in Soviet Jewish consciousness.

In the 1920s and 1930s Jewish Bolsheviks saw Yiddish songs as a powerful propaganda tool. These songs were widely distributed, published in newspapers, magazines, and books, and broadcast on national radio stations. More than fifty collections of Yiddish folk songs appeared during the interwar period, as well as approximately one hundred music sheets.[1] Many popular songs were altered one way or another in order to include new political messages. Entirely new genres of Yiddish songs emerged as well. While some of these songs became quite popular, others did not find a mass audience. While the reasons for success or failure will be analyzed in due course later in this chapter, it is noteworthy that every author of these songs attempted to create both new lyrics and the vocabulary of the Yiddish language in their work. Many hoped that this Soviet Yiddish language would speak directly to the Jewish working audience, and would make the songs instant hits. Ironically, one of the greatest reasons for the failure of newly minted Soviet Yiddish songs was the fact that their language was too artificial, almost "too Yiddish" for the rapidly acculturating Yiddish speakers of the 1930s.[2]

This chapter analyzes the subject matter and reception of various genres of Yiddish music, examining the texts both of songs that achieved popularity and those that remained entirely unknown. The transformation of Yiddish songs into propaganda vehicles provides revealing insights into how Jewish activists attempted to construct a new Soviet Jewish culture during the 1920s and 1930s.

The volume of official and unofficial Yiddish songs suggests that the Jewish public had an opportunity to choose within a wide variety of these songs, including revolutionary, romantic, or humorous songs, as well as lullabies, riddles, ditties, and hymns. For the purposes of my discussion here I have divided the entire body of Yiddish songs that I both found in print and collected from the oral histories into five groups: revolutionary songs, songs about Soviet leaders, about the new way of life, about the Red Army, and, finally, nostalgic and romantic songs. Some themes were more popular in the 1920s, and others flourished in the following decade. This chapter explores each theme separately and discusses their methods of creation in an effort to show how these songs shaped the emerging Soviet Jewish culture.

"Mutik, khaveyrim": Romance of the Revolution

The first revolutionary Yiddish songs were modifications of old folk tunes. In 1919 a collection of these works, *Red Freedom Songs,* was published in Petrograd.[3] The volume contains approximately twenty new versions of popular folk and theater melodies, such as Mark Warshavsky's "Sheyn, bin ikh sheyn" (Beautiful, I am beautiful) and "Di mizinke oysgegebn" (I married off my youngest daughter). The new versions retain the melodies, rhymes, and structure of the old songs, but their lyrics are altered. For example, the song "Frayhayt" (Freedom) is constructed from the popular children's song "Sheyn, bin ikh sheyn." The original version is the following:

> Sheyn, bin ikh sheyn,
> Sheyn iz oykh mayn nomen.[4]

> Beautiful, I am beautiful,
> Pretty, too, is my name.

The words of the new song are slightly modified but give a completely new meaning:

Sheyn, bin ikh sheyn,
Frayhayt is mayn nomen.[5]

Beautiful, I am beautiful,
Freedom is my name.

Here, a minor change of words turns a humorous children's song into a revolutionary anthem. The *Red Freedom Songs* collection features another reworked children's Yiddish song, "Arbeter's marsh" (Worker's March) based on Warshavsky's "Oyfn Pripetshik" (At the fireplace), first published in 1910. The new version uses the rhythm and structure of the refrain from the original but radically revises the lyrics. The original song speaks about children in kheder and encourages them to study because "knowledge of the Jewish alphabet will help to retain their Jewish identity and give them strength to struggle":

Vet ir fun di oysies
Koyakh shepn.
Kukt in zey arayn![6]

From the letters will you
Derive strength.
Look at them!

While the "Oyfn pripetshik" (written only eight years before the *Red Freedom Songs* collection appeared) promotes Jewish nationalism and culture, the Soviet parody encourages listeners to fight for freedom and the revolution:

Zing zhe arbeter, freylekh lebedik,
Breyter makh di trit,
S'kumt a naye glik, s'kumt a naye lid,
Zing a frayhayt lid![7]

Sing, worker, happily, merrily,
Make your step wider,
A new happiness is coming, a new song is coming,
Sing a freedom song!

"Oyfn pripetshik" contains many specifically Jewish-related terms. For example, the lyrics refer to learning the Jewish alphabet and to the experience of studying in kheyder. The Soviet version employs only the familiar melody and use of the Yiddish language to make it relevant to the Jewish ear and effective propaganda, omitting all other Jewish references. This approach was quite popular in the creation of early revolutionary songs in Yiddish, but parodies did not make a lasting impression on the contemporary Jewish public. This is not to say that the Jewish public ignored revolutionary Yiddish music altogether. Rather, people preferred other songs, namely marches written by American Jewish proletarian poets. Poems written by Dovid Edelshtadt (1866–1892), Moris Vintshevsky (1856–1932), Moris Rosenfeld (1862–1923), and Yosef Bovshover (1873–1915), filled with the "proletarian spirit," appealed to Jewish audiences not only through their language but also through specific notions familiar to

Jewish listeners. In fact, the works by these poets were the most popular Jewish political songs in the years immediately following the revolution. Their themes include references to heroic episodes from Jewish history or tradition. For example, Dovid Edelshtadt describes the rebellion of the Jews in Egypt as a social revolution:

> In dem land fun piramidn
> Geven a kenig beyz un shlekht.
> Zaynen dort geven di yidn,
> Zayne diner, zayne knekht.[8]

> In the land of pyramids
> Was an angry and evil king.
> The Jews were there,
> As his servants and his slaves.

Later in this song the author draws parallels between the exodus of Jews from Egypt and social revolution. He describes a new Jewish rebellion that allows the Jews to build a free society. Even though the Soviets presented the story of Passover entirely differently (see chapter 1), the song still was published many times during the Soviet period, perhaps because of its revolutionary spirit.

Another example of this genre is "Mayn tsavoe" (My will), which describes the death of a Jewish revolutionary. Written at the end of the nineteenth century, the song was widely sung in Russia. The dying soldier provoked pity and solidarity with his radical ideas:

> O gute fraynt, ven ikh vel shtarbn,
> Trogt tsu mayn keyver undzer fon,
> Di fraye fon, mit royte farbn,
> Bashpritst mit blut fun arbetsman.

> Oykh in mayn keyver vel ikh hern
> Mayn fraye lid, mayn shturem-lid.
> Oykh dort vel ikh fargisn trern
> Far dem farshklaftn krist un yid.[9]

> My dear friend, when I die,
> Carry our flag to my grave,
> Our free flag, red in color,
> Dabbed with the blood of the worker.

> Also, in my grave I will hear
> My free song, my storm song.
> I will shed tears
> For the enslaved Christian and Jew.

The notions in this verse, such as friendship and collaboration between Jews and non-Jews, respond to the need in Soviet ideology to emphasize the common proletarian background of different nationalities. Edelshtadt's poem, however, mentions *krist un yid* (Christian and Jew), which defined nationality by religion. Were this a Soviet song from the 1920s, it would read "a Russian and a Jew" or "a Ukrainian and a Jew." When Soviet Yiddish poets began to deal with the subject, they approached the issue from the Soviet position, which did not define nationality according to religion. In the ears of Soviet Jews, the poetic songs of Dovid Edelshtadt and other American proletarian composers sounded quite "revolutionary" but with a distinct "Jewish soul." They added the missing Jewish element to the revolutionary song and managed to introduce the ideas of radicalism into Jewish popular culture. Consequently they provided direction to the Soviet Yiddish verse that would follow later in the decade.

Yiddish revolutionary songs continued to be written well into the 1930s, but their content changed substantially. The tendency to completely negate old heroes from Russian history (which was typical in the early 1920s) shifted in the 1930s to a search for a "usable past." Heroes of Russian history, such as Stepan Razin (1630–1671), the leader of the seventeenth-century peasant movement, were presented as fighters for the public good and therefore as the first revolutionaries. The Jewish equivalent was supposed to demonstrate that the Jews dreamed of the new socialist system as well. Hirsh Lekert, an underground Bund activist from Vilna who was killed in 1905, was promoted as such a hero. Songs about Lekert were popularized and, in fact, were well liked by Jewish audiences. The content of these songs resembled their Russian equivalents. The hero was portrayed as a soldier for the common good, whose fate, more often than not, is a tragic one:

> Vi der gubernator iz fun tsirk aroysgegangen,
> Mit zayn oyg hot er gevorfn gants vayt.
> Azoy hot Hershke dem revolver aroysgenumen
> Un geshosn dem gubernator in a zayt.
> Azoy vi di tiranen hobn dem shos gehert,
> Azoy zaynen zey antkegn gekumen.
> Zey hobn im gants gut bamerkt.
> Azoy, brider, ir zolt mikh nit fargesn,
> Dem shtrik, vos me hot farvorfnt af mayn holdz.
> A tsavoe, brider, vil ikh aykh iberlozn,
> A raykhe zolt ir nemen far alts![10]

> When the governor came out of the circus,
> He threw a glance quite far.
> Then Hershke took his revolver out
> And shot the governor in his side.
> When the tyrants heard the shot,
> They immediately came toward him.
> They took good notice of him.
> So, brothers, you should not forget me,
> The rope that was thrown around my neck.
> My will, brothers, I leave you,
> That you should hold the rich responsible for everything!

Hirsh Lekert is portrayed in this song as a hero who searched for ways to improve his comrades' lives. The song combines an ideologically correct message, an easy-to-remember melody, an understandable sentimental plot, and, finally, a connection to national values. At the same time it has a significant melodramatic effect, which steers the Jewish audience to admire "the proper hero."

Radical songs with similar features enjoyed some levels of popularity during the 1920s and 1930s. Moyshe Beregovsky, who conducted folklore expeditions in the early 1930s, recorded more than two hundred of these songs, most of which were dated to prerevolutionary times.[11] Yet a majority of my Yiddish-speaking respondents did not remember Yiddish political songs, mentioning instead the existence and popularity of Yiddish translations of the Russian equivalents. In the mid-1920s Yiddish newspapers, magazines, and specialized collections published translations of many classic revolutionary songs such as the "International," "Boldly, Comrades, in Step," and "Varshavianka" and "Budennyi marsh" (Budenny's march).[12] Approximately half of my Yiddish-speaking respondents knew about these Yiddish translations and about a third of those were able to reproduce several examples. Klara G. (b. 1928), a former resident of Zhitomir, explains:

> I do not know who translated these songs into Yiddish, but we sang them in Yiddish. It was only later that I learned the Russian versions. Sometimes we knew the same song both in Russian and in Yiddish but sang only in Yiddish or only in Russian. It depended on the song . . . and I do not know why it was this way.[13]

An overwhelming majority of the Yiddish-speaking respondents, however, reported that they knew, listened, and sang revolutionary songs only in Russian. In fact, many misunderstood my question about Yiddish revolutionary songs, thinking that I was asking about songs in Russian. Thus, although the theme of revolution entered original Yiddish Soviet music, it did not remain in the memories of the consumers to the same extent as other products of Soviet Yiddish culture.

"*Stalin iz undzer firer*" (Stalin is our leader): Songs Glorifying State Officials

By the mid-1930s the rebellious themes that prevailed in political songs in the 1920s were gradually replaced by ones that glorified the state. Instead of promoting the struggle for worldwide revolution, Soviet mass culture of the 1930s called upon the country's citizens to cherish Soviet socialism. The songs from the 1930s encouraged the protection of Russian borders, as opposed to fighting for the revolution in other countries (as the earlier music had promoted). Images of Soviet leaders received a prominent place in this new culture, as the leaders were central to the success of the Soviet way of life: they protected, led, fed, educated, and cared. In the words of Vladimir Papernyi, the "horizontal" culture of the 1920s that proclaimed equality and the strength of the collective was replaced by a "vertical" culture, which centered on its leaders.[14]

The image of Stalin plays a prominent role in the texts of Yiddish popular songs. He appears in Yiddish marches, love songs, even lullabies. In marches Stalin is compared to celestial bodies because he shines "as bright as the sun" and is "a sign to follow" like the Polar Star. The most famous Yiddish Stalin praise song is Itsik Fefer's "A lid vegn firer" (A song about the leader):

> Er iz tifer fun di yamen,
> Er iz hekher fun di berg,
> Nokh aza iz nit faranen
> Af der kaylekhdiker erd!
>
> Iber ale vaytste ekn,
> Zingen mir di zelbe lid,
> Ukrainer un uzbeker,
> Der armener un der yid.[15]
>
> He is deeper than the seas,
> He is taller than mountains,
> There is no one like him
> On the round earth!
>
> In all distant corners,
> We sing the same song,
> A Ukrainian and an Uzbek,
> An Armenian and a Jew.

The image of Stalin appears frequently and is described in elaborate detail in Soviet folk songs in all languages.[16] Although such Yiddish pieces are not word-for-word translations of their Russian counterparts, the themes are identical. Stalin is revered as a guardian, a protector, and is compared to mountains, stars, and the sun. In the officially promoted songs, however, Stalin is never seen as a Jewish savior but rather as a nonpersonified divinity (as opposed to other genres that praised the Soviets for ending discrimination and protecting Jews from pogroms).

As in the Stalin marches mentioned earlier, the Soviet leader's physical and mental superiority is accompanied by divine features:

> S'hot gefregt mikh haynt mayn zun:
> Vos iz heler fun der zun?
> Tsi s'iz tifer nokh faran
> Funem taykh un fun dem yam?
>
> Vos iz sharfer fun a shverd?
> Vos iz raykher fun der erd?
> Vos iz gikher funem vint,
> Velkher flit azoy geshvind?

Un geentfert hob ikh dokh,
S'iz a mentsh aza faran.
Heler fun der helster zun,
Iz der mentsh, vos lernt undz;
In dem soyne treft zayn vort
Vi a shverd, glaykh afn ort.

Zayn gedank iz tifer fil
Fun dem yam, vos vert nit shtil.
Zayn gedank iz gikh—geshvind,
Gikher funem shnelstn vint.

Vi di erd zayn harts iz raykh,
Keyner iz tsu im nit glaykh.
Stalin—
Ruft zikh on der mentsh,
Zol zayn nomen zayn gebentsht!
Der iz heler fun der zun—
Zolstu visn, liber zun![17]

My son asked me today:
What is brighter than the sun?
What is deeper
Than a sea or a river?

What is sharper than the sword?
What is richer than the earth?
What is faster than the wind,
Which blows so fast?

And I answered him,
That there is such a person.
He is brighter than the brightest sun,
This is the man, who teaches us;
His words strike an enemy
Like a sword.

His thoughts are much deeper than
The sea, which is never quiet.
His mind is fast—very quick,
Quicker than the fastest wind.

His heart is as rich as the earth,
No one can be compared to him.
Stalin—
Is the name of this man,
Let his name be blessed!
He is brighter than the sun—
You should know this, my beloved son!

The range of things to which Stalin is compared, such as the sun, mountains, sea, and wind, comes from Russian folklore. The presence of the image of the "sun" is also quite important. Soviet scholars of the 1930s who wrote about Yiddish "folklore for Stalin" developed a theory of how these new images symbolized the new essence of Soviet Jewish folklore.[18] For example, Moyshe Beregovsky wrote:

> The image of the sun did not exist in Jewish folklore before the revolution. With the appearance of the image of Stalin, the sun entered Jewish folk songs. It might symbolize that, before the revolution, the life of the Jewish masses was dark and promised no hope. After the revolution, that life changed radically, and the sun, as a symbol of life and light, entered Jewish folk songs.[19]

Indeed, in almost every official song that dealt with the new way of life, the sun is usually present. Sometimes the lyrics even state that Stalin actually helped to light the sun:

Host gefirt undz in oktyaber,
Host far undz di zun tsehelt . . .
Fir undz itst tsu naye zign,
Nit geherte in der velt![20]

You led us in October,
You illuminated the sun for us . . .
Lead us to new goals,
Unheard of in the world!

Some songs use Yiddish idiomatic phrases to enliven the Soviet jargon of the text. For example, the expression "Zol zayn nomen zayn gebentsht" (Let his name be blessed) is a customary Yiddish phrase when speaking the name of God. In other songs Stalin's name is referred to as "zayn liber nomen" (his beloved name). In still others the expression "Play, my fiddle" is used at the start, for example, "Play, my fiddle, a song about Stalin." Although the remaining content of the songs usually has nothing to do with these particular Jewish expressions, such phrases probably were meant to create an impression of an "authentic" folk song. Similarly certain compositions use old klezmer melodies and feature attributes of songs associated with drinking parties. One example of this is "Lomir trinken a lekhaim" (Let us drink a toast):

S'hot gelebt bay undz a khaver,
Ay-ay-ay-ay.
Er iz geven a yat a braver,
Ay-ay-ay-ay.
Hodi kukn af di shtern,
Ay-ay-ay-ay.
A kolvirt zol bay undz vern!
Ay-ay-ay-ay.

Lomir trinken a lekhaim,
Ay-ay-ay-ay.
Far dem lebn, far dem nayem,

Ay-ay-ay-ay-ay.
Un der ershtn, zoln mir khvalyen,
Ay-ay-ay-ay,
Undzer liber khaver Stalin,
Ay-ay-ay-ay![21]

Among us lived a comrade,
Ay-ay-ay-ay.
He was a brave man,
Ay-ay-ay-ay.
Enough looking at stars,
Ay-ay-ay-ay.
We have to build a collective farm!
Ay-ay-ay-ay.

Let us drink a toast,
Ay-ay-ay-ay.
For life, for the new life,
Ay-ay-ay-ay.
And first, let us glorify,
Ay-ay-ay-ay,
Our beloved comrade Stalin,
Ay-ay-ay-ay!

"Lomir trinken a lekhaim" became one of the most successful official Yiddish songs of the era. Nearly every Yiddish-speaking respondent was familiar with this song. Some people saw it as a measurement of the high achievements of Jews in Soviet society. Sofia B. (b. 1928), a former resident of the Crimean Jewish collective farm Frayerdorf reproduced the song strikingly close to the original published text. During the interview she mentioned that she still likes to perform it, especially at private parties. But to make the song more appropriate for her new reality (she has lived in New York City since 1991), Sofiya changed the words but kept its original melody:

Mir hobn zikh tsenoyfgenumen
In amerike gekumen.
In der raykher land dernumen,
Yeder ken do vern raykh,
Hodi kukn af di shtern,
Aya ya ay ay ay!
A naye lebn zol do vern.
Lomir trinken a lekhaim,
Far dem lebn, far dem nayem,
Far di kinder un di shkheynim,
Un far alemen in eynem![22]

We got together,
And came to America.
We reached the rich land,
Where everyone can become rich,

Enough to look at stars,
Ay-ay-ay-ay!
We should make a new life here.
Let us drink a toast
For the new life,
For the children, for the neighbors,
And for everyone together!

Just as the original Soviet song encouraged its audience to "stop looking at the stars" and "build a collective farm," Sofiya's version tells her listeners to work toward "getting rich" and "building a new life." Even though Sofiya still believes that American ideology is radically different from, if not completely opposite to, Soviet ideology, she only needed to change a couple of lines in the Stalinist song to make it appropriate for her new reality. Sofiya speaks with equal enthusiasm about Soviet and American society, and especially how life in these two countries directly affected Jews:

There are some Jews (these are usually uneducated ones, but sometimes are even professors), who think that the Soviet regime gave nothing to Jews. This is not true. I think they are really wrong. The Soviet regime gave Jews education and took them out of the Pale of Settlement. Our family was the poorest of the poor, and we benefited from the revolution. I think only rich Jews say negative things about the Soviet Union. But they also say negative things about America. But for me, America is a paradise. This is my tenth year living here, and I am not tired of admiring this country. Bill Clinton is like our sun. It is impossible not to love him, he has done so much for Jews. . . . I do not like Jews who are not grateful to the Soviet Union or those who are not grateful to the United States![23]

Sofiya's ability to transform a song about Stalin into one about the richness of America demonstrates that Soviet ideology influenced her not only in terms of her political views but also in terms of how she thinks about state leaders and her own role in society. The importance of expressing gratitude to the state was an essential part of Soviet propaganda, and Sofiya thinks that she learned this lesson. Yet she left Russia in 1991 without hesitation and now is grateful to another system of government. Today she expresses this gratitude with methods she learned through Soviet propaganda.

Sofiya's admiration for the song is not shared by all the Yiddish-speaking respondents. While many did remember that "Lomir trinken a lekhaim" indeed was sung at private parties in the late 1930s and even the 1940s, some respondents emphasized that the song was commonly performed toward the end of parties, when most of the guests were under the influence of alcohol. They sang it not as a genuine anthem but rather as a parody.

Stalin is also a popular figure in *chastushkes* (ditties), a genre that appeared in official Soviet Yiddish folklore in the mid-1930s and whose structure consists of a four-line sung verse.[24] In these songs Stalin is present in the description of daily activities. For example, working in the field was described in one song as follows:

> Ikh gey aroys in feld,
> Bukt zikh mir der korn.
> Lebn zol der khaver Stalin
> Far di gute yorn![25]

> I go out into the field,
> And the corn bows to me.
> Let Comrade Stalin
> Live many long years!

The achievements of industrialization were also attributed to Stalin. There were songs that dealt with the building of new cities, factories, and the Moscow subway:

> Ikh bin in Moskve geven,
> Un geforn in metro.
> Lebn zol der khaver Stalin,
> Aza firer iz nito.[26]

> I was in Moscow,
> I took the subway.
> Long live Comrade Stalin,
> There is no leader like him.

Chastushkes sometimes connect Stalin with particularly Jewish experiences. Here his books replace Jewish prayer books:

> Kh'darf nit hobn itst sider,
> Ikh hob im shoyn farbrent,
> Kh'halt dokh itster Stalin's bikher
> In mayne feste hent.[27]

> I do not need the prayer book,
> I have already burned it,
> I now hold Stalin's books
> In my strong hands.

Stalin's famous expression of 1935, "Life has become better. Life has become more cheerful," entered the popular songs of the era. Here is a version that was translated into Yiddish and widely circulated:

> Dos lebn iz gevorn freylekh,
> Dos lebn is gevorn beser,
> Undz iz lebn zeyer gut,
> Esn mir mit gopl, meser.[28]

> Life has become merrier,
> Life has become better,
> For us it is very good to live,
> To eat with a fork, a knife.

In this ditty Stalin's image is not present, but his famous expression is preserved and reinterpreted. Eating with a fork and a knife symbolizes the higher level of culture (Soviet ideology asserted that in tsarist Russia people ate with a spoon, not with a knife and fork).[29] In short, Stalin is praised for all achievements of Soviet life, from the protection of the borders to the improvement of sanitary conditions in people's homes—in other words, for the modernization of Jewish life. However, Stalin is not the only leader praised in the Soviet Yiddish songs, even though he certainly took first place.

Similar to Russian Orthodox saints, different leaders were associated with various aspects of life. For example, Kliment Voroshilov (1881–1969), the commissar of military and naval affairs from 1925 to 1940, was referred to as a "protector" and the embodiment of physical strength. The president of VTsIK (Vserossiiskii Tsentral'nyi Ispolnitel'nyi Komitet [All-Russian Central Executive Committee]) Mikhail Kalinin (who actually had a peasant background) was responsible for agriculture.[30] Lazar Kaganovich (1893–1991), variously the commissar of heavy industry, the fuel industry, and transportation during the 1930s, is more often present in Yiddish chastushkes than in Russian ditties, simply because he was Jewish (however, that he was Jewish is not mentioned in these songs). It is quite curious that Vyacheslav Molotov (1890–1986), the commissar of foreign affairs, is often associated with a rabbi:

Arunter mitn golekh,
Arunter mitn rov,
Ikh klayb in deputatn
Dem khaver Molotov.

Mir zaynen gliklekh,
Mir zaynen zat,
Der khaver Kaganovich
Iz undzer deputat.[31]

Down with the priest,
Down with the rabbi,
I elect comrade Molotov
To be my deputy.

We are happy,
We are full,
Comrade Kaganovich
Is our deputy.

Other Soviet leaders were also included in love ditties. Kliment Voroshilov, the commander of the Red Army, was a popular sex symbol at the time. Songs portray young women as dreaming of boyfriends who are strong and outstanding soldiers (like Voroshilov):

Ikh vil az mayn gelibter
Zol kenen tantsn, shvimen,

Zayn zol er a roytarmeyer
Bay Voroshilov Klimen.[32]

I want my sweetheart
To dance and swim,
He should be a Red Army soldier
At Voroshilov Klim['s unit].

Yiddish ditties about Stalin and other Soviet leaders are perhaps the most authority-friendly genre of Soviet Jewish folklore. However, oral history is silent on whether people actually heard these ditties about Stalin and other Soviet leaders. These songs certainly did not make much of an impression on most of my respondents. None were able to sing Yiddish *chastushka* about Stalin or even remember their existence. Instead, when people heard the word *chastushka*, they thought I was referring to Russian or Ukrainian songs. Thus, although some Yiddish songs about Stalin such as "Lomir trinken a lekhaim" enjoyed significant success, many others, including those widely published such as chastushkes, were probably not very popular when they were created in the 1930s.

Oral history suggests that the Yiddish songs about Stalin that reached a wider audience were based musically on already popular melodies (such as "Lomir trinken a lekhaim" or the Stalinist "Tum Balalaika"). When asked about songs that were critical of Stalin, many respondents remembered that such pieces existed, but no one was able to reproduce them clearly. Singing an anti-Stalin song could lead to serious punishment, including imprisonment, which consequently made exposure to such songs extremely rare. Therefore only official Yiddish songs about Stalin are currently available. This is not the case with all the other themes in Soviet Yiddish mass culture. Topics such as collective farms, service in the Red Army, and the "new way of life" are portrayed differently in the officially published songs that were widely distributed than in the unpublished songs found in archival collections and described through oral history.

"*Hazeyrim vi di leybn shpatsirn af der gas*" (Pigs, like lions, walk in the streets): Songs about Jewish Collective Farms and Agricultural Settlements

The 1920s was a period of radical social change for Soviet Jews. Official policies actively tried to steer them away from religion and from prior entrepreneurial livelihoods in order to become workers in Soviet factories and farms. Beginning in 1925 a primary feature in official Soviet Yiddish songs was to encourage Jews, as a national group, to resettle and begin agricultural work. The most popular Yiddish song of the late 1920s was "Dzhankoye," named after the small town where a Crimean collective farm was organized in the late 1920s. The song promoted the Soviet solution to the "Jewish question":

Az men fort keyn Sevastopol,
S'z nit vayt fun Simferopol,
Dortn iz a stantsie faran.

Ver darf zukhn naye glikn,
S'z a stantsiye, an antikn,
In Dzhankoye, Dzhan, Dzhan, dzhan!

Entfert, yidn, oyf mayn kashe,
Vu iz mayn bruder, vu iz Abrashe?
S'geyt bay im a traktor vi a ban.
Di mume Leye bay der kosilke,
Beyle bay der molotilke,
In Dzhankoye, dzhan, dzhan, dzhan!

Ver zogt, az yidn kenen nor handlen,
Esn frishe yoykh mit mandlen,
Un nit zayn keyn arbetsman!
Dos kenen zogn nor di sonim.
Yidn, shpayt zey on in ponim,
Tut a kuk oyf Dzhan, dzhan, dzhan![33]

When one goes to Sevastopol,
Which is not far from Simferopol,
One finds a station there.
Who has to look for new happiness,
When there is a small, old station there,
In Dzhankoye, Dzhan, Dzhan, Dzhan!

Jews, answer my question,
Where is my brother, where is Abrasha?
His tractor moves like a train.
Auntie Leye is at the mower,
Beyle is at the thresher,
In Dzhankoye, dzhan, dzhan, dzhan!

Who says that Jews can only trade,
Eat fresh soup with almonds,
And not be workers!
Only enemies can say that.
Jews, spit in their faces,
Look at Dzhan, Dzhan, Dzhan!

The structure of the song parodies the traditional question-and-answer format commonly used by rabbis and teachers to quiz students at Jewish khaydorim and yeshives. The Yiddish word *kashe* (question, problem) usually applies to especially puzzling questions concerning aspects of Jewish tradition or law. The questions in the song both ridicule religious format and concern the unusual situation of a Jew working on the land.

"Dzhankoye" combines many elements that were popularized in Soviet Jewish songs in the 1920s and the early 1930s. The first is the inclusion of technical equipment. At least three agricultural machines are described—a mower, a thrasher, and a tractor; some versions also include a combine harvester. Another popular element in the song is the destruction of traditionally negative Jewish stereotypes. A third aspect is women's rights, a topic very much in the air in the 1920s. "Dzhankoye" demonstrates that Jewish women became farm workers and were acquainted with the latest technical achievements. The final verse is the culmination of these ideas. It describes the image of the ideal Soviet Jew, how he was officially seen, and how the "real Jew" was expected to behave. At the same time it criticizes the stereotypical image of the Jew, who only knows how to trade and eat fresh soup but not how to be a worker. Because of the song's catchy melody and memorable lyrics, "Dzhankoye" has remained popular for generations, even outside the Soviet Union. For that reason it is still included in the repertoire of many contemporary Yiddish musicians.

Jewish participation in agricultural settlements was treated as a way to destroy hostilities between Jews and other nationalities in the Soviet Union. A popular song by Sholem Lopatin (1902–1943) describes how common labor can unite former enemies, such as a Ukrainian peasant and a Jewish worker:

> Nekhtn shkheynim vayte,
> Haynt iz azoy noent,
> Ukrainer poyer, yidisher muzhik![34]
>
> Yesterday they were distant neighbors,
> Today they are so close,
> A Ukrainian peasant and a Jewish peasant!

The image of a Jewish and Ukrainian peasant working together emphasizes and promotes a common ground between people of different nationalities as part of the new way of life in the Soviet Union. This new lifestyle features the absence of religious customs, now substituted by antireligious behavior. The songs describe this behavior through indirect symbolism, such as portraying the importance for Jews to breed swine:[35]

> Hazeyrim, vi di leybn,
> Shpatsirn af der gas.[36]
>
> Pigs, like lions,
> Are walking in the street.

Further, preparing pork for holiday meals became the symbol of achievement in Soviet Yiddish songs:

> Ay, tseshpil zikh mayn harmoshke,
> Ay, tseshpil zikh mayn bayan,
> Ikh vel af yontev makhn grivn
> Fun mayn eygenem kaban.[37]
>
> Oh, play my accordion,
> Oh, play my squeeze-box,
> I will cook cracklings for the holidays
> From my own boar.

Grivn (cracklings) is a traditional Jewish dish, usually prepared during holidays from goose fat. In this song the holiday is Soviet and the meals are antireligious, but the dish itself remains the same, although it is made out of non-kosher boar.

Most published Yiddish songs of the new way of life are devoted to agricultural settlements and village life. They emphasize the antireligious nature of the Soviet Jewish community and promote friendship between Jews and non-Jews, once again based on agricultural experiences. Similar to the Yiddish press, published Yiddish songs fail to address issues important for the Jewish community of the time, such as urbanization, migration, and a change of language. Songs about the "Jewish Potemkin Village" were not about real issues and troubles but only concerned Jewish life as it was supposed to be in the ideal Soviet society.

Yet some of these songs achieved notable popularity. Respondents in my oral history project explained that these pieces fulfilled the need for positive images associated with the new regime. The songs provided an escape from everyday problems. Faina D. (b. 1918, in Novozlatopol, Ukraine) explains:

> We lived on a collective farm, and life there was very hard. I had to work twelve to fourteen hours a day, especially during summers. I did not even have the time to enjoy any leisure. But we had a radio at home, which sometimes broadcast Yiddish songs in the mornings. We all liked them because they had such great rhythm and energy, and catchy melodies. During the day when I was working, I often found myself singing some of the tunes that I heard in the morning. What were the songs? I liked, for example, the song "Dzhankoye."[38]

Sometimes new Soviet Yiddish songs were reinterpreted locally, and, in the process, their messages lost their ideological power (without any alteration of the words or melody). For example, Efim G. (b. 1918, in Parichi, Byelorussia) says that many people in his hometown did not take propaganda songs seriously and, in fact, laughed at the way this sort of official propaganda promoted Soviet policies. He remembers how one popular song about resettlement was interpreted sarcastically:

> During a performance in our amateur theater, actors, who were often children, performed songs about the new way of life. I remember once I was singing a song about Birobidzhan:

> > S'fort a yidene in mark,
> > Mit a groysn kheyshek.
> > Fort a yidene in Birobidzhan,
> > Hodeven a loshek!
> > Op-lya, op-lya, hodeven a loshek!

> > A Jewish woman is traveling to the market,
> > With lots of courage.
> > A Jewish woman goes to Birobidzhan,

To raise a calf!
Op-lya, op-lya, to raise a calf!

I was singing the song, and other children were acting during this performance. One girl played the *yidene* [Jewish woman]. She was wearing a
big dress with some pillows underneath. She was showing how she loved
to go to the market and how she did not want to go to Birobidzhan. However, she was encouraged by her young energetic sons, played by two boys,
to move there. While singing the "op-lya" refrain, we would take this quite
full-bodied girl and flip her up. It looked extremely funny, the audience
was laughing.[39]

The original idea of the song was to demonstrate that even a "backward"
yidene should be eager to travel to build a new life in Birobidzhan. Efim's recollection about this satirical play is revealing. The performance he took part in
shows that those who moved to settle in Birobidzhan were satirized rather than
admired.

Mixed attitudes toward the Soviet regime were expressed not only in the way
that published songs were performed but also in the fact that these were not the
only songs that Yiddish speakers enjoyed. Unpublished songs, found in archives
and recorded from respondents, also dealt with various aspects of contemporary Jewish life from this period, including shifts in the traditional family structure, and economic and social changes. But their treatment of the subject was
often far from favorable. Here is an example of how Jewish settlements were
perceived through the eyes of a person who was disappointed by the propaganda:

Geforn keyn Krym, gemeynt a kurort,
Esn vayntroybn un geyn zikh bodn dort.
Oy gastrolerele, gemeynt a kurort,
Esn vayntroybn un geyn zikh bodn dort.

Geforn keyn Krym, gemeynt es shprotst fontanen,
Nito keyn brunemer, me grobt artizanen.
Oy, gastrolerele, gemeynt se shprotst fontanen,
Nito keyn brunemer, me grobt artizanen.

Koyft er a ferdl, a neveyle koyft er dafke,
Paygert er avek, bakumt er a strakhovke.
Oy, gastrolerkele, a neveyle koyft er dafke,
Paygert er avek, bakumt er a strakhovke.

Dreyen, un dreyen, un dreyen, un dreyen,
Shpan kolektivne vil er nit geyn.

Baarbetn di erd—batrakes muz er dingen,
Di barishne baym shpigl romansn fleg zingen.
Oy, gastrolerele, batrakes muz er dingen,
Di barishne bam shpigl romansn flegn zingen.[40]

He went to Crimea, and thought it was a health resort,
Where one eats grapes and takes baths.
Oh, seasonal worker, you thought it was a health resort,
Where one eats grapes and takes baths.

He went to Crimea, he thought fountains were springing,
But there was no water, one had to dig wells.
Oh, seasonal worker, you thought fountains were springing,
But there were no wells.

He buys a horse, he buys a weak horse and a carcass,
The horse dies, and he gets insurance.
Oh, seasonal worker, he buys a carcass,
The horse dies, he gets insurance.

Whirling, and whirling, and whirling, and whirling.
He does not want to go with the *collective*.

To work the land—he must hire farm laborers,
The young lady near the mirror used to sing romances.
Oh, seasonal worker, he must hire serfs,
The young lady near the mirror used to sing romances.

The melody of this song is that of a Russian popular dance tune from the 1920s called "Krutitsya, vertitsya shar goluboy" (The blue ball is spinning). The lyrics paint an image of a Jewish collective farm that is in stark contrast to the one portrayed in the previously discussed, and officially created, "Dzhankoye." Images of Jews as fighters and progressive founders of new agricultural settlements are not present in this song. On the contrary, we see a stereotypically negative character who wants to take advantage of the government whenever possible. Almost everything in this song contradicts officially accepted methods for describing reality. The reason for resettlement, according to the protagonist, is to look for an "easy life"—"to eat grapes and swim." Signs of technical progress, such as artisan wells, are not portrayed as worthwhile achievements of the revolution but rather as annoying phenomena. The song describes the various tricks with which "unfaithful" Jews try to circumvent the system, for example, buying a dying horse and receiving insurance when the horse dies. The topic of women's emancipation is also discussed. In contrast to the women portrayed in "Dzhankoye" as working with threshers, here women want to "sing romances."

The style and structure themselves mock the Soviet ideology. In both "Dzhankoye" and "Geforn in Krym" Russian words are interspersed in the predominantly Yiddish compositions, although in the latter they are not associated with positive notions. Russian words are used in "Dzhankoye" to describe a tractor, a thrasher, and a mower (*traktor, kosilke,* and *molotilke*), all "positive" items, whereas in "Geforn in Krym" the Russian word for "lady" (*baryshnya*) has an overtone of a spoiled young lady. The other Russian words used in that song follow the same pattern: *gastrolerkele* implies not a serious worker but a casual one and *batrak* is a serf. In "Dzhankoye" the Russian words refer to moderniza-tion and technical progress, but in "Geforn in Krym" even the "positive" word *kolektivne* (collective) is misspelled and has an ironic connotation. Further, whereas "Dzhankoye" uses Russian words only where Yiddish terms do not ex-ist, the Russian words in "Geforn in Krym" are systematically substituted for existing Yiddish words. This usage plays a vital role in the construction of a satirical image. The negative character speaks in Russian instead of Yiddish in order to demonstrate advanced position in society. He decides that official So-viet policy allows him to have the privileges enjoyed by the "bourgeois" class before the revolution, such as a piano, household servants, fountains, and the ability to visit health resorts. Theoretically the song was supposed to ridicule such desires; in practice, however, listeners saw it instead as a satire of the re-gime. Because of this possibility of listeners misinterpreting the song and not understanding its "true meaning," "Geforn in Krym" was collected on a folklore expedition and was never officially published.

Even when unpublished folk songs are more sympathetic toward the regime, they differ from the state-supported songs in that they typically have a more "human face." Another difference is in the arrangements of the songs. Published songs are written predominantly for choral singing, whereas folk tunes are de-signed for individual performances. Also, despite the generally positive descrip-tions in these unpublished songs, they are filled with satirical images:

> Shemberg iz a traktorist,
> S'iz dokh a mekhaye.
> Dresht er eyn mol mit a traktor,
> Brekht er im in drayen.[41]

> Shemberg is a tractor driver,
> This is a pleasure.
> He threshes [the field] with his tractor,
> And the tractor splits into three.

The first two lines offer a positive description but lead to an unexpected twist: the hero is proud to be working on a tractor but does not know how to use it properly, and "the tractor splits into three." Only unpublished songs could contain satirical images, since the aim of Soviet publications was to promote the vision that Jews were competent agricultural workers. Challenging this notion was not permitted, even when the mockery was framed in a positive way.

A comparative analysis of the published and unpublished songs of the new lifestyle reveals a sharp discrepancy between the Jewish Potemkin Village and real villages. The published songs are in "purified Yiddish," that is, Yiddish cleansed of words with Hebraic and Slavic origins, and their characters work in collective farms and eat pork to commemorate Soviet holidays. Real villagers speak a mixture of Russian and Yiddish and often incorrectly, ridicule Soviet policies, suspect Jewish Communists of dishonesty, and ridicule new agricul-tural workers. Although the Jewish way of life was indeed changing rapidly dur ing the 1920s and 1930s, the unpublished songs recorded more ambivalent and perhaps more truthful attitudes toward these changes. Because unpublished songs were not widely distributed, however, nor performed in concert or on the radio, the officially published Yiddish songs were more familiar to the Jewish public. But the messages in state-supported music were taken lightly and often reinterpreted to fit the true feelings and mood of the audience. Similar trends can be seen in songs devoted to soldiers and to the Red Army.

"*Avek iz mayn bruder in royter armey*": Red Army Songs

Images of soldiers as protectors of the Soviet nation, their women, and their households entered popular culture in the 1930s; notably, during this period, the characters in the songs were not struggling for the good of the proletariat in other countries.[42] As the Red Army, the military service, and defense of the country came to dominate Soviet mass culture, Yiddish songs mirrored this trend. Their aim was to show the benefits of serving in the army, portraying soldiers as capable of dealing with any adversity:

> Dort, baym grenets,
> Dort, baym feld
> Roytarmeyer oysgeshtelt.
> Keynmol dorshtik, keynmol mid,
> Roytarmeyer shtendik hit.[43]

> There, near the border,
> There, in the field,
> A Red Army soldier stands.
> He is never thirsty, never tired,
> The Red Army soldier is always on duty.

Songs about soldiers had existed in Yiddish folklore since the beginning of the nineteenth century, when Nicholas I introduced the *cantonist* system, the compulsory recruitment of Jewish boys into the Russian army. Most of the Yiddish Nicholas-era military draft songs cursed the government. Yiddish songs about World War I, as well as the Russo-Japanese War of 1904–1905, seem to have been quite popular and were commonly sung through the 1930s. Soviet folklorists of the late 1930s recorded many such pieces during their expeditions and always included the following remark in their archival transcriptions: "The respondent heard the song before the revolution."[44] Songs containing this footnote often described military service and other state-related activities in a negative light. For example, the following song describes the feelings of a man who was drafted into the army:

> Zay zhe mir gezunt,
> Shkheynim funem gas,
> Ikh for fun aykh avek,
> Mayn ponim iz fun trern nas.[45]

Farewell,
Neighbors from the street,
I go away from you,
My face is wet from tears.

Oral history confirms that songs like this were not simply understood as representations of Jewish hardships from a prior era, namely, the tsarist regime; rather, they were seen by contemporaries as relevant social commentaries. When asked about antigovernment Yiddish songs, Bella G. (b. 1928), a former resident from the Ukrainian shtetl Kasatin, replied:

There was a song which people in Kasatin sang about Moyshe Stoliar [a Jewish soldier from her town]. The GPU took him because he did not pay his taxes or something. At that time people were arrested for nothing, they called it "speculation." . . . So he probably sold something wrong. . . . Or someone denounced him. . . . Anyway, the song was about his wife and how she did not see him after he was arrested. . . . Here is how it goes:

A naye lid vel ikh aykh mentshn zingen
Vos iz mit Moyshe Stoliar in Kasatin geshen.
A kholem hot mir gekhulemt far a nakht,
A kholem fraytik af der nakht
Az Moyshe Stoliar fun shtub hot men oysgebrakht.

I will sing you a new song, people,
What happened with Moyshe Stoliar in Kasatin.
I had a dream at night
A dream, Friday night,
That Moyshe Stoliar was taken away from his house

The next point of the song is about how the militia man came to arrest him:

Er iz gekumen zol mitgeyn mit dir.
Keyn gelt vel ikh nit nemen,
S'z gekumen di tsayt avekgeyn.

He came and said he should go with me.
I will not accept any money,
Your time has come to go away.

Then she went to the GPU to see him, but it was too late. He had already been killed; she only saw his feet:

Zi hot nor dos ershte vort gelozt a groys geveyn
Dray shtok hot zikh geton
Nor moysheles fiselekh gezen.
Der nachalnik hot mir aleyn geshikt
Moyshe'z mer nito.

She screamed out a great cry
Three floors she went
Only Moyshele's feet she saw.
The boss himself sent me to tell you
That Moyshe is not with us anymore.

You have to sing this song with a very tragic voice to make it more dramatic.[46]

Bella's recollection is actually a variation of a song published in Yekhezkel Dobrushin and A. Yuditskii's collection of Yiddish folk songs from 1940.[47] Dobrushin and Yuditskii's version describes a man who was killed during the Turkish War of 1877–78. Yet, for the respondent, this was a new song describing contemporary Soviet events. People modified prerevolutionary songs and adapted them to their current circumstances.

Meanwhile, published songs made a point of explaining the difference between then and now. For example, songs distinguished between the experiences of being drafted into the Soviet army versus the tsarist army. The explanations were quite comprehensive, dealing not only with political and patriotic aspects of the issue but also with matters of personal pride:

Taneysim hot gefast mayn mame,
Az kh'hob gedarft tsum priziv shteyn.
Tilim hot gezogt mayn tate,
S'zol tsu mayn kvitl nit dergeyn.

In der royter armey se darf geyn mayn zun—
S'nemt nit keyn shlof undzer oygn,
Tomer, kholile, di shol zol nit zayn,
Vet er ahintsu nit toygn.[48]

My mother fasted,
When I had to be drafted.
My father read Psalms,
They should not call my number.

My son has to go to the Red Army—
My eyes cannot be closed by sleep.
If, God forbid, he will not
Be useful to them.

The first part of the song describes a family in tsarist times, unhappy at the prospect of losing their son to the army. This is contrasted to a Soviet family later in the song who are proud of their patriotic son and only concerned with how successful he will be in the military service. In the description of the "backward" and therefore unhappy parents, many "Hebraisms" (Yiddish words with Hebrew origins) are used, such as *taneysim* (fasts) and *tilim* (psalms), as opposed to pure Yiddish—with the exception of the word "*holile*" (God forbid)—used in the "patriotic" segments.

Published songs demonstrated the appropriate reactions to the draft, namely, joy and pride. The subject of military service was also seen as romantic. Further, the notion of patriotism, which did not exist in Jewish folklore before the revolution, appeared throughout Soviet songs about the military, including service in the army as well as the border patrol.

The Far Eastern border is mentioned frequently because of the relevance of Birobidzhan. However, what makes most of the remaining Soviet military songs "Jewish," besides use of the Yiddish language, are the names of the heroes and the descriptions of shtetl life. It is noteworthy that people remember these songs as more nationalistic and Jewish-oriented than other Soviet Yiddish songs. Here is how Sofia B. remembers a song about the Red Army:

> S' geyen polkn royt armeyes
> S'geyen do in land
> Ergets vayt iz der soyne
> Loyert yidish land
> Ergetz loyert, iz der soyne,
> Loyert yidish land
> Af uraln ba taykh Yasin
> Un a Perekop
> Shlog dem soyne, shtarker, shtarker,
> Shlog dem soyne op!
> Shlog dem soyne, shtarker, shtarker,
> Shlog dem soyne op!
>
> There were regiments of Red Army soldiers
> They go here in this region
> Somewhere far is the enemy
> Hiding in the Jewish land,
> Somewhere hiding is the enemy
> Hiding in the Jewish land
> In the Urals, near the river Yasin,
> And at Perekop
> Beat the enemy, stronger, stronger,
> Finish the enemy!
> Beat the enemy, stronger, stronger,
> Finish the enemy![49]

Many attributes of official propaganda are present in this song: the Red Army soldiers protect the borders of their country, and they fight in the Ural mountains—a symbol of strength in Soviet propaganda—and in Perekop, the place where the Bolshevik Red Army won the civil war. Yet the soldiers in the song do not protect Soviet land but rather safeguard *yidish* (Jewish) land. Consciously or subconsciously the respondent, or possibly the composer, makes this song sound more Jewish than any official Yiddish publication would have allowed in the 1930s. Reinterpretation of this song can be seen as a way of adjusting to the new regime without necessarily accepting all its ideological values.

The popularity of old army songs provides proof of some ambivalence in popular reception. As with the songs about the new way of life, the published

Red Army songs were also reinterpreted. But, in the latter, the reinterpretations do not ridicule Soviet messages but rather add Jewish flavor to them. For the Yiddish speakers, the Yiddish language alone was not enough to make a song Jewish. They needed specifically Jewish notions to find the relevance. This attitude becomes clear through an analysis of published and unpublished romantic songs.

"Fun ale meydelekh iz Beylke bay mir shener" (Beylke is the most beautiful girl): Romantic and Nostalgic Songs

One of the most significant manifestations of "silent protest" expressed in Yiddish popular culture during the interwar period is the popularity of non-political songs. Topics include dishonest lovers, failed marriages, abandoned children, and tales of romantic heartbreak. In fact, approximately one-fourth of Yiddish sheet music publications from 1917 to 1930 are filled with this type of music, a percentage that rose in the following decade.[50] Some of the most popular composers in this genre are A. Kreyn and M. Milner.[51] Love and family songs in Dobrushin and Yuditskii's collection of Yiddish folk songs recorded in the late 1930s constitute approximately 60 percent of his entire book. One of the most popular Yiddish songs from this era was Mordechai Gebirtig's "*Kinder yorn*" (Childhood years), which tapped into the public longing for melodramaa and nostalgia:

> Kinder yorn, zise kinder yorn,
> Shtendik ligt ir mir in mayn zikorn.
> Ven ikh trakht fun ayer tsayt
> Oy, vi shnel bin ikh shoyn alt gevorn.
> Un di muter flegt mikh zeyer libn,
> Hotch in kheyder hot zi mikh getribn.[52]

> Childhood years, sweet childhood years,
> You are always in my memories.
> When I think about your time
> Oh, how quickly I grew old.
> My mother used to love me very much,
> Even though she dragged me to kheyder.

This song, like many others in this genre, mentions certain attributes of Jewish life, such as kheyder, but the content deals primarily with feeling generally nostalgic in a manner quite similar to that of Russian-language romantic songs. It is worth noting, however, that many Yiddish popular melodramatic songs focus on the mother-child relationship rather than on love affairs. For example, the most popular Yiddish song of the time was "A yidishe mame" (My Jewish mama), a hit that was known to virtually every Yiddish-speaking Jew.

Another massively popular song is "Papirosn" (Cigarettes) by Herman Yablokoff (1903–1981). This is essentially a Jewish version of the Russian "Bublichki" (Bagels), a song about a young homeless bagel seller. "Papirosn" tells the story of a Jewish boy who was orphaned and forced to sell cigarettes in the streets. The child first loses his parents and later witnesses the death of his sister on a cold bench in a park. The tale tapped into the Jewish consciousness in the Soviet Union. It also struck a chord with other Jewish audiences and became popular in Polish and American Yiddish theaters in the 1930s. Despite its grotesque elements, it still evokes tears from the people who first heard the song in the 1930s:

> Mayn tate in milkhome hot farloyrn zayne hent,
> Mayn mame hot di tsores mer oyskhaltn nit gekent,
> Yung in keyver zi getribn.
> Bin ikh af der velt farblibn
> Umgliklekh un elnt vi a shteyn.[53]

> My father lost his hands during the war,
> My mother could not bear her troubles any longer,
> And was driven to the grave at a young age.
> I was left on this earth
> Unhappy and alone like a stone.

Although "Bublichki" and "Papirosn" both had similar tragic stories, the two songs evolved differently.[54] The ending of the Russian "Bublichki" was eventually, and officially, altered to include a "happy ending," whereas "Papirosn" remained a tragic tale. The original "Bublichki," because of its negative imagery, was banned in the Soviet Union until the late 1980s; "Papirosn," on the other hand, was not officially prohibited but was performed primarily at private gatherings. Since Yiddish performers could argue that "Papirosn" only referred to Jews in Poland and America, and not in the Soviet Union, they were sometimes allowed to perform the song in public.

Many old Yiddish songs were performed during weddings. These were conducted as secular ceremonies as traditional religious weddings were not favored by the state. Still, that Yiddish songs were included made these weddings "Jewish." One of the most popular Yiddish songs at that time was a satirical wedding song, "Itsik hot shoyn khasene gehat" (Itsik got married). The song became so popular that even five decades after it was written no Jewish wedding party in the Soviet Union would be complete without it:

> Oy, lomir zikh tsekishn,
> Di mame meg shoyn visn,
> Az Itsik hot shoyn khasene gehat!
> Oy, Itsik iz a khosn,
> In tash nito keyn groshn,
> Oy, Itsik hot shoyn khasene gehat![55]

> Oh, let us all kiss,
> The mother already knows,
> That Itsik already got married!

Oh, Itsik is a groom,
He does not have a single kopeck in his bag,
Oh, Itsik got married.

Romantic lyrics appear widely in the Yiddish songs and often reflect non-socialist values. One of the most popular songs of this type is "A meydele in di yorn" (An old maid). The song details what an older woman offers to her suitor in order to convince him to marry her:

Ikh bin shoyn a meydele in di yorn,
Du host mir mayn kop fardreyt,
Ikh volt shoyn lang a kale gevorn,
Un efsher khasene gehat.
Un efsher vilstu gor nadn,
Di mame vet farkoyfn di shikh,
Un lomir shoyn beyde khasene hobn,
Vayl ikh hob dikh lib!
Un efsher vilstu gor yikhes,
Mayn zeyde iz gevezn a rov,
Lomir shoyn beser khasene hobn,
Un loz shoyn nemen a sof![56]

I am already an old maid,
You are fooling me,
I would have become a bride a long time ago,
And probably would have gotten married.
If it is only about dowry,
My mother will sell her shoes,
And let us get married,
Because I love you!
And probably you want some pedigree,
My grandfather was a rabbi,
Let us get married,
And that would be it!

Songs similar to Russian cruel romances[57] were performed at almost every informal meeting; examples are "Du darfst nit geyn mit pochaeve meydelekh" (You cannot go with the girls from Pochaev), "Oy, mayn stradaniye veyst nor got deremes" (Oh, my sufferings are only known to God), and "Ikh zits un shpil mikh af der gitare" (I am sitting here and playing my guitar). The melodies of these romantic Yiddish songs were frequently written by professional composers and were based on folk songs. They dealt with the universal questions intrinsic to personal relationships and family life. This genre survived throughout the entire prewar period and remained popular for decades.

In the 1920s and 1930s the state ideology began using popular and romantic songs to promote its own preferred family values, such as the rejection of a dowry or proper pedigree as marriage requirements. This was conveniently accomplished by introducing new ideas through the rewriting of old songs.[58] One example is "Nokhemke, mayn zun" (Nokhemke, my son). The original version

of the song was written at the turn of the century, structured as a dialogue between a father and his rebellious son:

—Un vifl git zi nadn, zunenyu?
—Keyn nadn git zi nit, tatenyu.
—Es gefelt mir nit der shidekh, zunenyu!
—Me fregt bay dir keyn deyes nit, tatenyu![59]

—And how big is her dowry, my son?
—She has no dowry, Father.
—I do not like this match, my son!
—No one asked for your opinion, Father![60]

The Soviet version from the 1930s reflects new changes in Soviet Jewish
family values:

Tsi hot zi epes nadn, zunenyu?
Tsvey goldene hent, mamenyu!
Tsi hot zi epes tsirung, zunenyu?
A kim af a bluzkele, mamenyu!
Ver vet dikh unter der khupe firn, zunenyu?
Der gantser komsomol, mamenyu.
Oy, ver zhe vet dir bentshn, zunenyu?
Oy, Stalin mit Kalininen, mamenyu.
Ver zhe vet dir esn gebn, zunenyu?
Di gantse ratnmakht, mamenyu![61]

Has she got any dowry, dear son?
Two golden hands, dear mother!
Has she got jewelry, dear son?
A badge on her shirt, dear mother!
Who will bring you under the wedding canopy, dear son?
The entire Young Communist League, dear mother!
Oh, who will bless you, dear son?
Stalin and Kalinin, dear mother.
Who will give you food, dear son?
Soviet Power, dear mother!

Here the general spirit of "Nokhemke, mayn zun" remains unchanged from
the original, as a rebellious young man named Nokhemke argues about his
choice of bride with his disapproving parents. The new version, however, ac-
quires a complete set of Soviet values: new treasures (strong hands are more
valuable than money), new spiritual authorities (rabbis are replaced by the Young
Communist League), and even new priests are named (Stalin and Kalinin). The
artificiality of this song is especially vivid when we compare its content to the
truly popular version discussed earlier. None of the respondents was familiar
with the Soviet version of "Nokhemke, mayn zun," but many remembered
"Meydele in di yorn" and other songs that retained traditional values such as
the importance of a dowry and one's pedigree. It is quite possible that singing
songs expressing tradition was a way to escape the overtly political messages

flooding popular culture during this period, but it is just as likely that published songs promoting new values may not have reached the targeted audience because of their artificiality, blunt ideological messages, and lack of memorable characters.

One can observe similar attitudes regarding Western values and civilization. The songs that were published featured characters who rejected Western nations for the sake of the Soviet Union:

> Af vos iz mir Amerike,
> Af vos iz mir Kanade?
> Ikh bin dokh a brigadir,
> Un brigadir—mayn Frade.[62]

> Why would I need America?
> Why would I need Canada?
> I am a brigade leader now,
> And my Frade is a brigade leader as well.

While the official chastushke confidently states the superiority of a Soviet collective farm over America and Canada, many unofficial songs often glorify Western values such as fashion. For example, Faina D. (b. 1918, in Novozlatopol, Ukraine) remembers the following popular couplets:

> Di dame fun Parizh mir ire shtiklekh,
> Perl in dekolte,
> S'gloybt zikh nit az
> Zi iz azoy gliklekh mit ir lokn pod kare.

> The lady from Paris with her things,
> Pearl in her cleavage,
> One cannot believe that
> She is so happy with her box-styled curls.[63]

This Yiddish song not only savors the details of the clothes worn by Western woman but also includes exotic words such as *dekolte* (cleavage) and *kare* (box, a hairstyle), which are described not as bourgeois decadence but as admirable features. This attitude is confirmed by contemporary sources. Leon Dennen, an American journalist who visited a Jewish collective farm in Ukraine in 1931, was amazed at the eagerness of Komsomol girls to learn about the latest trends in Western fashion and at their enthusiastic request that he teach them modern dances such as the fox-trot.[64] Thus, although officially published Yiddish songs preached against any appreciation of non-Soviet lifestyles, evidence, including eyewitness accounts, clearly reveals a more complex attitude toward Western values.

Still, the most striking difference between the reception of published and unpublished romantic songs can be seen in how the two dealt with the equality of ethnic groups. Official Yiddish songs stress the importance of equal rights for all nationalities but do not directly encourage intermarriage, as the characters who populate the romantic songs mostly have Jewish names. In contrast, unofficial Yiddish songs frequently relate tales of intermarriage, betrayal, and revenge set in exotic locations. Respected characters often marry non-Jews from different parts of the world. Klara G. remembers this popular song from the late 1930s:

Az der milkhome vet zikh kinchen
Drayen veln vern ale vegn.
Keyn Stambul, mame, vel ikh avekfurn,
Un opzikhn mit vayb mit mayn farmegn.

Az ikh bin keyn Stambul ongekimen,
Geblibn shteyn eyner bay der ban.
Oy, akegn kumt a giter brider:
"Dayn vaybl mit a negr far a man!"

Azoy ikh bin in shtib arayngekimen,
Ikh hob nisht sheyn Dvure nit derkont.
Zi drukt di zaydene halatn, un
Bronzoletn blitshen fun der hont.

Oy der negr in shtub arayngekumen:
"Vos tut bay mir an oreman in shtub?"
"Oy, in zibn yor hob ikh nit laykht gelitn,
Un far a negr hostu mikh farbitn!"[65]

When the war finally ends,
All my paths will turn.
Mother, I will go away to Istanbul,
To look for my wife and for my possessions.

When I came to Istanbul,
I stood alone by the train.
Then my good brother comes to meet me,
And says: "Your wife married a black man!"

So when I went into her house,
I did not recognize my beautiful Dvoreh.
She paints silk robes, and
Bracelets are shining on her wrists.

Then the black man entered the house:
"What is this poor man doing in my house?"
"Oh, in seven years I suffered so much,
And you traded me for a black man!"

The Ukrainian dialect of Yiddish in the song helps to establish its regional popularity.[66] The exotic setting of Istanbul is combined with the tale of a woman who "trades" a Jewish husband for a black one. Again, meticulous details of wealth are described: "silk robes" and "shiny bracelets" in contrast to the "badge on her shirt" referred to in the official Soviet version of "Nokhemke, mayn zun." Further, the deserted husband appears less upset about his wife remarrying than that she chose a man of a different ethnicity, which is in stark contrast to the official Soviet policy to promote the equality of races. Yet such songs were not commonly seen as direct criticism of Soviet ideology; instead, they were thought to serve as an escape from that ideology, a way to satisfy the public's desire for what was absent in official culture, specifically melodrama, decadence, and the exotic.

Although many of the unofficial love songs make use of a Soviet setting rather than an exotic one, still they feature attitudes that are contrary to official Soviet ideology:

> Fun ale meydelekh iz Beylke bay mir shener,
> Khotsh di lipn un di bakn royt zi nit.
> Mit ir in zags gevolt tsu geyn azh fir mener,
> Un zey shtarbn nokh atsind af ir trer. . . .
> Beylkele, mayn lebn, un a khupe, un a rebn,
> Lomir zikh farshraybn in zags arayn.
> Mir veln hobn sheyne yateles, di ale mames tateles,
> Oy, vi beyde glikhlekh veln mir zayn!

> In nayntsn yor hobn mir zikh mit beylkele farshribn,
> In komsomol iz zi farnumen tog un nakht.
> Derfar hot zi mikh ufgehert tsu libn,
> In komsomol iz zi farnumen tog un nakht.

> Zi kumt tsu loyfn, Beylkele, af kop aroyf farshenkelekh,
> Zi flit mit bikh mitgepakte beyde hent.
> Az ikh leyen nit keyn gazetn,
> Vil zi mir shoyn getn.
> Zi shrayt: "Du bist a temnyi element!"

> Ikh darf zikh lernen, nebekh, hob ikh shoyn farshribn,
> In sinagoge hobn ikh ufgehert tsu geyn.
> Derfar hot Beylkele mir ufgehert tsu libn,
> Un farblibn bin ikh elnt vi a shteyn.

> Ikh hob shoyn nit kin yatele, ikh bin shoyn nit kin tatele,
> Ikh hob nit vos tsu trogn vos tsu ton.
> Oy, ikh bin aroys fun a mentsh!
> Zi zogt tsu di kinder:
> "Volt er gramotne geshribn, volt er nit farblibn,
> A kustar, an odinochnyi element."

> Of all girls, Beylke is the most beautiful to me,
> Although she does not color her lips and cheeks.
> Four men wanted to go to ZAGS[67] with her,
> And they are still dying for a tear from her.
>   . . .
> Without a rabbi and without a wedding canopy,
> Let us register in ZAGS.

We will have beautiful sons, and become mothers and fathers,
Oh, how happy we both will be!

In 1919 Beylke and I were registered,
She was busy in the Komsomol all day and night.
That is why she stopped loving me,
Because she was in the Komsomol all day and night.

She runs around with her head up,
She flies with books in both hands.
Because I do not read any newspapers,
She wants to divorce me.
She shouts: "You are a backward element!"

I have to study, I am already registered,
I stopped going to the synagogue.
Because Beylkele stopped loving me,
I am alone like a stone.

I do not have a son anymore, I am not a father anymore,
I have nothing to wear, nothing to do.
Oh, I am not a man anymore!
She says to the children:
"That if he were literate, he would not have remained alone,
A craft worker, an isolated man."[68]

The structure of this song is reminiscent of the city ballad, a widespread genre from the 1920s. The melody resembles those used in "cruel romances" but contains elements from Jewish folk songs as well. The song is written in colloquial Yiddish and incorporates clichés from Soviet Russian slang. Expressions such as *temnyi element* (dark element) and *otstalyi element* (backward element) cannot be precisely translated into Yiddish. These labels come from contemporary newspapers and refer to "politically unconscious" people of the era who did not acquire Soviet values. Notably the Russian word *gazeta* is used for "newspaper" when the Yiddish word *tsaytung* would have been entirely appropriate. It is likely that newspapers, as well as other forms of agitation used by the Soviet regime, were identified with the Russian language since a new phenomenon introduced by the Soviet regime was the obligatory reading of newspapers. A significant feature of the song is the mention of ZAGS, the Soviet registry office, which stands in stark contrast to the traditional, religious Jewish wedding. This shows that the protagonist, despite his generally old-fashioned nature, associated the marriage ritual with a Soviet bureaucratic office and not with the presence of a rabbi or wedding canopy (*on a khupe, on a rebe*). Various Soviet programs, including literacy campaigns and antireligious propaganda, are also incorporated in the song, but probably the listeners' sympathies lie with the misfortunate, illiterate husband, who is out of step with the times and loses his wife and a child because of his political backwardness. Jeffrey Veidlinger noted a similar phenomenon in performances at the Moscow Yiddish Theater, when old-fashioned Jewish characters were portrayed more sympathetically than "positive, progressive heroes," with the result that audiences often sided more with negative, "backward" characters than the playwrights intended.[69]

In "Beylkele" the woman is shown to be advanced in political matters and more in step with the times than her groom, which agrees with the Soviet image of women as competitors who challenge men with their own hard labor. This representation of women was common in officially published songs, but because these songs were often rather stiff and lacking in charm, they were soon forgotten. For example, one ditty from the late 1930s states:

> Der aeroplan, er flit,
> Der motor, er dreyt zikh,
> Ikh bin a stakhanovke,
> Un mayn gelibter freyt zikh.[70]

> The airplane, it flies,
> The engine, it is running,
> I am a female Stakhanovite,[71]
> And my sweetheart is very happy.

The images of progressive women are prevalent in both published and unpublished romantic songs, but the two portray them quite differently. In published songs women themselves regularly boast about their achievements. The unpublished songs, on the other hand, commonly present women from the point of view of a man complaining about the "modern woman." The most crucial difference, however, is that, unlike the unofficial Yiddish love songs, the published songs lack drama, intimacy, appealing melodies, interesting characters, and, most important, the familiar Jewish notions that made the songs memorable and therefore popular. Although the poets and composers representing the official Soviet culture of the 1930s attempted to overcome these difficulties by trying to create works that were more engaging, Yiddish official culture rarely went beyond pale propaganda pieces.[72]

The unpublished Yiddish songs of the 1930s regularly center around love stories rather than social change, the latter merely serving as a "landscape" for the action:

> Gelibt hob ikh a meydl, geheysn hot zi Khashke,
> Gearbet hot zi af Minerkovs fabrik.
> Gelibt hot zi a yingl mit dem nomen Yoshke,
> Gearbet hot er af der fabrik.

> Fun pyate af desyate, desyate af pyate,
> Di teg geven ba Yoshken vikhodnoy.
> Vi azoy zhe zol zikh Khashke mit Yoshken haynt vstretshaye,
> Az Yoshke arbet morgn af notshnoy?

> Di tir hot im geefnt a kleyner oktyabrenok,
> "Mame," zogt er,—"s papoyu ushel."[73]

I loved a girl, her name was Khashke,
She worked at Minerkov's factory.
She loved a boy named Yoshke,
He also worked at the factory.

One thing led to another,
Yoshke had a day off.
How would Khashke meet Yoshke today,
If tomorrow he works the night shift?

A little Octobrist opened the door,
"Mother," said he, "left with Father."

The narrative uses some Yiddishized Russian idiomatic expressions, such as *fun pyate af desyate* (literally "from five to ten," but, idiomatically, "one thing led to another"). Most Russian phrases in published Soviet Yiddish songs, if used at all, are derived from official newspaper slang or from rhetoric glorifying the state, such as the use of Russian words for industrial machines. In songs the respondents recorded, the Russian expressions incorporated into Yiddish texts are often colloquial or even vulgar. They are also de-politicized. For example, in the song above, the Soviet term "Octobrist" (a member of the Communist organization for children) simply describes the child who opens the door. Moreover, the "Octobrist" is the son of a woman who apparently is cheating on her husband. The author of this song is obviously satirizing the official rhetoric of the 1930s. Here Khashke is portrayed not as a vanguard of Soviet society but rather as an immoral woman while the man is drawn as the victim. Thus the song has no positive characters. This contrasts sharply with the messages contained in the published songs of this period which gushed unrelenting optimism, and in which, in the words of James von Geldern, everyone had to be "an unswerving participant of the revolution."[74]

The language used in unpublished folk songs often included expressions of Russian and Hebrew origin, whereas published songs were predominantly written in a so-called purified Yiddish. Songs of mixed language, so called macaronic songs, are not new phenomena for Eastern European Jews in general nor for Russian Jews in particular.[75] During the Soviet period the dual-language song became more popular than ever, despite the fact that only in the Soviet Union did state officials conduct campaigns against these songs and satirize them in the official press. Yet both Soviet archival findings, and my respondents, enthusiastically combine both languages in one song:

Gorod Nikolaev, frantsuzskii zavod,
Gearbet hot a yingele *dvadtsat' pervyi god,*
Gearbet hot er shver, fardint hot er nit fil.
Bez zaslugi devushku vdrug on poliubil.

Slushai zhe ty Zlatke *chto ia skazhu tebe,*
Dem toyt vel ikh makhn *tebe i sebe.*

Un nit lang getrakht er, shost dem pistolet.
Ligt do a meydele, *ee uzh bol'she net.*[76]

City of Nikolaev, a French factory,
A boy worked here, he was *twenty-one years old.*
He worked hard, he did not earn much.
He fell in love with a dishonorable girl.

Listen to me, Zlatke, *I will tell you,*
I will kill *you and me,*
He does not think long, and shoots the revolver.
A girl lies here, *she is* no longer here.

State-sponsored Yiddish songs are filled with optimism and monolithic messages, whereas unofficial popular songs feature quite the opposite values. The above song effortlessly combines Russian and Yiddish lines that rhyme, an exotic setting such as a French factory within the Ukrainian city of Nikolaev, and a melodramatic ending. The main character who is not Jewish is portrayed as immoral in contrast to the people of all ethnicities shown in Soviet songs to be living in harmony. The song differs dramatically from most published Yiddish songs of the 1930s, which, deprived of their national color, present a bleached version of Soviet Jewish culture. The Yiddish melodramatic songs, which were far from uniform, monolithic, and often of low literary standards, continued to provide escape from the official Soviet rhetoric well into the late 1950s and beyond, whereas the official Yiddish pieces are largely forgotten.

Conclusions

In the 1920s and 1930s Soviet officials saw popular music as a powerful propaganda tool. They employed professional poets and composers to create works in an effort to Sovietize Yiddish speakers and establish a new Soviet Jewish culture.

Certain factors led to the success or failure of these state-sponsored Yiddish songs. Those with familiar Jewish notions gained popular reception, whereas those devoid of these motifs were frequently considered vacuous propaganda. The most popular revolutionary songs featured Jewish heroes such as Hirsh Lekert or were based on Yiddish folksongs such as "The Worker's March" that borrowed its melody from "Oyfn Pripetshik". Similarly the Yiddish songs praising Stalin and other Soviet leaders that enjoyed popularity were based on Jewish melodies or used Jewish imagery; for example, "Lomir trinken a lekhaim" was based on a klezmer tune. The key Jewish element that led many respondents to recall a song about collective farms was the portrayal of distinctly Jewish characters such as those described in "Dzhankoye." Published songs about the Red Army remained largely unpopular but found listeners when they were slightly modified to substitute the word "Soviet" for the word "Jewish," such as the song described by Sofia B. about protecting "Jewish land" from capitalist enemies. Finally, official romantic and melodramatic songs that rejected traditional Jewish values, such as negating a dowry or a proper pedigree, were frequently parodied. In short, the Yiddish-speaking population generally did not fully reject Soviet propaganda. The songs that reached the Jewish public operated within the notions understood by this audience such as familiar melodies and commonly used terms.

Analysis of the unpublished popular Yiddish songs from the 1920s and 1930s reveals that their content did not directly contradict the ideology of the Soviet regime. My research did not uncover any songs that directly opposed the idea of the revolution or the glorification of Stalin and other Soviet leaders. In the portrayal of collective farms, however, unpublished songs described Jews not as hard workers but rather as people who were unhappy and despised physical labor. This contrasted sharply to Soviet propaganda songs that proclaimed a "new strong Jew" who liked to work "with his hands." Similarly unpublished love songs glorified the values presumed dead in the official propaganda: the characters in these songs wanted dowries, appreciated a rabbinical pedigree, wished to marry other Jews, and condemned, even ridiculed, the idea of interracial relationships. In some ways the popularity of these songs signified a "silent" rejection of imposed ideology. Also, while official Red Army songs never became ingrained in the minds of their Jewish listeners, prerevolutionary, antimilitary Yiddish songs remained popular. Oral history suggests that Jews often understood these songs as an expression of protest against being drafted into the Red Army.

The producers of Soviet Jewish music had a dual purpose with their "official Yiddish songs": not only did they aim to use songs as a vehicle to bring propaganda messages to the Jewish listeners, but they also wanted to acculturate this audience. These songs were written in a purified Yiddish, cleansed of words with Hebraic and Slavic origins. Oral history suggests, however, that audiences preferred songs reflecting the everyday pattern of spoken Yiddish which included other linguistic elements. Unpublished Yiddish songs of the era examined here heavily incorporated Russian Soviet rhetoric into their lyrics and, in this way, ridiculed the policies of the regime.

The process of Russification of the Soviet Yiddish-speaking audience led to a diminishing interest in Yiddish culture. In the late 1930s most Jews (54 percent) declared Russian as their mother tongue, and many stopped speaking Yiddish every day. These songs thus became less effective for propaganda purposes. Yet their familiar melodies reminded listeners of their own ethnic identity and so, by the late 1930s, Yiddish songs, like theater, became a channel through which Jews expressed their ethnic sentiments. Unlike theatrical performances, which were more complicated to arrange, Yiddish songs were easy to perform at private parties, meetings, and other casual gatherings. The popularity of Yiddish songs exceeded all expectations. Singing Yiddish songs became one of the major expressions of Jewish identity in Soviet society when many other means were no longer available. Respect for Yiddish songs is still a part of modern Jewish post-Soviet identity. Although contemporary knowledge of the Yiddish language is rare, post-Soviet Jewish audiences continue to appreciate the melodies and comfort found in these songs.

5 Soviet in Form, National in Content: Russian Jewish Popular Culture

Former history professor Boris P. (b. 1926) retired from teaching at Leningrad State University in 1989. Two years later he began preparing to immigrate to the United States. He and his wife had only four suitcases. They had to decide which clothes, family heirlooms, books, photographs, and souvenirs were the most important to bring to their new home in America. The most difficult choice the couple had to make was deciding which books to take. Beautiful editions of Russian literary classics, Russian translations of world literature, children's stories, and hard-to-find novels competed for valuable space in the suitcases. Each volume underwent a careful examination: some books made it to the pile that would go to America, others were given to neighbors and friends, and still others, including magazines and newspaper clippings, were simply discarded. One box, however, was declared irreplaceable, and that was the one labeled "Jewish." In it were brochures, newspaper clippings, and books all dealing with Jewish issues. Some were published as far back as the 1920s and 1930s, and dealt with subjects concerning the struggle against antisemitism, the history of the Jewish workers' movement, the benefits of Jewish agricultural settlements, and reviews of performances at the Moscow State Yiddish Theater. The box also contained books published in the 1960s and 1970s, with infamous titles such as "The True Face of Judaism," a book that criticized Judaism in general and the state of Israel in particular. All these publications were in Russian, since Boris and his father, who had started the collection in the early 1920s, could only read Russian. Boris explained that, even though his family considered themselves to be "assimilated," still they wanted to learn about Jews. And even though these publications contained biased depictions, reading them was the only way to obtain any information about Jews. For Boris, reading such materials was also the only way he could assert his Jewishness. By reading the criticisms of Jewish religious doctrine, he learned the basics of the religion; by studying attacks on Zionism, he discovered the ideology of the movement. Reading between the lines enabled Boris to extract knowledge of Jewish history and tradition otherwise unavailable to him.

Among Boris's most prized documents was his collection of tattered materials devoted to the struggle against antisemitism. Most of these brochures and books were published by the Soviet government in the early 1930s and described Jews in a positive light. By reading these, Boris learned to be proud of being

Jewish. Also included in the pile to be brought to America were old vinyl records by Leonid Utesov, a Russian Jewish singer popular from the 1930s to the 1960s, as well as Russian translations of Yiddish literature, such as rare editions of collected works by Sholem Aleichem and Perets Markish. Boris explained that this was part of his Jewish identity and meant more to him personally than his other collections of Russian literature. In Boris's words, his Jewishness is "Utesov's Jewishness and the Jewishness of Russian Jewish culture."[1]

After 1917 the majority of Russian Jews began learning the Russian language with tremendous speed. In 1926 the percentage of those who declared Russian to be their mother tongue represented 26 percent of the Jewish population in the European part of the Soviet Union. By 1939 this percentage had increased to 54 percent.[2] This Russification can be directly traced to the migration of the Jews to the urban centers outside the former Pale of Settlement, especially Moscow, Leningrad, and Kiev.[3] In 1939 the proportion of those who declared Yiddish as their mother tongue was higher in rural regions (60.9 percent) than in urban centers with populations of over half a million (36.5 percent).[4] The process of migration to urban centers was not uniquely Jewish. Millions of Russian peasants also moved to bigger cities in the 1920s and 1930s. Yet the patterns of integration into urban society differed significantly.

David Hoffmann asserts that former Russian villagers often tended to retain their traditional lifestyles and recreational activities in Moscow, despite their newfound access to a wide variety of entertainment. Instead of enjoying new cultural outlets, they preferred to gather in parks—in Moscow, Izmailovsky Park—and to sing old Russian songs and perform traditional dances. Upon arriving in Moscow most of the new Muscovites lived in barracks and spent their free evenings in the kitchen, sharing food and playing cards. Many did not attend theaters, lectures, or cinemas, feeling they these activities did not correspond to their cultural needs.[5] Similarly some Jews tried to maintain their traditional shtetl lifestyle. In the 1920s, for example, the Moscow district of Zariade (not far from the Red Square) included wooden synagogues, ritual baths, a kosher bakery, and a meat shop. David B. (b. 1925) explains how his family retained their way of life in Zariade after arriving from Byelorussia:

> I was born in Zariade. I call it "shtetl Zariade." It consisted of small one- and two-story wooden houses. People used to live on the ground floor and work on the upper floor. My father was a tanner, he made things from leather. He had his workshop upstairs. Everyone lived like this. There was also a wooden synagogue there. My parents spoke Yiddish to us and to each other. Sometimes we even asked them questions in Yiddish, however the children mostly spoke Russian. My father even wanted to invite a tutor to teach me some Yiddish and some Hebrew, but I didn't want this and was already going to the Russian school. Now I am sorry I did not learn Hebrew.
>
> My parents had many other relatives who came from Lyazno [in Byelorussia] to settle in Moscow. They all lived with us until they found

their own places. My parents had only Jewish friends; their neighbors were all from Lyazno. I mostly hung out with Jewish kids. We used to go to the movies. There was a central children's movie theater. We saw *Chapaev* there and other movies about war.[6]

My friends came from Ukraine, Byelorussia, and different places. . . . My family celebrated Jewish holidays. My father took me to the Yiddish theater. I even went to the synagogue once or twice, but not to pray, just to look. It was only later, when we moved from Zariade to a different district, that I made some new friends who were not Jewish.[7]

Upon arriving in Moscow, David's parents tried to re-create many aspects of their shtetl life, including their circle of friends, religious practices, and leisure time. David, a first-generation Muscovite in his family, began assimilating into his new environment much faster than his parents did. This is evident in his kinships, language, and entertainment. Although David's father occasionally took him to the synagogue and the Yiddish theater, David preferred to spend his free time at the nearby movie theater, watching films like *Chapaev*. David asserted that his parents did not go to the movies because they were busy working, and yet they found time to go to the Yiddish theater. One may conclude, therefore, that David's parents consciously rejected a variety of urban entertainment options.

That many new migrants settled with their friends or family made it easier for them to retain their shtetl way of life in the urban environment, especially those who did not speak much Russian. Even the younger urban newcomers, who comprised the majority of migrants, initially socialized with other Yiddish speakers. At the age of fourteen Yurii B. moved from the Ukrainian shtetl Romanov to live in the city of Dnepropetrovsk, Ukraine, to attend a vocational school there. He shared his thoughts about his initial impressions:

When I first came to Dnepropetrovsk I wanted to study at a vocational school. My pals and I went to register, and we got a room in a dormitory. They told us the address: 2 Shirokaya Street. They said this in Russian. Our Russian was not very good at the time. We learned some in school, but in Romanov there was no one that we spoke Russian with. My mother knew Russian better than I did because she studied in a Russian gymnasium, but at home we only spoke Yiddish. Even when I came to Dnepropetrovsk, I went to study in a Jewish vocational school where the instruction was in Yiddish, because I was not able to study in Russian.

So they told us the address [in Russian]. I was the bravest of all five guys who came, and I remember how we wandered around the streets and asked people where is the "second Shirokaya street." You see, we did not know that the word "two" refers to the house number. We thought this was the "second street." This is how "well" I knew Russian then.

Yurii continued to speak Yiddish with his friends even after they moved to the urban environment, but, unlike David's parents, who preferred Yiddish theaters, Yurii immediately started taking advantage of the various entertainment venues offered in Dnepropetrovsk:

> We went to movie theaters, to drama theaters, to demonstrations, concerts, everywhere. It was so exciting to be part of the new life.[8]

Yurii found a compromise between his desire to retain his familiar environment, such as spending time with his Jewish friends, and his need to integrate into the new urban culture. Not all migrants arrived with friends, however. Many newcomers had to start adapting to their new way of life immediately, which included making new friends. And, like Yurii, many were not fluent in Russian. Consequently learning Russian went hand in hand with adjusting to their new lifestyle. Indeed, for the Jews, speaking, reading, and writing in Russian meant becoming Soviet. Thus their experiences were entirely different from those of the Russian peasants who migrated, since the peasants did not have to learn a new language in order to adjust.

When Lazar L. (b. 1905) moved from a small town to study in Moscow in 1921, he immediately stopped speaking Yiddish, partly because he felt it was inappropriate:

> I knew who was Jewish in our dormitory. But it did not matter. We were all friends, no matter what our nationality was, because we were all hungry. . . . As Jews, we only took advantage of the situation once a year. We heard rumors that a synagogue gave out matzo during Passover. And the rumor was that students who live in a dormitory do not have to pay. So we went, and it was a miracle, we got free food, free matzo. I could not believe it. . . . But even when we went to get matzo, we did not speak Yiddish, we just took advantage of the situation.[9]

Lazar's testimony demonstrates that although he befriended other Jews, and shared interests with them, he did not consider Yiddish his language of communication. Moreover, he did not view eating matzo as a Jewish activity in itself but rather as a way to take advantage of being Jewish. And when he and the other students went to get the free matzo they did not speak Yiddish, even though it was their mother tongue. After moving to Moscow Lazar began to consider Russian a superior language to Yiddish. Yiddish literature and theater did not correspond to his desire to integrate into Russian society as soon as possible. Lazar's behavior is reminiscent of that of other Jewish Muscovites. Jeffrey Veidlinger reminds us that the majority of those in the audience at the Moscow Yiddish Theater were visitors from the shtetlach.[10]

The desire for rapid assimilation also hastened the disintegration of the observance of traditional lifestyles. Students who lived in dormitories did not want to maintain a kosher diet, observe the Sabbath, and retain other traditional practices. As part of my research I asked approximately ninety Jews who had moved from shtetlach to big cities in the 1930s whether they kept kosher after the move, and many recalled that they stopped keeping kosher as soon as they arrived. Similarly the idea of reading and being entertained in Yiddish was seen by many young Jewish migrants as a sign of backwardness (*otstalost'*). It was around this time when the Russian adjective *mestechkovyi* (shtetl-like) became a pejorative term.

Oral history reveals, however, that although migrants gave many outward indications that they did not want to maintain their traditional Jewish lifestyles, they did hold onto many of their ethnic sentiments. Many of their friends were Jewish, and the majority of migrants kept in touch with their families back home. Moreover, they wanted to consume everything they could find relating to Jewish subjects, so long as the materials were written in Russian. But according to the ideology of korenizatsiia, or "nativization," Jews were unable to express their ethnic or national identity in any language other than Yiddish, so in the 1920s and 1930s virtually all literature and media products, even propaganda designed for Jews, were written in Yiddish. As a result, many Russian-speaking Jews did not have access to a Jewish Soviet press, Jewish literature, or Jewish theater precisely because they were produced in a language they did not understand.

At the same time the Soviet Russian-language press, literature, songs, theater performances, and films that mentioned Jews and Jewish subjects were extremely diverse in both content and form.[11] Most of this material was designed to present Jewish culture to the wider non-Jewish audience. In this chapter I look only at works specifically designed for propaganda purposes with a non-Jewish consumer in mind. Initially these materials were published as part of the regime's struggle against popular antisemitism, but later they were used to introduce the general public to the richness of Jewish culture. Because of the lack of any other materials dealing with Jewish issues, these publications found their greatest reception among rapidly assimilating urban Jews, who, despite losing their ties with the traditional expressions of their ethnicity, were still eager to read and hear about their heritage. I argue that the exposure to these positive descriptions of Jews during the prewar period played a crucial role in shaping urban Soviet Jewish culture. Analysis of this material also reveals how Soviet Stalinist propaganda often yielded unintended results.

The chapter first explores how Jewish themes were treated in Russian-language productions and compares the differences in the presentations of the same issues in Yiddish popular culture. It then takes a look at the Russian-speaking Jews who lived in the big cities outside the former Pale of Settlement, including their choices of literature and entertainment, and their general understanding of what it means to be Jewish. Because my aim here is to examine the cultural world of the average Jewish consumer during the interwar period, and not how the elite of Russian Jewish society understood and interpreted changes in their identity, the chapter omits any literary analysis of the works of famous Russian Jewish writers such as Isaak Babel, Vasilly Grossman, Joseph Utkin, Eduard Bagritsky, and even Iliya Erenburg.[12] For example, although works by Erenburg were extremely popular among the Soviet Jews from the 1940s to the 1970s, in the 1930s his name was largely unknown in the Jewish milieu. Therefore, I do not study the works of Erenburg in this chapter. On the other hand, I examine the career of singer Leonid Utesov, whose works seemed to reach the widest circle of the Russian Jewish public.

Russian Translations of Yiddish Literature

Soviet cultural ministers and activists believed that translating various forms of "local literature" was an important element in their goal to familiarize Russian speakers with the nation's minority cultures. In the early 1920s an entire industry for translating literary works was launched. Officials divided the works to be translated into two general categories: classics of ethnic literature from before the revolution that fit into the Soviet scheme of the "usable past" and contemporary authors whose views and artistic approaches were shaped by the revolution.

Jewish activists followed the same pattern in deciding which Hebrew and Yiddish prose and poetry would receive state-sponsored translations. Because the Hebrew language was considered the vernacular of clerics, Zionists, and other Jewish nationalists, only private publishers in the early 1920s were able to translate these works. From 1923 until the late 1950s not one work of Hebrew literature was translated into Russian.[13] On the other hand, since the state considered Yiddish to be the official language of the Jewish masses, by the mid-1920s the campaign to translate these works was gaining momentum. Before 1930 works of some Yiddish writers outside the Soviet Union, such as Sholem Ash and Joseph Opatoshu, appeared only in Russian translation but not in Yiddish. From 1931 to 1940 the government sponsored 145 translations of Yiddish belles-lettres, one-quarter of which were children's books.

The selection of Yiddish works for translation and publication followed the Soviet pattern of depicting the "usable past." The intent was to demonstrate that before the revolution Jews criticized tsarist policies and longed for change. Sholem Aleichem, therefore, represented "the old voice of the masses."[14]

New Yiddish writers, especially those who wrote according to the socialist realist principle of "national in form, socialist in content," were presented as new voices of Soviet multiethnic literature. Haim Gildin, Itsik Kipnis, Noteh Lurye, Itsik Fefer, and numerous others helped to bring contemporary Soviet Jewish works to a national audience.[15] This campaign even extended into children's literature and, consequently, Detgiz (the Children's State Publishing House) printed huge runs of Leyb Kvitko's poems.

Because there were not enough materials in Russian dealing with Jews, the Jewish public paid undivided attention to these translations from the Yiddish literature. Unlike before the revolution, when the Russian Jewish audience was small and highly educated, the early Soviet Jewish public was extremely large and diverse.[16] It did not consist primarily of newly assimilated Jewish intelligentsia who lived in the larger cities but was comprised mostly of former shtetl residents who wanted to read in Russian about Jews.

Oral history demonstrates that Russian translations of Yiddish literature were devotedly sought after by Jews. Many respondents suggested that reading these books, even having them in their homes, was the "most Jewish" thing they did after they stopped speaking and reading Yiddish on regular basis. David S. (b. 1920), a former resident of Leningrad, explains this phenomenon:

> When I read a book [in Russian], I always knew whether it is a Jewish book or a Russian book. There is something special about Jewish books, which is impossible to express in words. When you read a Russian book, it speaks to your mind; when you read a Jewish book, it touches your soul.[17]

Many of those I interviewed, however, had difficulty defining exactly what they mean by a "Jewish book." "It is impossible to explain, you have to feel it" was a common response. A favorable Jewish character, a description of an old shtetl, even a Jewish name could make the book Jewish.[18] For rapidly assimilating Soviet Jews, observance of religious rituals, even speaking Yiddish, had less significance than reading secular Jewish literature in translation. Just the act of buying translations of Yiddish writers was an expression of Jewish identity. Esfir A. elaborates:

> I took pride in my personal library. I had volumes of all the classics, the World Library series, and children's literature. My children are all educated, they liked reading. . . . But I also had Sholem Aleichem's collected works, and a book by Perets Markish. To tell you the truth, I did not care much about those writers. I just felt it was important to buy those books. Every Jew should have them at home.[19]

Many respondents shared Esfir's opinion, feeling that it was unnecessary to read translations of Yiddish books but essential to have them in one's home. Like Esfir A., some kept them because they thought it was important to support such translations. Others, like Mark P. (b. 1919, in Minsk, Byelorussia), owned such translations because they hoped that their children would read them, even though they themselves did not.[20] The majority agreed with the sentiments of Esfir A., "Every respectable Jew should have Sholem Aleichem at home."[21]

Yet Russian translations of Yiddish literature constitute only a fraction of the entire body of Soviet Jewish literature. The government made a special effort to develop original Russian-language cultural products with Jewish themes for "cultural education" and propaganda purposes. These works also found a sizable audience among Jews, even though, paradoxically, Jews were not the targeted public for these publications.

"Obman odin, chto pop, chto ravvin" (The same lie, whether from a priest or a rabbi): Judaism in Russian Publications

Propaganda publications that dealt with Jewish themes during the interwar period fall into three major categories: the campaign against religion, support for agricultural settlements, and the struggle against antisemitism.[22]

A large number of the books written in Russian that campaigned against the observance of Judaism also targeted other religions, particularly Christianity. The antireligious monthly *Bezbozhnik* (The godless) (1925–1941) and the newspaper *Bezbozhnik u stanka* (The godless at the work place) (1923–1931) published articles, stories, and discussions devoted to the campaign against Judaism, as did numerous brochures such as *Proiskhozhdenie iudeiskoi i khristianskoi paskhi* (The origins of Jewish Passover and Christian Easter) by Nikolai Nikolsky and *Bibliia dlia veruiushchikh i neveruiushchikh* (The Bible for believers and atheists) by Emelian Yaroslavsky.[23]

Judaism was presented to the Russian-speaking public in the context of two struggles: one against antisemitism, the other against Jewish clericalism and nationalism. The propaganda attempted to show that the observance of Judaism was an obstacle to the peaceful coexistence between different nationalities that otherwise had no grounds for hostility. Although the majority of Yiddish-language publications claimed that Judaism was at the heart of these problems, Christianity shared equal blame in the Russian-language publications. The aim here was to demonstrate that Judaism was no worse a threat than other religions and to avoid provoking religious-based antisemitism. Thus, paradoxically, the Russian-language publications justified, rather than criticized, Judaism.

The premier issue of *Bezbozhnik* ran a story entitled "The End of a Friendship." The plot describes a relationship between two neighbors: Van'ka Khrenov, a Russian, and Moyshe Shmulevich, a Jew. When Moyshe has a problem in his house on a Sunday, Van'ka does not offer to help, saying he cannot work on his Sabbath. The same situation occurs when Van'ka needs help on a Saturday, the Jewish Sabbath. The result is an abrupt end to their long-lasting friendship.[24] In the story both men are drawn as positive characters who simply find themselves in a difficult situation caused by their respective religions, both of which are seen as "equally harmful." The moral is straightforward: religion is a source of turmoil that unnecessarily turns workers into enemies.

Many publications included stories to demonstrate that practicing religious traditions causes difficulties for Jews and non-Jews who worked together. One story describes a factory that produces milk for a mixed community. One day a rabbi comes to inspect the facilities and proclaims that the milk manufactured there isn't kosher. Consequently Jewish citizens in the town stop buying dairy products there, eventually leading to the collapse of the business. The story is designed to illustrate that Jewish rabbis cause problems in their communities and provoke antisemitic riots.[25]

The authors of Russian Jewish publications presented rabbis and priests as enemies in two ways: first, they provoked conflicts between simple believers; and, second, these clerics actively helped each other to become rich at the public's expense. Because of their supposed similarities, priests and rabbis are portrayed as collaborators conspiring to destroy the Soviet regime. The story "Friends," by N. Neker, tells the tale of a rabbi who has to leave Russia after his synagogue is transformed into a proletarian club. At the same time a priest, and friend of the rabbi, suffers a similar dilemma when his church is turned into a factory warehouse. The rabbi helps his friend by raising money from Christian parishioners overseas, and the two clerics, portrayed as counterrevolutionaries, flee Russia.[26] The lead characters were modeled after Rabbi Joseph Shneerson and Patriarch Tikhon, and, midway through the story, the author points out actual similarities between the characters in the story and the genuine "traitors."[27] According to Neker's story, Tikhon also tries to organize a congress of Jewish religious activists in the Volynskaya region of Ukraine. To emphasize the point that priests and rabbis are the same, the story includes a caricature of Patriarch Tikhon wearing a tallis, the traditional Jewish garment worn by married Jewish men during prayer.

Ironically the story can also be read as an accusation that Patriarch Tikhon is Jewish, which would turn away some of his followers. Therefore, instead of promoting friendship between Jews and Russians, the article subversively plays on the antisemitic sentiments of some readers.[28] Indeed, in a different story, Tikhon is portrayed as the leader of a rabbinical congress whose goal is to overthrow the Soviet regime.[29] All these stories try to demonstrate that the religious elite, despite the religion at issue, consists of devious men who take advantage of ordinary parishioners.

By 1928 the collaboration between rabbis, priests, the bourgeoisie, and other "evil counterrevolutionaries" became the central focus of articles in *Bezbozhnik*. Rabbis were accused of creating ultra-nationalist organizations that promoted hostility between Jews and non-Jews, and were also portrayed as collaborators of the former tsarist regime. Many articles alleged that rabbis helped to organize anti-Jewish pogroms because the tsarist government paid them to do so.[30] One article contended that rabbis were responsible for atrocities that took place in England, South Africa, and other countries.[31]

Religion was also portrayed as a disruptive factor in family life. I. Gulbinskaya's "Babushka v brake" (Grandmother in a marriage) is a tragic story about a mixed marriage between two honorable communist citizens who come from different religious backgrounds. In this short story the marriage is almost destroyed because of the grandparents' religious prejudice. The Christian grandmother is outraged when she learns that her grandson has not been baptized, and the Jewish grandmother is furious when the boy is not circumcised when he is eight days old. At the end of the story the child catches a cold during a secret baptism performed by one of the grandmothers, is injured during a furtive circumcision conducted by the other set of grandparents, and eventually dies from these maladies.[32]

All these stories portray the activities of rabbis and priests, such as their religious behavior and collaborations, in the harshest light. On the other hand, friendships between people of different nationalities, often based on class similarities, are strongly encouraged. Neker's story, "Friends," shows how former believers, upon "seeing the light" by becoming politically literate, remember the injustices caused by the union between rabbis and priests.[33]

This pattern is repeated in the 1925 poem "Sviataia paskha" (Holy Easter) by M. Gurshman, which deals with a janitor's realization that rabbis and priests are criminals because they do not pay him for his work. In the poem the janitor goes to heaven to complain to God about these mischievous dealings. During the journey he learns that there is no God. The janitor also finds out that rabbis and priests created gods as a means to make money. At the end of the poem the worker exclaims:

Obman odin, chto Iegova,[34]
Chto syn, chto pop, chto ravvin![35]

The same lie—whether from Jehovah,
The Son, a priest, or a rabbi!

This conclusion of the poem demonstrates that literacy helped to destroy religion and to end ethnic hostility. According to Soviet doctrine, once someone became literate, he or she automatically stopped believing in God.[36] Many articles featured accounts by "former believers" who, after learning to read and write, became atheists. The publication of these stories was part of an ideological campaign which presumed that illiteracy was instrumental for religion to maintain its foothold and was also responsible for superstitions.[37] Thus these publications criticized not only rabbis but also Soviet officials who do not help to fight illiteracy. In June 1927 *Bezbozhnik* published a letter from a reader telling a story about a rabbi who invites a group of Jewish Red Army soldiers to attend a synagogue during Passover. The commander gave his permission for the soldiers to attend, but no one accepted the rabbi's invitation.[38] Here the commander is portrayed as more religiously backward than the soldiers.

A similar story set in a Jewish agricultural settlement was published in *Bezbozhnik* in 1929. In it a local branch of KOMZET[39] issued a ruling which stated that Jews were allowed to rest on Yom Kippur. The local Komsomol division, however, decided it would be a waste of resources to allow workers to take the day off during harvest time. Once again the official leaders of KOMZET were shown to be less aware than the rank and file. Portraying ordinary people rather than appointed state officials as the bearers of progress in society became a trend of Soviet propaganda during the early 1930s, which, incidentally, took place on the eve of the "Great Terror," an era when top Party and government officials were expunged from their posts based on accusations of disloyalty and specifically espionage. Thus antireligious propaganda fit into the general campaign of searching for "enemies in the midst."

All state ideological programs generally included antireligious connotations. For example, the state's campaign to improve sanitary conditions ran parallel with antireligious propaganda. The goal was to demonstrate that observing religious rituals can bring physical harm to practitioners. In the mid-1920s many publications described how kissing Christian icons spread infection. Similarly the state attacked Jewish ritual baths in V. Bronner's 1924 article "Mikva'" (Ritual bath). In his "exposé" Bronner described a series of dangers women face when they go to the ritual bath, such as becoming infected with syphilis or other communicable diseases. Accompanying the article was an illustration of a bath infested with bacteria.[40] The aim of such articles was to equate religion not only with backwardness but also with filth.

In addition to criticizing religion as a social organization and institution, Soviet propaganda also attacked the theoretical foundations of Judaism. A key element of the state's agenda in this campaign was to demonstrate that these Jewish rituals, which were presented as absurd and illogical, had no harmful impact *externally*. A. Karelin's *Zlye rosskazni pro evreev* (Pernicious stories about the Jews) is a vivid example of counterpropaganda to traditional antisemitic ideas.[41] Each story in the book tries to destroy negative stereotypes about Jews. It explains in popular language that the bourgeoisie provoked hostility between people on the basis of religion and used Jews as scapegoats. "Rational" explanations of every popular myth about Jews are offered. For example, arguments are given against the claim that the Jews killed Jesus:

1. The Jews did not kill Jesus, because Jesus never existed. Jesus is a myth invented by priests to make simple people pay taxes and is used to provoke hostility between Jews and Christians.
2. Even if Jesus were a historical personality, he lived a very long time ago, and the Jews who lived at the same time as Jesus have already died. Modern Jews have nothing to do with them.
3. Bourgeois Jews wanted to kill Jesus because they wanted to exploit other peoples. Simple Jews protested against this.
4. Actually the Romans killed Jesus. They also oppressed Jews at that time.[42]

Karelin's book also included other antisemitic stereotypes, such as Jews drinking Christian blood during Passover. The author explains that this in fact dates back to the very first Christians, who called the wine that was used for the Eucharist "the blood of Christ." This expression was used to provoke hostility between Jews and Christians.[43] Thus, using historical arguments, Karelin addressed many issues of religious-based antisemitism in an attempt to destroy its foundations.

This method of spreading Soviet antireligious propaganda was common and was used in both Russian and Yiddish publications. In the Russian-language materials, however, because Soviet activists believed that antisemitism was a greater evil than religion, this form of propaganda was used not to criticize Judaism but to defend it. Frequently official Russian-language brochures focused on the positive aspects of Judaism, for example, presenting the Jewish Holy Scriptures and the Talmud in a positive light. Karelin uses the Talmud to disprove many inconsistent accusations against Jews and quotes the lines in these texts that describe Jews as a hard-working people. Karelin's book points out that Jews loved and respected productive labor but were not allowed to reach their potential under the cruel tsarist regime. "The Jewish faith," states the author "teaches kindness and goodness. There are many good people among the Jews."[44]

Vladimir Mikhailovsky took a similar approach in his brochure, *Jews in the Fight against the White Army*. In it he portrays religious Jews positively and describes prominent rabbis who fought against the White Army during the civil war. According to the author, "Rabbis realized that it was better for Jews to lose their faith than their lives."[45]

These works by Mikhailovsky and Karelin are poignant examples of the fundamental difference between Russian and Yiddish Soviet propaganda. Even the most critical descriptions of Judaism in Russian publications were less aggressive than in Yiddish publications, which were designed for Jewish readers, because each was serving an entirely different purpose. Whereas the Russian-language publications were designed to counter public antisemitism, the Yiddish publications aimed to discourage religious practices. Largely ignoring the religious feelings of believers, the Yiddish propaganda blatantly criticized, even parodied, various aspects of Jewish traditions in an attempt, presumably, to divert readers from celebrating the holidays. Especially visible were attacks against Passover and Rosh Hashanah. Russian-language publications, on the other hand, had to strike a balance. Here the effort was to ridicule Passover as a religious holiday in order to spread antireligious feelings but at the same time to guard against too negative a portrayal so as not to provoke antisemitism. In fact, many Jewish respondents report that they were not offended by the Soviet anti-Passover campaigns, since these paralleled those directed against Christian and Muslim holidays. The Russian publications that criticized Passover stressed that the holiday presented no "physical danger" to the public and was no more mysterious than Easter.

Some stories about Passover contained "rational" explanations of why various rituals of the festival were nonsensical. For example, according to Jewish tradition, after the Passover meal is finished the door is opened in the hope that the prophet Elijah will enter. Soviet antireligious publications described and ridiculed this rite. Ts. Bobrovskaya wrote that she stopped believing in God following an incident at a Passover seder when a goat came through the door that had been as left open for the prophet Elijah.[46] Another "real-life story" described how robbers broke into a house and stole all the property while the door was open for the Messiah.[47] Such stories combine several ideological messages. First, they demystify the meaning of the custom of leaving the door open during the Passover seder. Second, they ridicule the idea of the religious custom and demonstrate how the observance of Judaism made people believe in illogical customs. Finally, the tales show that ordinary Jews gradually decided to abandon their religion.

Sometimes the ideologists combined anti-Passover propaganda with other campaigns such as combating alcoholism. Passover was criticized as a holiday that encouraged excessive drinking, because Jews are required to drink four glasses of wine during the Passover seder. The poem "Elijah at Passover," published in the magazine *Bezbozhnik,* even accused the Jewish prophet of being an alcoholic:

> Kak po seyderam Ilia
> Nalizalsia kak svin'ia.
> Za evreiskoi p'ianoi paskhoy,
> Byl k butylke ochen' laskov.[48]

> During [many] seders [the prophet] Elijah
> Got as drunk as a swine.
> During the Jewish drunken Passover,
> He was very tender to the bottle.

Here the prophet Elijah—God's messenger, herald of the Messiah—is said to have gotten "drunk as a swine" and the holiday itself is labeled "drunken Passover" from the tradition of having four glasses of wine during the seder, both pointed references to alcoholism. In addition to criticizing Judaism, the author wishes to demonstrate that everyone, whatever their religion, is subject to a similar problem, namely, alcoholism. The aim of the poem is also to encourage people of various religions to unite based on the common problem of alcoholism.

Another popular theme in anti-Passover propaganda concerned how the holiday allegedly fostered social and economic injustice. Many publications accused rabbis of organizing Passover rituals for personal financial gain. Various stories spoke of the covert techniques rabbis employed to approve food as kosher for Passover, including a "guarantee" that was purportedly based entirely on bribes.[49] Further, ordinary believers are portrayed simply as victims who lose their money to the schemes of the religious elite, while atheists are portrayed as the wisest citizens of all. One story made the comparison explicit in the portrait it draws of two friends: the one who observes Passover is constantly in debt, and the other is a thrifty atheist, able to save enough money for his family to build a new house.[50]

The claim that rabbis and kosher butchers profited excessively from the observance of Jewish holidays played a central role in anti-religious publications. Like Passover, Yom Kippur includes various rituals that non-Jewish readers would find unusual, especially that of *kapoyres.*[51] The propaganda campaign against Yom Kippur was conducted in a manner similar to the anti-Passover campaign; both aimed to communicate that the observance of rituals caused adherents to suffer economically, socially, and morally.

According to Jewish tradition, Yom Kippur is the day when all Jews, regardless of their social and economic position, fast, go to a synagogue, and wear white clothing. Performing these rituals signifies the symbolic equality of all Jews, despite whether they are of the upper- or lower-class or are rich or poor. Anti-Yom Kippur propaganda aimed to prove that the appearance of equality was simply a tool used by rich Jews to keep those who were poor under their rule. The 1928 poem "Holiday Parallels" summarized the major Soviet accusations against the Jewish High Holidays:

> Pomniu: v prazdnik Rosh Gashone,
> Kantor pel kak oglashennyi.
> I za kantorom narod,
> Razeval korytom rot.
>   . . .
> I grebla vo imia boga.
> Den'gi s greshnykh sinagoga.
>   . . .
> Bogomol'nyi po privychke
> K nuzhdam bednykh glukh i slep.
> V sinagogu khodit NEP,
> No soznatel'nyi Rabochii
> S bogom del imet' ne khochet.
>
> Bog, Talmud i Rosh Gashone . . .
> A Yom Kippur,
> Otradnyi post,
> On poslal k chertiam pod khvost.
>
> Budem zhdat', chto k piatiletke
> Mrakobesy stanut redki.
> A bogam ravvin i pop
> Pust' gotoviat obshchii grob![52]

> I remember the holiday of Rosh Hashanah,
> The cantor sang like crazy.
> People followed the cantor,
> Opening their mouths like troughs.
>   . . .
> In the name of God,
> The synagogue raked in money from the sinners.
>   . . .
> The prayerful man is usually
> Blind and deaf to the needs of the poor.
> NEP[men] go to synagogue,
> But a conscious worker does not want
> To have anything to do with God.
>
> God, the Talmud, and Rosh Hashanah . . .
> But on Yom Kippur,
> The fasting day,
> He sent all these holidays to hell.
>
> We shall hope that by the end of the Five-Year Plan
> Obscurantists will be rare.
> And let the rabbi and priest
> Prepare a common coffin for the gods!

In this poem rabbis, synagogue servants, businessmen, and priests are all portrayed negatively as obscurantists. Ordinary believers are shown as non-thinking individuals who blindly follow the lead of religious opportunists. The poem, however, does not portray Jews as helpless victims who cannot make decisions for themselves. Instead, it emphasizes that not all Jews attend synagogue and that "conscious" Jewish workers openly ignore God. The "prayerful man" is described as selfish (i.e., immoral), since he is "blind and deaf" to the needs of the poor. This statement is used to paint religious people as hypocrites who preach justice but, in reality, do nothing to help the less fortunate.

During meetings with Jews who had lived in the USSR in the 1930s, I noticed that those who lived in urban areas were often more sympathetic toward religion and traditional Jewish life than those who remained in the shtetlach until the outbreak of World War II. It may be that city Jews, who knew far less than those in the shtetlach about religious traditions, may have held those traditions in greater awe and perhaps even harbored nostalgic feelings for customs they had never known. It is possible, too, that Jews who moved to bigger cities were more exposed to positive Russian-language information about the Jewish religion than their rural counterparts. Whereas shtetl Jews were exposed to mass campaigns against religion such as the Red Seder, persecution of underground khaydorim, and antireligious education in Yiddish-language schools, urban Jews' experience with these activities was comparatively painless. Their voluntary acculturation spared them the coerced assimilation visited upon the majority of shtetl Jews.

The views held by urban Jews about religion are often strikingly similar to those cited in antireligious pamphlets from the 1930s. For example, Anna M. (b. 1923, in Moscow) explains her attitude toward Judaism in this way:

> I do not believe in religion. I believe in some power that exists above. There is some universal truth. I believe in it. But I do not believe in religion or in observing little rituals. I have a hard time thinking that God really cares whether I go to a synagogue or a church. I honestly think that many religious people are hypocrites. They say they believe in God and do dishonest things.[53]

Anna's views toward organized religion summarizes approximately a hundred similar statements I heard from Jews born in Soviet cities in the 1920s and early 1930s. While many emphasize that they are not hostile toward the Jewish religion in general, a significant number of respondents state that they do not trust the clergy. I conducted the interviews from 1999 to 2002, many years after it became possible to practice religion openly in Russia. It is difficult to say whether Anna consciously learned her ideas from Soviet antireligious pamphlets, but she, like Boris, quoted at the beginning of this chapter, had saved some of the Russian-language brochures of the 1930s era designed to discourage the observance of Jewish traditions.

Propaganda initially created for non-Jews had, in fact, responded to the need of urban Jews to find a way to express their Jewish identity but stripped of its traditional forms and manifestations. Some Jews saw these publications as unavoidable, because, to them, if all religions were being attacked, it seemed only logical that Judaism should be no exception. Indeed, the criticism of Judaism in the Russian-language publications was generally accompanied by attacks against Christianity and other religions. Some respondents recalled that they were even happy to see antireligious propaganda directed against Judaism so that they could respond to antisemitic accusations, among them that Russia is ruled by the Jews and that the Bolsheviks are all Jews. In fact, these Russian-language brochures against antisemitism were especially remembered and appreciated by the rapidly assimilating Jewish public of the 1930s.

Pogroms, Antisemitism, and Agriculture: Jewish Life through Soviet Lenses

During the Russian civil war (1918–1921) Jews suffered waves of pogroms and slaughter. In some cases these involved virtually entire communities. In this period approximately thirteen hundred pogroms and anti-Jewish attacks took place in seven hundred Ukrainian localities, and between sixty and seventy thousand Jews were killed in similar attacks in Byelorussia.[54] As Benjamin Pinkus noted, "Russia's centuries-old anti-Semitism found expression in the outrages of the Civil War period."[55]

When the Bolsheviks gained power they took a firm stance against antisemitism and pogroms. The Council of People's Commissars issued a special decree on July 27, 1918, condemning all antisemitic manifestations. Informative literature about the harm of antisemitism was published on a large scale and distributed through the military ranks and public workplaces.[56] In Russia alone, between 1917 and 1922, antisemitism was the subject of forty-six of the one hundred books published with Jewish themes.[57] Propaganda against pogroms was the focus of many publications. Numerous short brochures, newspaper articles, and flyers explained that pogroms were a horrific legacy of the old regime and that the former rulers used them to redirect the public's anger against the tsarist regime toward innocent victims, in this case the Jews. After the revolution, however, this explanation was weakened.[58] Brochures emphasized that the Jewish poor suffered from Jewish capitalists, just like the Russian poor remained downtrodden because of Russian capitalists.

When the civil war ended and the Soviet regime was established, the ideological campaign against antisemitism, together with penalties imposed on rioters, led to a substantial decrease in pogroms and other violent anti-Jewish behavior. Still, as Bernard Weinryb noted, "it would have been remarkable for an old and firmly established prejudice to vanish in so short a time. In fact, in the mid-1920s, according to Soviet publications, mass antisemitism once more swept through the population, including industrial workers and the new Soviet intelligentsia."[59] Indeed, popular antisemitism was now associated not only with religious prejudices but with the negative aspects of the new regime itself. The prominent place of Jews in the Soviet government and in economic and educational institutions enabled antisemitic circles to spread the idea that "the Jews have taken over Russia."[60] The influx of Jews into heavy industry and their move from small towns to industrialized regions of Russia led to confrontations with populations that had, until then, rarely known any Jews. Antisemitism was intensified by the presence of Jews in the secret police and militia, organizations responsible for the confiscation of Church property during this period. Peasants clearly associated Jews with the destruction of churches.[61] Jewish settlement in Crimea caused dissatisfaction, expressed in the complaint that "they're being given everything at the expense of the Russian people."[62]

State-sponsored publications tried to address the root causes of antisemitism. At a 1928 meeting of Party activists held in Moscow, one topic discussed was the stereotypes and allegations that provoked these prejudices. These were addressed in the form of questions:

> Why does the Russian worker disdain Jews more than he does Georgians, Germans, and other nationalities?
> Why is it that Jews do not want to do heavy work?
> How is that Jews always manage to obtain good positions?
> Why are there so many Jews attending universities? Isn't it because they forge their papers?
> Why were Jews in the Crimea given good land, whereas the land the Russians received is not as fertile?[63]

These questions were countered in the Russian-language press in the late 1920s and early 1930s in its materials about Jews, Judaism, and the Jewish question. Books and pamphlets analyzed the harm caused by antisemitism and stressed the need to combat it. Antisemitic expressions were presented as the antithesis of socialism.

Some of these issues are summarized and addressed in a 1927 brochure by the Soviet president Mikhail Kalinin called *The Jewish Question* (*Evreiskii vopros*). Kalinin expressed the official view on the Jewish question, emphasizing that although many Jews were indeed speculators, an overwhelming majority had nothing to do with this activity. He emphasized that proletarian and honest Jews supported the Soviet regime.[64] Moreover, the brochure explains that when the Russian intelligentsia refused to accept the revolution in 1917, Jewish citizens filled the niche and became actively involved in Soviet organizations. According to Kalinin, this initially provoked antisemitism.[65] He also addressed the topic of the rapidly changing Soviet Jewish identity. "If I were a rabbi," continued Kalinin, "I would have cursed all Jews who were moving to Moscow, because there they lose their Jewish identity very quickly and become assimilated Soviet citizens."[66] Regarding the alleged Jewish privileges, Kalinin stressed that Jews were not strangers to Russia and had, in fact, always lived there but had been deprived of their civil rights by the unjust policies of the tsarist regime. The Soviet regime had returned these rights.[67]

There were some similarities in the ways that the Russian media and its Jewish equivalent responded to the Jewish question in their descriptions of the Jewish agricultural settlements. In both, the settlements were presented with enthusiasm and described in the brightest of terms. The Russian publications emphasized a seamless transformation of Jewish workers from occupations in crafts and small businesses to successful agricultural farm workers, and the Yiddish propaganda materials featured numerous "success stories" of those who had made the transition. Thus the propaganda literature in both languages aimed to show that Jews were extremely successful in the agricultural arena and that their involvement improved the Soviet economy. One article went so far as to say that "the lack of [Jewish] agricultural traditions, centuries-old conservatism, and, therefore, ease in accepting modern methods of agriculture, such as adapting new techniques and advice from experts, made Jews better stewards of the land than traditional peasants."[68]

However, important distinctions were also apparent in the ways that the agricultural collectives were depicted by the two languages. The Yiddish press spoke of great financial support from both abroad and the state, whereas the Russian publications emphasized that the government provided no support at all in the move to previously uninhabited lands.[69] Further, the Russian-language publications deliberately underrepresented the actual numbers of Jewish agricultural settlements, perhaps so as not to provoke additional bursts of public antisemitism. Because the Yiddish propaganda was designed to encourage Jews to move to these settlements, they correctly stated that the number of existing collective farms was thirty-two.[70] B. Berezhanskaia has compared the data concerning Soviet Jewish collective farms published in the official literature with data from the archives. She concludes that, according to a contemporary report published in Russian, there were only fourteen Jewish collective farms in Crimea, although the official Soviet archival reports list some thirty-two in the region.[71]

A 1936 brochure by Shmuel Godiner and D. Lifshits describes a meeting that supposedly took place between representatives from Jewish and Cossack collective farms.[72] In order to share their experiences, a delegation from a Jewish collective farm in Novozlatopol, Ukraine, goes to visit a Cossack farm.[73] The Jewish agricultural workers find numerous problems at the Cossack collective farm, including unproductive use of the land. Their biggest concern is that the Cossack pig farms are not as well equipped as those on Jewish collective farms.[74] Jewish swine breeders advise the Cossacks on how to cope with various problems. At the end of the meeting the Cossacks and the Jews exchange letters in which they decide to launch a socialist competition between the two collective farms after carrying out mutual training programs. The Jewish advisers promise to teach the Cossacks about agriculture, and the Cossacks agree to show the Jews how to shoot guns, the only area in which Jews are portrayed as inferior to the Cossacks in the publication. The brochure concludes, "The Jews used to be scared of Cossacks, but now they are ready to accept them as brothers and to help them and to receive their help."[75] By promoting friendship between Jews and Cossacks, the two most unlikely groups to make peace given their long history of mutual hatred, the publication tried to convince readers that they lived in a new society devoid of religious and ethnic prejudice. The brochure was published in both Yiddish and Russian and was designed for a Jewish as well as a non-Jewish audience.

To sum up, Russian-language Soviet propaganda portrayed Jews in the following ways: although their religion was just as negative as other religions, it was not as frightening as popular antisemitism presented it; their cultural and historical heritage was progressive since Jews were active in the revolutionary movement; and they were loyal to the Soviet regime, and well integrated into the new society economically, socially, and culturally. The publications concluded, therefore, that antisemitism was an unjust remnant of the tsarist regime.

The key question is whether these messages reached their intended audiences. Numerous studies of popular antisemitism in the 1990s demonstrate that antisemitic stereotypes are still valid in modern Russian society. A sociological survey conducted in 1992 revealed that 13.3 percent of Russians agree with the statement that "Jews deserve to be punished because they killed Christ," and 34 percent are uncertain about this allegation.[76] When asked to respond to the statement, "Jews would choose money over friends," 34 percent of Russians agreed or strongly agreed, and 41 percent were uncertain.[77] The data demonstrate that, at the end of the twentieth century, Russian popular opinion still reflects misconceptions about the Jewish religion and about Jews in general. Another survey concluded that members of the older generation are more likely to express antisemitic statements.[78] Of course, this "older generation" is the one that grew up in the 1920s and 1930s, and was the "target audience" for the antisemitic propaganda described above. Any effects of the Soviet ideological campaign in the 1930s certainly no longer remained with its targeted audience. Yet oral history demonstrates that this literature had a profound influence on the Jewish audience, which was still in place seventy years later.

Oral history reveals nuances of how the campaign against antisemitism helped to shape the cultural identity of urban Jews. Some read the literature in order to be able to counter antisemitic accusations. Ilya S. (b. 1919, in Byelorussia) explains:

[In 1935] I arrived in Leningrad and settled in a dormitory at the Electrical Engineering Institute. Most of the students were from villages and were uneducated peasants. They did not know that I was Jewish, I did not look Jewish at all, so I heard all these [antisemitic] comments. They used to say, Jews ran the government, Jews sold out Russia, Jews this, Jews that. First, I wanted to hit them. I was a strong man, I liked sports, and I was not afraid of anything. But then I thought, "What would it do for me?" They would hate me even more. So I did nothing. Then I was in the library and stumbled across a book with stories about Jewish pogroms written by Korolenko. I read it, and thought, "If only my roommates read it, they would stop saying those things about Jews." But then again, what did these guys read? They only liked playing cards and drinking vodka. Then

I saw another book, which was entitled something like "Our Answer to Antisemites." I started flipping through the pages and realized that the book dealt with all the issues I was interested in. It spoke about Jewish collective farms, explained that Jews were involved in the revolutionary movement. I started reading and could not stop. I knew nothing of Jewish history, and it was fascinating. . . . I did not tell anything to my roommates, but I was no longer hurt by their comments.[79]

Ilya did not advise his roommates to read any of the publications designed to combat discrimination. That was why, in his view, they did not change their opinions about Jews. Thus the message that had been deliberately intended for Ilya's roommates never reached them, at least not through Ilya. But Ilya, a Jewish student who was troubled by antisemitic comments, so enjoyed these books that sympathetically described Jews that they boosted his national pride.

Another respondent, Mikhail Sh. (b. 1914, in Novoustyitsa, Ukraine) describes how the literature that spoke out against antisemitism actually helped him to believe in the goals of Soviet ideology:

My mother was raped during a pogrom in 1918, and she went crazy after that. I was four at the time, and I did not see anything. My older brother, Srulik, hid me under the bench, and I remember he put his hand on my eyes so that I do not see it. He died in the 1930s from pneumonia. I left Novoustyitsa in 1929. I went to study in Kharkov [Ukraine]. . . . When I got there, I went to the housing office of the vocational school where I wanted to study and stood in line with other kids. Then one said: "Those Yids, they rule everywhere, too bad they were not all killed in pogroms!" I became so mad that I hit him in the face, real hard. The militia came, and they took us both to the militia station. After a couple of hours they let me go, but he stayed there. . . . Oh, I was so angry. I then read a book about Jewish victims of pogroms. And I thought to myself, if this is the government that protects Jews, I will support this government, I am with the Communist Party. I then joined the Party, and I still think that, no matter what people say, the Communist Party was right in everything.[80]

In this case the brochures about the pogroms had reached Mikhail, who, in turn, became more sympathetic toward the Soviet regime. But, again, it is not clear whether non-Jewish audiences read such publications and, even if they had, whether they were convinced by the arguments. Yet, as oral history reveals, at least some Jewish readers actively read and discussed these works that were primarily not designed for them. Moreover, as some respondents testified, these brochures had an important influence on the formation of their Jewish identity. Other state-sponsored genres on the same subject, namely, theatrical trials and films, also had a tremendous impact since they found even wider Jewish audiences.

Antisemitism on Trial

The Soviet government used amateur and semi-amateur theatrical performances to combat antisemitism. Agitation sketches, buffooneries, and oral newspapers all dealt with the subject. Yet it was the public theatrical trials against antisemitism that made the greatest impression on both Soviet citizens and foreign travelers.

Leon Dennen, an American journalist who visited Kiev in 1932, described a play he attended that consisted of a theatrical trial against antisemitism. Unlike the mock trials described in chapter 3, this play was conducted in Russian and was purely theatrical: the judges, jury, attorney, and prosecutor were all actors. The plot features a clerk named Raznochintseva, who is accused of saying, "The Jews have already forgotten what a pogrom is like, but soon there will be another war and we shall remind them what it means to capture Russia's government, land, factories, and everything else."[81] Raznochintseva shares her views with her colleagues and customers. A peasant named Gnivenko, influenced by Raznochintseva, begins to complain that the Soviet government is giving away land, seed, credit, and agricultural implements to Jews, while taking everything away from Russian peasants. Gnivenko and Raznochintseva are put on trial based on a complaint by a local citizen, Shapiro, for inciting hatred against a national minority. During the trial other witnesses confirm the pair's antisemitic behavior.[82]

The trial equates antisemites with counterrevolutionaries and with people of bourgeois origins. The investigation reveals that Raznochintseva was a graduate of the tsarist gymnasium, where she was presumably taught to hate Jews and other minorities, and that her former husband was a White Army colonel who fled Russia after the revolution. The theatrical trial highlights this testimony to symbolize that the antisemitism of the accused had its origins in the failed values of the old regime. The trial also reveals that Raznochintseva has no facts to back up her antisemitic statements:

> RAZNOCHINTSEVA: Don't you know that they [the Jews] have always been after easy money?
> ATTORNEY FOR THE DEFENSE: How well do you know any Jews?
> RAZNOCHINTSEVA: Personally I know very few of them. I always avoid them.
> PROSECUTOR: Did you ever read any literature about Jews?
> RAZNOCHINTSEVA: I was not interested enough.[83]

The judge concludes that Raznochintseva's ignorance regarding Soviet educational literature about Jews led her to the false assumptions that Jews run the country. The most serious charge against Raznochintseva is that she encouraged a pogrom. This accusation is confirmed by other witnesses, including Boychenko, a worker who testifies that he knows Jews personally and considers them "good fellows." However, when people begin criticizing them, Boychenko agrees. Later in the trial the prosecutor reveals that Boychenko does not read newspapers. The message here is that those who do not read Soviet newspapers can easily be corrupted by biased individuals such as Raznochintseva; thus antisemitism is equated with ignorance. Testimonies of other witnesses confirm that their antisemitic ideas came from a lack of information and not from any empirical knowledge about Jews. Even a Jew is put on trial in the theatrical performance: Raznochintseva's boss, a Jew named Kantorovich, is accused of hearing antisemitic statements from his workers and doing nothing to stop them.[84] The result of the trial is that Raznochintseva is fired from her post, expelled from the trade union, and sentenced to a two-year prison term for the counterrevolutionary activity of inciting antisemitism.[85]

Such performances were staged throughout the Soviet Union. These theatrical trials typified Soviet propaganda of the era in that they had negative characters voicing popular concerns about antisemitism. By presenting antisemites as uneducated, illiterate, and aggressive people, the authors hoped to educate the public about bigotry.[86] It is not known whether the message reached non-Jewish audiences in the Soviet Union, but evidence suggests that many Jews attended the performances. When asked about Jewish-related trials from the 1920s and 1930s, many respondents specifically described this type of performance. They reiterated that the public trials of antisemites made them proud of the Soviet regime. Oral history shows that such performances also taught Jews to respond to antisemitic assaults. In the words of Asya G. (b. 1922, in Kiev):

> I went to a [theatrical] trial against antisemites. One man was tried because he beat up his fellow worker just because he was Jewish. It was not a real trial, just a performance, but everything looked real, and there was a judge, a bench, and everything. The prosecutor explained about antisemitism, that it was wrong to hate Jews, and that bastard [on trial] got two years in jail. A couple of days later, I took a tram. There was a man there, and he said something like, "There is no escape from those Yids, they are everywhere. I am a real proletarian, and I have to stand in the tram, and they all have their own cars!"
>
> I heard all that, approached him, and hit him in the face with all my force. You see, I am tall now, and I was tall then, and I am very strong. I used to work on a collective farm. My arms and fists are really strong. He fell down. People were watching, but no one said anything. Then I yelled to the driver: "Stop the car!" He stopped at the next stop, and I took this man to the militia station. I wrote a complaint that he assaulted Jews. But while I was waiting for the next tram, I saw this guy coming out of the station. They did not do anything to him. Well, at least I hit him with my strong fist![87]

Of course the trial that Asya saw at a theater in Kiev did not advocate physical assaults on antisemites. Rather, the intention was to encourage the use of logical and intellectual explanations to combat prejudice. Yet her recollection from this performance was that Jews should protect themselves and should not be intimidated by antisemitic abuse.

Trials against antisemites were not always purely theatrical. Sometimes real people were tried publicly for expressing antisemitic remarks. In Efim G.'s view (b. 1919, in the Byelorussian shtetl Parichi), such trials represented the triumph of Jews over antisemitism and antisemites:

> There was absolutely no antisemitism before World War II. I can give you an example. We lived in a building where a former rich man used to live. Another person, a Russian man, lived in a different apartment of this building. My brother was very strong and had a bad temper. Once, he insulted this Russian man. That man began to shout at him, "Zhidenok [Little Yid]." My mother appealed to the court, and the Russian man had to apologize publicly.[88]

Efim's comment that there was no antisemitism before the war—a belief shared by the majority of respondents—essentially referred to the absence of state-sponsored antisemitism as opposed to popular antisemitism. Indeed, trials against antisemitism certainly prove that the state exerted much effort in the struggle to end discrimination.

It is noteworthy that the Soviet Yiddish press rarely dealt with antisemitism, although both Russian- and Yiddish-speaking Jews were interested in the subject. Russian-language events dealing with antisemitism were widely attended by both Yiddish- and Russian-speaking Jews, because these events not only criticized antisemites but also indirectly praised Jews and the Jewish heritage. Once again we see how an audience was able to make independent choices within a limited framework of political and cultural freedom. Similar phenomena can be observed in popular attitudes toward the portrayal of Jews and Jewish issues on the Soviet screen.

The Jewish Question on the Soviet Screen

After taking power the Soviet government began to create silent propaganda films to combat popular antisemitism. Two early examples are *The Struggle for the Light Kingdom of the Third Internationale* and Alexander Razumnyi's *Comrade Abram*.[89] *Comrade Abram* (1919) is the story of a young Jewish man from a shtetl (played by a star of prerevolutionary cinema, Dmitrii Bukhovetsky) who survived the pogroms and discrimination of tsarist Russia and was later drawn into the revolutionary workers' milieu. The film shows the viewer the painless path by which Jews, regardless of class, could enter the future kingdom of internationalism.[90] Short films like *Comrade Abram*, which depicted the horrors of the pogroms, were designed to evoke sympathy for Jews. They were part of a prevailing tendency in the official press of that period to idealize everything associated with Jews and Judaism in order to fight antisemitism.

In the 1920s there were approximately forty silent movies based on Jewish themes.[91] Some of these movies, such as *Cross and Revolver* (1925) directed by Vladimir Gardin, concerned false accusations of Jews killing Christians.[92] Others emphasized the participation of Jews in the revolution and the suffering they endured from anti-Jewish riots; examples of these films include *Mabul* (1925), *Hirsh Lekert* (1927), *Motele Shpindler* (1928), and *Prison Labor* (1929). In the 1930s this theme was repeated in Russian-language sound movies such as *Five Brides* (1935) and *Dnepr on Fire* (1937).

Jews were also portrayed in movies as progressive socialists. A notable example is the only Yiddish talkie produced in the Soviet Union, *Natan Beker Comes Home* (1932), a film that portrays an American Jew who returns to the Soviet Union to work in a factory in Magnitogorsk.[93] Similarly the 1931 short film *Remember Their Faces* tells a story about Nakhum Beychik, a Jewish worker who invents a new tool that enables his factory to become more efficient. The head of the factory, a former NEPman named Lopatin, does not like the invention and attempts to have Nakhum killed by a group of non-Jewish workers. The Komsomol organization uncovers the conspiracy, however, and Lopatin is arrested. Both films portray Jews as being sympathetic to socialism and to the new Soviet ideology.

Although Jewish subjects were regularly featured on the Soviet screen, there is no evidence of their widespread popularity, even among Jewish viewers, with one notable exception, namely, *Iskateli shchastia* (Seekers of happiness) produced in 1936 by the Byelorussian State Cinema.[94] No other movie about Jews received as much attention at the time or made such an impact. The film is about a young Jewish woman, Roza, and her extended family who travel from Palestine to Birobidzhan to begin new lives on a collective farm. The entire family is enthusiastic about the move. However, Pinya—Roza's brother-in-law, played by Veniamin Zuskin, a star of the Moscow State Yiddish Theater—is plotting ways to profit from the situation. Instead of working on the collective farm like the other members of the household, he leaves to search for gold. When he thinks he has found precious metal, he wants to go to China. Leva, Roza's brother, discovers Pinya's intentions and tries to stop him, but the result is that Pinya hits Leva, leaving him unconscious. Everyone thinks that Leva was attacked by Korney, a non-Jewish Russian worker who is in love with Roza. When the truth is finally revealed, Leva recovers, Pinya goes to jail, and Roza marries Korney.

Seekers of Happiness presented Soviet Jews from an ideal perspective. The traditional Jewish identity was represented by the older generation, namely, Roza's mother who opposes the intermarriage at the end of the film. The "positive" Jews sing optimistic songs, as a clarinetist plays, pessimistically, "The Lament of Israel on the Bank of the Amur." In this film assimilation is presented as the solution to the Soviet Jewish question.

When originally released *Seekers of Happiness* was described as a Russian-language film intended for a broad, namely Russian, audience. However, its popularity among Jews exceeded all expectations. Overnight the soundtrack became a hit, the dialogue remained in viewers' memories, and countless respondents reported that they saw the movie at least three or four times. Many Jews of the 1930s generation remembered that when *Seekers of Happiness* was show-

Anna Shternshis conducts interviews at the Moscow Jewish Charity Kitchen, June 2001. Photograph by Natan Koifman.

ing locally on the screen, it was like a "holiday in a Jewish street." In the words of Mikhail O., a former resident of Kiev:

> When the movie theater in Kiev began showing this movie, it looked like a synagogue. The audience was filled with Jews: mothers with children, teenagers, and grandparents. Once, after the movie was over, the audience did not want to go home but asked the operator to show it again. The cashier went around the audience and collected more money for tickets. It was that popular.[95]

First among the various reasons for the film's popularity was that it was about Jews and Jewish life in the Soviet Union. A former resident of Kiev, Naum F. (b. 1918) describes the Jewish reaction to *Seekers of Happiness* in this way:

> We knew it was a propaganda movie, but that did not matter. This did not convince us to pick up and move to Birobidzhan. . . . Still, it was a movie about us, about Jews. We sang the songs they sang, we memorized their jokes. Until now, I remember this popular verse from that movie—"Pinia zoloto iskal, a nashel prostoi metal" [Pinya was looking for gold and found simple metal]. When the movie was shown in Kiev, it was always sold out. The audience was almost exclusively Jewish. The cinema hall looked like a synagogue.[96]

A second reason for the movie's enormous popularity was the presence of the actor Venyamin Zuskin. His portrayal of the "negative" Pinya in *Seekers of Happiness* received both popular and critical acclaim. In a memorable scene in the film Pinya, instead of working for the greater goal of building socialism, travels to Birobidzhan for personal gain. While on the boat to Russia from Palestine he continually asks the captain and the passengers: "Skazhite, pozhaluista, skol'ko stoit etot parokhod?" (Could you tell me, please, how much does this boat cost?) Although Pinya speaks Russian with a strong Yiddish accent and intonation, his character in the movie, through Zuskin's considerable talents as an actor, conveys anti-Soviet sentiments. Indeed, Pinya is the most likable and memorable character in the movie. Of the 225 respondents I interviewed, 211, among them respondents from Germany, the United States, and Russia, were all able to quote Zuskin's line from the movie, even though many could not recall the details of the plot. In preferring Pinya's "negative" character over the apparently propagandistic "positive" figures in the film, the Jewish viewers were expressing their silent protest against Soviet rhetoric and ideology. Pinya provoked so much sympathy that some respondents considered that his downfall was intended to connote antisemitism. In the view of Semyon Sh. (b. 1918):

> I saw this movie, everyone saw it. "How much does the boat cost?" Zuskin played the main character. This was antisemitic. When Jews were given Birobidzhan, the movie was created to show how they organized a collective farm there. Now, why did they have to use this expression to show specific Jewish negative characteristics? Why, of all things, did they emphasize this?[97]

For Semyon, Pinya's grimaces, smirks, and groveling were all negative Jewish characteristics. Because this was how Jews were seen by antisemites, Semyon saw no reason to legitimize these views on the movie screen. But his opinion was not shared by most respondents. Even his wife, Lyusya G. (b. 1925, in Kiev), disagreed. Here is her response to her husband's claims of antisemitism in *Seekers of Happiness*:

> This was a beautiful movie. And it had a fantastic song, it was called "Fisherman." I can sing it for you. And why does Senya [Semyon] call it antisemitic? It was wonderful, it had Jewish music in it, and it even portrayed Jews positively. I liked this movie, and all my friends did, too.[98]

Elizaveta Z. (b. 1924), a former resident of the Ukrainian town of Nemirov, also commented on how much she liked the music in the film: "I especially liked that fiddle. It played a Jewish melody. . . . It was so rare to hear Jewish music [publicly] at that time."[99]

Sofiya B. from Birobidzhan spares no superlatives when speaking about *Seekers of Happiness*:

> I absolutely loved it. I think it was perfect. The actor who played Dvoyra [Roza's mother] was Russian, but she acted amazingly well. Plus, they

showed absolutely beautiful nature, this was the best movie about Jews. And the music, of course, this music. That song "Fisherman" was so beautiful. I think this is the best song ever written.[100]

There were two important pieces of music in the movie. The first, "Plach u beregov Amura" (The lament of Israel on the bank of the Amur), was an instrumental selection played by a Jewish violinist who did not want to go to Birobidzhan. This piece symbolized the lack of connection between the Soviet times and the Jewish or religious past and was ridiculed by other figures in the film for being inappropriate. The second, "U rybalki u reki" (Fishing by the river), featured an appealing melody written by Isaak Dunaevsky (1900–1955), a famous Russian Jewish composer. The tune resembled that of the Hebrew song "Eliyahu HaNavi," which is usually sung during the Passover seder. The lyrics, by Yekhezkel Dobrushin, a Yiddish poet, actually have no relevance to any specifically Jewish experience. They speak about fishing, productive labor, and being kissed by a girl at the end of a hard day's work. In fact, the song is first introduced in *Seekers of Happiness* by non-Jews, who are singing as they work at the collective farm. When the Jewish characters, for example, Roza, become more enthusiastic about the collective farm, they, too, begin to sing this song. Thus, acceptance of the song is portrayed as a symbol of accepting the new Soviet way of life. Yet, as oral testimonies about the film reveal, the public viewed the song as Jewish. Moreover, when I asked respondents which Jewish songs they remembered, without referring to the film, many hesitated to sing anything in Yiddish but almost everyone was able to reproduce the melody and words of the song "from that Jewish movie," the song "Fishing by the River." In fact, they referred to it as "our Soviet Jewish song." "Fishing by the River" was even sold separately under the title "Evreiskaia komsomol'skaia" (Jewish Komsomol song). What made the song "Jewish" was that it was performed by Jews in a movie devoted to Jewish issues.

It is significant that, when asked if they remembered the plot of the movie *Seekers of Happiness*, many respondents had difficulty doing so. Most remembered a few episodes, such as Zuskin's asking about the price of the boat or the rendition of the "Fisherman" song. The messages the Soviets wanted to convey in the film—about productive labor, intermarriage, and so on—left no significant impressions on the audience, in contrast to the unintended elements described above. None of the respondents remembered the intermarriage that concluded the film, which, in keeping with the writers' intention, was supposed to demonstrate the full integration of Jews into Russian society. Miron Chernenko, a scholar of Soviet film who belongs to the first generation of Soviet Jews, relates his experience of watching and analyzing *Seekers of Happiness*:

Once I reread the synopsis of *Seekers of Happiness,* I suddenly saw that the film was a typical social drama with a bit of melodramatic flavor and peppered with a "mystery" plot. However, in my childhood memories I saw this picture as a comedy, because hilarious Pinya [Zuskin] wore a funny vest and a hat. . . .

It was Pinya, and not rapidly assimilating Birobidzhan farmers, who provoked the sympathies of viewers. Pinya came from the extensive tradition of Jewish literature, from Sholem Aleichem, Sholem Asch, and Mendele Moykher Sforim. Although Soviet authors wanted to present this character as negative, tradition held sway. Therefore it is not the authors' fault that viewers remembered the charming Pinya through Venyomin Zuskin's impressive performance rather than through the performances of other "positive" characters.[101]

Chernenko's attitude is an indication that members of his generation who saw this movie chose to remember what best suited their understanding of Jewish identity and the place of Jews in Soviet society. *Seekers of Happiness* had a relatively small release and was shown in only a limited number of theaters. Yet oral history demonstrates that watching *Seekers of Happiness* became one of the important manifestations of Soviet Jewish identity in the late 1930s. Similarly, as in the case of literature against antisemitism, Jews themselves became the primary consumers for a work originally intended for a broad Russian-speaking audience, who in fact remained quite indifferent to the film's message.

"Yasha is a Pilot, He is a Good Boy": Jewish Images in Russian Songs

Russian popular culture of the 1920s was filled with exoticism associated with people of different domestic ethnic groups, especially Jews and gypsies. Songs of this genre are often set in Jewish shtetlach and advocate intermarriage. The typical plot revolves around a Jewish girl who marries a non-Jew much to her family's chagrin. Such songs often combine frivolous descriptions with political messages. Linguist Robert Rothstein cites an example, "Sarah: A Jewish Shtetl Melody," written by Timofeev and Prozorovskiy:[102]

> V mestechke Ol'shanakh zhila byla Sarra,
> Kak veshnee solntse svezha,
> Vsia polnaia negi i taynogo zhara,
> Krasavitsa, tra-la-la-la.
>
> . . .
>
> U rebe Leybovicha dom s mezaninom,
> Kvartiry i sklady stekla.
> Gorditsia mestechko ego magazinom,
> I den'gami, tra-la-la-la.
>
> . . .
>
> No v serdtse u Sary zakralos' drugoe,
> Ei zhizn' po inomu mila,
> Ona poliubila veselogo goya,
> Krasivaia, tra-la-la-la![103]

> In the town of Ol'shany lived Sarah,
> Radiant as the spring sun,
> Full of voluptuousness and secret ardor,
> A beauty, tra-la-la-la.
>
> . . .

Rebe Leybovich has a house with a patio,
An apartment and a warehouse with glass.
The shtetl is proud of his store,
And of his money, tra-la-la-la.

. . .

But someone else stole Sarah's heart,
She prefers a different kind of life,
She fell in love with a merry gentile,
She is beautiful, tra-la-la-la![104]

Rothstein notes that, unlike other songs by Timofeev and Prozorovsky, this one was not banned by the Main Repertoire Committee (Glavrepetkom), perhaps because of its progressive portrayal of interethnic relations.[105] It is notable that Sarah is described as an exotic beauty, passionate and independent, and rejects the rich Jew, Leybovich, to marry a gentile. The presentation of Jews as overly sexual was common in the popular culture of this period. Criticism of Jewish traditions, and capitalism, occupies a key place in this song, and the captivating melody appeals to both Jewish and non-Jewish audiences.

Although Sarah rebels against Jewish traditions, her family and the entire shtetl remain unchanged. The song "Daughter of the Rabbi" also deals with intermarriage. Here a young woman's behavior actually has an effect on her family. Klara R., a former resident of Odessa, remembers the song:

Zachem vam, grazhdane, chuzhaia Argentina?
Vot vam istoriia Kahovskogo ravvina
Kotoryi zhil v stolichnom gorode Kakhovka
V takoi prekrasnoi i roskoshnoi obstanovke.

V Kakhovke nravilas' vsem doch' ravvina, Enta,
Takaia stroinaia, kak shelkovaia lenta,
Takaia chistaia, kak mytaia posuda,
Takaia umnaia, kak tselyi tom Talmuda.

I zhenikhov imela mnogo deva nasha,
Miasnik Abrasha i parikhmakher Yasha,
I kazhdyi den' meniaia Yashu na Abrashu
Ona svodila etim vsekh s uma.

No revoliutsiia proizoshla v Kakhovke,
Perevorot sluchilsia v Entinoy golovke,
Priekhal novyi predsedatel' gubprodtresta,
I nasha Enta ne nakhodit sebe mesta.

Ivan Ivanovich, krasavets chernobrovyi,
Takoi krasivyi, i na vid pochti zdorovyi,
Na nem botinochki i sapogi shevrovie,
A galife na nem sovsem pochti kak novie.

Vot raz prikhodit ravvin iz sinagogi,
Ego uzh Enta ne vstrechaet na poroge,

A na stole lezhit pis'mo v chetyre slova:
Proschai. Uekhala. Grazhdanka Ivanova.

Oy, oy, oy, oy, da chto zh eto takoe!
Priekhal frayer i natvoril takoe!

I perestal togda molit'sia ravvin Bogu,
Ne khodit bol'she on v subbotu v sinagogu,
Pobril on borodu, usy, i stal on frantom,
Interesuetsia valiutoi, brilliantom.

Why do you need to hear about strange Argentina?
Here is a story for you about a Kakhovkian rabbi
Who lived in the capital city of Kakhovka
In a beautiful and luxurious atmosphere.

Everyone in Kakhovka liked the daughter of the rabbi, Enta,
She was as slim as a silk ribbon,
As clean as washed dishes,
As smart as an entire volume of the Talmud.

She had many boyfriends, our girl,
The butcher Abrasha and the barber Yasha,
And every day she switched between Yasha and Abrasha
And drove everyone crazy.

But a revolution took place in Kakhovka,
A coup happened in Enta's head,
A new chairman of the regional trade mission came,
And Enta is confused.

Ivan Ivanovich is handsome, he has black eyebrows,
He is so handsome and looks almost healthy,
He has shoes and leather boots,
His riding breeches are almost new.

One day, the rabbi comes back from the synagogue,
Enta does not meet him at the entrance,
And on the table there is a short four-word letter:
Good-bye. Left. Citizen Ivanova.

Oy-oy-oy-oy, what is this!
A trendy chap came and started all this mess!

And the rabbi stopped praying to God,
He does not go to the synagogue on Saturdays,
He shaved his beard and mustache, and became a dandy,
Now he is interested in hard currency and diamonds.[106]

The song criticizes Jewish traditions and features an adventurous plot in an exotic setting. However, the description of the gentile, the chairman of a Soviet organization, is drawn not as idealistic but instead is described ironically: he has "almost new" pants and looks "almost healthy." Yet Enta prefers him to her Jewish boyfriends. Like Sarah in the previous song, Enta is presented as sexual, and Jewish men cannot satisfy her passion. Thus intermarriage is provoked not by political reasons but rather by physical ones. Even though the political message of the song, namely, intermarriage, supports Soviet ideology, Enta's motivation for choosing her Communist husband is not inspired by state dogma. It is worth noting that contemporary respondents rarely remembered songs such as "Sarah" or "Enta." Even Klara, who recounted "Enta," does so apologetically: "Only some uneducated people used to sing it, maybe students with guitars, but it was not widely known."[107]

Indeed, an overwhelming number of respondents refer to such songs as "antisemitic" and "vulgar." However, this is not to say that Russian-speaking Jews are not eager to listen to Russian songs with Jewish characters in them. Quite the contrary.

Oral history demonstrates that even though urban Jews listened to a wide range of popular music, including Russian-language songs, jazz pieces, gypsy folk tunes, and romances, many still preferred music that they thought of as "Jewish." When asked about their favorite music from the 1920s and 1930s, an overwhelming majority of respondents mention Leonid Utesov (1895–1982) and Alexander Tsfasman (1906–1974), two prominent figures in Soviet jazz from that period. Both men are of Jewish origin, and their music contains recognizably Jewish motifs and styles. What Frederick Starr refers to as "Jewish music transferred into Russian form" was seen by many Jews as new, distinctly Jewish music.[108] Venyamin S. (b. 1906), who moved from Zhitomir, Ukraine, to Moscow in the early 1930s, explains:

> I did not distinguish between Russian and Jewish music. But once I heard Utesov's singing . . . He sang nice songs, and you know what is interesting? I recognized some of the old Yiddish melodies! Do you know the song, "Uncle Elia"? Utesov sang it. It is a lovely song, and it reminds me of Yiddish music. But not only Jews loved Utesov, everyone did. I just think Jews liked him more.[109]

Venyamin's perceptive remark, "Jews liked Utesov more," correctly describes the popular attitude toward Utesolv's music. Born in Odessa with the given name Lazar Weisbeyn, Utesov performed songs that eventually were heard across the Soviet Union. From the early 1930s through the late 1960s he traveled across the country, giving sold-out concerts. Starting his career by performing Soviet jazz music, Utesov soon included in his repertoire couplets, romances, marches, parodies, and sentimental songs. Because Utesov was open about his being Jewish, many Jews saw him as their representative.[110] Mila G. (b. 1920, in Moscow) describes this response to Utesov:

> You see, Utesov's songs were all Jewish. He used Jewish melodies and sang with Russian words. Everyone thought that all these were new Soviet songs, but they were Jewish. Jews knew these were Jewish songs. Utesov

also sang in Yiddish. I have not heard them myself, but I know for sure that he did.[111]

Like Venyamin, Mila asserts that many of Utesov's songs were either Jewish or based on Jewish melodies. The reality is, however, that Utesov's repertoire—more than five hundred songs—includes only five that are directly tied to Yiddish compositions. The first, "Evreiskaia rapsodiia" (Jewish rhapsody), was recorded in 1932 and featured a klezmer melody written by Isaak Dunaevsky. "Jewish Rhapsody" starts with a Hasidic tune. The lyrics describe the luxurious lifestyle of the last Russian tsar, Nicholas II:

> Skazhi mne, dedushka,
> Oy, skazhi zhe mne, oy skazhi zhe mne, oy skazhi,
> Kak zhil tsar' Nikolai?
>
> Esli govorit' otkrovenno, to tsar'
> Nikolai zhil taki ochen' khorosho!
>
> Kak tsar' Nikolai pil chai?
> A chai on, byvalo, pil tak.
> Bral bol'shuiu sakharnuiu golovu,
> I delali v etoi golove dyrku,
> V etu dyrku nalivali odin stakan chaiu
> I iz etoi sakharnoi golovy
> Tsar' Nikolai pil chay.
>
> Skazhi zhe mne, dedushka, kak tsar' Nikolai spal?
> A spal on byvalo tak.
> Brali bol'shuiu bol'shuiu komnatu
> I nasypali ee s lebiazhim pukhom
> Sverkhu lozhilsia tsar' Nikolai i zasypal.
>
> A krugom stoiali kazaki, streliali iz pushek i krichali,
> "Stat', chtoby bylo tikho, tsar' Nikolai spit!"
> I tak on prospal vse svoe tsartsvo.[112]

> Tell me, grandfather,
> Oh, please tell me, please tell me,
> Tell me, how did Tsar Nicholas used to live?
>
> To tell you the truth, Tsar
> Nicholas used to live really very well!
>
> How did he use to drink tea?
> He used to drink tea like so.
> He took a large sugar head,[113]
> Made a hole in this head,
> In this hole one poured one glass of tea
> And from this sugar head
> Tsar Nicholas used to drink tea.

Tell me, grandfather, how did Tsar Nicholas use to sleep?
He used to sleep like so.
They took a large room
And filled the room with swan's down.
Tsar Nicholas used to lie down on top and fall asleep.

And Cossacks stood around, shot from their cannons and yelled,
"Quiet, there should be quiet, Tsar Nicholas is asleep!"
So he slept through his entire tsardom.

The lyrics of the song are taken from a well-known Yiddish folksong (at one time the song was even performed by the American singer Paul Robeson). When Utesov sang it, he put on a strong Yiddish accent when singing the grandfather's lines. It is worth noting that "Jewish Rhapsody" did not follow the trend in the use of Yiddish in Soviet propaganda whereby old liturgical melodies were used to highlight negative aspects of the traditional Jewish lifestyle.[114] In "Jewish Rhapsody," the "sadness" of the liturgical melody is meant to illustrate the misery of Jewish life caused by the tsar. It therefore indirectly justifies traditional Jewish practices. In the second half of the song, the sad melody changes into a new, cheerful Yiddish tune, borrowed from Mark Warshavsky's (1840–1907) wedding song "Di mizinke oysgegebn" (I gave away my youngest daughter):

A dal'she, detki,
Nastala nastoiashchaia zhizn', tak davaite zhe potantsuem!

And then, children,
Real life came! So let us dance!

In the song the word "then" clearly refers to the postrevolutionary period. The cheerful melody symbolizes the new, worry-free life of the Jewish people. Notably none of the respondents of the oral history project noticed the propaganda message in the song. Rather, contemporaries emphasized that Utesov performed Jewish songs from the Russian stage. For many this meant that Yiddish music was popularized and certainly not used for propaganda purposes.

One song performed by Utesov in the late 1930s, "Uncle Elia," borrowed heavily from a Yiddish tune. The song closely resembles "Az der rebe Elimeylekh" (When Rabbi Elimeylekh), written by the American Yiddish poet Moshe Nadir (1885–1943). The original Yiddish lyrics describe how Rabbi Elimeylekh becomes drunk and invites musicians to share in his happiness. Utesov's version uses the same melody but changes Rabbi Elimeylekh into uncle Elia. Instead of the satirical description of a drunken rabbi originally intended by the American Communist Nadir, Utesov presents a lyrical, almost nostalgic image of an adorable Jewish uncle, Elia:

I kogda nash diadia Elia
V serdtse chuvstvoval veselye,
V serdtse chuvstvoval veselye,
Diadia Elia

Podkhodil k zavetnoi stoike.
Vypival stakan nastoiki
Vyvodil s bol'shoiu truboiu trubachei.

Trubachi trubi trubili,
Trubachi trubi trubili,
Trubachi trubi trubili,
Trubachi.
I togda u diadi Eli
Vse kruzhilos' ot vesel'ia,
Vse kruzhilos' ot vesel'ia,
Diadia Elia.[115]

And when our uncle Elia
felt happiness in his heart,
felt happiness in his heart,
Uncle Elia,
Came to the precious bar.
He drank a glass of liquor
And invited trumpeters with large trumpets.

Trumpeters trumpeted,
Trumpeters trumpeted,
Trumpeters trumpeted,
Trumpeters.
Then uncle Elia
Became dizzy from merriness
Became dizzy from merriness.
Uncle Elia.

Utesov often adjusted the melody and the key of his compositions so that the audience could sing along with him.[116] In the case of "Uncle Elia," this strategy worked successfully. Many respondents of my oral history project remembered this song, were able to sing it, and considered it a Russian Jewish song.

In the late 1930s two other songs performed by Utesov, "Ten Daughters" and "Little Bells Ring and Play," enjoyed immense popularity among Jewish audiences. The music and lyrics for both songs were written by Evgenii Zharkovskiy and Leyb Kvitko, respectively, and the subject of both is weddings. "Little Bells" is about a rebellious bride who does not like the groom and is opposed to her parents' plans for an arranged marriage. "Ten Daughters" tells the story of a father who has to deal with the problems of having so many daughters. In a verse from the first half of the song he bemoans the burden of having to marry them off:

Devki zdorovennie, neobyknovennye,
Kto b ne vzial ikh,
Ia otdam uzh,
Ne berut bez deneg zamuzh.

The girls are the healthiest, extraordinary,
Whoever decides to take them,
I will give them away,
But no one wants to marry them without money.

The song later becomes more cheerful. Its tune incorporates melodies from two Yiddish classics: "Lomir ale in eynem" (Let us all together) and "Sheyn, bin ikh sheyn" (Beautiful, I am beautiful):

A teper' ia vot kakov!
Molod, vesel i zdorov.
Desiat' dochek ne beda,
Desiat' dochek erunda.
Ne ponadobilsia svat,
Sami vyshli zamuzh!

But now look at me!
I am young, happy, and healthy.
Ten daughters are no trouble,
Ten daughters are no trouble at all.
I did not need a matchmaker,
They got married without any help!

Still later in the song the father explains that he doesn't need money because everything in the country belongs to him. In other words, the Soviet regime has eliminated all sorts of problems associated with a traditional way of life such as the need for a dowry. Just as in the song "Jewish Rhapsody," the cheerful conclusion of "Ten Daughters" is linked with the Soviet regime, even though the words "Soviet" or "revolution" appear nowhere in the song. Aside from the melody, the only other direct Jewish reference in the song comes with names of the daughters, for example, Esther, Beyle, Shprintse, Khave, and Tsaytl.

The average Jewish listener from that period undoubtedly would associate "Ten Daughters" with Sholem Aleichem's well-known novel, *Tevye the Dairyman,* which portrays a father who has little control over his daughters' marriages. The brides names in the song are the same as Tevye's daughters, and, in both novel and song, a father is the narrator. The difference is, however, that whereas Sholem Aleichem depicts Tevye as bereft of everything he believed in because his daughters chose grooms he did not approve of, the father in "Ten Daughters" is proud, even relieved, that he doesn't have to become involved in matchmaking. The presumption here is that had Tevye lived in Soviet times, his life would not have been a tragic one.

Oral history demonstrates that many of Utesov's listeners noticed the connection between the novel and the song. Rozaliya U. (b. 1903) explains,

Sholem Aleichem was my favorite writer. I was telling my Russian girlfriends to read his works. We loved to read. They could not find copies of his books. . . . We were so poor. Then I heard Utesov's song "Ten Daughters," and I thought that this was like Sholem Aleichem but in Russian. . . .

I do not quite know why I thought that, but it reminded me of the shtetl and of my poor parents. . . . There was some ending, but I do not remember it. I just liked the Jewish melody at the beginning, and the words broke my heart. It was a very sad song.[117]

Rozaliya's testimony typifies the opinions of many of the respondents. They knew the song, remembered hearing it, but did not recall the lyrics and were confident that the song was a nostalgic look at a Jewish shtetl. Thus, although Utesov's "Jewish songs" all presented a picture of how the traditional Jewish lifestyle was becoming a new Soviet way of life, the public seems to remember the songs as old-fashioned, nostalgic melodramas.

Leonid Utesov's repertoire also included many songs with Ukrainian and Russian folk origins. "Jewish Rhapsody" appeared as part of a series that included Russian and Ukrainian rhapsodies.[118] Utesov brought the idea to his songwriter friend, Isaak Dunaevsky, of composing rhapsodies based on four themes: Russian, Ukrainian, Jewish, and Soviet. The two friends agreed, because "Russian is the basis of Soviet culture, Ukraine is where we [Dunaevsky and Utesov] were born, and Jewish, because it is close to our hearts."[119] Their initial intention was to incorporate Jewish melodies as an integral part of Soviet multinational society. Yet the assimilated Jewish public found in these songs precisely what they were looking for: Jewish melodies with Russian lyrics, Jewish characters, and, most important, a positive portrayal of Jewish culture. This was sufficient to create a popular image of Utesov as a national Jewish singer and Isaak Dunaevsky as a Jewish composer, despite the fact that most of the music the two men created had no Jewish relevance.

Another hit of the late 1930s was the sentimental "Synovia" (Sons). The music and lyrics, respectively, were by Boris Fomin and Ilia Fink. The melody was not tied to any particular Jewish folk song, but the characters in the song had Jewish names. Also, the story told was about the experience of parents when their children grow up and move away, something many Jewish families would relate to. The following are sample verses:

> Yasha—letchik, molodets.
> On letit za granitsu,
> On po poliusu mchitsia,
> Polius blizhe, chem otets.
>
> I esli shum motora v nebe nashem
> Prekrasnym utrom veter prineset,
> Togda byt' mozhet eto syn nash Yasha,
> K rodnomu domu gonit bystryi samolet.
>
> Nalei zhe riumku, Roza, mne s moroza,
> Ved' novyi god vstrechaem my vdvoem.
> Ved' gde eshche naydesh ty, Roza,
> Takikh rebiat, kak nashi synovia?

Yasha is a pilot, a good boy.
He flies in foreign lands,
He goes around the North Pole,
He is closer to the Pole than to his own father.

If the noise of a motor in the sky
Will one day be carried by the wind,
Maybe this is our son, Yasha,
Taking his fast aircraft home.

Pour me a glass, Roza, I was out in the frost,
We are celebrating the New Year, just the two of us.
Where else will you find, Roza,
Such children as our sons?

Although the characters in the song have Jewish names, no reference is made to any specific Jewish experience. The professions depicted in the song are those of a pilot, an engineer, and an actor/singer which are among the most prestigious in Soviet society of the 1930s. The parents, who praise their sons and take pride in their achievements, are celebrating the New Year, and, since the action takes place in winter, the holiday is clearly not Rosh Hashanah, the Jewish New Year, which occurs in the fall. But even though the song was not based on a Jewish melody, and not even performed by a Jewish artist,[120] it spoke directly to the Jewish audience. The nature of the characters, and of course their names, created a special feeling for the song among the Jewish public, and Jews even came to refer to it as "Evreiskaia novogodniaia" (The Jewish New Year song).

An anecdote is illustrative here. On December 19, 1999, I presented a paper in Minneapolis, Minnesota, about Russian Jewish culture to an audience of Russian Jews who were born in the 1920s. To illustrate my points about the use of propaganda in Soviet songs, I played a 1938 recording of "Sons," performed by Klavdiia Shulzhenko, a famous star of the 1930s–1950s. When the song was over, almost the entire audience of three hundred was in tears. I then explained that the images of the successful Jewish sons in the song were created in order to promote the integration of Jews into Soviet society. I added that the characters in the song were depicted as celebrating the January New Year to illustrate the success of Soviet antireligious propaganda among Jews. The tears vanished, and the previous sentimental mood of the audience was replaced by anger. Dozens of people raised their hands to speak. They asserted that the song was genuinely Jewish and not propaganda. One audience member, Mikhail (b. 1910) even stood up to proclaim:

This is who we are, we are Jews born in the Soviet Union. We had very little to be happy about, as all we heard about our Jewishness were the antisemitic comments from neighbors and humiliating remarks from our bosses at work. But this was our pride, our outlet, our life. If you call this

Attendees at the Moscow Jewish Charity Kitchen, June 2001. Photograph by Natan Koifman.

propaganda, then all our lives are propaganda. These are pearls of Jewish culture, and one has to grow up there to understand it!

Mikhail received a standing ovation from the audience.

Indeed, in the decades following World War II, songs like "Sons" retained their popularity. A new recording of "Sons" is even included on a 2001 compact disc by Joseph Kobzon, a well-known contemporary Russian singer of Jewish origin. And in the 1950s other songs that loosely dealt with Jewish themes became popular, at least among Jewish audiences. One such song, "Ballad about a Tailor," describes a man who loses his son during World War II. The only indication that the tailor in the song is Jewish is the use of the word *mestechko* (shtetl), which occurs only once.

Another popular song from this period, "Red and Black," deals with red-haired and dark-haired sons who fought in World War II. The Jewish element of the song is seen simply through the representation of hair color, for, according to Russian stereotypes, Jews are more likely to have red or dark-colored hair. Thus the legacy of Russian songs with Jewish characters remained valid even in the postwar years, when other forms of Russian-language media were no longer sympathetic toward Jews. The ability to recognize "Jewishness" between the lines played an important part in Soviet Jewish identity. Moreover, these official Russian Jewish songs became "anthems" of new Soviet Jewish culture.

Not all Soviet songs that mentioned Jews became popular among Jewish audiences, however. For example, frivolous pieces such as "Sarah" or "The Rabbi's Daughter" never became very popular. This was not only because they were rarely performed publicly, but, perhaps more significant, their content did not fit the Soviet Jewish ideal that saw Jews as educated achievers. Nor did the songs that depicted Jews as exotic speak to the rapidly assimilating Jewish audience that were eager to become full-pledged members of Soviet society. Whereas Yiddish-speaking audiences preferred songs that were distinctly apolitical, Russian-speaking Jews enjoyed Soviet official songs that portrayed Jews in a positive light.

This dichotomy can be explained by the fact that Jews had different expectations from Yiddish and Russian Jewish songs. Yiddish was seen as a vernacular for "insider" information, and thus Yiddish songs could be more frivolous, even vulgar, since only Jews would understand the lyrics. But because Russian-language songs about Jewish culture were understood by non-Jews as well, the Jewish audience instinctively wanted to be seen as advanced, modern, and fully integrated into mainstream society. Thus songs about successful Jewish pilots or engineers enjoyed much greater popularity in Russian than their counterparts did in Yiddish.

Conclusions

The cultural choices made by Jewish audiences took place under the strict control of a totalitarian state. However, even in these circumstances, the Soviet Jewish community was able to maintain two distinct cultures: one Yiddish, the other Russian. Soviet Russian Jewish culture was full of contradictions. The state-sponsored campaign against popular antisemitism, which was intended for non-Jewish audiences, had a profound impact on the cultural identity of Russian-speaking Jews. Movies, brochures, magazines, and theatrical performances portrayed Jews positively in order to fight racial prejudice. Yet the most attentive audience of these works consisted of Jews who were deprived of other ways to openly express their ethnic identity.

The majority of the Soviet Jews born in the early 1920s consider themselves to be "culturally Russian": they adore Russian ballet, theater, classical literature, and even folksongs. On the other hand, they also love the old Yiddish folksongs, read Russian Jewish newspapers, attentively follow the careers of successful Jewish actors and politicians, and take notice of all aspects of antisemitism. Whether they live in New York, Berlin, or Moscow, the majority do not attend a synagogue to partake in religious services but do so simply to meet fellow Jews or to receive financial help. Many never even step foot into a synagogue. In short, Soviet ideology and discourse shaped the identity of these Soviet Jews, but, in the process, there were unintended consequences as people found a source of Jewishness in unexpected places. And this is the Jewish identity that they have passed on to their children and grandchildren, one that continues to shape the Jewish community of modern Russia.

Conclusion

The antireligious propaganda and cultural policies promoted by the Soviet regime in the 1920s and 1930s had a tremendous impact on Jewish religious observance, yet at the same time these programs, in many ways, actually fostered a unique set of Jewish identities. Jews from Yiddish-speaking shtetlach had very little in common with those who lived in the big cities not only because they spoke Yiddish and not Russian but also because of the differences in the information conveyed to them by Soviet cultural productions. World War II and the Holocaust led to the complete destruction of the Yiddish-speaking Jewish community within the Soviet Union. Only one Jewish identity survived the war, that of urban Jews. This identity, which was held by Jews who were largely assimilated and integrated into Soviet society, was a vague one and became the basis for the development of cultural trends among Soviet Jewry during the postwar years. Being deprived of traditional ways to express their ethnic sentiments, Jews developed a specific worldview, one that differed from that of the Soviet non-Jewish citizens as well as from Jews who lived abroad. The phrase "kosher pork" noted in the introduction is not simply intended as a comic phrase to illustrate that Sara F. does not understand Jewish dietary laws. Rather, it is an expression of Soviet Jewish identity that formed during the 1920s and the 1930s in the Soviet Union.

The mixture of Jewish and Soviet, traditional and new, was expressed in a wide range of cultural activities of the Yiddish-speaking population. The Soviet government used cultural programs exclusively for utilitarian purposes. The ideology of official Yiddish mass culture aimed to transform Jews into new Soviet citizens. From a literary point of view, the primary intent of all genres of the Soviet Yiddish mass media and arts was not to mirror reality but instead to paint a picture of a utopian Jewish life in the Soviet Union: stories of the perfect shtetlach inhabited by ideal Jews appeared in the press, and Yiddish skits and songs promoted government policies. Essentially all genres of Soviet Yiddish mass culture taught their audience to see reality through "Soviet glasses" or at least not to notice certain disadvantages or problems. The systems designed to perpetuate the messages fell into several categories.

One common method to defeat ideological enemies, both individuals and their ideas, was across-the-board negation. Maxim Gorky's expression, "Who is not for us, is against us," became proverbial. The origins of an enemy, as well as the reason for his or her hostility to the Soviet regime, did not matter. In the 1920s this meant that Jewish religious activists were considered just as dangerous as White Army officers. That many White Army actions were directed against Jews, and often caused the physical destruction of Jewish communities and rabbis, did not stop the creators of Soviet antireligious carnivals from label-ing White Army generals such as Denikin and Kolchak "rabbis." At the same time famous rabbis such as Yosef Shneerson were even accused of being White Army collaborators who helped to organize pogroms. Later, in the 1920s and early 1930s, when the Soviet regime began campaigns designed to combat the growing Soviet bureaucracy, some Yiddish theatrical performances portrayed Soviet officials as religious Jews, and vice versa, and negative characters often performed parodies of Jewish religious songs (*nigunim*) with lyrics generally critical of the Soviet regime. The message was that "enemies" were masking their antigovernment ideas under the cover of "innocent" religious songs.

An important goal of the propaganda was to emphasize the legitimacy of the Soviet regime, if not legally than at least morally. The arts and literature were used to create the impression that support for the arrival of the Soviet regime dated back to the nineteenth century. The press published stories about the ex-ceptionally difficult living conditions for Jews in tsarist Russia, including the frequent violent pogroms that eventually fostered Jewish participation in the Russian Revolution. New interpretations of literature and historical events were invented, and traditional heroes of the past were replaced by new ones. Impor-tant Jewish works that had been revered for centuries, such as the Holy Scrip-tures, were replaced by the works of modern Yiddish writers such as Sholem Aleichem, Mendele Moykher Sforim, and Yitzhok Leybush Perets, and were studied from the new Soviet perspective. Revolutionary or at least antireligious motifs were highlighted in these works and given disproportionate attention. Of all the heroic characters in Jewish history, Hirsh Lekert, a young revolution-ary from Vilna, was suddenly deemed to be the leading hero in Jewish history, replacing even the figures of Jewish prophets and ancient kings.

The Yiddish language itself was not only the medium through which propa-ganda was directed at Jews but was also a tool to manipulate the ideological message. During korenizatsiia the government promoted the development of Yiddish and even organized Yiddish courts, Yiddish local councils, and Yiddish schools. Creation of a Yiddish mass culture was officially explained by the in-tention to develop a new Soviet Jewish culture based on the language of the Jewish proletariat. But the development and use of Yiddish was not only dis-cussed in theoretical books but was used in plays, popular stories, and songs. Despite official support for everything Soviet, the use of Soviet-created Russian words and bureaucratic terms by Yiddish speakers was not formally encouraged. Only negative Jewish characters in plays and stories mixed Russian Soviet neo-logisms into their Yiddish. Ideal Soviet Jews spoke and wrote purified Yiddish, and not its "Soviet dialect." New Yiddish words, such as *kolvirt* (collective farm) and *komyug* (Komsomol), were invented and encouraged rather than the use of the established Russian Soviet neologisms *kolkhoz* (collective farm) and *Kom-somol*. In fact, Yiddish was the most significant part of the Jewish cultural heri-tage that Jews were officially allowed to retain while converting to Soviet citi-zens. However, the notions associated with being Jewish, such as observing religious holidays and rituals, and attending traditional Jewish primary schools, largely disappeared. Jewish laypersons, persuaded that their traditional religious values should be forgotten, easily recognized that they did not need an additional barrier, such as Yiddish, that would prevent them from becoming full Soviet citizens. Consequently the new Yiddish culture was probably doomed from the day of its creation.

Nevertheless Jews who stopped using Yiddish as their daily language retained their ethnic identity. They expressed their national sentiments by reading anything that mentioned the Jewish question or by watching movies and theater performances that included Jewish characters. The bulk of this material, however, was intended for a Russian-speaking, non-Jewish audience and was designed as a struggle against popular antisemitism. Consequently Russian-speaking Jews were far more exposed to positive information about Jews than were their Yiddish-speaking counterparts.

The results of state-sponsored cultural activities were often unforeseen, both by the Soviet government and by Jews themselves. For example, Jewish activists considered that the establishment of Soviet Yiddish schools was a way to bring political messages to Yiddish-speaking children without necessarily fostering their ethnic identity. Moreover, the Soviets hoped that these Jewish children would, in turn, educate their parents to depart from their traditionally religious ways. However, that Jewish children studied in Yiddish and were taught by Jewish teachers did help them to develop a positive association with their Jewish ethnicity. Children did not see school as an alternative to their parents and eventually did not notice the contradictions between the atheistic curriculum in school and their religious upbringing at home. As a result, the tremendous efforts by the regime to direct Jews away from religion came to naught. Soviet Jews mostly retained respect for tradition and traditional rituals, but, to them, being Jewish no longer meant observing Jewish religious laws or leading a traditional way of life.

Another example of the unforeseen consequences of Soviet policies toward Jews is the popular attitude toward Yiddish theater and songs. The Soviets used them as tools to direct propagandistic messages toward Jews. However, the promotion of certain Yiddish literary classics led to a growing pride in the Jewish cultural heritage. Similarly, Yiddish theater became an expression of Jewish identity. By the 1930s attending the theater had replaced going to the synagogue as a leading manifestation of what it meant to be Jewish in the Soviet Union.

The results of my oral history project shed light on the formation of this Jewish identity and the effectiveness of antireligious propaganda and other Soviet cultural policies. Using oral history enables us to reconstruct the changes in Jewish cultural identity between 1917 and 1941 and to observe the effects of Soviet policies as reflected in the lives of real people. The difference between the various generations that I interviewed is dramatic: those who were born before 1917 have quite different views on Judaism, Yiddish culture, and Jewish history than those born between 1917 and 1928 or after 1929. The older generation, born before the revolution, fondly remembered attending a synagogue, celebrating religious holidays, and studying in Jewish traditional schools. The existence of these Jewish institutions, as well as the observance of Jewish religious laws, constituted their understanding of what it meant to be Jewish. Antireligious propaganda in its various manifestations came as a shock to this generation. Jewish antitraditional and Jewish secular institutions signified a break from Jewish tradition, and were viewed as symbols that were created to transform Jews into atheistic Soviet citizens.

Being Jewish meant something entirely different to the generation born between 1917 and 1928 that grew up in the mid-1920s and 1930s. These people attended Yiddish schools and took part in activities organized at local Yiddish clubs. These Soviet secular institutions represented their Jewish identity in a positive fashion. They grew up in a Soviet Yiddish culture that, in a sense, was the embodiment of the nineteenth-century *Maskilic* ideals, combining Jewish holidays at home with being a Soviet citizen in the street. To be a Jew meant speaking Yiddish, watching Yiddish plays, reading Yiddish newspapers, and attending a Yiddish school; it did not mean being an observant, religious Jew. During the mid-1920s and early 1930s the specifically Soviet "Jewish soul" mentioned by Sara F. came into existence. This was the time when the notions of what it meant to be "kosher" and to be "Jewish" changed radically. This transformation was fundamental and continued for subsequent generations of Soviet Jews. Indeed, these notions have still not changed greatly for Jews now living in the European republics of the former Soviet Union.

The youngest prewar generation, born in the late 1920s and 1930s, went to Russian, Ukrainian, or Byelorussian schools and lost all positive associations with their Jewish identity. This generation usually viewed being Jewish as a misfortune. They equated being Jewish with secret minyans and speaking Yiddish behind closed doors so as not to provoke antisemitism. To be Jewish meant to be persecuted and insulted. However, they also shared many aspects of what it meant to be Jewish with the group born a decade earlier, such as a love for attending plays with Jewish motifs and hearing Yiddish songs. This generation also became the greatest consumers of Russian-language cultural products that portrayed Jews positively, materials that originally were designed to combat antisemitism. This generation did not consider the observance of any religious rituals to be a necessary attribute of being Jewish.

In post-Soviet Russia religious observance is largely supported by the state. The grandchildren of those born in the 1930s are now, once again, a transitional generation. Their parents have socialist upbringings and their own children will grow up in a different, post-Soviet society. Only the future will show how this dramatic sea change from an atheistic Soviet nation to a country filled with many religious and cultural options will fully transpire in the twenty-first century.

Notes

Introduction

1. Sara F., interview by author, Brooklyn, New York, August 1999.

2. Song written by Herman Yablokov. For the published text, see Eleanor Mlotek, *Perl fun yidish lid: 115 yidishe folks arbeter kunst un teater* (New York, 1989), 170.

3. Zvi Gitelman, "Thinking about Being Jewish in Russia and Ukraine," in *Jewish Life after the USSR,* ed. Zvi Gitelman, Musya Glants, and Marshall Goldman (Bloomington, 2003), 49.

4. Valeriy Chervyakov, Zvi Gitelman, and Vladimir Shapiro, "*E Pluribus Unum?* Post-Soviet Jewish Identities and Their Implications for Communal Reconstruction," in Gitelman, Glants, and Goldman, *Jewish Life after the USSR,* 71.

5. Steven M. Cohen and Arnold M. Eisen, *The Jew Within: Self, Family and Community in America* (Bloomington, 2000), 185.

6. Ibid.

7. In 1917 there were about 6 million Jews in Russia. In 1923–24 there were 2,431,000 Jews in Soviet-held territories after new borders had been drawn that removed Poland, the Baltic states, and Bessarabia from the Soviet Union. By 1926 the total had reached 2,680,823. In the 1939 census, 3,020,000 people declared themselves to be Jews (Mordechai Altshuler, *Soviet Jewry on the Eve of the Holocaust* [Jerusalem, 1998], 35).

8. The goals of these Jewish sections included dissemination of Soviet propaganda among Jewish workers, support of the Yiddish language, and efforts to diminish the importance of both Judaism and the Hebrew language. *Evsektsii* were closed in 1930, officially because their task of Sovietizing the Jewish population was considered complete, but in fact because all nationality-specific sections of the Party were shut down at this time. See Zvi Gitelman, *Jewish Nationality and Soviet Politics: The Jewish Sections of the CPSU, 1917–1930* (Princeton, 1972), 121–44.

9. David Shneer, "A Revolution in the Making: Yiddish and the Creating of Soviet Jewish Culture" (Ph.D. diss., University of California, Berkeley, 2001), xxv.

10. Recent scholarship, namely, works by Jeffrey Veidlinger, Gennady Estraikh, Katerina Clark, and David Shneer, argues that these Jewish activists, including some members of the *Evsektsii,* took advantage of Soviet opportunities and intended to build a secular Yiddish culture with a distinct, albeit non-religious, Jewish content. For example, Veidlinger argues that producers, actors, and directors of the Moscow State Yiddish Theater were able to incorporate hidden Zionist and religious messages into their plays (*The Moscow*

State Yiddish Theater: Jewish Culture on the Soviet Stage [Bloomington, 2000], 17–18). Estraikh demonstrates that the government-sponsored cultural and political institutions seriously treated the Yiddish language as a basis for the "new Jewish culture of the Soviet Union" (*Soviet Yiddish: Language Planning and Linguistic Development* [Oxford, 1999]). Clark introduced a useful metaphor, "cultural ecosystem," in which Party leaders created a special climate, and others contributed one way or another to its development and maintenance (*Petersburg: Crucible of Cultural Revolution* [Cambridge, Mass., 1995], ix–x). Similarly Shneer suggests that Soviet Jewish activists were striving for the creation of a Jewish ecosystem with Yiddish as an official language and defining cultural feature ("A Revolution in the Making," 19).

11.   Although Jews did not have a territory of their own (unlike other minorities, such as Poles and Latvians, for example), Lenin acknowledged that Jews had their own language, which meant that they were an "official minority." At the time the government set up agencies to conduct Soviet propaganda among Latvian, Byelorussian, and Polish populations in their native languages (Gitelman, *Jewish Nationality and Soviet Politics*, 105).

12.   Zvi Gitelman, *Century of Ambivalence: The Jews of Russia and the Soviet Union, 1881 to the Present*, 2nd ed. (Bloomington, 2000), 104.

13.   The Yiddish language was even recognized as one of the official languages of Byelorussia (1922–38), four regions of Ukraine (1925–41), and, of course, in Birobidzhan.

14.   H. Kazakevich, "Der ershter alfarbandisher tsuzamenfor fun yidishe kultur-tuers 25.11–2.12 1924," *Di royte velt* 1 (1925): 29.

15.   Gitelman, *Century of Ambivalence*, 89–93.

16.   For more, see Ben Cion Pinchuk, *Shtetl under Soviet Rule: Eastern Poland on the Eve of the Holocaust* (Oxford, 1991).

17.   Shneer, "A Revolution in the Making," 3.

18.   Kazakevich, "Der ershter alfarbandisher," 29.

19.   Ibid., 28–29.

20.   I include only the European Jewish community. "Other" Jews, namely Georgian, Bukharan, and Mountain Jewish communities lived in the Soviet Union during the period reviewed here. However, their culture and Soviet policies toward them were radically different from those of Ashkenazic Jews and deserve a separate study. For an overview history of these communities, see Gitelman, *Jewish Nationality and Soviet Politics*, 196–211.

21.   Nicholas B. Dirks, Geoff Eley, and Sherry Ortner, eds., *Culture/Power/History: A Reader in Contemporary Social Theory* (Princeton, 1994), 5.

22.   Hilary Pilkington, *Russia's Youth and Its Culture: A Nation's Constructors and Constructed* (London, 1994), 22.

23.   Veidlinger, *Moscow State Yiddish Theater*, 79.

24.   See Richard Stites, *Russian Popular Culture* (Cambridge, 1992); Peter Kenez, *The Birth of the Propaganda State: Soviet Methods of Mass Mobilization, 1917–1929* (Cambridge, 1985); James von Geldern, *Bolshevik Festivals, 1917–1920*

(Berkeley, 1993); James von Geldern and Richard Stites, eds., *Mass Culture in Soviet Russia: Tales, Poems, Songs, Movies, Plays, and Folklore, 1917–1953* (Bloomington, 1995); Robert Rothstein, "Popular Song in the NEP Era," in *Russia in the Era of NEP*, ed. Sheila Fitzpatrick, Alexander Rabinowitch, and Richard Stites (Bloomington, 1991), 268–94; Isabel Tirado, *The Village Voice: Women's Views of Themselves and Their World in Russian Chastushki of the 1920s* (Pittsburgh, 1993); Anne Gorsuch, *Youth in Revolutionary Russia: Enthusiasts, Bohemians, Delinquents* (Bloomington, 2000).

For analysis of popular religion, see William Husband, *"Godless Communists": Atheism and Society in Soviet Russia, 1917–1932* (DeKalb, 2000). Glennys Young examined aspects of peasant resistance to antireligious propaganda, and elaborated resistance at the family level. See Glennys Young, *Power and the Sacred in Revolutionary Russia: Religious Activists in the Village* (Pennsylvania, 1997), 89–94. For an overview of the League of Godless activities, see Daniel Peris, *Storming the Heavens: The Soviet League of the Militant Godless* (Ithaca, 1998). On Soviet policies regarding Judaism, see Zvi Gitelman, "Jewish Nationality and Religion," in *Religion and Nationalism in Soviet and East European Politics,* ed. Pedro Ramet (Durham, 1989), 59–80.

Analysis of the Soviet press has led to extensive research on public opinion during the 1930s. For more on this, see Sarah Davies, *Popular Opinion in Stalin's Russia* (Cambridge, 1997), and Jeffrey Brooks, *Thank You, Comrade Stalin: Soviet Public Culture from Revolution to Cold War* (Princeton, 2000). For more on amateur Russian theater, see Lynn Mally, *Revolutionary Acts: Amateur Theater and the Soviet State, 1917–1938* (Ithaca, 2000).

Studies of the popular response to official policies include Sheila Fitzpatrick, *Everyday Stalinism: Ordinary Life in Extraordinary Times: Soviet Russia in the 1930s* (New York, 1999); Davies, *Popular Opinion in Stalin's Russia;* and David Hoffmann, *Peasant Metropolis: Social Identities in Moscow, 1929–1941* (Ithaca, 1994).

25. Stites, *Russian Popular Culture,* 3.

26. For scholarship on the official status of Jewish religion, see Joshua Rothenberg, *The Jewish Religion in the Soviet Union* (New York, 1972); Zvi Gitelman, "Jewish Nationality and Religion in the USSR and Eastern Europe," in Ramet, *Religion and Nationalism in Soviet and East European Politics,* 59–77; and David Fishman, "Preserving Tradition in the Land of Revolution: The Religious Leadership of Soviet Jewry 1917–1930," in *The Uses of Tradition,* ed. Jack Wertheimer (New York, 1992), 85–118.

For more on language policy, see Estraikh, *Soviet Yiddish.*

For more on Soviet Yiddish theater, see Moshe Litvakov, *Finf yor melukhisher yidisher kamer-teater (1919–1924)* (Moscow, 1924); Yosef Sheyn, *Arum moskver yidishn teater* (Paris, [1964?]); Mordechai Altshuler, ed., *ha-Teatron ha-Yehudi bi-Verit ha-Moatsot: mehkarim, iyunim, teudot* (Jerusalem, 1996); and Veidlinger, *Moscow State Yiddish Theater.*

For more on the Soviet Yiddish press, see Shneer, "A Revolution in the Making."

For an overview of Soviet Yiddish literature, see Chone Chmeruk, "Yiddish Literature in the USSR," in *The Jews in Soviet Russia,* ed. Lionel Kochan (London, 1968), 232–68; and Shmuel Niger, *Yidishe shrayber in Sovet-Rusland*

(New York, 1958). For the texts, see Chone Chmeruk, ed., *Shpigl oyf a shteyn: antologye: poezye un proze fun tsvelf farshnitene, Yidishe shraybers in Ratn-Farband* (Jerusalem, 1987).

For more on Russian-language Jewish literature, see Alice Stone Nakhimovsky, *Russian Jewish Literature and Identity* (Baltimore, 1992); Shimon Markish, *Babel' i drugie* (Moscow, 1997); and Efraim Sicher, *Jews in Russian Literature after the October Revolution: Writers and Artists between Hope and Apostasy* (Cambridge, 1995).

For more on education, see Zvi Halevy, *Jewish Schools under Czarism and Communism: A Struggle for Cultural Identity* (New York, 1976); and Elias Schulman, *A History of Jewish Education in the Soviet Union* (New York, 1971).

For more on scholarships, see Avram Greenbaum, *Jewish Scholarship and Scholarly Institutions in Soviet Russia, 1918–1953* (Jerusalem, 1978). For studies of Jewish folklore in the Soviet Union during the period studied, see Mark Kiel, "A Twice Lost Legacy: Ideology, Culture and the Pursuit of Jewish Folklore in Russia until Stalinization, 1930–1931" (Ph.D. diss., Jewish Theological Seminary of America, 1992); and Paul Soifer, *Soviet Jewish Folkloristics and Ethnography: An Institutional History, 1918–1948* (New York, 1978).

The historian David Shneer studies cultural products created by the Soviet Jewish elite, designed for the "masses." See his "Revolution in the Making."

27. Kenez, *The Birth of the Propaganda State,* 3. See also Lynne Viola, *Peasant Rebels under Stalin: Collectivization and the Culture of Peasant Resistance* (New York, 1996); and Sheila Fitzpatrick, *Stalin's Peasants: Resistance and Survival in the Russian Village after Collectivization* (New York, 1994).

28. The Russian State Library contains most, if not all, periodicals and brochures that have been published in the Soviet Union during the 1920s and 1930s. The Yiddish-language materials are kept at the Department of Rarely Requested Literature in the library's branch in the town of Khimki.

Records of the Jewish sections of the Communist Party, or *Evsektsii,* are held in the Russian State Archive for Social and Political Research (Rossiiskii gosudarstvennyi arkhiv sotsial'no-politicheskikh issledovanii [hereafter, RGASPI], f. 445, Evreiskie sektsii Kommunisticheskoi Partii, 1918–30).

The scripts and lectures, as well as additional documents, are in the state archives in Moscow, Kiev, and Minsk, as well as some regional archives. For more on this, see Vasilli Schedrin, ed., *Obzor dokumental'nykh istochnikov po istorii evreev v arkhivakh SNG. Tsentral'nye gosudarstvennye arkhivy. Gosudarstvennye oblastnye arkhivy Rossiiskoi Federatsii* (Moscow, 1994); and Mark Kupovetskii, E. Savitskii, and Marek Web, eds., *Dokumenty po istorii i kul'ture yevreyev v arkhivakh Belarusi: putevoditel'* (Moscow, 2003).

29. Paul Thompson, *The Voice of the Past* (Oxford, 2000), 101–104.

30. For more on the limitations and problems of using oral history, see Anthony Seldon and Joanna Pappworth, *By Word of Mouth: "Elite" Oral History* (London, 1983), 16–32.

31. I conducted this project jointly with Professor Zvi Gitelman (University of Michigan). It was sponsored by the Conference for Material Claims against Germany, and by the University of Michigan and the University of Toronto. Interviews were recorded digitally, in Russian and in Yiddish, and were then

transcribed. All transcriptions are available from the author, on request. By 2007 the interviews will be available from the Frankel Center of Judaic Studies at the University of Michigan, Ann Arbor.

32. As a basis for the structure of the questionnaire, I used the methodological instructions of Paul Thompson, *The Voice of the Past,* 296–307. I also consulted the questionnaire by Zvi Gitelman for the Soviet Jewish Veterans Project at the Frankel Center for Judaic Studies, University of Michigan.

33. The worker correspondents movement was a wide-scale campaign organized by the Soviet government in the early 1920s. Its aim was to encourage workers to write articles and letters to the local and central press.

34. In 1939, 54 percent of Soviet Jews declared Russian to be their mother tongue (Altshuler, *Soviet Jewry on the Eve of the Holocaust,* 95).

1. Antireligious Propaganda and the Transformation of Jewish Institutions and Traditions

1. Lyubov B., interview by author, Berlin, June 2002.

2. Grigorii P., interview by author, Berlin, June 2002.

3. Will Herberg, *Protestant-Catholic-Jew: An Essay in American Religious Sociology* (New York, 1960), 172–210.

4. In the All-Soviet Union Census of 1937, 57 percent of respondents said they believed in God (Mordechai Altshuler, *Soviet Jewry on the Eve of the Holocaust* [Jerusalem, 1998], 100).

5. Robert Conquest, ed., *Religion in the USSR,* Soviet Studies series (London, 1968), 4.

6. David Powell, *Antireligious Propaganda in the Soviet Union: A Study of Mass Persuasion* (Cambridge, 1975), 34.

7. Philip Walters, "A Survey of Soviet Religious Policy," in *Religious Policy in the Soviet Union,* ed. Sabrina Ramet (Cambridge, 1993), 13.

8. Zvi Gitelman, *Century of Ambivalence: The Jews of Russia and the Soviet Union, 1881 to the Present,* 2nd ed. (Bloomington, 2000), 93.

9. Nicholas Timasheff, *Religion in Soviet Russia, 1917–1942* (London, 1944), 39.

10. Ibid., 40.

11. Walters, "A Survey of Soviet Religious Policy," 14.

12. Timasheff, *Religion in Soviet Russia,* 49.

13. Zvi Gitelman, "Jewish Nationality and Religion in the USSR and Eastern Europe," in *Religion and Nationalism in Soviet and East European Politics,* ed. Pedro Ramet (Durham, 1989), 59.

14. Igor Krupnik, "Soviet Cultural and Ethnic Policies toward the Jews: A Legacy Reassessed," in *Jews and Jewish Life in Russia and the Soviet Union,* ed. Yaacov Ro'i (London, 1995), 67–86.

15. Joshua Rothenberg, *The Jewish Religion in the Soviet Union* (New York, 1972), 100–109.

16. Joshua Rothenberg, "Jewish Religion in the Soviet Union," in *The Jews in Soviet Russia since 1917,* ed. Lionel Kochan (London, 1970), 165–66.

17. Ibid.

18. Calculations were based on Yoseph Cohen, *Pirsumim Yekhudim bivrit haMoatzot, 1917–1960* (Jewish publications in the Soviet Union, 1917–1960) (Jerusalem, 1961).

19. Peysi Altshuler and Nodel Khatskl, *Gekasherte neshomes (Vegn kheyder)* (Kharkov, 1922). See also L. Abram, I. Khinchin, and K. Kaplan, eds., *Der mishpet ibern kheyder* (Vitebsk, 1922).

20. Abram, Khinchin, and Kaplan, *Der mishpet,* 11.

21. Ibid., 12.

22. Ibid., 11.

23. Ibid., 12.

24. Hillel Lurye, *Shabes: Vos men zogt vegn im un fun vanen er hot zikh in der emesn genumen* (Odessa, 1922); and idem, *Toyre: ir antviklung, vi un ven iz geshafn gevorn. Vos meynt vegn dem di traditsye un vegn dem di visnshaft* (Kharkov, 1922).

25. Lurye, *Toyre: ir antviklung,* 3–6.

26. *Vos yeder krigirisher apikoyres darf visn* (Kharkov, 1929), 4–5.

27. Some examples are *Anti-religyeze lernbukh* (Moscow, 1929); *Bloknot fun agitator: kegn di religyeze yontovim* (Minsk, 1933); L. Goldin, *Di yidishe yontovim* (Kharkov, 1929); M. Verite, *Mir—krigirishe apikorsim* (Kharkov, 1932); L. Khaytov, *Der vilder minheg mile* (Kharkov, 1930); and *Der klerikalizm in kamf kegn arbeteres bavegung* (Moscow, 1936).

28. This happened in Homel, Byelorussia, in 1921 (see Mordechai Altshuler, "The Rabbi of Homel's Trial in 1922," *Michael* 6 [1980]: 9–18); Vitebsk in 1922 (see Zvi Gitelman, *Jewish Nationality and Soviet Politics: The Jewish Sections of the CPSU, 1917–1930* [Princeton, 1972], 310–11); St. Petersburg in 1937 (see Mikhail Beizer, *Evrei Leningrada, 1917–1939. Natsional'naia zhizn' i sovetizatsiia* [Moscow-Jerusalem, 1999], 217–23).

29. For more on what happened to synagogues in the Soviet Union during the 1930s, see A. Gershuni, *Yahadut mi-Baad le-Soreg u-veRiah* (Jerusalem, 1978). See also Rothenberg, *The Jewish Religion in the Soviet Union,* 39–66.

30. Bernard Weinryb, "Anti-Semitism in Soviet Russia," in Kochan, *The Jews in Soviet Russia,* 301.

31. See, for example, Vladimir Tan-Bogoraz, ed., *Evreiskoe mestechko v revoliutsii* (Moscow, 1926), 203.

32. See for example, M. Shteyn, "Koloniya Novozlatopol," in *Evreiskoe mestechko v revoliutsii,* ed. Tan-Bogoraz, 140–141.

33. David Fishman, "Judaism in the USSR, 1917–1930: The Fate of Religious Education," in *Jews and Jewish Life in Russia and the Soviet Union,* ed. Yaacov Ro'i (Essex, 1995), 251–62.

34. Beizer, *Evrei Leningrada,* 230–33.

35. *Minkhe* is the Jewish afternoon prayer and *mayrev* the evening prayer.

36. Ian D., interview by author, Brooklyn, New York, February 1999. This testimony seems trustworthy. Even though some facts are omitted and some dates confused, the testimony serves as a vivid portrayal of how the respondent understood and digested the synagogue's closing, and how he wanted to present the story to the interviewer.

37. Powell, *Antireligious Propaganda in the Soviet Union*, 15.

38. Gitelman, *Jewish Nationality and Soviet Politics*, 306. Sometimes rabbis did offer interpretations of the Soviet regime in the context of Judaism. For example, one rabbi in a Berdichev synagogue drew a parallel between Moses, Karl Marx, and Lenin, arguing that all three were struggling to bring peace to Jews (*Otchet o deiatel'nosti Evsektsii v Berdicheve za 1923 god* [Report on the activities of the Jewish sections, 1923], RGASPI, f. 445, d. 8, l. 65). See also Gitelman, *Jewish Nationality and Soviet Politics*, 302–303.

39. Sara Fr., interview by author, Brooklyn, New York, March 1999.

40. Viktor Kh., interview by author, Brooklyn, New York, August 1999.

41. Manya L., interview by author, Detroit, December 2000.

42. For more on this, see Rothenberg, "Jewish Religion in the Soviet Union," 162.

43. Gitelman, *Jewish Nationality and Soviet Politics*, 272.

44. Fishman, "Judaism in the USSR, 1917–1930," 252.

45. Ibid.

46. Ibid., 255–56.

47. Fira T., interview by author, Brooklyn New York, April 1999.

48. I recorded about sixty testimonies of people who simultaneously attended both kheyder and a Soviet school.

49. Ian D., interview by author, Brooklyn, New York, February 1999.

50. Ida V., interview by author, Philadelphia, November 2001.

51. Rothenberg, "Jewish Religion in the Soviet Union," 341.

52. Gitelman, *Jewish Nationality and Soviet Politics*, 337.

53. The original Yiddish pronunciation of the respondent has been kept intact.

54. Semyon S., interview by author, Brooklyn, New York, August 1999.

55. Semyon K., interview by author, Brooklyn, New York, March 1999.

56. Gitelman, *Jewish Nationality and Soviet Politics*, 338–40.

57. Elias Schulman, *A History of Jewish Education in the Soviet Union* (New York, 1971).

58. Tsirl B., interview by author, Brooklyn, New York, June 1999.

59. For more about new rituals, see Richard Stites, "Bolshevik Ritual Building in the 1920s," in *Russia in the Era of NEP: Explorations in Soviet Society and Culture*, ed. Sheila Fitzpatrick, Alexander Rabinowitch, and Richard Stites (Bloomington, 1991), 297–98.

60. Timasheff, *Religion in Soviet Russia*, 35.

61. Hillel Lurye, *Yom Kippur* (Kharkov, 1923).

62. *Der apikoyres* (fall 1923).

63. Ibid., 2.

64. *Ani maamin* are the thirteen principles of the Jewish faith. These are that (1) the Creator creates and controls everything; (2) there is only one God, and all Creation is unified with Him; (3) God is not a physical being; (4) God is without beginning or end, and precedes all existence; (5) it is proper to pray only to the Creator; (6) God communicates through his Prophets; (7) the prophecy of Moses, greatest of all Prophets, is true; (8) the entire Torah was given to Moses; (9) this Torah will never be changed; (10) the Creator is aware of all of man's deeds and thoughts; (11) we are rewarded for obeying the commandments and punished for disobeying; (12) although he may tarry, the coming of the Messiah is eagerly awaited each day; and (13) the dead will be resurrected.

65. P. Lafarg, "Der kapitalistisher ani maamin," *Der apikoyres* (fall 1923): 9.

66. Philip Birnbaum, *Daily Prayer Book* (New York, 1977), 154.

67. *Der apikoyres* (fall 1923): 9.

68. Ibid.

69. Ibid.

70. Maks Goldin, ed., *Evreiskaia narodnaia pesnia* (St. Petersburg, 1994), 121.

71. All translations are mine unless otherwise stated.

72. *Der apikoyres* (fall 1923): 21–22.

73. GARF, *Otchet evsektsii Gomel'skoi oblasti za sentiabr'-dekabr' 1923 goda* (Report of the Jewish Sections of Gomel for September–December 1923), f. 2313, op. 123, d. 8, l. 10.

74. Similar anti–Yom Kippur ceremonies were conducted three decades earlier in London by Jewish anarchists, who created Yom Kippur balls. At these events Jews were encouraged to say the *Kol Nidre* (the starting prayer of the Yom Kippur service) in the Berners Street Club (William Fishman, *East End Jewish Radicals, 1875–1914* [London, 1995], 211). Similar ceremonies were conducted at the time in New York, Chicago, Montreal, and other North American cities.

75. Yakov M., interview by author, Brooklyn, New York, March 1999.

76. This calculation is based on a survey of the activities of the Evsektsii of the Communist Party recorded in RGASPI, f. 445 (Jewish Sections of the Communist Party, 1918–30).

77. Edward Portnoy, "Interwar Parodies of the Passover Haggadah," paper presented at the Thirty-first Annual Conference of the Association for Jewish Studies, Chicago, December 19–21, 1999.

78. Moyshe Altshuler, *Hagode far gloybers un apikorsim* (Moscow, 1923). See reprint in *Pen* 35 (1998): 67–80. Quotations are from the original publication. The circulation of the first edition was six thousand copies; the circulation of the second edition, published in 1927, was six thousand.

79. The first edition of the *Komsomolishe Haggadah* says: "Five years before the

first Komsomol Passover." The phrase "ten years ago" refers to the October Revolution of 1917 and is taken from the second edition, which was published in 1927.

80. The first edition *Di komsomolishe* adds that all other *shlim-mazls* (losers) and parasites should be burned in the flame of revolution.

81. GPU is the acronym for *Gosudarstvennoe politicheskoe upravlenie,* or State Political Administration (secret police). The entire sentence refers to a customary saying that is pronounced when one burns *khometz* before Passover: "Any *khometz,* or leaven, that is in my possession that I have not seen, have not removed, and do not know about should be annulled and become ownerless, like dust of the earth." The particular expression rephrases the saying by identifying *khometz* with the representatives of ideologically hostile political parties.

82. Altshuler, *Hagode far gloybers un apikorsim,* 5.

83. Ibid., 7.

84. Tan-Bogoraz, *Evreyskoe mestechko v revoliutsii,* 81; quoted in Avraham Yarmolinsky, *The Jews and Other Minor Nationalities under the Soviets* (New York, 1928), 119.

85. Tan-Bogoraz, *Evreyskoe mestechko v revoliutsii,* 81.

86. This refers to one of the miracles described in the Passover Haggadah. When Jews were escaping from Egypt, the sea divided and they were able to travel through it. When the Egyptians followed them, the sea became one again and swallowed the Egyptians.

   The battle near Perekop was the last battle of the civil war (November 7, 1920), which led to the complete destruction of the White Army and victory for the Bolshevik Red Army.

87. *Der apikoyres* (April 15, 1929): 4.

88. Ibid., 5.

89. I. Veytsblit, "Daryevke. A pruv fun monografishe bashraybung fun shtetl," *Di royte velt,* nos. 7–12 (1928).

90. Ibid., no. 12 (1928): 75–77.

91. GARF, *Otchet evsektsii Gomel'skoi oblasti za ianvar'-mart 1924 goda* (Report of the Jewish Sections of Gomel, January–March 1924), f. 2313, op. 123, d. 9, l. 6.

92. See also Boris Goldenberg, "Der yidisher klerikalizm un der antireligyezer kultur marsh," *Di royte velt* 7 (1929): 97–105; S. Lvov, "Dos kontrrevolyutsionere ponim fun yidishn klerikalizm," *Der shtern* 273 (1939): 2; M. Sheyngold, "In ongrif kegn der religye," *Ratnbildung* 3 (1929): 18–23; and B. Melamed, "Di antireligyeze derfarung in arbeter shul," *Ratnbildung* 2 (1929): 22–29.

93. Sh. Gutyansky and Sh. Bryansky, "Vi batsien zikh etlekhe kinder tsu peysakh," *Ratnbildung* 4 (1930): 52–63; and K. Khadoshevich, "Afn antireligyezn front," *Shtern* 8–9 (1928): 76–137.

94. Khadoshevich, "Afn anti-religyezn front," 76–137.

95. Ibid., 77.

96. Gutyanskii and Bryansky, "Vi batsien zikh etlekhe kinder tsu peysakh," 59.

97. Ibid.

98. Ibid., 136.

99. Ibid., 59–60.

100. Efim G., interview by author, Brooklyn, New York, February 1999.

101. Velvl K., interview by author, Brooklyn, New York, February 1999.

102. Etya G., interview by author, Brooklyn, New York, February 1999.

103. *Simkhes Toyre* (Simhat Torah) literally means rejoicing in the Torah, and is celebrated on 23 Tishrei. The celebration usually involves reading from the Torah, singing, and dancing with the Torah scrolls. Children are generally given decorative flags or miniature scrolls, and they, too, follow the torah scrolls in the processions.

104. Ian D., interview by author, Brooklyn, New York, February 1999.

105. Ibid.

106. Philip G., interview by author, Brooklyn, New York, February 1999.

107. Thus the idea of the nineteenth-century Jewish enlighteners (*maskilim*) became a reality under the Soviets. This idea is associated with Yehuda Leyb Gordon (1830–1892), a *maskilic* thinker and poet. His phrase "Heyeh Yehudi be'oholecha, uven adam betsaytecha" (Be a Jew at home, a human being in the street) was central to the nineteenth-century Hebrew enlightenment movement.

108. Samuil G., interview by author, Brooklyn, New York, May 1999.

109. Efim G., interview by author, Brooklyn, New York, January 1999.

110. Yurii B., interview by author, Brooklyn, New York, March 1999.

111. The word *Paskha* in Russian means both Easter and Passover. In the case of Passover, it is customary to say *Evreyskaya Paskha* (Jewish Easter).

112. Galina K., interview by author, Bronx, New York, June 1999.

113. William Husband, *"Godless Communists": Atheism and Society in Soviet Russia, 1917–1932* (DeKalb, 2000), 6.

114. For more on nuances in popular religion in Russia, see Moshe Lewin, "Popular Religion in Twentieth-Century Russia," in *The World of Russian Peasant: Post-Emancipation Culture and Society,* ed. Ben Eklof and Stephen Frank (Boston, 1990), 155–69; and especially William Husband, *"Godless Communists."*

115. David Fishman, "Preserving Tradition in the Land of Revolution: The Religious Leadership of Soviet Jewry, 1917–1930," in *The Uses of Tradition: Jewish Continuity in the Modern Era,* ed. Jack Wertheimer (New York, 1992), 86.

2. From Illiteracy to Worker Correspondents

1. Fira S., interview by author, Moscow, June 2001.

2. For the most recent study of Yiddish printed culture of early Soviet Russia, see David Shneer, *Yiddish and the Creation of Soviet Jewish Culture* (New York, 2004).

3. David Shneer, "A Revolution in the Making: Yiddish and the Creating of Soviet Jewish Culture" (Ph.D. diss., University of California, Berkeley, 2001), xxiii.

4. *Doklad tovarischa Gildina na Vseukrainskom s"ezde proletarskikh pisatelei* (Report by Comrade Gildin at the All-Ukrainian Congress of Proletarian Writers), RGASPI, f. 445, op. 1, d. 172, l. 34.

5. Jeffrey Brooks, *When Russia Learned to Read: Literacy and Popular Literature, 1861–1917* (Princeton, N.J., 1985), 304.

6. Steven Lovell, *The Russian Reading Revolution: Print Culture in the Soviet and Post-Soviet Eras* (New York, 2000), 11.

7. Solomon Schwartz, *The Jews in the Soviet Union* (Syracuse, 1951), 13.

8. Zvi Gitelman, *Jewish Nationality and Soviet Politics: Jewish Sections of the CPSU 1917–1930* (Princeton, N.J., 1972), 24.

9. Mordechai Altshuler, *Soviet Jewry on the Eve of the Holocaust: A Social and Demographic Profile* (Jerusalem, 1998), 104.

10. *Resolutsii zasedaniia Vserossiiskoi gosudarstvennoi komissii likvidatsii bezgramotnosti na 1921 god. Sektsiia Natsmen'shinstv* (Resolutions from the meeting of the All-Russian State Commission on the eradication of illiteracy in 1921. Section of National Minorities), GARF, f. 2314, op. 6, d. 6, ll. 1–3.

11. "Instruktsiya o likvidatsii negramotnosti sredi natsional'nykh men'shinstv na territorii RSFSR, 27 marta 1920 g." in *Kul'turnoe stroitel'stvo v RSFSR 1917–1927gg.* (Moscow, 1983), 216–18.

12. *Otchet Evsektsii pri Donskom Gubnarobraze* (Report of the Jewish Sections at the Don Ministry of Education), 1921, RGASPI, f. 445, op. 1, d. 68, l. 197.

13. *Otchet Evsektsii pri Severo-Novgorodskom Gubnarobraze za 1923 god* (Report of the Jewish Sections at the Severo-Novgorod Ministry of Education for 1923), RGASPI, f. 445, op. 1, d. 68, l. 21.

14. This happened, for example, in the Byelorussian shtetl of Parichi. According to Efim G., his father went to the Russian *likbez* (literacy courses) because he already knew some Yiddish. His mother attended similar courses in Yiddish, because she was completely illiterate and spoke no Russian at all. Efim G., interview by author. New York, February 1999.

15. *Vypiska iz protokola Glavbiuro ot 14/12–21* (Extract from the minutes of the meeting of the headquarters, December 14, 1921) RGASPI, f. 445, op. 1, d. 43, l. 1.

16. *Vypiska iz protokola zasedaniia Evsektsii Kharkovskogo biuro, 13/05–1924* (Extract from the minutes of the meeting of the Kharkov Jewish Sections, May 13, 1924), RGASPI, f. 445, op. 1, d. 68, l. 192.

17. *Otchet o likvidatsii negramotnosti sredi evreiskogo naseleniia v Vitebskom raione, ianvar' 1921* (Report on the eradication of illiteracy in the Vitebsk Region, January 1921), GARF, f. 2314, op. 6, d. 16, l. 26.

18. *Rezolutsiia ob izpol'zovanii zhurnala Iungvald, 27/X-1924* (Resolution about the use of the magazine *Yungvald*, October 27, 1924), RGASPI, f. 445, op. 1, d. 121, l. 75.

19. Noyakh Lurie, "Porits—volf," *Pioner* 1 (1926): 6.

20. Hershl Shub, "Dodke der leninets," *Pioner* 3 (1926): 1–6.

21. Ester Frumkin (Malkah Frumkin) (1880–1943) was an important ideologue who was active in the Jewish Sections of the Communist Party (previously a prominent Bundist leader). She translated Lenin's works into Yiddish, edited *Der emes,* and wrote extensively about the role of women in Communist society. She was arrested in 1938 and died in a Stalinist camp in Karaganda.

22. Nikolai Ivanovich Bukharin (1888–1938) was a Russian Communist leader and theoretician. He was the editor of the Soviet newspaper *Pravda.* In 1924 he was made a full member of the Politburo. Bukharin was an advocate for slow agricultural collectivization and industrialization (the position of the so-called right opposition). In 1929 he was defeated by the Stalinist majority in the party. He wrote and translated many works on economics and political science. His works have received greater attention and a larger readership in the late twentieth century.

23. P. Birman, "A mayse mit Shmerlen, velkher ruft zikh Zhak, un a komyugistke Rivechke Faynbak," *Yungvald* 2 (1925): 20.

24. L. Zelik, "In undzer otryad," *Yunger arbeter* 5 (1927): 16.

25. M. Beker, "Di lebedike tsaytung baym klub roze liuksemburg," *Der odeser arbeter* 5 (1927): 11.

26. B. Shlosberg, "Nadn, piesn, piter far beheymes," *Der odeser arbeter* 18 (1928): 4–5.

27. E. Metschinski, "Vi azoy darf a pioner aynteyln zayn tog," *Pioner* 9 (1925): 18.

28. "Vi azoy darf men leyenen a bikhl," *Oys ameratses!* (April 1927): 11.

29. For more on Russian peasants' difficulties in understanding the vocabulary in newspapers, see Regine Robin, "Popular Literature of the 1920s: Russian Peasants as Readers," in *Russia in the Era of NEP: Explorations in Soviet Society and Culture,* ed. Sheila Fitzpatrick, Alexander Rabinowitch, and Richard Stites (Bloomington, 1991), 256–58.

30. I. Veytsblit, "Daryevke," *Di royte velt* 10 (1928): 111.

31. Robin, "Popular Literature of the 1920s," 263.

32. Peter Kenez, *The Birth of the Propaganda State: Soviet Methods of Mass Mobilization, 1917–1929* (Cambridge, 1985), 233.

33. V. N. Alferov, *Vozniknovenie i razvitie rabsel'korovskogo dvizheniia v SSSR* (Moscow, 1970), 103–15.

34. Gennady Estraikh, *Soviet Yiddish: Language Planning and Linguistic Development* (Oxford, 1999), 57.

35. N. Natanzon, *Kolektivizatsie un kultur-arbet in yidishn dorf* (Moscow, 1931), 31–32.

36. Estraikh, *Soviet Yiddish,* 64.

37. David Raytnbarg, "Vegn pedkorn," *Af di vegn tsu der nayer shul* 2 (1924): 64.

38. V. Markin, "Kolektivchikes," *Der odeser arbeter* 14 (1928): 10–12.

39. Riva Gvirtsman, "Vi azoy ikh hob ufgehert gloybn in got," *Der apikoyres* 1 (1930): 5.

40. Ibid., 7.

41. Sholem Zelikson, "Di kheyder-yinglekh kumen af der farzamlung," *Pioner* 6 (1928): 22.

42. "Fun der redaktsye," *Pioner* 6 (1928): 22.

43. Ibid.

44. Oyzer Klotsman, "In undzer *shtetl*," *Pioner* 1 (1927): 20.

45. Eyner, "Afn nayem front," *Arbeter korespondent* (Moscow, 1924): 6.

46. "Vegn vos shraybn undz," *Der apikoyres* 1 (1931): 14.

47. "Der alukrainisher baratung fun der arbkomprese," *Arbdorfkor* (Kharkov, 1933), 3.

48. Sheila Fitzpatrick, *Stalin's Peasants: Resistance and Survival in the Russian Village after Collectivization* (New York, 1994), 262.

49. L. G., "Aroys mit der makht fun klerikaln," *Kremenchuger arbeter* 12 (1932): 3.

50. Sofa G., interview by author, New York City, February 1999.

51. Many respondents used the term "golden night" to describe actions by local activists who came to their homes to search for gold, usually during the nights of the mid-1920s. Gold was taken "for the needs of the state" (similar to confiscating the golden cupolas of Russian Orthodox Churches).

52. Saul M., interview by author, Brooklyn, New York, May 1999.

53. M. Ayzenshtadt, *Masn-arbet in leyenshtibl* (Moscow, 1929), 8.

54. Ibid., 190.

55. Ibid., 191.

56. Poyley Tsien (Poalei Zion) is a political movement that combined Zionism and socialism. It functioned in Russia throughout the early 1920s.

57. Khaults (He-Halutz), literally "Pioneer," is an association of Jewish youth whose aim was to prepare its members to settle in the land of Israel. It operated in Russia during 1917–28.

58. Turkin, Rokhlin, Ruderman, "Undzer kemerl, Bykovo, Molever rayon" *Yungvald* 3 (1927): 22.

59. Veytsblit, "Daryevke," 111.

60. I. Pul'ner, "Iz zhizni goroda Gomelya," in *Evreyskoe mestechko v revoliutsii,* ed. Vladimir Tan-Bogoraz (Moscow, 1926), 174.

61. Sonya G., interview by author, Brooklyn, New York, March 1999. Segments published in Anna Shternshis, "Soviet and Kosher in the Ukrainian *Shtetl*," in *The Shtetl: Image and Reality,* ed. Gennady Estraikh and Mikhail Krutikov (Oxford, 2000), 148.

62. Philip G., interview by author, Brooklyn, New York, February 1999.

63. Ian D., interview by author, Brooklyn, New York, April 1999.

64. Ian T., interview by author, New York, March 1999.

65. Veytsblit, "Daryevke," 112.

66. Pul'ner, "Iz zhizni goroda Gomelia," 174.

67. He is probably referring to Yekhezkel Dobrushin, Iosif Rabin, and Lev Godlberg, *Deklamator fun der yidisher sovetisher literatur* (Moscow, 1934).

68. Ian D., interview by author, Brooklyn, New York, February 1999.

69. Grigorii B., interview by author, New York, April 1999.

70. L. Rosenblum, "Der kleyner pioner," *Pioner* 1 (1926): 18.

71. In 1928 guidelines for writers were included in an editorial in the Yiddish literary journal *Prolit* (Proletarian literature) that defined "true proletarian literature" as "prose that depicts the revolution, the civil war, and the development of socialist society. It should portray a worker, not a coachman [*balegule*] as the main character" ("Undzere oyfgabn," *Prolit* 1 [1928]: 3–5).

72. This novel, by the French writer Emile Zola, is known by the title *Germinal*.

73. Efim G., interview by author, Brooklyn, New York, February 1999.

74. Ioan K., interview by author, Berlin, June 2002.

3. Amateur Local Yiddish Theaters

1. Mila and Moisei Sh., interview by author, Brooklyn, New York, April 1999.

2. Jeffrey Veidlinger, "Let's Perform a Miracle: The Soviet Yiddish State Theater in the 1920s," *Slavic Review* 57, no. 2 (summer 1998): 374.

3. Habimah, a highly regarded Hebrew theater, was established in Russia in 1917. It functioned until 1926, during a period when almost all other Hebrew bodies were abolished. Habimah featured three hundred performances in the Soviet Union alone and was praised by leaders of Soviet Russian culture like Maxim Gorky, Fedor Shaliapin, and Konstantin Stanislavsky, and by the political figures Anatolii Lunacharsky and Lev Kamenev. The Habimah actors troupe left the Soviet Union in January 1926 for a tour of Europe and the United States, and never came back. It became the national theater of Yishuv in Palestine and later in Israel. For more on the history of the Habimah, see Jehoshua Gilboa, *A Language Silenced: The Suppression of Hebrew Literature and Culture in the Soviet Union* (Rutherford, N.J., 1982).

4. Jeffrey Veidlinger, *The Moscow State Yiddish Theater: Jewish Culture on the Soviet Stage* (Bloomington, 2000), 90.

5. For a full history of the Moscow Yiddish Theater, an analysis of its repertoire, theater personalities, and its role in Soviet Jewish culture, see Veidlinger, *Moscow State Yiddish Theater*.

6. Zvi Gitelman, *Century of Ambivalence: The Jews of Russia and the Soviet Union, 1881 to the Present*, 2nd ed. (Bloomington, 2000), 114.

7. Veidlinger, *Moscow State Yiddish Theater*, 57.

8. There is no published research on Kultur lige. Kenneth Moss has made the first attempts to analyze its work and impact on Jewish shtetl life of 1917–20. See Kenneth Moss, "Tarbut/Kultur/Kultura in a Revolutionary Key: Rethinking and Remaking 'Modern Jewish Culture' in Russia and Ukraine, 1917–19,"

paper presented at the annual meeting of the Association of Jewish Studies, Los Angeles, December 17, 2002.

9. *Polozhenie o blizhaishikh zadachakh politichesko-prosvetitelskoi raboty RKSM sredi evreiskoi trudiashcheisia molodezhi* (Statement on the immediate tasks of political and educational work of the Russian Communist Youth League among Jewish working youth), RGASPI, f. 445, op. 1, d. 16, l. 44.

10. *Informatsionnie svedeniia o deiatelnosti evsektsii v razlichnykh chastiakh za 1923 god* (Information on the activities of Jewish sections in a number of regions in 1923), RGASPI, f. 445, d. 169.

11. *Otchet o rabote evsektsii za 1920–1921 god* (Report on the work of the Jewish sections for 1920–21), RGASPI, f. 445, d. 68, l. 94.

12. Shlomo Rubin, "Der yidisher teater," in *Yisker bukh fun Rokisis, Lite,* ed. M. Bakalczuk-Felin (Johannesburg, 1952), 261.

13. *Otchet evsektsii Belorussii za fevral' 1922 goda* (Report of the Jewish Sections of Byelorussia for February 1922), RGASPI, f. 445, d. 120, l. 53.

14. *Otchet Novgorod Severskoi Evsektsii* (Report of the Jewish sections of Novgorod Severskii), RGASPI, f. 445, d. 68, l. 196.

15. M. Kruglyak, "Dramkrayz in shtetl," *Ratnbildung* 6 (1929): 35.

16. Lynn Mally, *Revolutionary Acts: Amateur Theater, and the Soviet State, 1917–1938* (Ithaca, 2000), 6.

17. Philip G., interview by author, Brooklyn, New York, February 1999.

18. Veidlinger, *Moscow State Yiddish Theater,* 207.

19. Ibid.

20. This is actually a play by Avrom Goldfaden.

21. Sonya G., interview by author, Brooklyn, New York, March 1999.

22. "Iz zolotogo fonda radio" (O Solomone Mikhailoviche Mikhoelse). From the All-Russian radio archive. The song "Shimele Soroker" was performed by Solomon Mikhoels, the director of, and actor in, the Moscow Yiddish Theater.

23. Iona K., interview by author, Berlin, June 2002.

24. Faina D., interview by author, Bronx, New York, August 1999.

25. Semyon Sh., interview by author, Brooklyn, New York, August 1999.

26. Sonya G., interview by author, Brooklyn, New York, March 1999.

27. I recorded about fifteen interviews with people who took part in antireligious plays when they were students in Soviet Yiddish schools, even though their fathers were rabbis and ritual slaughterers. All these respondents reported that their parents, despite their traditional Jewish backgrounds, attended these amateur productions to see their children perform.

28. For a description of living newspapers on the Russian stage, see Richard Stourac and Kathleen McCreery, *Theatre as a Weapon: Worker's Theater in the Soviet Union, Germany, and Britain, 1917–1934* (London, 1986); and Peter Kenez, *The Birth of the Propaganda State: Soviet Methods of Mass Mobilization, 1917–1929* (Cambridge, 1985).

29. *Otchet o deiatel'nosti evsektsii Minska za 1920/21 gg.* (Report on the activity of the Jewish sections of Minsk for 1920/21), RGASPI, f. 445, d. 37, l. 108.

30. *Otchet o deiatel'nosti smolenskogo otdela evsektsii za 1920 god* (Report on the activity of the Smolensk Department of the Jewish sections for 1920), RGASPI, f. 445, d. 130, l. 169.

31. *Otchet o deiatel'nosti evsektsii Belorussii za vesnu 1923 goda* (Report on the activity of the Jewish sections of Byelorussia for the spring of 1923), RGASPI, f. 445, d. 118, l. 36.

32. Semyon R., interview by author, Moscow, June 2001.

33. M. Rubinshteyn, *Dramkrayz* (Moscow, 1928), 95–96.

34. A. Aris, "A yor arbet fun yugt drankrayz baym kharkover klub dritn internatsional," *Di royte velt* 5 (1925): 47.

35. *Pioner* 3 (1927): 15.

36. Etya G., interview by author, Brooklyn, New York, March 1999.

37. Aris, "A yor arbet fun yugt drankrayz baym kharkover klub dritn internatsional," 43–47.

38. Mally, *Revolutionary Acts,* 83.

39. These calculations are based on the bibliography by Yoseph Cohen, *Pirsumim Yekhudim bivrit haMoatzot, 1917–1960* (Jewish publications in the Soviet Union, 1917–1960) (Jerusalem, 1961), and the catalogue of the Russian State Library, Moscow.

40. The term "kulak" (literally, "fist" in Russian) is Soviet jargon for a rich peasant.

41. Cited in Abraham Vevyorke, *In midber,* in *Oys religye! Zamlung fun literatur, material tsum oysfirn af antireligyeze ovntn,* ed. Shmuel Godiner and Abraham Vevyorke (Moscow, 1929), 39–53.

42. Ibid., 43–44.

43. The author recommended using the melody of the popular Yiddish folksong *Ikh bin a balegule* (I am a horse cabby).

44. Mary Douglas, "Jokes" (1975), reproduced in *Rethinking Popular Culture: Contemporary Perspectives in Cultural Studies,* ed. Chandra Mukerji and Michael Schudson (Berkeley, 1991), 295.

45. For more of this type of play, see *Apikoyres zamlung* (Bobruysk, 1928); *Moskover apikoyres* (Moscow, 1931); *Di programen far dem kolvirtishn apikorsishn krayz* (Moscow, 1933); *Oys religye* (Moscow, 1929); Yekhezkel Dobrushin, *Far bine* (Moscow, 1929); B. Orshansky, *Teatr* (Moscow, 1931); Yekhezkel Dobrushin, *Der kolvirtisher teater* (Moscow, 1932); and Yekhezkel Dobrushin, *Der gerikht geyt* (Moscow, 1929).

46. Yekhezkel Dobrushin, "Mitn ponem tsum khazer," in *Der kolvirtisher teater* (Moscow, 1925), 4.

47. I. I. Yaffe, "Fun Haslovich kin Kherson," *Yungvald* 8 (1926): 14.

48. *Yevsek* is an abbreviation for a member of the Jewish sections.

49. Isaac Verite, "Fun yener velt," *Yungvald* 11–12 (1925): 25.

50.   Ibid.

51.   Ibid.

52.   Ibid., 24.

53.   Some words are not conjugated or declined properly and nouns are accompanied by an articles (absent in Russian). For example, in the original Yiddish above, "*di povestke dnia*" (agenda of the day), the word *di* is a Yiddish article accompanying a feminine noun. The other two words are Russian: *Povestka* means "agenda" and *dnia* is "of the day." Yet, in proper Russian construction, *povestka* would be in the genitive case (*povestku*), whereas the song uses the instrumental case (*povestke*).

54.   Shveyprom—*Shveinaia promyshlennost'*—is the (State) Department of the Tailoring Industry; Kozhetrest—*Kozhevennyi trest*—is the (State) Department of the Leather Industry; and Skorokhod (fast-walking) is the name of the first state shoe firm (I. Shrayer, "Nay broyt," *Pioner* 11 (1925): 15.

55.   *Shkotsim* and *shikses* are slightly derogative terms for non-Jewish men and women, respectively.

56.   *Netrudovoi element* is a Soviet neologism of the 1920s that entered Yiddish as an idiom. It literally means a "nonworking element" (someone who does not work).

57.   Shrayer, "Nay broyt," 16.

58.   Dovid Kats, "Yiddish Stylistic," lectures, University of Oxford, 1996.

59.   I. Yafe, "Fun Khaslovich keyn Kherson," *Yungvald* 8 (1926): 16.

60.   D. Mayerovich, "A tuml afn mark," *Yungvald* 6 (1925): 16.

61.   Yafe, "Fun Khaslovich," 14.

62.   Sofiya B., interview by author, Brooklyn, New York, August 1999.

63.   Ian D., interview by author, Brooklyn, New York, April 1999.

64.   Richard Stites, "Trial as Theater in the Russian Revolution," *Theater Research International* 1 (1998): 8.

65.   Elizabeth Wood, *Performing Justice: Agitation Trials in Early Soviet Russia* (Ithaca, N.Y., 2005), 4–5.

66.   Ibid., 7.

67.   *Otchet o provedenii suda nad kheiderom v g. Polotske, 23/11–1920* (Report on the trial against *Kheyder* in Polotsk, November 23, 1920), RGASPI, f. 445, d. 37, l. 91.

68.   Zvi Gitelman, *Jewish Nationality and Soviet Politics: The Jewish Sections of the CPSU* (Princeton, 1972), 301.

69.   "Borba s klerikalizmom v evreiskoi srede" (Struggle against clericalism among Jews), RGASPI, f. 445, d. 97, l. 130.

70.   Ibid.

71.   *Otchet o deiatel'nosti evsektsii Odessy za 1923 god* (Report on the activities of the Jewish sections of Odessa for 1923), RGASPI, f. 445, op. 1, d. 169, l. 48.

72.   Grigorii Koltunov, "Disput v odesskom opernom teatre o vrede obrezaniia

(vospominaniia poluintelligenta)," unpublished manuscript. I would like to thank Dr. Carol Avins of Rutgers University for sharing this work with me.

73. A. Tcherikover, "Der mishpet iber der yidisher religye," in *In der tkufe fun revolutsiye*, ed. Tcherikover (Berlin, 1924), 385; quoted in Gitelman, *Jewish Nationality and Soviet Politics*, 301.

74. Musar is a religious movement within Judaism that arose in the nineteenth century and continued into the twentieth, and was popular in yeshivas in Lithuania (and part of modern Byelorussia). The movement was established by Israel Lipkin (Salanter) and developed by Isaac Blazer. By the beginning of the twentieth century Musar had become a prevailing trend in Lithuanian yeshivas. Yeshiva students (*yeshibotniks*) were required to read ethical words from the Midrash and the Talmud, and to recite verses from the Bible out loud. This served as a vehicle for creating a certain mood. The Musar movement was an educational system that strove to integrate youthful emotions into a deeply instilled defense system of a rigorous Jewish life ("Musar," *Encyclopedia Judaica*, CD-Rom edition).

75. In 1921 similar trials were arranged against the kheyder in Vitebsk and against the yeshiva in Rostov. Circumcision was put on trial in Kharkov in 1928.

76. *Otchet o deiatel'nosti evsektsii v Belorussii za mart 1923 goda* (Report on the activities of the Jewish sections of Byelorussia for March 1923), RGASPI, f. 445, op. 1, d. 118, l. 64.

77. Ibid., l. 65.

78. Ibid., l. 66.

79. *Otchet ob agitatsionnoi rabote na Ukraine za period s aprelia 1920 po 1921 gg.* (Report on the agitation work in Ukraine from April 1920 to 1921), RGASPI, f. 445, op. 1, d. 37, l. 91.

80. *Otchet o deiatel'nosti evreiskoi sektsii Kremenchuga za oktiabr' 1922* (Report on the activities of the Jewish sections of Kremechug for October 1922), RGASPI, f. 445, op. 1, d. 116, l. 24.

81. For example, see *Rekomendatsii dlia provedeniia sudov protiv ravvinov, melamedov i lits, sviazannykh s otpravleniem ereiskogo religioznogo kul'ta* (Recommendations on how to conduct trials against rabbis, *melamdim*, and persons connected with the Jewish religious cult), RGASPI, f. 445, op. 1, d. 37, l. 47.

82. Other trials were conducted that used this model in many cities of Ukraine, Russia, and Byelorussia, for example, Kiev, Minsk, Khar'kov, Shepetovka, Elizavetgrad, and Kherson (RGASPI, f. 445, op. 1, d. 169).

83. *Informatsionnye svedeniia o deiatel'nosti evsektsii v razlichnykh chastiakh strany* (Information on the activities of Jewish sections in different parts of the country), RGASPI, f. 445. op. 1, d. 169, l. 72.

84. Ibid., ll. 38–72.

85. Ibid., l. 34.

86. Ibid., l. 26.

87. *Sud nad klubom* (Trial against the club), RGASPI, f. 445, op. 1, d. 121, l. 200.

88. Ibid.

89. "Informatsionnye svedeniia o deiatel'nosti evsektsii v razlichnykh chastiakh strany," l. 100.

90. B. Zlatov, "Kul'trazvlecheniia v klube," *Rabochii klub* 2 (1924): 30–32.

91. *Metodicheskie ukazaniia k provedeniiu litsudov na evreiskom iazyke* (Methodological recommendations on how to conduct literature trials in Yiddish), RGASPI, f. 445, op.1., d. 47, ll. 186–88.

92. Ibid., l. 186.

93. Ibid.

94. Ibid.

95. Ibid., l. 188.

96. Katerina Clark, *The Soviet Novel: History as a Ritual* (Chicago, 1981), 35. Also see Geoffrey Hosking, *Beyond Socialist Realism: Soviet Fiction since Ivan Denisovich* (London, 1981), 4.

97. *Otchet o deiatel'nosti evsektsii za mart 1923 goda v Belorussii (Minsk)* (Report on the activities of Jewish sections for March 1923 in Byelorussia [Minsk]), RGASPI, f. 445, op. 1, d. 118, l. 227.

98. In the novel Menakhem Mendl was a *luftmench,* a person without a profession, who left his shtetl in order to find a source of income and to invest the money from his wife's dowry. As a result, he found himself conducting unproductive "businesses," such as speculating in the stock market, matchmaking, and working as a travel agent. All his enterprises failed.

99. Yakov T., interview by author, Brooklyn, New York, February 1999.

100. For more on theatrical trials as predecessors of Soviet show trials, see Julie Cassiday, *The Enemy on Trial: Early Soviet Courts on Stage and Screen* (DeKalb, 2000); and, especially, Wood, *Performing Justice.*

101. Semyon Sh., interview by author, Brooklyn, New York, August 1999; Isai K., interview by author, New York City, March 1999.

102. Grigorii Braziler, *Razbuzhennye vospominaniia* (New York, 1997).

103. Mariya S., interview by author, New York City, April 1999.

104. Semyon S., interview by author, Moscow, June 2001.

4. Soviet Yiddish Songs as a Mirror of Jewish Identity

1. The most notable were Yekhezkel Dobrushin and A. Yuditskii, *Yidishe folks-lider* (Moscow, 1940); Itsik Fefer, Mikhail Kotlyar, and Fayvl Sito, *Ferzn un chastushkes* (Kiev, 1937); Rive Boyarskaya, *Klingen khamerlakh: lider zamlung far for-shul kinder* (Moscow, 1925); and Moyshe Beregovskii and Itsik Fefer, *Yidishe folks-lider* (Kiev, 1938).

2. During this period the state "purified" printed Yiddish by removing many Slavic and Hebrew words from the language, and by altering conventional spelling. Words of Hebrew origin were now spelled phonetically, and, after

1929, end letters were abolished. However, this printed language differed greatly from the Yiddish spoken by a majority of the Jewish population.

3. *Royte frayhayt lider* (Petrograd, 1919).

4. Yekhezkel Shtern, *Kheyder un beys-medresh* (New York, 1948), 69–70.

5. *Royte frayhayt lider*, 4.

6. Text as in Eleanor Mlotek and Yoseph Mlotek, *Mir trogn a gezang* (New York, 1977), 2–3.

7. *Royte frayhayt lider*, 5.

8. Quoted as in Moyshe Beregovskii, *Evreiskii muzykal'nyi fol'klor* (Moscow, 1934), 187.

9. Moyshe Beregovskii, *Jidiser muzik-folklor* (Moscow, 1934), 117.

10. S. Polonski, *Far yugnt. Lider zamlung* (Moscow, 1931).

11. Beregovskii, *Jidiser muzik-folklor: Band 1*.

12. These translations can be found practically in every collection of Yiddish Communist songs. For the most representative example, see I. Bakst and Mikhail Gnesin, *Naye lider: muzikalishe zamlung* (Moscow, 1927): the Yiddish version of "Boldly, Comrades, in Step" ("Mutik, khaveyrim"), 20; "International," 23, "*Vy zhertvoyu pali—A korbn gefaln*" ("You Were Sacrificed"), 22; "'*Zamucheny v temnoi nevole'—Farmuchet in fintsterer tfise*" ("Tortured in Dark Confinement"), 22.

13. Klara G., interview by author, Berlin, June 2002.

14. Vladimir Papernyi, *Kultura "Dva"* (Moscow, 1996).

15. Text as in Rive Boyarskaya, ed., *Lomir zingen, Lider zamlung mit notn* (Moscow, 1940), 6–7.

16. For an analysis of similar pieces in Russian, see Frank Miller, *Folklore for Stalin: Russian Folklore and Pseudo-folklore of the Stalin Era* (Armonk, N.Y., 1990).

17. Beregovskii and Fefer, *Yidishe folks-lider*, 4.

18. I borrow the phrase "folklore for Stalin" from Miller, *Folklore for Stalin*.

19. Moyshe Beregovskii, "Shrikhtn fun di yidisher sovetisher folkslid," *Sovetish heymland* 4 (1972): 175.

20. Beregovskii and Fefer, *Yidishe folks-lider*, 6–7.

21. First published in Solomon Fayntukh, *A yat a braver: s'hot gelebt bay undz a khaver: kolhoznaya zastol'naya pesnya dlia vokal'nogo ansamblia (hora)* (Kiev, 1939).

22. Sofia B., interview by author, Brooklyn, New York, August 1999.

23. Ibid.

24. In 1936 a brigade of Yiddish poets, consisting of Itsik Fefer, Fayvl Sito (1909–1945), and Yosef Kotlyar (1908–1962), went to shtetlach near Kiev to "collect" some Yiddish chastushkes. These poets published the first volume of Soviet Yiddish verses and chastushkes in 1937 from the research they collected on this trip (Itsik Fefer, Yosef Kotlyar, and Fayvl Sito, *Ferzn un chastushkes* [Kiev,

1937]). Subsequently more than thirty other collections of Yiddish chastushkes appeared in 1937–40. See, for example, Dobrushin and Yuditskii, *Yidishe folks-lider,* 440–59; *Folks-lider vegn Leninen* (Kiev, 1937); *Folks-lider vegn Stalinen* (Kiev, 1937); Mark Fradkin, *Yidishe folkslider* (Odessa, 1940); *Frayhayt lider [Lider tsu zingen]* (Odessa, 1940); Nikolai Golubev, *Yidishe folsklider* (Moscow, 1936); M. Grinblat and Leon Dushman, *Stalin in der yidisher folksshafung* (Minsk, 1939); Arn Kushnirov, *Dos gezang fun di felker fun FSSR vegn Leninen un Stalinen* (Moscow, 1939); Osher Shvartsman, *Lider vegn der royter armey* (Moscow, 1938); *Lider vegn Stalinen* (Kiev, 1937); *Yidishe folks lider vegn der royter armey* (Minsk, 1938); *Yidishe sovetishe folkslider mit melodies* (Kiev, 1940); Boyarskaya, *Lomir zingen.*

25. Fefer, Kotlyar, and Sito, *Ferzn un chastushkes,* 13.

26. Ibid., 59.

27. Dobrushin and Yuditskii, *Yidishe folks-lider,* 451.

28. Fefer, Kotlyar, and Sito, *Ferzn un chastushkes,* 5.

29. For the latest research on "culturedness" in the 1930s, including propaganda of "cultured" eating habits, see David Hoffman, *Stalinist Values* (Madison, 2003); and Vadim Volkov, "The Concept of *Kul'turnost'*: Notes on the Stalinist Civilizing Process," in *Stalinism: New Directions,* ed. Sheila Fitzpatrick (London, 2000), 210–30.

30. Vsesoiuznyi tsentral'nyi ispolnitel'nyi komitet (All-Union Central Executive Committee).

31. Dobrushin and Yuditskii, *Yidishe folks-lider,* 452.

32. Ibid.

33. Quoted as published in ibid., 424–25. This book offers two versions of the song. I quote the second, more popular one.

34. Sholem Lopatin, "Kegn gold," in *Lomir ale zingen. Zamlung fun yidishe, hebreyshe un englishe lider* (New York, 1956), 31.

35. Because pork is not kosher, it is not allowed for consumption according to the Jewish law. Pig breeding therefore would never be possible on a Jewish agricultural settlement that followed traditional religious dietary laws.

36. Dobrushin and Yuditskii, *Yidishe folks-lider,* 426.

37. Ibid., 448.

38. Faina D., interview by author, Brooklyn, New York, August 1999.

39. Efim G., interview by author, Brooklyn, New York. February 1999.

40. "Geforn in Krym, gemeynt a kurort," Kiev State Library, file 961/3, p.1. Recording of Mani Strasheske, a fifteen-year-old schoolgirl, Belotserkov, March 1936. The collector wrote a comment below the original text: "In this song the speculative elements, which came to Jewish colonies in Crimea in recent years, are mocked."

41. The Vernadsky National Library of Ukraine, Manuscript Department, File 940/2, Kviat, Kalinindorf, 1936.

42. James von Geldern and Richard Stites, eds., *Mass Culture in Soviet Russia:*

Tales, Poems, Songs, Movies, Plays, and Folklore, 1917–1953 (Bloomington, 1995), xix.

43. Itsik Fefer, "*Dort baym grenets,*" in Boyarskaya, *Klingen khamerlakh,* 12.

44. The Vernadsky National Library of Ukraine, Department of Manuscripts, Collection of Beregovskii Folklore Expedition (1936–1939), Document 177.

45. Ibid.

46. Bella G., interview by author, Berlin, July 2002.

47. Dobrushin and Yuditskii, *Yidishe folks-lider,* 315.

48. Ibid., 15–16.

49. Sofia B., interview by author, Brooklyn, New York, August 1999.

50. Based on *Jewish Sheet Music. From the Vernadsky Library in Kiev, Ukraine. Guide* (Washington, D.C., 1992).

51. Aleksander Kreyn, *Dray lider des ghetto* (Moscow, 1929); Aleksander Kreyn, *Ya nartsiss Sarona. Liliya dolin* (Moscow, 1922); M. Milner, *Di farshterte khasene* (Leningrad, 1930); M. Miner, *Farn obsheyd. Kleyne rapsodie* (Leningrad, 1930).

52. Song by Mordechai Gebirtik. Recorded as sung by Efim Gorelik, February 28, 1999, New York. For the published text, see Mlotek and Mlotek, *Mir trogn a gezang,* 222.

53. Text as in Eleanor Mlotek, *Perl fun yidish lid: 115 yidishe folks arbeter kunst un teater* (New York, 1989), 267.

54. For the text of "Bublichki," see von Geldern and Stites, *Mass Culture in Soviet Russia,* 70–71.

55. Words as in Mlotek, *Perl fun yidish lid,* 165.

56. Words as in The Vernadsky National Library of Ukraine, File 959/1. Recorded in Belotserkov, n.d. See also Mark Kipnis, *80 folkslider* (Warsaw, 1918). This song has been popularized by Michael Alpert, a New York–based klezmer musician. Alpert recorded this song from Bronya Sakina (b. 1908).

57. Cruel romance is a genre of Russian city ballads that often feature romantic plots with sad endings.

58. The same process took place in Russian song writing. See Robert Rothstein, "How It Was Sung in Odessa: At the Intersection of Russian and Yiddish Folk Culture," *Slavic Review* 4 (2001): 287.

59. Mlotek, *Perl fun yidish lid,* 161.

60. Translation as in ibid., 161.

61. Dobrushin and Yuditskii, *Yidishe folks-lider,* 461–62.

62. Ibid., 448.

63. Faina D., interview by author, Brooklyn, New York, August 1999.

64. Leon Dennen, *Where the Ghetto Ends: Jews in Soviet Russia* (New York, 1934), 98–102.

65. Klara G., interview by author, Berlin, June 2002. To demonstrate the use of

Yiddish dialects, the song is transliterated phonetically and not according to YIVO rules.

66. For example, *hont* is a Ukrainian Yiddish dialectal pronunciation of *hant* (hand), which rhymes with *derkont,* a variation of *derkent* (recognized).

67. ZAGS is a registry office where couples went to officially get married.

68. Recorded August 1999, from Moyshe P. (street interview). He said that this was his favorite song. My grandmother, Faina Hromaya (1918–1988), born in Lenskorun, Ukraine, also used to sing this song.

69. Jeffrey Veidlinger, *The Moscow State Yiddish Theater: Jewish Culture on the Soviet Stage* (Bloomington, 2000), 117.

70. Dobrushin and Yuditskii, *Yidishe folks-lider,* 449.

71. A Stakhanovite is a worker in the Soviet Union who regularly surpassed production quotas and was specially honored and rewarded.

72. As James von Geldern explains, "new heroes arrived with the mid-thirties: simple-hearted but wise country folk, kind and fatherly professors, wives and mothers who stayed on the factory floor while they raised families" (introduction to *Mass Culture in Soviet Russia,* ed. von Geldern and Stites, xviii).

73. Kiev State Library, File 941/2.

74. Von Geldern, introduction, xviii.

75. Rothstein, "How It Was Sung in Odessa."

76. Recorded from Sofia B., Brooklyn, New York, August 1999. The Russian words are italicized.

5. Soviet in Form, National in Content

1. Boris P., interview by author, Minneapolis, December 2000.

2. Mordechai Altshuler, *Soviet Jewry on the Eve of the Holocaust* (Jerusalem, 1998), 91.

3. According to the 1939 census, 86.9 percent of Soviet Jews lived in urban centers. Accelerated urbanization in the Soviet Union led to the emergence of eleven large cities with populations exceeding half a million. More than a third (39.8 percent) of all Soviet Jews lived in these cities, most of them located outside the former Pale, and were predominantly Russian-speaking (ibid., 35).

4. Ibid., 36.

5. David Hoffman, *Peasant Metropolis: Social Identities in Moscow, 1929–1941* (Ithaca, 1994), 158–60.

6. *Chapaev* is a 1934 film, directed by the Vasiliev brothers, that was based on a socialist realist novel by Dmitry Furmanov.

7. David B., interview by author, Moscow, June 2001.

8. Yurii B., interview by author, Brooklyn, New York, February 1999. Yurii B. preferred to be interviewed in Russian, since he felt he had forgotten his Yiddish. Later in the interview he added that he stays in touch with his old Jew-

ish friends, many of whom live in his same Brooklyn neighborhood, but that they speak Russian, not Yiddish, to one another.

9. Lazar L., interview by author, Philadelphia, November 2001.

10. Jeffrey Veidlinger, "Let's Perform a Miracle: The Soviet Yiddish State Theater in the 1920s," *Slavic Review* 57, no. 2 (1998): 372–97.

11. For the literature published in the Soviet Union in Russian about Jews and the Jewish question, see Dmitrii El'yashevich and Viktor Kelner, *Bibliografiya istorii evreev na russkom yazyke, 1860–1994* (St. Petersburg, 1995); and Benjamin Pinkus, Avraam Grinbaum, and Mordechai Altshuler, *Pirsumim Rusiim al Yehudim ve-Yahadut Vi-vrot ha-Moazot* (Russian publications on Jews and Judaism in the Soviet Union, 1917–1967: A bibliography) (Jerusalem, 1970).

12. For the Russian Jewish elite, see Alice Stone Nakhimovsky, *Russian-Jewish Literature and Identity: Jabotinsky, Babel, Grossman, Galich, Roziner, Markish* (Baltimore, 1992); Efraim Sicher, *Jews in Russian Literature after the October Revolution: Writers and Artists between Hope and Apostasy* (Cambridge, 1995); and Maxim Shrayer, Russian Poet/Soviet Jew: The Legacy of Eduard Bagritskii (Lanham, 2000).

13. Altshuler, "Summary," in Pinkus, Grinbaum, and Altshuler, *Pirsumim Rusiim,* xiv.

14. Ibid.

15. For a full list of translations from Yiddish literature published in Russian, see Pinkus, Grinbaum, and Altshuler, *Pirsumim Rusiim,* 112–82. In 1927–29 the Puchina publishing house released translations of the principal works of Sholem Aleykhem such as *Jewish Luck, Bloody Joke, From the Marketplace, Tevye the Dairyman,* and *Actors.* In 1929 a translation of Mendele Moykher Sforim's *Fishke the Lame* was published. In Odessa translations of Sholem Aleykhem were also published in the Library of Jewish Writers series. Avrom Reyzen's *Stories* was published in 1929, as well as David Bergelson's *In the Dangerous Days.* In 1929–30 a seven-volume set of the collected works of Sholem Asch was published in Russian in Odessa. In the early 1930s all these publishing houses were closed. A Jewish Literature series was established in 1931 and lasted until 1933. Translations of Soviet Yiddish writers revolved largely around the Jews' participation in the revolutionary movement and demonstrated the various positive changes that had taken place in the Jewish community after 1917. Most of these works were translations of David Bergelson, Eliyahu Gordon (b. 1903), Itsik Kipnis (1896–1974), and Yekhezkel Shraybman (b. 1913), although translations of some Russian-language works of Isaak Babel (1894–1941) were also published. Another body devoted to Yiddish literature in Russian translation was the Ukrainian Publishing house of National Minorities. In 1935–40 it published many works by Sholem Aleykhem, Khayim Gildin, Dovid Hofshteyn, Itsik Kipnis, Noteh Lurye, and Itsik Fefer.

16. Nakhimovsky, *Russian Jewish Literature and Identity,* 14–23.

17. David S., interview by author, New York, January 1999.

18. During the postwar period the very word "Jew" became pejorative. When it appeared in a work of literature, it often became a subject of heated private debate and discussion among the Russian Jewish intelligentsia. For an excellent overview of Jewish images in late Soviet and post-Soviet literature, see Mikhail Krutikov, "Constructing Jewish Identity in Contemporary Russian Fiction," in *Jewish Life after the USSR,* ed. Zvi Gitelman, Musya Glants, and Marshall Goldman (Bloomington, 2003), 252–74.

19. Esfir A., interview by author, Potsdam, June 2002.

20. Mark P., interview by author, Brooklyn, New York, August 1999.

21. Etya G., interview by author, Brooklyn, New York, March 1999.

22. One-fifth (20.4 percent) were translations of antireligious works written in West European languages, and more than half (twenty-eight out of fifty-four) dealt with early Judaism, particularly the Bible (Altshuler, "Summary," xiv).

23. Emelyan Yaroslavskiy (Gubelman Minei Izrailovich, 1878–1943). For more on his biography, see Daniel Peris, *Storming the Heavens: The Soviet League of the Militant Godless* (Ithaca, 1998).

24. I. A., "Konets Druzhbe," *Bezbozhnik* 1 (1923): 10.

25. M. Brut, "Trefnoe moloko," *Bezbozhnik* 4 (1926): 23.

26. N. Neker, "Druz'ia," *Bezbozhnik* 2 (1925): 12.

27. Rabbi Yoseph Shneerson (1880–1950) was a famous Hassidic leader of KHABAD, which was especially active in the Soviet Union. The initials KHABAD stand for "khohmah, binah, da'at"—wisdom, understanding, knowledge—a Hassidic movement founded in Byelorussia by Shneur Zalman of Lyady. He was deported in 1928. Tikhon (Vasilyi Ivanovich Belavin, 1865–1925) was Patriarch of the Russian Orthodox Church following the Bolshevik Revolution of 1917. At first he sharply resisted the new anti-ecclesiastical legislation of the Soviet state and refused to cooperate with the schismatic, state-supported, and politically oriented element of the clergy known as the Living Church. Later he sought mitigation of government repression and assumed a more flexible position.

28. I thank David Shneer for his comment on this possible interpretation.

29. S. Pen, "Ne staia voronov sletelas," *Bezbozhnik* 1 (1928): 26.

30. See, for example, Ploshchansky, "Sionistskie shpiony i provokatory," *Bezbozhnik* 11 (1928): 7–8; and I. Intsertov, "Paskha—znamia kontr-revolutsii," *Bezbozhnik* 7 (1931): 2.

31. A. Yurko, "Smychka," *Bezbozhnik* 11 (1928): 6–7. See also S. Pen, "Voron voronu glaz ne vykliuet," *Bezbozhnik* 2 (1928): 15.

32. Il. Gul'binkaia, "Babushka v brake," *Bezbozhnik* 5 (1927): 14.

33. Neker, "Druz'ia," 11.

34. The use of the name of the Jewish God in a poem is blasphemous. Saying it in Russian in this context might seriously offend Jewish believers. At the same time its use de-mystified the name of the Jewish God for non-Jewish readers.

35. M. Gurshman, "Sviataia paskha," *Bezbozhnik* 5 (1926): 14.

36. Altshuler, *Soviet Jewry on the Eve of the Holocaust,* 100.

37. In the sociological census of 1937 all citizens sixteen years old and older were asked, in one question, whether they were literate and religious (ibid.).

38. Parovozov, "Umnyi ravvin," *Bezbozhnik* 6 (1927): 13.

39. KOMTET—Komitet po zemleustroistvu evreev (Committee for the Rural Resettlement of the Jews). For more on KOMZET see the introduction to this book.

40. V. Bronner, "Mikva," *Bezbozhnik* 6 (1924): 16–17.

41. A. A. Karelin, *Zlye rosskazni pro evreev* (Moscow, 1919).

42. Ibid., 4–5.

43. Ibid., 5.

44. Ibid., 6–8.

45. Vl. Mikhailovsky, *Evrei pri belykh* (Rostov-on-Don, 1922), 29.

46. Ts. Bobrovskaia, "Belaia koza," *Bezbozhnik* 2 (1923): 10.

47. E. Cherniak, "Ilia prorok vse produkty uvolok," *Bezbozhnik* 2 (1926): 15.

48. "Ilia na Paskhe," *Bezbozhnyi krokodil. Spetsial'noe prilozhenie k zhurnalu Bezbozhniku* 15 (1924): 1.

49. D. Gelman, "Sviatoe edinenie," *Bezbozhnik* 4 (1924): 11.

50. E. Cherniak, "Dva priiatelia," *Bezbozhnik* 5 (1926): 14.

51. *Kapoyres* (meaning expiation, in Hebrew) is the custom that symbolically transfers the sins of a person to a fowl. In certain Orthodox circles on the day before Yom Kippur, the Day of Atonement, particular psalms are recited and then a cock for a male, or a hen for a female, is swung around the person's head three times as the following phrase is pronounced: "This is my substitute, my vicarious offering, my atonement, this cock [or hen] shall meet death, but I shall find a long and pleasant life of peace."

52. Tsvi, "Prazdnichnye Paralleli," *Bezbozhnik* 19 (1928): 19.

53. Anna M., interview by author, Moscow, June 2001.

54. Bernard Weinryb, "Anti-Semitism in Soviet Russia," in *Jews in Soviet Russia,* ed. Lionel Kochan (London, 1972), 292.

55. Benjamin Pinkus, *The Jews of the Soviet Union: The History of a National Minority* (Cambridge, 1988), 85.

56. Ibid., 84–85.

57. Pinkus, Grinbaum, and Altshuler, *Pirsumim Rusiim,* 51–56.

58. *Doloi pogromy* (Odessa, 1920), 3–4.

59. Weinryb, "Anti-Semitism in Soviet Russia," 298.

60. Pinkus, *The Jews of the Soviet Union,* 86.

61. Merle Fainsod, *Smolensk under Soviet Rule* (Cambridge, Mass., 1958), 437.

62. Pinkus, *The Jews of the Soviet Union,* 87.

63. Quoted in Weinryb, "Anti-Semitism in Soviet Russia," 301.

64. Mikhail Kalinin, *Evreiskii vopros* (Moscow, 1927), 5. See also Pinkus, *The Jews of the Soviet Union,* 87–89; and Weinryb, "Anti-Semitism in Soviet Russia," 302–305.

65. Kalinin, *Evreiskii vopros,* 31.

66. Karelin, *Zlye rosskazni pro evreev;* Kalinin, *Evreiskii vopros.*

67. Kalinin, *Evreiskii vopros,* 14.

68. D. M., "Bez boga na zemle," *Bezbozhnik* 9 (1928): 11–12.

69. See, for example, P. Kantselyarskii, *Sovetskaia vlast' i evreiskoe naselenie v SSSR* (Dnepropetrovsk, 1929), 20.

70. See A. Glensky, *Dergrayhungen un felern in der arbet tsvishn di natsionale mindehaytn* (Kharkov, 1931), 28.

71. For the contemporary public report, see N. Den, *Krym* (Moscow, 1930), 29; and B. Berezhanskaia, "Evreiskie Kolkhozy v Krymu," in *Evrei Kryma: ocherki istorii,* ed. Ella Solomonik (Simferopol, 1997), 71–85. Pinkus noted that Soviet published data on the number of national Jewish councils was inconsistent. See Pinkus, *The Jews of the Soviet Union,* 67. Also see, for example, Y. Kantor, *Natsional'noe stroitel'stvo sredi evreev SSSR* (Moscow, 1934), 13.

72. Shmuel Godiner and D. Lifshits, *Vstrecha v Tsymle* (Moscow, 1936).

73. Jews and Cossacks were two of the most mutually antagonistic groups in Soviet society. This hostility became manifest when the Cossacks initiated the most cruel, anti-Jewish riots during the civil war.

74. Godiner and Lifshits, *Vstrecha v Tsymle,* 23–25.

75. Ibid., 27.

76. James L. Gibson, "Understanding Anti-Semitism in Russia: An Analysis of the Politics of Anti-Jewish Attitudes," *Slavic Review* 53, no. 3 (autumn 1994): 797.

77. Ibid.

78. Robert Brym and Andrei Degtyarev, "Anti-Semitism in Moscow: The Results of an October 1992 Survey," *Slavic Review* 52, no. 1 (spring 1993): 10.

79. Iliya Sh., interview by author, Brooklyn, New York, April 1999.

80. Mikhail Sh., interview by author, Moscow, June 2001.

81. Leon Dennen, *Where the Ghetto Ends: Jews in Soviet Russia* (New York, 1934), 38.

82. Ibid.

83. Ibid, 39.

84. Ibid, 45.

85. Ibid, 49.

86. Elizabeth Wood describes an early example of a trial designed to combat anti-Semitism, entitled "Trial of Jewry," staged in 1919 in Kharkov, Ukraine (*Performing Justice,* 46–48).

87. Asya G., interview by author, Berlin, June 2002.

88. Efim G., interview by author, Brooklyn, New York, February 1999.

89. Neither the script nor the film of the former survives today, but copies of the latter can be found in both the Russian and Brandeis University archives.

90. For more on Russian and early Soviet films devoted to Jews, see Rashid Iangirov, "Jewish Life on the Screen in Russian, 1908–1919," *Jews and Jewish Topics in the Soviet Union and Eastern Europe* (spring 1990): 15–32.

91. Miron Chernenko, *Iudaika na ekrane: kinematograficheskaia istoriia evreistva v SSSR 1919–1934* (Moscow, 1990). Also available at http://www.jewishheritage.org.

92. For a detailed description of this movie, see ibid., 10.

93. P. Markish, B. Shnis, and R. Mil'man, *Vozvrashchenie Natana Bekkera* (Moscow, 1932). This was the only film from this era produced in both Russian and Yiddish. See Daniel Romanovsky, "An Unpublished Soviet Film of 1940 with a Jewish Theme," *Jews in Eastern Europe* (spring 1996): 32.

94. For an excellent overview of Jewish characters and motifs in the Soviet cinema, see Miron Chernenko, *Krasnaia zvezda, zheltaia zvezda (kinematograficheskaia istoriia evreistva v Rossii, 1919–1999 gg.)* (Vinnitsa, 2001).

95. Mikhail O., interview by author, New York, June 1999.

96. Naum F., interview by author, Brooklyn, New York, February 1999.

97. Semyon Sh., interview by author, Brooklyn, New York, August 1999.

98. Lyusya G., interview by author, New York, August 1999.

99. Elizaveta Z., interview by author, Berlin, June 2002.

100. Sofiya B., interview by author, Brooklyn, New York, August 1999.

101. Miron Chernenko, *Kinematograficheskia istoriia Sovetskogo evreistva 1934–1941* (Moscow: Evreiskoe nasledie, 2001), 17.

102. The words of this song were written by Boris Timofeev, an author of many Russian gypsy songs, and the music was arranged by Boris Prozorovsky but taken from the Yiddish song "Margaritkelekh" (Daisies).

103. Robert Rothstein, "Popular Song in the NEP Era," in *Russia in the Era of NEP: Explorations in Soviet Society and Culture,* ed. Sheila Fitzpatrick, Alexander Rabinowitch, and Richard Stites (Bloomington, 1991), 276. The original song by Zalman Shneur tells a story of a young girl seduced by a handsome man in the woods (Eleanor Mlotek and Yoseph Mlotek, *Mir trogn a gezang* [New York, 1977], 40–41). I would like to thank Dr. Rothstein for introducing me to the full version of this song and for sending me the photocopy of the original publication (n.d., n.p.).

104. Translation of this verse by Robert Rothstein ("Popular Song in the NEP Era").

105. Ibid.

106. Five different versions of this song are available at http://www.caida.org, a website that lists folk songs recorded by Russians from 1990 to 2000.

107. Klara R., interview by author, Brooklyn, New York, August 1999.

108. For more on Jews in Soviet music, see Frederick Starr, *Red and Hot: The Fate*

of *Jazz in the Soviet Union, 1917–1980* (New York, 1983); Rothstein, "Popular Song in the NEP Era," 263–83.

109. Venyamin Sh., interview by author, Moscow, June 2001.

110. Utesov published three books of memoirs: the first in 1939, the second in 1955, and the third in 1976. In all three he describes his experiences growing up in a Jewish family and in a Jewish environment. See Leonid Utesov, *Spasibo serdtse* (Moscow, 1976); and idem, *S pesnei po zhisni* (Moscow, 1961).

111. Mila G., interview by author, Moscow, June 2001.

112. Words by anonymous, music by Isaak Dunaevsky, performed by Leonid Utesov, "Evreiskaia rapsodiia" (Jewish rhapsody), recorded in 1932. See also Leonid Utesov, *Para Gnedykh (1937–1940)* (Moscow, 1995), "Iz repertuara Leonida Utesova" Series. May be downloaded from http://www.retromusic.2u.ru.

113. Sugar head is a piece of hard sugar shaped like a large rock with a hole in the middle. The hole serves as a cup in which one can pour tea. Because sugar was considered a delicacy, drinking tea from a sugar head was seen as a sign of extravagant luxury.

114. For more on this, see chapter 3.

115. Music by N. Pustylnik, words by E. Polonskaya (Utesov, *Para Gnedykh*).

116. Yakov Basin, "Ia pesne vse otdal spolna," *Mishpokha* 5 (1999): 17.

117. Rozaliya U., interview by author, Moscow, August 2002.

118. "Ten Daughters" and "The Little Bells Ring and Play" were on the same LP as the famous Russian song "Raskinulos' more shiroko" (The sea is wide) and Stalin's favorite Georgian tune, "Suliko."

119. Utesov, *Spasibo serdtse,* 116.

120. "Synovia" was first performed by a star of the Russian popular stage, Klavdia Shulzhenko (1906–1984).

Bibliography

Archival Collections

GARF—Gosudarstvennyi arkhiv Rossiiskoi Federatsii (State Archive of the Russian Federation), Moscow.

Fond 296. Sovet po prosvescheniiu narodov nerusskogo iazyka Narkomprosa RSFSR. Evreiskoe tsentral'noe biuro (The Council on Enlightenment of Peoples of Non-Russian Language. Jewish Central Bureau).

Fond 1575. Glavnoe upravlenie sotsial'nogo vospitaniia i tekhnicheskogo obrazovaniia NKP RSFSR. Biuro sovnatsmen (The Head Department of Social Work and Technical Education of the People's Committee of Enlightenment of the Russian Federation. National Minorities Section).

Fond 2313. Glavnyi politiko-prosvetitel'nyi komitet respubliki RSFSR. Biuro propagandy. Otdel natsional'nykh men'shinst (State Committee of Political Education of the Russian Federation. Propaganda Section. Department of National Minorities).

Fond 2314. Vserossiiskaia gosudarstvennaia komissiia po likvidatsii bezgramotnosti. Sektsiia natsmen'shinstv (All-Russian State Committee for Eradication of Illiteracy. National Minorities Section).

Brandeis University Jewish Film Archive

FILMS

Comrade Abram (1919)
Yidishe glik (Jewish luck) (1925)
Natan Beker Comes Home (1932)
Iskateli shchast'ia (Seekers of happiness) (1936)

RGASPI—Rossiiskii gosudarstvennyi arkhiv sotsial'no-politicheskoy istorii (Russian State Archive for Social and Political History)

Fond 445. Evreiskie sektsii Kommunisticheskoi Partii (1918–1930) (Jewish sections of the Communist Party [1918–1930]).

The Vernadsky National Library of Ukraine

DEPARTMENT OF MANUSCRIPTS

Collection of Beregovskii and Engel Folklore Expedition (1922–1926)

Self-Published Memoirs

Braziler, Grigorii. *Razbuzhennye vospominaniia.* New York, 1997.
Koltunov, Grigorii. *Disput v odesskom opernom teatre o vrede obrezaniia (vospominaniia poluintelligenta).* N.d.
Yagman, Vladimir. *Moi puti dorogi.* St. Petersburg, 2000.

Oral History Interviews

Texts of all interviews are available from the author on request. By 2007 each interview will be available from the Frankel Center of Judaic Studies at the University of Michigan.

Anna M., Moscow, June 2001.
Asya G., Berlin, June 2002.
Bella G., Berlin, July 2002.
Boris P., Minneapolis, December 2000.
David B., Moscow, June 2001.
David S., Brooklyn, New York, January 1999.
Efim G., Brooklyn, New York, February 1999.
Elena K., Moscow, June 2001.
Elizaveta Z., Berlin, June 2002.
Esfir A., Potsdam, June 2002.
Etya G., Brooklyn, New York, March 1999.
Faina D., Brooklyn, New York, August 1999.
Fira S., Moscow, June 2001.
Fira T., Brooklyn, New York, April 1999.
Galina K., Bronx, New York, June 1999.
Grigorii B., New York, April 1999.
Grigorii P., Berlin, June 2002.
Ian D., Brooklyn, New York, April 1999.
Ian T., New York, March 1999.
Ida V., Philadelphia, November 2001.
Ilya Sh., Brooklyn, New York, April 1999.
Ioan K., Berlin, June 2002.
Isai K., New York City, March 1999.
Klara G., Berlin, June 2002.
Klara R., Brooklyn, New York, August 1999.
Lazar L., Philadelphia, November 2001.
Lyubov B., Berlin, June 2002.
Lyusya G., Brooklyn, New York, August 1999.
Manya L., Detroit, December 2000.
Mariya S., New York City, April 1999.
Mark P., Brooklyn, New York, August 1999.
Mikhail O., Brooklyn, New York, June 1999.
Mikhail Sh., Moscow, June 2001.
Mila G., Moscow, June 2001.
Mila Sh., Brooklyn, New York, April 1999.
Moisei Sh., Brooklyn, New York, April 1999.
Moyshe P., Brooklyn, New York, August 1999.
Naum F., Brooklyn, New York, February 1999.
Philip G., Brooklyn, New York, February 1999.
Rozaliya U., Moscow, August 2002.
Samuil G., Brooklyn, New York, May 1999.
Sara F., Brooklyn, New York, August 1999.
Sara Fr., Brooklyn, New York, March 1999.
Saul M., Brooklyn, New York, May 1999.

Semyon K., Brooklyn, New York, March 1999.
Semyon R., Moscow, June 2001.
Semyon S., Brooklyn, New York, August 1999.
Semyon Sh., Brooklyn, New York, August 1999.
Sofa G., New York City, February 1999.
Sofiya B., Brooklyn, New York, August 1999.
Sonya G., Brooklyn, New York, March 1999.
Tsirl B., Brooklyn, New York, June 1999.
Venyamin Sh., Moscow, June 2001.
Velvl K., Brooklyn, New York, February 1999.
Viktor Kh., Brooklyn, New York, August 1999
Yakov M., Brooklyn, New York, March 1999.
Yakov T., Brooklyn, New York, February 1999.
Yurii B., Brooklyn, New York, March 1999.

Published Primary Sources

Periodicals (in Yiddish and Russian)

Af di vegn tsu der nayer shul (Moscow, 1924–28)
Afn shprakhfront (Minsk, 1932–35)
Arbeter korespondent (Moscow, 1924)
Bezbozhnik (newspaper) (1922–41)
Bezbozhnik u stanka (Moscow, 1923–32)
Birobidzhaner shtern (Birobidzhan, 1930–41)
Der apikoyres (Moscow, 1931–35)
Der arbeter (Berdichev, 1927–35)
Der emes (Moscow, 1920–38)
Der odeser arbeter (Odessa, 1927–37)
Der royter shtern (Vitebsk, 1920–23)
Der shtern (Minsk, 1918–21)
Farmest (Kiev, 1933–37)
Forpost (Birobidzhan, 1936–40)
Kremenchuger arbeter (Kremenchug, 1925–31)
Kolvirt shtern (Kiev, 1931–35)
Oktyaberl (Kiev, 1930–39)
Oktyabr (Minsk, 1925–41)
Oys amaratses! (Minsk, 1920–21)
Oys amaratses! (Moscow, 1925–27)
Pioner (Moscow, 1925–28)
Rabochii klub (Moscow, 1923–27)
Shlogler (Odessa, 1932–35)
Shtern (Kharkov, 1925–41)
Shtern (Minsk, 1925–41)
Sovetish (Moscow, 1934–41)
Visnshaft un revolyutsye (Kiev, 1934–36)
Vitebsker arbeter (Vitebsk, 1925–28)
Yungvald (Moscow, 1923–27)
Zay greyt! (Kharkov, 1928–37)

Abchuk, Avrom. *Etyudn un materialn. Tsu der geshikhte fun der yidisher literatur-bavegung in FSSR. Ershter bukh, 1917–1927.* Kharkov: Literatur un kunst, 1934.

———. "Vegn naye literatishe zhanres." *Prolit* 1 (1928): 41–8.

Abram, L., I. Khinchin, and K. Kaplan, eds. *Der mishpet ibern kheyder.* Vitebsk: Vitebsker gubernyaler byuro fun di Idishe sektsyes R.S.F., 1922.

Alberton, Meyer. *Biro-Bidzhan.* Kharkov: Tsentrfarlag, 1929.

Aleksandrov, Hilel. *Der veg tsum ershtn may. Zamlung.* Minsk: Melukhe-farlag, 1926.

Alfa-Omega: khristianskie i evreiskie prazdniki, ikh iazycheskoe proiskhozhdenie i istoriia. Moscow: Gosizdat, 1924

Alsvaysruslendishe konferents fun yidishe kultur un bildungs-tuer. Rezolyutsies (28 Yanvar'– 4 Fevral' 1931). Minsk: Tsentrfarlag, 1931.

Altman, Petro, and Khatskl Nadel. *Antireligyeze kinstlerishe zamlung.* Kiev: Ukrmelukh-natsmindfarlag, 1939.

Altshuler, Moyshe. *Antireligyezer lernbukh.* Moscow: Tsentrfarlag, 1929

———. *Hagode far gloybers un apikorsim.* Moscow: Tsentrfarlag, 1927.

———. *Hagode shel peysekh, Komsomolishe agode.* Moscow: Tsentrfarlag, 1922.

———. *Komyugishe polit-shmuesn.* Moscow: Tsentrfarlag, 1929–30.

———. *Vi azoy darf men firn antireligyeze propagande. Metodishe briv.* Moscow: Tsentrfarlag, 1929.

Altshuler, Peysi, and Khatskl Nadel. *Gekasherte neshomes (vegn kheyder).* Kharkov: Melukhe-farlag, 1922.

Arbdorfkor. Kharkov: n.p., 1933.

Arbeter lider. Kiev: Der hamer, 1918.

Aris, A. "A yor arbet yugnt dramkrayz baym kharkover klub." *Di royte velt* 4 (1925): 43–47.

Arnshteyn, Mark. *Der arbeter klub (Organizatsiye un metodik).* Moscow: Shul un bukh, 1926.

———. *Dramatishe shriftn.* Moscow: Kunst un lebn, 1918.

———. *Masn-arbet in leyenshtibl.* Moscow: Tsentrfarlag, 1929.

———. *Shvester un brider: tragikomedye in eyn akt.* Moscow: Kunst un lebn, 1918.

Bakst, I., and Mikhail Gnesin. *Naye lider: muzikalishe zamlung.* Moscow: Tsentrfarlag, 1927.

Barkovsky, Mikhail. *Chto nado znat' kazhdomu o khristianskom i evreiskom prazdnike paskhi.* Novgorod: Okruznoi, raionnyi i gorodskoi sovet soiuza bezbozhnikov, 1931.

Beregovskii, Moyshe. *Evreiskie narodnye pesni.* Moscow: Sovetskii kompozitor, 1962.

———. *Evreiskii muzykal'nyi folklor.* Moscow: Muzgiz, 1934.

———. *Jidiser muzik-folklor. Band I.* Moscow: Melukhisher muzik farlag, 1934.

———. "Shriftn fun der yidisher sovetisher folkslid." *Sovetish heymland* 4 (1972): 172–76.

Beregovskii, Moyshe, and Itsik Fefer. *Yidishe folks-lider.* Kiev: Ukrmelukhnatsmind-farlag, 1938.

Beregovskii, Moyshe, and Ruvim Lerner. "Yidishe folks-shafung baym der foterlendisher milkhome." *Sovetish heymland* 5 (1970): 143–46.

Berezhanskaia, B. "Evreiskie Kolkhozy v Krymu." In *Evrei Kryma: ocherki istorii,* ed. Ella Solomonik. Simferopol: Mosty, 1997.

Bergoltz, B. *Far estrade.* Kharkov: Literatur un kunst, 1933.

Beznosik, K., Max Erik, and Isroel Rubin. *Antireligyezer literarisher leyenbukh.* Moscow: Tsentrfarlag, 1930.

Bilov, Shloyme. "Undzer sovetishe proze." *Prolit,* 1 (1928): 29–32.

Bilski, I., *Far a bolshevistisher tsaytung.* Zhitomir: Shlogler fun profintern, 1933.

Birebidzhan. Literarishe zamlung. Moscow: Der emes, 1936.

Birnbaum, Philip. *Daily Prayer Book.* New York: Hebrew Publishing, 1977.

Bloknot fun agitator: kegn di religyeze yontoyvim (Rosheshone, Yonkiper). Minsk: Partey-farlag, 1929.

Bonch-Bruevich, Vera [Velichkina]. *O sviashchennykh knigakh.* Moscow: Zhizn' i znanie, 1922.

Boyarskaya, Rive, ed. *Arbet, shpil, gezang (Kinder-Lider).* Moscow: Der emes, 1932.

———. *Kleyne boyer.* Moscow: Der emes, 1938.

———. *Klingen hemerlakh: lider zamlung far for-shul kinder.* Moscow: Melukhe-farlag, 1925.

———. *Lomir zingen: Lider zamlung mit notn.* Moscow: Tsentrfarlag, 1940.

———. *Pesni na stikhi evreiskikh poetov dlia golosa i khora.* Moscow: Muzyka, 1962.

———. *Yontev in biro-feld.* Moscow: Tsentrfarlag, 1940.

Bragin, Aleksei, and Mikhail Kol'tsov. *Sud'ba evreiskikh mass v Sovetskom Soiuze.* Moscow: Mospoligraf, 1924.

Bronshteyn, Isaak. "Oyf di vegn tsu der yidisher proletarishe proze." *Di royte velt* 7 (1928): 136–47.

Bryanski, Shlomo, and Binyamin Gutyanski, "Vi batsien zikh etlekhe kinder tsu pey-sekh," *Ratnbildung* 4 (1930): 52–63.

Burganski, P. *Far antireligyezer dertsiyung in shul.* Kharkov: Tsentrfarlag, 1929.

———. "Polit-ufkler arbet in shtetl." *Ratnbildung,* 3 (1929): 31–7.

Chernenko, Miron. *Iudaika na ekrane: kinematograficheskaia istoriia evreistva v SSSR 1919–1934.* Moscow: Evreiskoe nasledie, 1990.

———. *Kinematograficheskia istoriia Sovetskogo evreistva 1934–1941.* Moscow: Evreiskoe nasledie, 1997.

———. *Krasnaia zvezda, zheltaia zvezda (kinematograficheskaia istoriia evreistva v Rossii, 1919–1999 gg.).* Vinnitsa: Globus, 2001.

Chernyak, B. *Evreiskaia lirika sovetskoi epokhi.* Moscow: Radioizdat, 1935.

Davidov, Al. "Di rolye fun radio inem lebn." *Di royte velt* 5 (1925): 71–73.

Den, N. *Krym.* Moscow, 1930.

Deych, Alexander. *Maski evreiskogo teatra.* Moscow: Russkoe teatral'noe obshchestvo, 1927.

———. "Vegn yidishn kamer-teater." *Di royte velt* 1 (1924): 22–27.

Dimanshteyn, Semen. *Di problem fun der natsionaler kultur.* Moscow: Tsentrfarlag, 1930.

———. *Evreiskaia avtonomnaia oblast'—detishche Oktiabr'skoi revoliutsii.* Moscow: Der emes, 1934.

———, ed. *Yidn in FSSR.* Moscow: Mezhdunarodnaia kniga and Der emes, 1935.

Dobin, Efim. *Pravda o evreiakh.* Leningrad: Krasnaia gazeta, 1928.

Dobrushin, Yekhezkel. *In iberboy.* Moscow: Der emes, 1932.

———. *Literaturno-kriticheskie stat'i.* Moscow: Sovetskii pisatel', 1964.

———. *Programen far kolvirtishn anti-religyezn dram-krayz.* Moscow: Der emes, 1933.

———. *Sovetishe yidishe folks-lider.* Moscow: Der emes, 1939.

———. "Vegn undzer kunst-kultur." *Di royte velt* 2 (1924): 43–47.

———. *Yidishe folks maysiyes.* Moscow: Der emes, 1939.

Dobrushin, Yekhezkel, and A. Yuditskii. *Evreiskie narodnye pesni*. Moscow: Gospolitizdat, 1947.

———. *Yidishe folks-lider*. Moscow: Der emes, 1940.

Dobrushin, Yeheskil, Iosif Rabin, and Lev Godlberg. *Deklamator fun der yidisher sovetisher literatur*. Moscow: Der emes, 1934.

Doloi pogromy. Odessa, 1920.

Dubilet, Moisey. "Dos ort fun literatur un anti-religyeze propagande in arbeter shul." *Ratnbildung* 10 (1929): 35–37.

Dunaevskiy, Isaak. *Birobidzhanskaia rybatskaia*. Moscow: Muzgiz, 1940.

Dunets, Khatskl. *Vegn der masn-arbet af yidish*. Minsk: Melukhe-farlag, 1929.

Engel, Yurii *Yudishe kinder lider far kinder-heymen, shuln un familie*. Moscow: Gezelshaft far yudishe muzik, 1919.

Epshteyn, Shakhne. "Oyfn sheydveg fun tsvey trupes." *Di royte velt* 5–6 (1929): 134–49.

Ershter may; zamlung fun kinder-lider un dertsylungen. Homel: Proftekhnishe shul fun druker, 1920.

Eydelman, E. *Ot cherty osedlosti k avtonomnoi oblasti*. Moscow: Der emes, 1934.

Far der bine (Dertseylungen, pyeses, lider). Moscow: Tsentrfarlag, 1929.

Farn proletarishn gerikht; protses ibern farhagvaltiker-farbrekher dem shoykhet (Yankev-Tevye) Rapoport. Minsk: Melukhe-farlag, 1934.

Fayntukh, Solomon. *A yat a braver: s'hot gelebt bay undz a khaver: kolhoznaya zastol'naya pesnya dlia vokal'nogo ansamblia (hora)*. Kiev: Tsentralnyi dom narodnogo tvorchestva URSR, 1939.

———. *Grentets lid: Bay di ratn: u granitsy ezdila, dlia hora*. Kiev: Tsentralnyi dom narodnogo tvorchestva URSR, 1939.

———. *Ot azoy neyt a shnayder: narodnaya pisnya dlia mishanogo khoru*. Kiev: Tsentralnyi dom narodnogo tvorchestva URSR, n.d.

———. *Urozhay: my vazhimo pshenitseyu*. Kiev: Tsentralnyi dom narodnogo tvorchestva URSR, 1931.

———. *Zaynen haynt gekumen: a kolvirte lid*. Kiev: Tsentralnyi dom narodnogo tvorchestva URSR, 1931.

Fefer Itsik. *A lid vegn firer*. Moscow: Der emes, 1940.

———. *Radio tsu alemen*. Kiev: Ukrmelukhnatsmindfarlag 1940.

Fefer, Itsik, Mikhail Kotlyar, and Fayvl Sito. *Ferzn un chastushkes*. Kiev: Ukrmelukhnatsmindfarlag, 1937.

Feldman, D. "Kultur-fragn, tsum VI-tn alfarbandishn profesionaln tsuzamenfor." *Di royte velt* 4 (1924): 32–34.

Folks-lider vegn Leninen. Kiev: Ukrmelukhnatsmindfarlag, 1937.

Folks-lider vegn Stalinen. Kiev: Ukrmelukhnatsmindfarlag, 1937.

Fradkin, Mark. *Yidishe folkslider*. Odessa: Melukhe-farlag, 1940.

Frayhayt lider (Lider tsu zingen). Odessa: Frayhayt, 1919.

Freydkina, Lyubov. *Korol' Lir v Moskovskom gosudarstvennom evreiskom teatre*. Moscow: Der emes, 1935.

Fridman, Vladimir. *Bibleiskie chudesa i zakony prirody*. Leningrad: Priboi, 1925.

Frumkina, Mariya [Esther Frumkina]. *Doloi ravvinov, ocherk anti-religioznoi bor'by sredi evreiskikh mass*. Moscow: Krasnaia nov', 1923.

Gilboa, Jehoshua. *A Language Silenced: The Suppression of Hebrew Literature and Culture in the Soviet Union*. Rutherford, N.J.: Associated University Press, 1982.

Gildin, Khaim. *Royte purim-shpil; bufanades*. Moscow: Yidsektsie, 1923.

Glensky, A. *Dergrayhungen un felern in der arbet tsvishn di natsionale mindehaytn.* Kharkov: Tsentrfarlag, 1931)

Godiner, Shmuel, and D. Lifshits. *Vstrecha v Tsymle.* Moscow: Der emes, 1936.

Godiner, Shmuel, and Avrom Vevyorke, eds. *Oys religye! Zamlung fun literatur, material tsum oysfirn af antireligyeze ovntn.* Moscow: Bezbozhnik, 1929.

Goldenberg, Boris. "Der yidisher klerikalizm un der antireligyezer kultur-marsh." *Di royte velt* 7 (1929): 97–105.

Goldin, Leybl. *Yidishe yontoyvim.* Kharkov: Tsentrfarlag, 1929.

Goldreyn, B. *In klub arayn.* Moscow: Tsentrfarlag, 1928.

Golubev, Nikolai. *Yidishe folsklider.* Moscow, 1936.

Gordon, Eliyahu, Peretz Markish, and Arn Kushnirov, eds. *Komyug; Literarish-kinstlerisher zamlung.* Moscow: Der emes, 1938.

Gordon, Eliyahu. *Fun nayem shteyger.* Minsk: Shul un bukh, 1925.

———. *Kolvirtishe bine.* Moscow: Der emes, 1932.

———. *Mayz.* Moscow: Der emes, 1936.

———. *Tsebrokhene stamen.* Minsk: Melukhe-farlag, 1927.

Grinblat, M., and Leon Dushman. *Stalin in der yidisher folksshafung.* Minsk: Vaysrusishe Visnshaft Akademie, 1939.

Grinzayt, I. *Litkomyug: a komyugishe zamlung: proze un kritik.* Kharkov: Ukrmelukhnatsmindfarlag, 1933.

Gurshteyn, Aron. *Izbrannye stat'i.* Moscow: Sovetskii pisatel', 1959.

Gutyansky, Sh., and Sh. Bryansky. "Vi batsien zikh etlekhe kinder tsu peysakh." *Ratnbildung* 4 (1930): 52–63.

Hantbukh far antireligyezer propaganda. Kiev: Kooperativer farlag fun kultur-lige, 1927.

Hantbukh fun yungn pioner. Moscow: Tsentrfarlag, 1925.

Hershenboym, Y. *A shtetl in rekonstruktivn period.* Minsk: Vaysrusishe visnshaft akademie, 1931.

Hindes, A. *Tomer iz dos a got?* Kharkov: Tsentrfarlag, 1929.

Iaroslavsky, Emel'ian. *Bibliia dlia veruiushikh i neveruiushikh.* Moscow: Bezbozhnik, 1923–1925.

Ivanovich, St. *Ravnopravie evreev.* Petrograd: Izdanie soiuza soldat respublikantsev, 1917.

Kahan A., ed. *Komyugishe zamlung: lider, dertseylungen.* Kharkov: Melukhe farlag fun Ukrayne, 1926.

Kalmanson, A. "Kremenchuge yidishe prof-tekhnishe shul." *Di royte velt* 5 (1925): 69–70.

Kantor, Iakov. *Natsional'noe stroitel'stvo sredi evreev SSSR.* Moskow: Vlast' Sovetov, 1934.

———. *Ratnbildung in der yidisher svive.* Kiev: Kultur-lige, 1928.

Kantselyarskii, P. *Sovetskaia vlast' i evreiskoe naselenie v SSSR.* Dnepropetrovsk: Partrabitnik dnipropetrovshini, 1929.

Karelin, A. A. *Zlye rosskazni pro evreev.* Moscow: Izdatel'stvo VTsIKS, 1919.

Kats, M. *Religiye iz nit keyn privat zakh.* Moscow: Tsentrfarlag, 1930.

Kazakevich, Kh. "Der ershter tsuzamenfor fun di yidishe kultur-tuers, 25.11–1.12.1924." *Di royte velt* 1 (1925): 27–30.

Kegn got un peysekh. Moscow: Der emes, 1939.

Kegn peysekh. Materialn fun propagandistn un fartreger tsu der anti-peysekh kampanye. Moscow: Tsentrfarlag, 1929.

Kegn religye. Dnepropetrovsk: n.p., 1931.

Kegn religye. Kharkov: n.p., n.d.

Kegn religye. Minsk: n.p., 1929.

Khadoshevich, K. "Oyf anti-religyezn front." *Shtern* 8–9 (1931): 76–84.

Khanzhi, Ch. E. *Evreiskaia sovetskaia literatura, annotirovannyi katalog.* Moscow: Mosgiz, 1936.

Kharik, Izi. *Broyt.* Moscow: Tsentraler felker farlag fun F.S.S.R., 1930.

Khashchevatski, Moisey, and Fayvl Sito. *Estrade.* Kiev: Melukhe farlag fardi natsyonale minderhaytn in USSR, 1938.

Khasnilevitsh, S. "Anti-religyeze kampanies." *Ratnbildung* 3 (1930): 48–52.

Khayt, Yu. A. *Khekher un khekher.* Moscow: Der emes, 1940.

Khaytov, L. *Der vilder minheg mile.* Moscow: Tsentrfarlag, 1923.

Kholodenko, D. *Kino.* Kiev: Ukr. Teater-Kino-Farlag, 1930.

Kiper, Motl. *Der antireligyezer kultur march in di kultur boyungen der yidisher svive.* Kharkov: Tsenrfarlag, 1930.

———. *Dos yidishe shtetl in Ukraine.* Kharkov: Melukhe farlag fun Ukraine, 1929.

———. *Evreiskoe mestechko Ukrainy.* Khar'kov: Proletarii, 1930.

Kipnis, Menakhem. *80 folkslider.* Warsaw: n.p., 1918.

Kirzhnits, Abram. *Di heylike shediker un undzer kultur-revolyutsie.* Moscow: Bezbozhnik, 1929.

———. *Trudiashchiesia evrei v bor'be s religiei.* Moscow: Bezbozhnik, 1931.

Klangen; Revolyutsionere lider. Ershte heft. Vitebsk: Yidishe Sektsiye RKP, 1920.

Klingen khamerlakh: Lider zamlung far for-shul kinder. Moscow: Melukhe-farlag, muzikalishe serie, 1925.

Klitenik, Shmuel. *Di kultur-arbet tsvishn di yidishe arbetndike inem Ratnfarband.* Moscow: Tsentrfarlag, 1931.

Koblents, B. *Far arbdorf korishe brigades.* Moscow: Tsentrfarlag, 1931.

———. *Vegn vos un vi azoy shraybn: tsum hilf dem arfdorf korespondent.* Moscow: Tsentrfarlag, 1930.

Kogan, L. Z. *Evreiskie narodnye pesni.* Moscow: Sovetskii kompozitor, 1958.

Kompaneets, Zinovii. *Geshtorbn iz dos alte. A satirish lid.* Moscow: Muzgiz, 1932.

Kompaneets, Zinovii. *Piat' pesen na slova evreiskikh sovetskikh poetov.* Moscow: Sovetskii kompozitor, 1960.

Kompaneets, Zinovii, ed. *Evreiskie narodnye pesni.* Moscow: Sovetskii kompozitor, 1961.

Komyugishe bufanade shel peysekh. Minsk: n.p., 1927.

Komyugishe lider: zamlbukh fun revolutsionere, komyugishe un pionerishe lider tsum zingen. Moscow: Tsentrfarlag, 1926.

Konstantinovski, M. "Eltern, kinder, klubn, leyenshtibl, shul." *Ratnbildung* 2 (1929): 30–32.

———. "Vi azoy darf men onfirn polit-ufkler arbet in shtetl un dorf zumertsayt." *Ratnbildung* 5 (1929): 1–5.

Korman, Ezra. *In fayerdikn doyer. Zamlung fun revolyutsionerer lirik in der nayer yidisher dikhtung.* Kiev: Melukhe-farlag, 1921.

Kostik, P. *Di klerikaln kegn dem agrominimus.* Kharkov: Knigospilke, 1930.

Kotlyar, Yosef. *Tsen lider.* Kharkov: Tsentrfarlag, 1927.

Kovaliv, N. D. *Di arbet fun leyens-shtibl bemeshekh fun posev-kampanie.* Kharkov: Tsentrfarlag, 1929.

Kreyn, Aleksander. *Dray lider des ghetto.* Moscow, 1929.

———. *Tsen yidishe lider far shtime un piano.* Moscow: Melukhe-farlag, 1940.

———. *Ya nartsiss Sarona. Liliya dolin.* Moscow, 1922.

Krishtal, D. *Khomets (Bufanade).* Kharkov: Tsentrfarlag, 1929.

Kruglyak, M. "Dramkrayz in shtetl." *Ratnbildung* 6 (1929): 35–38.

Kupershmid, Sh. "Folklor-Arbet in Shul." *Ratnbildung* 2 (1936): 84–87.

Kushnirov, Aharon. *Dos gezang fun di felker fun FSSR vegn Leninen un Stalinen.* Moscow: Der emes, 1939.

———, ed. *Dos land darf kenen zayne heldn. Literarisher zamlung.* Moscow: Der emes, 1932.

Kvitko, Leyb. *Deklamator.* Kharkov: Tsentrfarlag, 1929

Kvitko, Leyb, and Heneh Kozakevich. *Deklamator.* Kharkov: Tsentrfarlag, 1929.

Lev, Aba. *Der yidisher klerikalizm un zayn kamf kegn der yidisher arbeter-bavegung.* Moscow: Shul un bukh, 1928.

———. *Kleykoydesh in kamf mit der arbeter-bavegung.* Moscow: Shul un bukh, 1928.

———. *Religye un kleykoydesh in kamf kegn der yidisher arbeter-bavegung.* Moscow: Der emes, 1923.

Lewin, Moshe. "Popular Religion in Twentieth-Century Russia." In *The World of Russian Peasant: Post-Emancipation Culture and Society,* ed. Ben Eklof and Stephen Frank, 155–69. Boston: Unwin Hyman, 1990.

Leychkover, Yekhezkel. *Kegn religye, kegn peysekh.* Moscow: Tsentrfarlag, 1931.

Lezman, Y. *Dos muz visn yeder komyugist.* Moscow: Shul un bukh, 1928.

Lidelekh far kinder in kindergortn. Moscow: Ukrmelukhenatsmindfarlag, 1934.

Lider vegn Stalinen. Kiev: Ukrmelukhnatsmindfarlag, 1937.

Lifshits, Sh. *Vegn shtetl.* Kharkov: Ukrmelukhnatsmindfarlag, 1932.

Limone, M. *30 lider far kinder.* Minsk: Vaysruslendisher melukher farlag, 1928.

Literarishe zamlung far kinder-gertner. Minsk: Melukhe-farlag, 1936.

Litvakov, Moshe. *Finf yor melukhisher yidisher kamer-teater (1919–1924).* Moscow: Shul un bukh, 1924.

Loginov, A. *Nauka i bibliia.* Moscow: Bezbozhnik, 1925.

Lomir ale zingen. Zamlung fun yidishe, hebreyshe un englishe lider. New York: Yidisher muzik farband, 1956.

Lomir zingen, Lider zamlung mit notn. Moscow: Der emes, 1940.

Lopatin, Sh. "Lider." *Prolit* 1 (1928): 25.

Lurye, Hillel. *Shabes; vos men zogt vegn im un fun vanen er hot zikh in der emesn genumen.* Odessa: Melukhe-farlag, 1922.

———. *Toyre, ir antviklung, vi un ven iz zi geshafn gevorn. Vos meynt vegn vegn dem di visnshaft.* Kharkov: Melukhe-farlag, 1922.

———. *Yom Kippur* (Kharkov: Melukhe-farlag, 1923).

Lvov, S. "Dos kontrrevolyutsionere ponim fun yidishn klerikalizm," *Der shtern* 273 (1939).

Lyubomirski, Yevsei. *Der revolyutsyonerer teater.* Moscow: Shul un bukh, 1926.

———. *Kinematograf: vunder fun kino un zayn derklerung.* Moscow: Tsentrfarlag, 1930.

———. *Vi azoy tsu greytn spektakl (Hantbukh far dramkrayzn).* Moscow: Der emes, 1937.

Makagon, Ahron. *Anti-religyezer kultur-marsh.* Kharkov: Tsentrfarlag, 1929.

———. "Far ideologisher un efener zelbst-kritik in der yidisher kultur-arbet." *Ratnbildung* 12 (1929): 1–6.

———. *Kegn got un zayn diner.* Moscow: Der emes, 1940.

Makagon, Ahron, and Ephraim Shprakh. *Polituf kler arbet in shtetl. Hantbukh far yidishe polituf kler-tuers.* Kiev: Kultur-Lige, 1928.

Mardershteyn, I., and P. Solov'ev. *Paskha khristianskaia i evreiskaia.* Stalin: Okruzhnoi Sovet Bezbozhnikov, 1929.

Mashchenko, V. A. *Proiskhozhdenie i klassovaia sushchnost' evreiskoi paskhi.* Moscow: Der emes, 1931.

Maurenbrekher, M. *Proroki, ocherk razvitiia izrail'skoi religii.* Petrograd: Antei, 1919.

Melamed, B. "Di antireligyeze derfarung in arbcters shul." *Ratnbildung* 2 (1929): 22–29.

Melamud, Khaim. *Antireligyeze arbet in shul: praktik un metodik.* Kharkov: Tsentrfarlag, 1930.

Mikhailovsky, Vl. *Evrei pri belykh.* Rostov-on-Don, 1922.

Mikhoels, Solomon. *Sbornik.* Moscow: Iskusstvo, 1965.

———. *Stat'i, besedy, rechi.* Moscow: Iskusstvo, 1960.

Milner, M. *A gute nakht; far shtim mit piano.* Kiev: Kultur-Lige, 1921.

———. *Di farshterte khasene.* Leningrad: Muzsektsia evreiskogo istoricheskogo obshchestva, 1930.

———. *Farn obsheyd. Kleyn rapsodye.* Leningrad: Muzsektsia evreiskogo istoricheskogo obshchestva, 1930.

Mirer, Sholem. *Antiklerikale folks-maysyes.* Moscow: Der emes, 1940.

Mogulo, F. *Dos royte vinkl un di felder.* Kharkov: Tsetrfarlag, 1931.

Molodym bezbozhnikam: materialy k komsomol'skomu rozhdestvu: Sbornik. Biblioteka rabochei molodezhi. Moscow: Novaia Moskva, 1924.

Moss, Kenneth. "Tarbut/Kultur/Kultura in a Revolutionary Key: Rethinking and Remaking 'Modern Jewish Culture' in Russia and Ukraine, 1917–19." Paper presented at the annual meeting of the Association of Jewish Studies, Los Angeles, December 17, 2002.

Nadel', Kh. *Bibliografiia anti-religioznoi literatury. 46 nazvanii broshur i statei na russkom i ukrainskom iazykakh.* Kharkov: Tsentral farlag, 1931.

Natanzon, N. *Kolektivizatsie un kultur-arbet in yidishn dorf.* Moscow: Der emes, 1931.

Nesterenko, V. *Di arbreterin un di religye.* Kharkov: Di arbet palats, 1928.

Nikol'skii, Nikolai. *Proiskhozhdenie evreiskikh prazdnikov i khristianskogo kul'ta.* Gomel': gomelskii rabochii, 1926.

———. *Yidishe yontoyvim.* Minsk: Melukhe-farlag, 1925.

Nisnevich, D. N. *Dve evreiskie pesni dlia golosa s soprovozhdeniem fortep'iano.* Moscow: Sovetskii kompozitor, 1957.

Novakovski, Yehuda. *Got strapochet: kleykoydesh.* Kiev: Kultur-Lige, 1928.

Novakovski, Yehuda. *Yidishe yontoyvim: heylike minhogim un zeyere vortslen.* Kiev: Kultur-lige, 1929.

Obrastsov, M. I. *Moisei i piatiknizhie.* Astrakhan: Kommunist, 1925.

Oktyaber zamlung. Kiev: Melukhe-farlag, 1925.

Okun, Z. *Antireligyeze mayses un vertlekh.* Moscow: Der emes, 1939.

Orshanskiy, Ber. *Di yidishe literatur in vaysrusland nokh der revolyutsie.* Minsk: Tsentraler felker farlag fun FSSR, 1931.

———. *Horepashne froy—zay aktiv!* Moscow: Der emes, 1938.

Otsmakh, B. *Anekdoty i ostroty iz evreiskogo byta.* Krasnodar: Kubpoligraf, 1927.

Pionerishe lider. Minsk: Tsentrfarlag, 1927.

Polonski, S., and Izya Kharik. *Broyt.* Moscow: Tsentrfarlag, 1930.

Pul'ner, I. "Iz zhizni goroda Gomelya." In *Evreyskoe mestechko v revoliutsii,* ed. Vladimir Tan-Bogoraz. Moscow: Gosizdat, 1926.

Rabinovich, A. B. *Evreiskie osennie prazdniki.* Moscow: Moskovskii rabochii, 1929.

Rabinovich, A. B. *Iudeiskaia religiia.* Moscow: Gosudarstvennnoe anti-religioznoe izdatel'stvo, 1934.

Rabinovich, Israel, ed. *Der arbeter in der yidisher literatur.* Moscow: Tsentrfarlag, 1931.

———. *Froyen.* Moscow, 1928.

Rabinovich, Kh. A. *Vos dertseyln far kinder.* Kharkov: Tsentrfarlag, 1928.

Rafalski, M. *Zamlung far dramkrayz*. Minsk: Melukhe-farlag, 1936.

Ranovich, A., and F. Olezhchik. *Di yidishe religye un ir klasove rolye*. Kiev: Ukrmelukh-natsmindfarlag, 1938.

Riskind, B. *Tsen lider*. Kharkov: Tsentrfarlag, 1927.

Rosin, Shmuel. *Tsu der tsayt*. Moscow: Melukhe-farlag Der emes, 1939.

Royte frayhayt lider. Petrograd: Petrogradskii revolutsionnyi sovet, 1919.

Roytman, V. *A gedenk-bikhl far a kultarmeyer: vi tsu lernen matematik in likpunktn*. Kharkov: Melukhisher natsmindfarlag, 1932.

Rozenfeld, P. *Kadren far der kultur revolyutsye in der yidisher svive*. Moscow: Tsentrfarlag, 1927.

Rozentsvayg, A. *Sotsiale diferensatsye inem yidishn folklor lid*. Kiev: Alukrainishe visnshaftlekhe akademye, 1934.

Rubenchik, Yankl. *Akhter mart*. Minsk: Melukhe-farlag, 1926.

Rubinshteyn, M. *Dramkrayz*. Moscow: Tsentrfarlag, 1928.

Rumyantsev, A. *Paskha, ee proiskhozhdenie i znachenie*. Moscow: Bezbozhnik, 1927.

Ruzin, M. *Tsu hilf dem yunkor-krayz*. Kharkov: Yunge gvardie, 1927.

Sabaneev, Leonid. *Evreiskaia natsional'naia shkola v muzyke*. Moscow: Obshchestvo evreiskoi muzyki, 1924.

Salistra, Sh., and H. Holdrat. *Apikorsim vegn peysekh*. Kiev: Kultur-Lige, 1929.

Savikovski, E. *Far yunge zingers*. Minsk: Melukhe-farlag, 1927.

Shakhnovich, Mikhail. *Komu sluzhit religiia Izrailia*. Leningrad: Priboi, 1930.

———. *Sotsial'naia sushchnost' Talmuda*. Moscow: Ateist, 1929.

Sheyngold, M. *Der yunger apikoyres; antireligyezer leyenbukh*. Kharkov: Ukrmelukh-natsmindfarlag, 1932.

———. *Higienishe mitsves (Kosher un treyf)*. Kharkov: Tsentrfarlag, 1931.

———. "In ongrif kegn der religye (peysekh, der lerer, klub un dos leyenshtibl)." *Ratnbildung* 3 (1929): 18–23.

———. *Mit vos iz shedlekh di religye*. Kharkov: Tsentrfarlag, 1930.

Sheynin, E. *5 yidishe lider far a khor*. Kharkov: Ukrmelukhnatsmindfarlag, 1929.

———. *27 lider far kinder khor in eyn shtim mit piano bagletung*. Kiev: Ukrmelukh-natsmindfarlag, 1932.

———. *Zhovten*. Kiev: Mystetstvo, 1936.

Sheynman, Mikhail. *O ravvinakh i sinagogakh*. Moscow: Bezbozhnik, 1928.

Shlogler. Zamlung fun di minsker arbeter-shlogler, gerufene in der literature. Minsk: Melukhe-farlag, 1932.

Shlogler; Almanakh. Literarisher zamlung fun arbeter-shloglers in der literature. Kharkov: Ukrmelukhnatsmindfarlag, 1932.

Shloglerishe trit. Minsk: Melukhe-farlag, 1932.

Shostakovich, Dmitrii. *Iz evreiskoi narodnoi poezii, vokal'nyi tsikl dlia soprano*. Moscow: Muzykal'nyi fond SSSR, 1955.

Shprakh, Efraim. *Komyugishe politshmuesn*. Moscow: Tsentrfarlag, 1929.

Shtern, Yekhezkel. *Kheyder un beys-medresh*. New York: YIVO, 1948.

Shteynbakh A. *Masn-lider*. Minsk: Melukhe-farlag, 1934.

Shvartsman, Osher. *Lider vegn der royter armey*. Moscow: Der emes, 1938.

Skuditski, Zalman, and Meir Viner. *Folklor-lider; naye materialn-zamlung*. 2 vols. Moscow: Der emes, 1933.

Solts, B., and Note Vaynhoyz, *Yomim neroim*. Minsk: Chervonaya zmena, 1926.

Stalintses. (Zamlung fun litkrayz bam Moskver avtozavod af kh. Stalins nomen). Moscow: Der emes, 1932.

Sud nad bibliei (Instsenirovka). El'nya: Otdelenie narodnogo obrazovaniia, 1925.

Sudarski, Ya. *Far vos kemfn mir kegn religye.* Kharkov: Tsentrfarlag, 1931.

Sukhov, A. A. *Iudaism i khristianstvo.* Odessa: Gosizdat Ukrainy, 1925.

Tan-Bogoraz, Vladimir, ed. *Evreiskoe mestechko v revoliutsii.* Moscow: Gosizdat, 1926.

Terman, Moyshe. *Kultur un der arbeter klas.* N.p.: Di velt, 1918.

Tsentraler bildungs-komisarat. Yidishe opteylung. Rezolyutsies fun dem ershtn Alruslendishn tsuzamenfor fun yidishe tuer afn gebit fun sotsialistisher kultur un bildung in Moskve dem 16–26 Iyuli 1920. Moscow: Komunistishe velt, 1920.

Tsentraler bildungs-komisariat. Yidishe opteylung. Rezolyutsyes funem tsveytn Alfarbandishn tsuzamenfor fun di yidishe kultur-tuer. Kharkov: Tsentrfarlag, 1928.

Tsu Leninen. Dertseylungen far kinder. Moscow: Tsentrfarlag, 1927.

Utesov, Leonid. *S pesnei po zhizni.* Moscow: Iskusstvo, 1961.

———. *Spasibo, serdtse: vospominaniia, vstrechi, razdumia.* Moscow: VTO, 1976.

Vapnyarski, Sh. *Di yidishe horepashne froy in der sotsialistisher iberboyung.* Kharkov: Tsentrfarlag, 1925.

Verite, M. *Mir krigirishe apikorsim (Antireligyeze shmuesn).* Kharkov: Ukrmelukhnatsmindfarlag, 1932.

Vevyorke, Avrom. *Der shlogler hot a vort. Zamlung fun shloglers verk.* Kharkov: Tsentrfarlag, 1932.

———. *In shturem.* Kharkov: Ukrmelukhnatsmindfarlag, 1932.

———. *Revizye.* Kharkov: Literatur un kunst, 1931.

Veytsblit, I. "Daryevke. A pruv tsu gebn a monografishe bashraybung fun haynttsaytik yidish shtetl." *Di royte velt* 7–12 (1928).

———. *Derazhnia. Sovremennoe evreiskoe mestechko.* Moscow: Gosizdat, 1929.

———. *Vegn altn un nayem shtetl.* Kharkov: Tsentrfarlag, 1930.

Vigdorov, A. *Antireligyeze dertsiyung in der yidisher shul fun der ershter shtufe: metodishe briv.* Kharkov: Tsentrfarlag, 1929.

Viner, Meir. *Problemes fun folkloristik: zamlung..* Kiev: Ukrmelukhnatsmindfarlag, 1932.

Vishnevskaya, Elizaveta. *Antireligioznye skazki narodov SSSR. Antireligioznaia khudozhestvennaia biblioteka.* Moscow: Gosudarstvennoe antireligioznoe izdatel'stvo, 1939.

Vishnyak, Mark *Polozhenie evreev v Rossii.* Moscow, Zemlia i volia, 1917.

Vos yeder krigisher apikoyres darf visn. Kharkov: Tsentrfarlag, 1929.

Vozvrashchenie Natana Bekera, kino-libretto i metodichekie ukazaniia k besede. Moscow: Roskino, 1932.

Vsesoiuznyi s"ezd sovetskikh pisatelei. Stenograficheskii otchet. Moscow: Khudozhestvennaia literatura, 1934.

Yampolski, Leyb. *A kharavod.* Leningrad: Muzsektsia sektsiia evreiskogo istoriko-etnograficheskogo obchestva, 1930.

———. Yampolski, Leyb. *Birobidzhan.* Kiev: Ukrderzhnatsmenvydav, 1938.

———. *Blonde komsomolkes.* Minsk: Melukhe-farlag, 1935.

———. *Itster, kinder, helft undz mit.* Kiev: Ukrderzhnatsmenvydav, 1931.

———. *Ruf.* Minsk: Melukhe-farlag, 1935.

———. *Shteyt der vald.* Minsk: Melukhe-farlag, 1935.

———. *Yidishe kinder lider.* Minsk: Melukhe-farlag, 1935.

Yaroslavskii, Yemelyan. *Di bibl far gloybike un nit gloybike.* Moscow: Der emes, 1937.

Yidishe sovetishe folkslider mit melodies. Kiev: Ukrmelukhnatsmindfarlag, 1940.

Yom Kiper; hilfsbukh far propagandistn. Kharkov: Put prosveshchenie, 1923.

Zagorskii, Mikhail. *Mikhoels.* Moscow: Kinopechat', 1927.

Zamlbukh fun kinder lider. Homel: Melukhe-farlag, 1921.

Zamlbukh fun pionerishe dertseylungen. Minsk: Melukhe-farlag, 1927.

Zaslavskii, David. *Evrei v SSSR.* Moscow: Der emes, 1933.

Zavadovskii, B. M. *Moisei ili Darvin.* Moscow: Bezbozhnik, 1927.

Zhukov, B., and B. Kin. *Kultur arbet tsvishn kustarn un baley-melokhes.* Moscow: Der emes, 1936.

Zhukovski, S. "Vegn der yidisher literatur inem ibergang period." *Di royte velt* 9 (1928): 160–64.

Zinger, L. *Evreiskoe naselenie v Sovetskom Soiuze.* Moscow: OGIZ, 1933.

Published Secondary Sources

Alferov, Vladimir. *Vozniknovenie i razvitie rabsel'korovskogo dvizheniia v SSSR.* Moscow: Mysl', 1970.

Altshuler, Mordechai. *ha-Yevsektsyah bi-Verit ha-Moatsot 1918–1930: ben Leumiyut le-Komunizm.* Tel Aviv: Sifriyat Poalim, 1980.

———. "The Rabbi of Homel's Trial in 1922." *Michael* 6 (1980): 9–18.

———. *Soviet Jewry on the Eve of the Holocaust.* Jerusalem: Center for Research on East European Jewry, 1998.

———, ed. *ha-Teatron ha-Yehudi bi-Verit ha-Moatsot: mehkarim, iyunim, teudot.* Jerusalem: ha-Merkaz le-heker ule-teud Yahadut mizrah Eropah, ha-Universitah ha-Ivrit bi-Yerushalayim, 1996.

Anderson, John. *Religion, State, and Politics in the Soviet Union and Successor States.* Cambridge: Cambridge University Press, 1994.

Apter, David. "Political Religion in the New Nations." In *Old Societies and New States: The Quest for Modernity in Asia and Africa,* ed. Clifford Geertz, 57–104. London: Fress Press, 1963.

Azadovskii, A. "Novyi fol'klor." In *Sovetskii fol'klor,* 24–90. Leningrad: Nauka, 1939.

Baron, Salo Wittmayer. *The Russian Jew under Tsars and Soviets.* Rev. 2nd ed. New York: Macmillan, 1976.

Basin, Yakov. "Ia pesne vse otdal spolna." *Mishpokha* 5 (1999): 15–19.

Beizer, Mikhail. *Evrei Leningrada, 1917–1939. Natsional'naia zhizn' i sovetizatsiia.* Moscow: Gesharim, 1999.

Bickermann, Joseph, ed. *Ten Years of Bolshevik Domination: A Compilation of Articles.* Berlin: S. Scholem, 1928.

Blum, Jacob. *The Image of the Jew in Soviet Literature: The Post-Stalin Period.* New York: Ktav, 1984.

Blum, Zeev. *Poyle tsien in ratnfarband: zikhroynes, gedanken un dokumentn.* Tel-Aviv: Y. L. Perets, 1978.

Boym, Svetlana. *Common Places: Mythologies of Everyday Life in Russia.* Cambridge, Mass.: Harvard University Press, 1994.

Brandist, Craig. *Carnival Culture and the Soviet Modernist Novel.* Basingstoke: Macmillan, 1996.

Braun, Joachim. *Jews and Jewish Elements in Soviet Music: A Study of a Socio-national Problem in Music.* Tel Aviv: Israeli Music Publications, 1978.

Braun, Leopold L. S. *Religion in Russia, From Lenin to Khrushchev.* Paterson, N.J.: St. Anthony Guild Press, 1959.

Brooks, Jeffrey. *Thank you, Comrade Stalin: Soviet Public Culture from Revolution to Cold War.* Princeton, N.J.: Princeton University Press, 2000.

——. *When Russia Learned to Read: Literacy and Popular Literature, 1861–1917.* Princeton, N.J.: Princeton University Press, 1985.

Brym, Robert, and Andrey Degtyarev. "Anti-Semitism in Moscow: The Results of an October 1992 Survey." *Slavic Review* 52, no. 1 (spring 1993): 1–12.

Buss, Gerald. *The Bear's Hug: Religious Belief and the Soviet State.* London: Hodder and Stoughton, 1987.

Chernenko, Miron. *Krasnaia zvezda, zheltaia zvezda (kinematograficheskaia istoriia evreistva v Rossii, 1919–1999 gg.).* Vinnitsa: Globus, 2001.

Chervyakov, Valerii, Zvi Gitelman, and Vladimir Shapiro. "*E Pluribus Unum?* Post Soviet Jewish Identities and Their Implications for Communal Reconstruction." In *Jewish Life after the USSR,* ed. Zvi Gitelman, Musya Glants, and Marsall Goldman, 61–75. Bloomington: Indiana University Press, 2003.

Chmeruk, Chone. "Yiddish Literature in the USSR." In *The Jews in Soviet Russia since 1917,* ed. Lionel Kochan, 232–68. London: Oxford University Press, 1972.

——, ed. *Shpigl oyf a shteyn: antologye: poezye un proze fun tsvelf farshniten, Yidishe shraybers in Ratn-Farband.* Jerusalem: Magnes, 1987.

Clark, Katerina. *Petersburg: Crucible of Cultural Revolution.* Cambridge, Mass.: Harvard University Press, 1995.

——. *The Soviet Novel. History as Ritual.* Chicago: University of Chicago Press, 1981.

Coe, Steven Robert. "Peasants, the State, and the Languages of NEP: The Rural Correspondents' Movement in the Soviet Union, 1924–1928." Ph.D. diss., University of Michigan, 1993.

Cohen, Steven, and Arnold Eisen. *The Jew Within: Self, Family, and Community in America.* Bloomington: Indiana University Press, 2000.

Cohen, Yoseph. *Pirsumim Yekhudim Bivrit haMaoetzot, 1917–1960.* Jerusalem: Historical Society of Israel, 1961.

Conquest, Robert. *Religion in the USSR.* Soviet Studies series. London: Bodley Head, 1968.

Cooke, Richard Joseph, Bp. *Religion in Russia under the Soviets.* New York: Abingdon, 1924.

Dark, Sidney. *The War Against God.* New York: Abingdon, 1938.

Davis, Sarah. *Popular Opinion in Stalin's Russia.* Cambridge: Cambridge University Press, 1997.

Dennen, Leon. *Where the Ghetto Ends: Jews in Soviet Russia.* New York: A. H. King, 1934.

Dirks, Nicholas, Geoff Eley, and Sherry Ortner, eds. *Culture/Power/History: A Reader in Contemporary Social Theory.* Princeton, N.J.: Princeton University Press, 1994.

Dobrenko, Evgenii. *Formovka sovetskogo chitatelia. Sotsial'nye i esteticheskie predposylki retseptsii sovetskoi literatury.* St. Petersburg: Akademicheskii proekt, 1997.

Dobroszycki, Lucijan, and Jeffrey Gurock, eds. *The Holocaust in the Soviet Union.* Armonk, N.Y.: M. E. Sharpe, 1993.

Douglas, Mary. "Jokes." In *Rethinking Popular Culture: Contemporary Perspectives in Cultural Studies,* ed. Chandra Mukerji and Michael Schudson, 291–310. Berkeley: University of California Press, 1991.

Druzhinikov, Yurii. *Informer 001. The Myth of Pavlik Morozov.* New Brunswick, N.J.: Transaction, 1997.

Eliyashevich, Dmitrii. "Russko-evreiskaia kul'tura i russko-evreiskaia pechat' 1860–1945." In *Literatura o evreiakh na russkom iazyke, 1890–1947. Knigi, broshury, ottiski statei, organy periodicheskoi pechati. Bibliograficheskii ukazatel',* ed. Viktor Kel'ner and Dmitrii Eliyashevich, 37–78. St. Petersburg: Akademicheskii proekt, 1995.

Estraikh, Gennady. *Soviet Yiddish: Language Planning and Linguistic Development.* Oxford: Oxford University Press, 1999.

Etinger, Shmuel. "Istoricheskie korni antisemitizma v Sovetskom Soiuze." In *Evrei v kul'ture russkogo zarubezh'ia: sbornik statei, publikatsii, memuarov i esse.* Jerusalem: M. Parkhomovskii, 1992.

Fainsod, Merle. *Smolensk under Soviet Rule.* Cambridge, Mass.: Harvard University Press, 1958.

Fishman, David, "Judaism in the USSR, 1917–1930: The Fate of Religious Education." In *Jews and Jewish Life in Russia and the Soviet Union,* ed. Yaacov Ro'i, 251–62. Tel-Aviv: Frank Cass, 1995.

——. "Preserving Tradition in the Land of Revolution: The Religious Leadership of Soviet Jewry, 1917–1930." In *The Uses of Tradition,* ed. Jack Wertheimer, 85–118. New York: Jewish Theological Seminary, 1992.

Fishman, William. *East End Jewish Radicals, 1875–1914.* London: Duckworth, 1995.

Fitzpatrick, Sheila. *The Cultural Front: Power and Culture in Revolutionary Russia.* Ithaca, N.Y.: Cornell University Press, 1992.

——. *Cultural Revolution in Russia, 1928–1931.* Bloomington: Indiana University Press, 1978.

——. *Education and Social Mobility in the Soviet Union, 1921–1934.* Cambridge: Cambridge University Press, 1979.

——. *Everyday Stalinism. Ordinary Life in Extra-Ordinary Times: Soviet Russia in the 1930s.* New York: Oxford University Press, 1999.

——. *The Russian Revolution.* Oxford: Oxford University Press, 1982.

——. *Stalin's Peasants: Resistance and Survival in the Russian Village after Collectivization.* New York: Oxford University Press, 1994

Fitzpatrick, Sheila, Alexander Rabinowitch, and Richard Stites, eds. *Russia in the Era of NEP: Explorations in Soviet Society and Culture,* Bloomington: Indiana University Press, 1991.

Frank, Stephen, and Ben Eklof, eds. *The World of the Russian Peasant: Post-Emancipation Culture and Society.* Boston: Unwin Hyman, 1990.

Frank, Stephen P., and Mark D. Steinberg, *Cultures in Flux: Lower-Class Values, Practices, and Resistance in Late Imperial Russia.* Princeton, N.J.: Princeton University Press, 1994.

Frankel, Jonathan. *Prophecy and Politics: Socialism, Nationalism, and the Russian Jews, 1862–1917.* Cambridge: Cambridge University Press, 1981.

Friedberg, Maurice. "Jewish Themes in Soviet Russian Literature." In *The Jews in Soviet Russia since 1917,* ed. Lionel Kochan, 188–207. London: Oxford University Press, 1972.

Friedlaender, Israel. *The Jews of Russia and Poland: A Bird's-Eye View of Their History and Culture.* New York: Hebrew Publishing, 1920.

Frumkin, Vladimir. "Tekhnologiia ubezhdeniia." *Obozrenie* 5 (1983): 17–20; 6 (1983): 23–26.

Gans, Herbert J. *Popular Culture and High Culture: An Analysis and Evaluation of Taste.* New York: Basic Books, 1975.

Geertz, Clifford. *The Interpretation of Cultures.* London: Anchor, 1973.

——. *Old Societies and New States. The Quest for Modernity in Asia and Africa.* London: Free Press, 1963.

Gershuni, A. *Yahadut mi-Baad le-Soreg u-veRiah.* Jerusalem: Misrad Ha-hinukh Veha-tarbut, ha-Mahlakah Le-tarbut Toranit, 1978.

Gezets fun der Ruslendisher Sovetisher Federativer Sotsyalistisher Republik Vegn der Yid-isher Avtonomer Gegnt. Bibliotek fun Sovetish Heymland 5. Moscow: Sovetskii pisatel', 1984

Gibson, James L. "Understanding Anti-Semitism in Russia: An Analysis of the Politics of Anti-Jewish Attitudes." *Slavic Review* 53, no. 3 (autumn 1994): 829–56.

Gitelman, Zvi. *A Century of Ambivalence: The Jews of Russia and the Soviet Union, 1881 to the Present.* 2nd ed. Bloomington: Indiana University Press, 2000 [1988].

———. "Jewish Nationality and Religion in the USSR and Eastern Europe." In *Religion and Nationalism in Soviet and East European Politics,* ed. Pedro Ramet, 59–77. Durham and London: Duke University Press, 1989.

———. *Jewish Nationality and Soviet Politics: The Jewish Sections of the CPSU, 1917–1930.* Princeton, N.J.: Princeton University Press, 1972.

———. *The Jewish Religion in the USSR.* New York: Institute for Jewish Policy Planning and Research of the Synagogue Council of America, 1971.

———. *Soviet Reforms and Soviet Jewry: The Perils and Potentials of Perestroika.* Los Angeles: Susan and David Wilstein Institute of Jewish Policy Studies, 1989.

———. "Thinking about Being Jewish in Russia and Ukraine." In *Jewish Life after the USSR,* ed. Zvi Gitelman, Musya Glants, and Marsall Goldman, 49–60. Bloomington: Indiana University Press, 2003.

———, ed. *Bitter Legacy: Confronting the Holocaust in the Soviet Union.* Bloomington: Indiana University Press, 1997.

Gitelman, Zvi, Musya Glants, and Marshall Goldman, eds. *Jewish Life after the USSR.* Bloomington: Indiana University Press, 2003.

Gleason, Abbot, Peter Kenez, and Richard Stites, eds. *Bolshevik Culture: Experiment and Order in the Russian Revolution.* Bloomington: Indiana University Press, 1985.

Gol'din, Maks, ed. *Evreiskaia narodnaia pesnia.* St. Peterburg: Kompozitor, 1994.

Gorsuch, Anne. *Youth in Revolutionary Russia: Enthusiasts, Bohemians, Delinquents.* Bloomington: Indiana University Press, 2000.

Greenbaum, Avraam. *Jewish Scholarship and Scholarly Institutions in Soviet Russia, 1918–1953.* Jerusalem: Hebrew University of Jerusalem, 1978.

Grinko, E., and L. Efanova, eds. *Fol'klor Rossii v dokumentakh sovetskogo perioda 1933–1941. Sbornik dokumentov.* Moscow: Gosudarstvennyi respublikanskii tsentr russkogo fol'klora, 1994.

Grossman, Leonid Petrovich. *Ispoved' odnogo evreia.* Jerusalem: Izdatel'stvo Ia. Vaiskopfa, 1987.

Groys, Boris. *Iz dnevnika filosofa.* Paris: Posev, 1989.

Grunwald, Constantin de. *The Churches and the Soviet Union.* New York: Macmillan, 1962.

Gudashnikov, Ya. I. "Vidy i tipy peredelannykh literaturnykh pesen v Sovetskom fol'klore." *Russkii fol'klor* 9 (1964): 115–21.

Halevy, Zvi. *Jewish Schools under Czarism and Communism: A Struggle for Cultural Identity.* New York: Springer, 1976.

Hecker, Julius Friedrich. *Religion under the Soviets.* New York: Vanguard, 1927.

Herberg, William. *Protestant–Catholic–Jew: An Essay in American Religious Sociology.* Garden City, N.Y.: Doubleday, 1960.

Hobsbawm, Eric, and Terence Ranger. *The Invention of Tradition.* Cambridge: Cambridge University Press, 1983.

Hoffman David. *Peasant Metropolis: Social Identities in Moscow, 1929–1941.* Ithaca, N.Y.: Cornell University Press, 1994.

———. *Stalinist Values*. Madison: University of Wisconsin Press, 2003.

Hosking, Geoffrey. *Beyond Socialist Realism: Soviet Fiction since Ivan Denisovich*. London: Granada, 1981.

Hubbs, Joanna. *Mother Russia: The Feminine Myth in Russian Culture*. Bloomington: Indiana University Press, 1988.

Husband, William. *"Godless Communists": Atheism and Society in Soviet Russia, 1917–1932*. DeKalb: Northern Illinois University Press, 2000.

Iangirov, Rashid. "Jewish Life on the Screen in Russian, 1908–1919." *Jews and Jewish Topics in the Soviet Union and Eastern Europe* (spring 1990): 15–32.

Il'in, Vladimir. *Religiia revoliutsii i gibel' kul'tury*. Paris: YMCA-Press, 1987.

"Instruktsiya o likvidatsii negramotnosti sredi natsional'nykh men'shinstv na territorii RSFSR, 27 marta 1920 g." In *Kul'turnoe stroitel'stvo v RSFSR 1917–1927gg*. Moscow, 1983.

Jacobs, Dan, and Ellen Paul, eds. *Studies in the Third Wave: Recent Migration of Soviet Jews to the United States*. Boulder, Colo.: Westview, 1981.

Jahn, Hubertus. *Patriotic Culture in Russia during World War I*. Ithaca, N.Y.: Cornell University Press, 1995.

Jewish Sheet Music. From the Vernadsky Library in Kiev, Ukraine. Guide. Washington, D.C.: Museum of the Holocaust, 1992.

Kagedan, Allan. *Soviet Zion. The Quest for a Russian Jewish Homeland*. New York: St. Martin's, 1994.

Kaletskii, P. "O poetike chastushki." *Literaturnyi Kritik* 9 (1936): 186–201.

Kalinin, Mikhail. *Evreiskii vopros*. Moscow: Proletarii, 1927.

Kampars, Petr. *Sovetskaia grazhdanskaia obriadnost'*. Moscow: Mysl', 1967.

Kel'ner, Viktor. "Russkoe evreiskoe knizhnoe delo 1980–1947." In *Literatura o evreiakh na russkom iazyke, 1890–1947. Knigi, broshury, ottiski statei, organy periodicheskoi pechati. Bibliograficheskii ukazatel'*, ed. Viktor Kel'ner and Dmitrii Eliyashevich, 5–41. St. Petersburg: Akademicheskii proekt, 1995.

Kel'ner, Viktor, and Dmitrii Eliyashevich. *Literatura o evreiakh na russkom iazyke, 1890–1947. Knigi, broshury, ottiski statei, organy periodicheskoi pechati. Bibliograficheskii ukazatel'*. St. Petersburg: Akademicheskii proekt, 1995.

Kenez, Peter. *The Birth of the Propaganda State: Soviet Methods of Mass Mobilization, 1917–1929*. Cambridge: Cambridge University Press, 1985.

———. *Cinema and Soviet Society, 1917–1953*. Cambridge: Cambridge University Press, 1992.

———. *Varieties of Fear: Growing up Jewish under Nazism and Communism*. Washington, D.C.: American University Press, 1995.

Kent, Geiger. *The Family in Soviet Russia*. Cambridge, Mass.: Harvard University Press, 1968.

Kharkhordin, Oleg. *The Collective and the Individual in Russia. A Study of Practices*. Berkeley: University of California, 1999.

Kiel, Mark. "A Twice Lost Legacy: Ideology, Culture, and the Pursuit of Jewish Folklore in Russia until Stalinization, 1930–1931." Ph.D. diss., Jewish Theological Seminary of America, 1992.

Klier, John. *Russia Gathers Her Jews: The Origins of the "Jewish Question" in Russia, 1772–1825*. Dekalb: Northern Illinois University Press, 1986.

Kochan, Lionel, ed. *The Jews in Soviet Russia since 1917*. London: Oxford University Press, 1972.

Kolarz, Walter. *Religion in the Soviet Union*. New York: St. Martin's, 1961.

Korsch, Boris. *Soviet Publications on Judaism, Zionism, and the State of Israel, 1984–1988: An Annotated Bibliography.* Garland Reference Library of Social Science, vol. 482. New York: Garland, 1990.

Kotkin, Stephen. *Magnetic Mountain. Stalinism as a Civilization.* Berkeley: University of California Press, 1995.

Krupnik, Igor. "Cultural and Ethnic Policies toward Jews." In *Jews and Jewish Life in Russia and the Soviet Union,* ed. Yaacov Ro'i, 67–86. Tel-Aviv: Frank Cass, 1995.

Krutikov, Mikhail. "Constructing Jewish Identity in Contemporary Russian Fiction." In *Jewish Life after the USSR,* ed. Zvi Gitelman, Musya Glants, and Marshall Goldman, 252–74. Bloomington: Indiana University Press, 2003.

Kupovetskii, Mark. *Dokumenty po istorii i kul'ture evreev v arkhivakh Belarusi: putevoditel'.* Moscow: RGGU, 2003.

Kupovetskii, Mark, E. Savitskii, and Marek Web, eds., *Dokumenty po istorii i kul'ture yevreyev v arkhivakh Belarusi: putevoditel'* (Moscow: Rossiiskii gos. Gumanitarnyi universitet, 2003).

Lane, Cistel. *The Rites of Rulers. Ritual in Industrial Society: The Soviet Case.* Cambridge: Cambridge University Press, 1981.

Laskovaia, M. [Marina]. *Bogoiskatel'stvo i bogostroitel'stvo prezhde i teper'.* 2nd ed. Moscow: Moskovskii rabochii, 1976.

Lederhendler, Eli. "Did Russian Jewry Exist Prior to 1917?" In *Jews and Jewish Life in Russian and the Soviet Union,* ed. Yaacov Ro'i, 15–27. Tel-Aviv: Frank Cass, 1995.

———. *The Road to Modern Jewish Politics: Political Tradition and Political Reconstruction in the Jewish Community of Tsarist Russia.* New York: Oxford University Press, 1989.

Levin, Nora. *Jews in the Soviet Union since 1917: Paradox of Survival.* New York: New York University Press, 1988.

Lewin, Moshe. *Russia in the Making of the Soviet System: Essays in Social History.* New York: Patheon Books, 1985.

Lifshits, Solomon. *History of the Jewish Kolkhoz in Siberia (1926–1934).* Jerusalem: Soviet Institution series, 1975.

Livshits, Giler Markovich. *Ocherki po istorii ateizma v SSSR: 20–30-e gody.* Minsk: Nauka i tekhnika, 1985.

Lokshin, Alexander, ed. *Evrei v Rossiiskoi imperii XVII–XIX vekov.* Moscow: Izdatel'stvo evreiskogo universiteta, 1995.

Lovell, Steven. *The Russian Reading Revolution: Print Culture in the Soviet and Post-Soviet Eras.* New York: St. Martin's, 2000.

Luckert, Yelena. *Soviet Jewish History, 1917–1991: An Annotated Bibliography.* Garland Reference Library of Social Science, vol. 611. New York: Garland, 1992.

Luukkanen, Arto. *The Party of Unbelief: The Religious Policy of the Bolshevik Party, 1917–1929.* Helsinki: Suomen historiallinen seura, 1994.

———. *The Religious Policy of the Stalinist State: A Case Study. The Central Standing Commission on Religious Questions, 1929–1938.* Helsinki: Suomen historiallinen seura, 1997.

L'vov-Rogachevskii, V. (Vasilii). *A History of Russian Jewish Literature.* Ann Arbor: Ardis, 1979.

Mally, Lynn. *Culture of the Future: The Proletkult Movement in Revolutionary Russia.* Berkeley: University of California Press, 1990.

———. *Revolutionary Acts: Amateur Theater, and the Soviet State, 1917–1938.* Ithaca, N.Y.: Cornell University Press, 2000.

Maltinski, Chaim. *Der moskver mishpet iber di Birobidzshaner.* Tel-Aviv: Farlag nay-lebn, 1981.

Markish, Esther. *Stol' dolgoe vozvrashchenie: vospominaniia.* Tel-Aviv: Izdatel'stvo avtora, 1989.

Markish, Perets, B. Shnis, and R. Mil'man. *Vozvrashchenie Natana Bekkera.* Moscow: Der emes, 1932.

Markish, Shimon. *Babel' i drugie.* Moscow: Mikhail Shchigol, 1997.

Markowitz, Fran. *A Community in Spite of Itself: Soviet Jewish Émigrés in New York.* Washington: Smithsonian Institution, 1993.

McGuigan, Jim. *Cultural Populism.* New York: Routledge, 1992.

Medem, Vladımır. *Vladımır Medem, The Life and Soul of a Legendary Jewish Socialist.* New York: Ktav, 1979.

Mendelsohn, Ezra. *Class Struggle in the Pale: The Formative Years of the Jewish Workers' Movement in Tsarist Russia.* Cambridge: Cambridge University Press, 1970.

Middleton, David, and Derek Edwards. *Collective Remembering.* London: Sage, 1990.

Miller, Frank. *Folklore for Stalin: Russian Folklore and Pseudo-folklore of the Stalin Era.* Armonk, NY: M. E. Sharpe, 1990.

Mints, S. *Khronika chastnykh sobytii.* Tel-Aviv: Tri bogatyria, 1983.

Mlotek, Eleanor. *Perl fun yidish lid: 115 yidishe folks arbeter kunst un teater.* New York: Education Department of Workmen Circle, 1989.

Mlotek, Eleanor, and Yoseph Mlotek. *Mir trogn a gezang.* New York: Arbeter Ring, 1977.

Mogilner, Boris. *Far alts farantvortlekh.* Bibliotek fun Sovetish Heymland 6. Moscow: Sovetski pisatel', 1986.

Mukerji, Chandra, and Michael Schudson, eds. *Rethinking Popular Culture.* Berkeley: University of California Press, 1991.

My nachinali eshche v Rossii: vospominaniia. Biblioteka Aliia 97. Tel-Aviv: Biblioteka-Aliia, 1983.

My porvali s religiei; rasskazy byvshikh veruiushchikh. Nauchno-Populiarnaia biblioteka. 2nd ed. Moscow: Voennoe izdatel'stvo, 1963.

Nakhimovsky, Alice Stone. *Russian Jewish Literature and Identity: Jabotinsky, Babel, Grossman, Galich, Roziner, Markish.* Baltimore, Md.: Johns Hopkins University Press, 1992.

Niger, Shmuel. *Yidishe shrayber in Sovet-Rusland.* New York: S. Niger bukh-komitet baym Alteltlekhn Yidishn Kultur-Kongres, 1958.

Oinas, Felix. *Folklore, Nationalism, and Politics.* Columbus: Slavica, 1978.

Orleck, Annelise. *The Soviet Jewish Americans.* Detroit: Greenwich, 1999.

Ostrovski, Mikhail. *Keyn beser land, vi Rusland, iz af der velt nit faran.* Bibliotek fun Sovetish Heymland 4 (76). Moscow: Sovetskii pisatel', 1987.

Papernyi, Vladimir. *Kul'tura "Dva."* Moscow: Novoe literaturnoe obozrenie, 1996.

Peled, Yoav. *Class and Ethnicity in the Pale: The Political Economy of Jewish Workers' Nationalism in Late Imperial Russia.* London: Macmillan, 1989.

Peris, Daniel. *Storming the Heavens: The Soviet League of the Militant Godless.* Ithaca, N.Y.: Cornell University Press, 1998.

Petrone, Karen. *Life Has Become More Joyous, Comrades: Celebrations in the Time of Stalin.* Bloomington: Indiana University Press, 2000.

Pilkington, Hillary. *Russia's Youth and Its Culture: A Nation's Constructors and Constructed.* London: Routledge, 1994.

Pinchuk, Ben-Cion. *Shtetl Jews under Soviet Rule, Eastern Poland on the Eve of the Holocaust, Jewish Society and Culture.* Oxford: Blackwell, 1990.

Pinkus, Benjamin. *The Jews of the Soviet Union: The History of a National Minority.* Cambridge: Cambridge University Press, 1988.

Pinkus, Benjamin, Avraam Grinbaum, and Mordechai Altshuler. *Pirsumim Rusiim al Yehudim ve-Yahadut Vi-vrot ha-Moazot, 1917–1967.* Jerusalem: Historical Society of Israel, 1970.

Piscator, Erwin. *The Political Theatre.* London: Eyre Methuen, 1980.

Portnoy, Edward. "Interwar Parodies of the Passover Haggadah." Paper presented at the Thirty-first Annual Conference of the Association for Jewish Studies, Chicago, December 19–21, 1999.

Pospielovsky, Dimitry. *History of Soviet Atheism in Theory and Practice, and the Believer.* Vol. 1, *A History of Marxist-Leninist Atheism and Soviet Anti-Religious Policies.* Houndmills, Basingstoke, Hampshire: Macmillan, 1987.

———. *History of Soviet Atheism in Theory and Practice, and the Believer.* Vol. 2, *Soviet Anti-Religious Campaigns and Persecutions.* Houndmills, Basingstoke, Hampshire: Macmillan, 1988.

Powell, David. *Antireligious Propaganda in the Soviet Union: A Study of Mass Persuasion.* Cambridge, Mass.: MIT Press, 1975.

Ramet, Pedro. ed. *Religion and Nationalism in Soviet and East European Politics.* Durham and London: Duke University Press, 1989.

Ramet, Sabrina. *Cross and Commissar: The Politics of Religion in Eastern Europe and the USSR.* Bloomington: Indiana University Press, 1987.

———, ed. *Religious Policy in the Soviet Union.* Cambridge: Cambridge University Press, 1993.

Ro'i, Yaacov. ed. *Jews and Jewish Life in Russia and the Soviet Union.* Bath, England: Frank Cass, 1995.

Robin, Regine. "Popular Literature of the 1920s: Russian Peasants as Readers." In *Russia in the Era of NEP: Explorations in Soviet Society and Culture,* ed. Sheila Fitzpatrick, Alexander Rabinowitch, and Richard Stites. Bloomington: Undiana University Press, 1991.

———. *Socialist Realism: An Impossible Aesthetic.* Stanford: Stanford University Press, 1992.

Romanovsky, Daniel. "An Unpublished Soviet Film of 1940 with a Jewish Theme." *Jews in Eastern Europe* (spring 1996): 32–36.

Rosental, Bernice Glatzer, ed. *The Occult in Russian and Soviet Culture.* Ithaca, N.Y.: Cornell University Press, 1997.

Rothenberg, Joshua. "Jewish Religion in the Soviet Union." In *The Jews in Soviet Russia since 1917,* ed. Lionel Kochan, 159–87. London: Oxford University Press, 1970.

———. *The Jewish Religion in the Soviet Union.* New York: Ktav, 1972.

———. *Judaism in the Soviet Union: A "Second-class" Religion?* Washington, D.C.: B'nai B'rith International Council, 1971.

Rothshild, Sylvia. *An Oral History of Soviet Jewish Émigrés in the United States.* New York: Simon and Schuster, 1985.

Rothstein, Robert. "How It Was Sung in Odessa: At the Intersection of Russian and Yiddish Folk Culture," *Slavic Review* 4 (2001): 287.

———. "Popular Song in the NEP Era." In *Russia in the Era of NEP: Explorations in Soviet Society and Culture,* ed. Sheila Fitzpatrick, Alexander Rabinowitch, and Richard Stites, 263–83. Bloomington: Indiana University Press, 1991.

Rozin, Aharon. *Darki Ha-baitah: Zikhronot Shel Asir-Tsiyon bi-Verit-ha-Moatsot.* Jerusalem: Y. Markus, 1983.

Rubin, Ruth. *Voices of a People: The Story of Yiddish Folksongs.* Philadelphia: Jewish Publication Society of America, 1979.

Rubin, Shlomo. "Der yidisher teater." In *Yisker bukh fun Rokisis, Lite,* ed. M. Bakalczuk-Felin, 261. Johannesburg: Rakishker Society, 1952.

Savel'ev, S. N. [Sergei Nikolaevich]. *Ideinoe bankrotstvo bogoiskatel'stva v Rossii v nachale XX Veka: Istoriko-religiovedcheskii ocherk.* Leningrad: Izdatel'stvo Leningradskogo Universiteta, 1987.

Schedrin, Vasilli, ed. *Obzor dokumental'nykh istochnikov po istorii evreev v arkhivakh SNG. Tsentral'nye gosudarstvennye arkhivy. Gosudarstvennye oblastnye arkhivy Rossiiskoi Federatsii.* Moscow: Ob-vo "Evreiskoe nasledie," 1994.

Schulman, Elias. *A History of Jewish Education in the Soviet Union.* New York: Ktav, 1971.

Schwartz, Solomon. *The Jews in the Soviet Union.* Syracuse, N.Y.: Syracuse University Press, 1951.

Seldon, Antony, and Joanna Pappworth. *By Word of Mouth: "Elite" Oral History.* London: Methuen, 1983.

Sheptaev, L. "Sovetskaia chastushka." In *Sovetskii Fol'klor,* 264–97. Leningrad: Khudozhestvennaya literatura, 1939.

Sheyn, Yosef. *Arum Moskver yidishn teater.* Paris, [1964?].

Shneer, David. "A Revolution in the Making: Yiddish and the Creating of Soviet Jewish Culture." Ph.D. dissertation, University of California, Berkeley, 2001.

———. *Yiddish and the Creation of Soviet Jewish Culture.* New York: Cambridge University Press, 2004.

Shrayer, Maxim. *Russian Poet/Soviet Jew: The Legacy of Eduard Bagritskii.* Lanham, Md.: Rowman and Littlefield, 2000.

Shternshis, Anna, "Soviet and Kosher in the Ukrainian *Shtetl.*" In *The Shtetl: Image and Reality,* ed. Gennady Estraikh and Mikhail Krutikov, 133–51. Oxford: Legenda, 2000.

Sicher, Efraim. *Jews in Russian Literature after the October Revolution: Writers and Artists between Hope and Apostasy.* Cambridge: Cambridge University Press, 1995.

Siegelbaum, Lewis H. *Soviet State and Society between Revolutions, 1918–1929.* Cambridge Soviet Paperbacks, 8. Cambridge: Cambridge University Press, 1992.

———. *Stakhanovism and the Politics of Productivity in the USSR, 1935–1941.* Cambridge: Cambridge University Press, 1988.

Smith, Gerald Stanton. *Songs to Seven Strings: Russian Guitar Poetry and Soviet "Mass Song."* Bloomington: Indiana University Press, 1984.

Smolar, Hersh. *Fun ineveynik: zikhroynes vegn der yevsektsye.* Tel-Aviv: Y. L. Perets farlag, 1978.

———. *Vu bistu khaver Sidorov?* Tel-Aviv: Y. L. Perets farlag, 1975.

Soifer, Paul. *Soviet Jewish Folkloristics and Ethnography: An Institutional History, 1918–1948.* New York: YIVO, 1978.

Sokolov, A., ed. *Golos naroda. Pis'ma i otkliki riadovykh sovetskikh grazhdan o sobytiiakh 1918–1932gg.* Moscow: Rospen, 1998.

Sokolov, Yurii M. "Fol'klor i pisatel'skii s"ezd." *Sovetskoe kraevedenie* 10 (1934): 4–10.

Solomonik, Ella, ed. *Evrei Kryma: ocherki istorii.* Simferopol: Mosty, 1997.

Stanislawski, Michael. *Tsar Nicholas I and the Jews: The Transformation of Jewish Society in Russia, 1825–1855.* Philadelphia: Jewish Publication Society of America, 1983.

Starr, Frederick. *Red and Hot: The Fate of Jazz in the Soviet Union, 1917–1980.* New York: Oxford University Press, 1983.

Stites, Richard. "Bolshevik Ritual Building in the 1920s." In *Russia in the Era of NEP:*

Explorations in Soviet Society and Culture, ed. Sheila Fitzpatrick, Alexander Rabinowitch, and Richard Stites, 295–309. Bloomington: Indiana University Press, 1991.

———. *Revolutionary Dreams: Utopian Vision and Experimental Life in the Russian Revolution* (New York: Oxford University Press, 1989).

———. *Russian Popular Culture, 1917–1990.* Cambridge University Press, 1992.

———. "Trial as Theater in the Russian Revolution." *Theater Research International* 23, no 1 (1999): 7–13.

———, ed. *Culture and Entertainment in Wartime Russia.* Bloomington: Indiana University Press, 1995.

Stourac, Richard, and Kathleen McCreery. *Theatre as a Weapon: Workers' Theatre in the Soviet Union, Germany, and Britain, 1917–1934.* London: Routlege and Kegan Paul, 1986.

Szajkowski, Zosa. *An Illustrated Sourcebook of Russian Antisemitism, 1881–1978.* New York: Ktav, 1980.

Tcherikover, A. "Der mishpet iber der yidisher religye." In *In der tkufe fun revolutsiye,* ed. idem. Berlin: Yidisher literarisher frlag, 1924.

Thompson, Paul. *The Voice of the Past.* Oxford: Oxford University Press, 2000.

Thrower, James. *Marxism-Leninism as the Civil Religion of Soviet Society: God's Commissar.* Studies in Religion and Society 30. Lewiston: Mellen, 1992.

Timasheff, Nicholas. *Religion in Soviet Russia, 1917–1942.* New York: Sheed and Ward, 1942.

Tirado, Isabel. "The Revolution, Young Peasants, and the Komsomol's Antireligious Campaigns, 1920–1928." *Canadian American Slavic Studies* 26, nos. 1–3 (1992): 97–117.

———. *The Village Voice: Women's Views of Themselves and Their World in Russian Chastushki of the 1920s.* Pittsburgh: Center for Russian and East European Studies, University of Pittsburgh, 1993.

Tumarkin, Nina. *Lenin Lives! The Lenin Cult in Soviet Russia.* Cambridge, Mass.: Harvard University Press, 1983.

Ul'ianov, Mikhail. *Kul'turnoe obsluzhivanie truzhenikov sela—zabota obshchaia.* Moscow: Profizdat, 1973.

Utesov, Leonid. Para gnedykh. CD disk. Moskow: Kominform, 1995.

Veidlinger, Jeffrey. "Let's Perform a Miracle: The Soviet Yiddish State Theater in the 1920s." *Slavic Review* 57, no. 2 (summer 1998): 372–97.

———. *The Moscow State Yiddish Theater: Jewish Culture on the Soviet Stage.* Bloomington: Indiana University Press, 2000.

Vereshchagin, A. *Pesni dlia uchashchikhsia 6–7 klassov.* Kiev: Muzychna Ukraina, 1975.

Vergelis, Arn. *16 stran, vkliuchaia Monako: putevye ocherki.* Moscow: Sovetskii pisatel', 1979.

Vinkovetskyi, Aharon. *Anthology of Yiddish Folksongs.* 4 vols. Jerusalem: Mount Scopus Publications by the Magnes Press, 1983–87.

Viola, Lynne. *Peasant Rebels under Stalin: Collectivization and the Culture of Peasant Resistance.* New York: Oxford University Press, 1996.

Volkov, Vadim. "The Concept of *Kulturnost*': Notes on the Stalinist Civilizing Process." In *Stalinism: New Directions,* ed. Sheila Fitzpatrick, 210–30. London: Routledge, 2000.

von Geldern, James. *Bolshevik Festivals, 1917–1920.* Berkeley: California University Press, 1993.

von Geldern, James, and Richard Stites, eds. *Mass Culture in Soviet Russia: Tales, Poems, Songs, Movies, Plays, and Folklore, 1917–1953.* Bloomington: Indiana University Press, 1995.

von Hagen, Mark. *Soldiers in the Proletarian Dictatorship: The Red Army and the Socialist State, 1917–1930.* Ithaca, N.Y.: Cornell University Press, 1990.

Walters, Philip. "A Survey of Soviet Religious Policy." In *Religious Policy in the Soviet Union,* ed. Sabrina Ramet, 3–30. Cambridge: Cambridge University Press, 1993.

Weinberg Robert. *Stalin's Forgotten Zion: Birobidzhan and the Making of a Soviet Jewish Homeland: An Illustrated Story, 1928–1996.* Berkeley: University of California Press, 1998.

Weinryb, Bernard. "Anti-Semitism in Soviet Russia" In *Jews in Soviet Russia,* ed. Lionel Kochan. London: Oxford University Press, 1972.

Wertheimer, Jack, ed. *The Uses of Tradition.* New York: Jewish Theological Seminary, 1992.

White, Stephen. *The Bolshevik Poster.* New Haven, Conn.: Yale University Press, 1998.

Wood, Elizabeth. *The Baba and the Comrade.* Bloomington: Indiana University Press, 1997.

———. *Performing Justice: Agitation Trials in Early Soviet Russia.* Ithaca: Cornell University Press, 2005.

Yarmolinsky, Avraham. *The Jews and Other Minor Nationalities under the Soviets.* New York: Vanguard, 1928.

YIVO Institute of Jewish Research, *Revolutions in Print: Jewish Publishing under Tsars and Soviets.* New York: YIVO, 1990.

Young, Glennys. *Power and the Sacred in Revolutionary Russia. Religious Activists in the Village.* University Park: Pennsylvania State University Press, 1997.

Index

Italicized page numbers refer to illustrations.

day care, 15
"Dayenu" (Passover song), 34, 38
de-Stalinization, 45
Denikin, Gen. A. I., 27, 28, 35, 183
Dennen, Leon, 134, 163
denunciations, 60–62
Detgiz (Children's State Publishing
  House), 148
"Directions and Methods for Conducting
  Trials of Literary Works in the Yiddish
  Language," 101
Dnepr on Fire (film), 166
Dnepropetrovsk (Ukraine), 145–46
Dobrushin, Yekhezkel, 84, 128, 130, 169
Dodke der leninets [Dodke the Leninist] (short
  story), 50, *51*
Douglas, Mary, 83
"Du darfst nit geyn mit pochaeve meydelekh"
  [You cannot go with the girls from Po-
  chaev] (song), 132
Dunaevsky, Isaak, 169, 174, 178
"Dzhankoye" (song), 119–21, 122, 124–25, 140

Easter, Russian Orthodox, 1, 2, 20, 42, 196n111
Edelshtadt, Dovid, 108, 109, 110
Eesovtses (political party), 27
Eisen, Arnold, xiv
"Elijah at Passover" (poem), 154–55
"Eliyahu HaNavi" (song), 169
Emes, Der [The truth] (newspaper), 4, 54, 65,
  198n21
émigrés, 10
"End of a Friendship, The" (magazine
  article), 150
Erenburg, Iliya, 147–48
"Erev yom kiper" [Yom Kippur eve] (Pin-
  sky), 101–102
Esers (political party), 27
Esesovtses (political party), 27
Estraikh, Gennady, 187–88n10
ethnography, xx
Ettinger, Solomon, 52
Europe, Eastern, 7, 26
"Evreiskaia komsomol'skaia" (Jewish Komso-
  mol song), 169
"Evreiskaia novogodniaia" [The Jewish New
  Year song] (song), 179
"Evreiskaia rapsodiia" [Jewish rhapsody]
  (song), 174–75, 177
Evsektsii (Jewish sections of Communist
  Party), xv, xviii, 9, 36; archival records of,
  190n28; closing of, 187n8; Jewish educa-
  tional system and, 14; Jewish holidays
  and, 20–21, 24, 26; literacy campaigns

and, 48; living newspapers and, 78, 80; on
  popularity of Zionism, 63–64; Red Passover
  and, 27; synagogue closings and, 9; theatrical trials and, 94, 96, 98, 101; Yiddish theater and, 72, 73, 76
Exodus, story of, 27, 35, 109, 195n86. *See also*
  Passover
exoticism, 134, 170
Experimental Theater (Kiev), 72
exploitation, by bourgeoisie, 5

factories, 119
family: as center of Jewish tradition, 39, 41;
  denunciations within, 60–62; socialist revolution and, 102; Soviet family values, 132–
  34; theatrical trials and, 98
Farkishefter shnayder, Der [The bewitched
  tailor] (Aleichem), 74
Farvos hot Itsik nit khasene gehat [Why Itsik
  did not get married] (play), 74
fascism, 7
fashion, Western, 134
Fefer, Itsik, 44, 45, 67, 68; *chastushkes* collection and, 206n24; socialist realism and, 148;
  song about Stalin, 112; theater and, 72
film (motion pictures). *See* cinema
Fink, Ilia, 178
Fishman, David, 9, 15, 43
Fitzpatrick, Sheila, 60
Five Brides (film), 166
folk songs, xiii, xx, 38; collections of, 106, 128,
  130; "cruel romances" and, 137; images of
  Stalin in, 112; in literacy courses, 49; as ma-
  terial for professional composers, 132; paro-
  dies in buffoon theater, 85; of Russian or
  Ukrainian origin, 178, 181. *See also* songs
folklore, Russian, 113
folklore, Soviet Jewish, 114, 119
Folksbine, xiii
Fomin, Boris, 178
food, xiii, 121–22
Frankel Center for Judaic Studies (University
  of Michigan), xix
Fray, Sonya, 72
"Frayhayt" [Freedom] (song), 107–108
"Friends" (Neker), 150–51, *151*
Frumkin, Ester, 52, 198n21
"Fun ale meydelekh iz Beylke bay mir shener"
  [Of all girls, Beylke is the most beautiful to
  me] (song), 130, 136–38
Fun Kaslovich keyn Kherson [From Kas-
  lovich to Kherson] (Yafe), 85, 90–91
Fun yener velt [From the other world]
  (Verite), 85–89

treatment of, 166, 169; in propaganda litera-
ture, 151; songs about, 170–73
International Day of Youth, 40
International Women's Day, 39
"Internationale" (song), 34, 111
Iskateli shchastia [Seekers of happiness]
(film), 166–70
Israel, 66, 200n3
"Itsik hot shoyn khasene gehat" [Itsik got
married] (song), 131–32
Izvestiia (newspaper), 65

jazz, 173
Jesus, 153
Jewish Commissariat (*Evkom*), xv
"Jewish question," 119, 159, 165–70
Jewish Question, The [*Evreiskii vopros*]
(Kalinin), 159
"Jewish worrier," image of, 91
Jews and Jewish communities, xvii, 9, 44, 60;
as beneficiaries of Soviet revolution, 3, 10–
11, 69, 116; "chosen people," 5; cinema and,
166–70; class division within, 97, 98–99,
101–102, 155; community centers, 14; conflict between real and ideal, 62; destroyed
in Holocaust, 182; dual culture of, 181; as
ethnicity, 2; Jewish "masses," xvii; Judaism disassociated from Jewishness, xiii;
non-Ashkenazic Soviet Jews, 188n20; in
post-Soviet Russia, 181; relations with
other Soviet nationalities, 121; as religious minority, 2; resettlement from
shtetlach, 56; Russification of, 141, 144;
switch to agricultural labor, 89, 119–26;
in tsarist Russia, 183; urban migration of,
59, 209n3
Jews in the Fight against the White Army
(Mikhailovsky), 154
journalists, 46, 60, 63
Judaism, 5, 21, 143, 184; antireligious campaigns and, 3; attacked by Jewish Communist activists, 9–10; defended against antisemitism, 153–54; dietary laws (*kashrut*),
xiii, xiv, 1, 182; enlightenment (19th century), 7, 196n107; idealization of, 165;
Musar movement, 96–98, 204n74; Orthodox, 33, 77, 97, 212n51; principles of belief
(*ani maamin*), 21, 194n64; prohibitions of
Jewish law, 84; Russian-language propaganda against, 149–58; state persecution of,
43; theatrical attacks on, 82, 84–85, 94–96;
as tribal religion, 3; ultra-Orthodox, xiv. *See
also* Orthodox Judaism; rabbis; synagogues;
Talmud; Torah

Kadet Party, 27
Kaganovich, Lazar, 118
Kalatun, Grigori, 95
Kalinin, Mikhail, 118, 133, 159
Kamenev, Lev, 200n3
"Kapitalistisher ani maamin, Der" (The capi-
talist principles of belief), 21, *22*, 23, 24
Karelin, A., 153, 154
Kasatin (Ukrainian shtetl), 127
kashrut (Jewish dietary laws), xiii, xiv, 1, 182
Kenez, Peter, xvii
Khadoshevich, K., 36
Khaluts (He-Halutz), 64, 199n57
Kharik, Izi, 67
Kharkov (Ukraine), 55, 65, 72, 80
kheyder/khaydorim (Jewish primary schools),
4–5, 57; Bolshevik literacy programs and,
47, 48; instructors (*melamdim*), 15–16, 88,
98; replaced by Soviet schools, 14–20; songs
referring to, 108; teaching method at, 120;
theatrical trials against, 93, 96, 98, 204n75;
underground, 157; worker correspondents
and, 58
Khots (Gots), Abram, 27
Kiev, 5, 45, 55; cinema in, 167; Jewish migra-
tion to, 144; theater in, 72; theatrical trials
against antisemitism in, 163, 164
"Kinder yorn" [Childhood years] (song), 130
Kipnis, Itsik, 148, 210n15
Kishefmakherin [The witch] (Goldfaden), 73–74
klezmer, 114, 174
Kobzon, Joseph, 180
Kolchak, Adm. A. V., 27, 35, 183
"Kolektivchikes" [Small collectives]
(Markin), 56
Kolvirtishe shtern [Collective farm star]
(newspaper), 55
Komsomol (Communist Youth League), 3,
82, 152, 183; amateur theater and, 80; antireligious activities, 41; appeal of, 11; denunciations and, 61; girls and fashion in, 134;
Jewish members of, 17, 26; Komsomol Haggadah, 27–30; literacy campaigns and, 50–
52; songs referring to, 133, 137; synagogue
closings and, 9; theatrical trials and, 98,
100; worker correspondents and, 64
Komunistishe fon [Communist flag] (newspaper), 55
komyugistn. See Komsomol (Communist
Youth League)
Kopaigorod (Ukrainian shtetl), 70, 80
korenizatsiia ("nativization"), xv, 65, 69, 183;
Russian-speaking Jews and, 147; slogans of,
84; theater and, 71

kosher food, xiii, 1–2, 3, 37, 146–47, 207n35.
    See also kashrut (Jewish dietary laws);
    shoykhet/shokhtim (kosher butchers)
"kosher pork," xiii–xiv, 182, 185, 207n35
Kotlyar, Yoysef, 84, 206n24
Kozhetrest, 89
Kremenchug (Ukraine), 98
Kremenchuger arbeter [Kremenchug worker]
    (newspaper), 56, 59, 60–61
Kreyn, A., 130
Krupnik, Igor, 3
"Krutitsya, vertitsya shar goluboy" [The blue
    ball is spinning] (song), 124
kulaks, 82, 101, 202n40
Kultur lige (Culture League), 72, 200n8
Kunstvinkl (Art corner), 72
Kushnirow, Aron, 72
kustars (handicraftsmen), 37, 84, 88, 89
Kvitko, Leyb, 148, 176

Lafarg, P., 21
language, xiii, 122
Latvian language, 188n11
laughter, Freudian theory of, 83
League of the Militant Godless, 3, 4
Lekert, Hirsh, 80, 110–11, 183
Lenin, V. I., 5, 20, 188n11, 193n38; death of,
    56; in song, 38; worker correspondent move-
    ment and, 64; writings translated into Yid-
    dish, 198n21
Leningrad, 9, 17, 68, 104, 144, 149
Leninism, 50, 52
Lermontov, Mikhail, 68
"Lid vegn firer, A" [A song about the leader]
    (song), 112
Lifshits, D., 160
Lipkin, Israel (Salanter), 204n74
Lipkina, Sofiya, *13*
lishentsy (persons deprived of civil rights),
    3, 61
literacy campaigns/courses, 45, 46–54, 69,
    197n14; antireligious propaganda and, 152;
    theater and, 89
literary heroes, theatrical trials of, 101–103
literature, Yiddish, 19, 66–69, 148–49, 200n71,
    210n15
Lithuania, 1, 73, 80, 96, 204n74
"Little Bells Ring and Play" (song), 176,
    215n118
"Lomir ale in eynem" [Let us all together]
    (song), 177
"Lomir trinken a lekhaim" [Let us drink a
    toast] (song), 114–16, 119
London, xiv

London, Jack, 66
Lopatin, Sholem, 121
loshn koydesh. See Hebrew language
Loyter, Efraim, 72
Lubavicher Rebbe, 9
Lunacharsky, Anatolii, 200n3
Lurye, Hilel, 5
Lurye, Noteh, 148, 210n15

Mabul (film), 166
macaronic songs, 139–40
Maeterlinck, Maurice, 71
Main Repertoire Committee (Glavrepetkom),
    171
Markin, V., 56
Markish, Perets, 67, 144, 149
marriages, arranged, 105, 176
Martov, Yulii, 27, 31
Marx, Karl, 38, 193n38
Marxism, 48, 90
Maskilic culture, 52, 185, 196n107
matchmakers, 1, 105, 177
May Day, 29–30, 35; international character
    of, 42; living newspapers and, 78; parades,
    39; Passover as more popular holiday, 37;
    theatrical trials on, 101
"Mayn tsavoe" [My will] (song), 109–110
"Mayse mit Shmerlen, A" [A story with
    Shmerl] (short story), 50–52
melamed/melamdim (*khaydorim* instructors),
    15–16, 88, 98
melodrama, 130, 136, 140, 141, 169
Mendele Moykher Sforim (Sholem Abramo-
    vich), 67, 80, 170, 183, 210n15; taught in
    Soviet Yiddish schools, 19; theater and, 73
Mensheviks, 27, 31
merchant class, 49, 101
Meserl, Dos [The knife] (Aleichem), 74, 76
"Meydele in di yorn, A" [An old maid] (song),
    132, 133
migration, urban, 59, 122, 147, 159, 209n3
Mikhailovsky, Vladimir, 154
Mikhoels, Solomon, 71, 201n22
"Mikva" [Ritual Bath] (Bronner), 152–53
mikves (ritual baths), 3–4, 7, 152–53
Milner, M., 130
minorities, national, 47, 48
Minsk, 14, 55, 65, 72, 78, 96–98
Mirele Efros (Gordin), 73
Mitn ponim tsum khazer [Turn your face to-
    ward the pig] (Dobrushin), 84–85
"Mizinke oysgegebn, Di" [I married off my
    youngest daughter] (song), 107, 175
modernization, xx, 72, 118

heroes in literary works, 101; "Jewish question" and, 160; Jews as, 90; nationality and, 121; Potemkin villages and, 60; Russian urban migrants, 144, 146; workers in relation to, 89. *See also* kulaks

pedkorn (pedagogical correspondents), 56

Perets, Itskhok Leybush, 67, 71, 73, 80, 102, 183

Petlyura, Symon, 27

Petrograd, *104*, 107

pigs, breeding of, 121, 160, 207n35. *See also* pork, as "kosher" food

Pilsudskii, Gen. Jozef, 27

Pilyava (Ukrainian shtetl), 12

Pinsky, David, 73, 101

Pioner [Pioneer] (periodical), 49, *51, 53;* oral newspapers and, 80; worker correspondents and, 56, 58, 59

"Plach u beregov Amura" [The lament of Israel on the bank of the Amur] (musical piece), 169

playwrights, 84, 138

Poalei Zion (Poyley Tsien), 27, 64, 93, 199n56

poetry, xvii, 108–109

pogroms, 44, 45, 91, 112, 163; in civil war, 158; films condemning, 165; rabbis accused of abetting, 151, 183; in tsarist era, 158, 165, 183

Poincaré, Raymond, 31

Poland, xv, 2, 27, 131, 187n7

Poles, 42, 188n11

politics, international, 82–83

pork, as "kosher" food, xiii–xiv, 182, 185, 207n35. *See also* pigs, breeding of

Potemkin culture, 60, 69, 122, 125

Poyley Tsien (Poalei Zion), 27, 64, 93, 199n56

Pravda (newspaper), 54, 65, 198n22

priests, Christian, 4, 5, 11, 150–52, 156, 158. *See also* Orthodox Church, Russian

Prison Labor (film), 166

Proiskhozhdenie iudeiskoi i khristianskoi paskhi [The origins of Jewish Passover and Christian Easter] (Nikolsky), 150

proletariat, xvi, 29, 30, 183

Proletarisher emes [Proletarian truth] (newspaper), 56

propaganda, xix, 4, 52, 183; across-the-board negation, 83; antireligious, 2, 18, 59, 91, 92, 149–58, 182, 185; antisemitism as target of, 163–70; buffoonery and humor in service of, 82; categories of, 149; "enemies in our midst" theme, 91, 152, 183; equal opportunity as theme, 64; literacy campaigns and,

46, 54; literature and, 101–103, 149; methods of, 28; popular reception of, 122–24; positive and negative elements of, 57; songs and, xx, 34–35, 106–107, 116, 122, 129, 141, 175, 179; theater as vehicle of, 71, 98, 104–105. *See also* ideology, Soviet

proverbs, 24

Prozorovsky, Boris, 170, 171, 214n102

Pulner, Ivan, 66

Purim, 37

Pushkin, Alexander, 68, 76

rabbis, 4, 5, 57, 193n38; accused of abetting pogroms, 151, 183; closing of synagogues and, 7; Hassidic, 59; as *lishentsy*, 61; propaganda against, 150–52; in shtetlach, 36; songs about, 175; in Soviet history of Passover, 29; Soviet ideology and, 11, 33; teaching method of, 120; theatrical attacks on, 86–89, 101; wedding ceremonies and, 136, 137. *See also* Judaism

Rabinowich, Alexander. *See* Aleichem, Sholem

Rabochii klub [Worker's club] (magazine), 100, 103

radio, 122, 126

Rafal'skii, Mikhail, 72

ration cards, 3

Ratnbildung [Soviet education] (periodical), 36, 37

Razin, Stepan, 110

Razumnyi, Alexander, 165

"Red and Black" (song), 180

Red Army, xx, 30, 107, 118–19, 126–30, 141

"Red Dayenu" (song), 38

Red Freedom Songs (song collection), 107–108

Red Haggadah/Passover, xix, 27–30, *28, 30–33,* 33–35; popular reception of, 39; songs, 37–38

religion, xiii, xix, 2, 38; nationality and, 3, 109–110; opponents of Soviet regime and, 35; "pattern stories" rejecting, 57; songs against, xx; "Soviet and kosher" concept, 35–43; theatrical criticism of, 84–89; urban nostalgia for traditions of, 157. *See also* Judaism; Orthodox Church, Russian

Remember Their Faces (film), 166

Reznik, Lipe, 72

Robeson, Paul, 175

Rokiskisk (Lithuanian shtetl), 73

romance, songs of, 132–33, 141

Romania, xv

Romanov (Ukrainian shtetl), 42, 145

Rosenblum, L., 68

Rosenfeld, Moris, 108

Rosh Hashanah, xiv, 37; living newspapers and, 78; Russian-language propaganda against, 154, 156; in song, 179; Soviet Jewish schools and, 20; theatrical trials against, 96; Yiddish-language propaganda against, 20–21, *22*, 23–24, *25*, 26–27

Rothstein, Robert, 170, 171

Royte nodl, Dos [The red needle] (tailors' journal), 55

Royte velt, Di [The red world] (periodical), 36

Rozental, Moshe, 96

Rubin, Shlomo, 73

Russia, post-Soviet, xiv, 142, 157, 161, 181, 185

Russia, tsarist, 3, 47, 49, 89, 118; antisemitism in, 161; Jews restricted and persecuted by, 91; pogroms in, 158, 165, 183; song about, 174–75

Russian history, heroes of, 110

Russian language, xv, xix, 100; antireligious propaganda in, 149–58; assimilated Jews and, 143; classical poetry in, 68; decline of Yiddish culture and, 141, 144, 184; films in, 166; Jewish literature in, xvii; Jewish popular culture in, xxi; lack of proficiency in, 48, 72; literacy courses in, 45, 47; modernization and, xx; newspapers associated with, 137; in *Pravda*, 54; press in, 64–65; school instruction in, 17; songs in, 111, 130, 170–81; theatrical trials in, 93, 94, 165; transliteration of, xxiii; Yiddish literature in translation, 148–49; Yiddish mixed with, 44, 88–89, 124–25, 139–40, 183

Russian Republic, in USSR, 72

Russo-Japanese War (1904–1905), 126

Sabbath, xiv, xxiii, 5, 7; candles lit for, 67, 77; evening prayers, 40; Jewish and Christian, 150; six-day work week and, 3, 12; theatrical trials against, 93, 94, 99; travel on, 36; urban migrants and, 146

Sabbath: What One Says about It and Where It Indeed Came From (Lurye), 5, 6

samogon (homemade alcohol), 99

sanitary conditions, 152–53

"Sarah: A Jewish Shtetl Melody" (song), 170–71, 181

satire, 125

Schneerson, Rebbe Joseph Isaac, 14

schools: antireligious performances in, xix, 3, 39, 41; competition between, 19; literacy courses in, 54; Soviet versus Jewish traditional, 14–20, 184; synagogues transformed

into, 14. *See also kheyder/khaydorim* (Jewish primary schools)

secularism/secularization, 3, 7, 11, 43

Seekers of Happiness (film), 166–70

sexual equality, 49, 57

sexuality, 171, 173

Shalom theater, 106

Shepetovka (Ukraine), 100

Shevchenko, Taras, 76

"Sheyn, bin ikh sheyn" [Beautiful, I am beautiful] (song), 107–108, 177

"Shimele" (Rosenblum), 67–68

Shlosberg, B., 52

Shneer, David, 46

Shneerson, Rabbi Yosef, 151, 183

Shneur Zalman of Lyady, 211n27, 214n103

shop owners, 61, 89

shoykhet/shokhtim (kosher butchers), 3, 7, 60; depicted as reactionary figures, 57, 70; as *lishentsy*, 61; theatrical attacks on, 86, 97, 99. *See also* kosher food

Shrayer, I., 89

Shtern, Der [The star] (Kharkov newspaper), 65, 66

Shtern [Star] (periodical), 36

shtetlach, xv, xviii, 180; Communist institutions in, xix; Kaslovich as general name for, 85; languages spoken in, 48; living newspapers in, 78; May Day celebrations in, 42; merchant class in, 49; nostalgia for, 178; Party campaign against shtetl life, 71; religious belief in, 36–37; resettlement to agricultural colonies, 56; in Russian songs, 170; sanitary conditions in, 58–59; theater in, 72–73; urban migrants and lifestyle of, 59, 144–45

Shtrayml, Der [The fur-trimmed hat] (Perets), 102

Shulzhenko, Klavdiia, 179

Shveyprom, 89

Siddur, 69

Sito, Fayvl, 84, 206n24

Six-Day War, 66

Skhorokhof, 89

socialism, 5, 23, 57; antisemitism as antithesis of, 159; legacy of, 185; songs about, 111; theater and, 90

socialist realism, 60, 63, 102, 148

songs, 15, 23–24, 106–107, 140–42; about agricultural settlements, 119–26; *chastushkes* (ditties), 116–19, 134, 206–207n24; Jewish images in Russian songs, 170–81; parodies of religious songs, 34–35; Red Army songs,

Utesov, Leonid, 144, 148, 173–78, 215n110
Utkin, Joseph, 147

Vaad Rabbanei SSR (Committee of Rabbis of the USSR), 14
"Varshavianka" (song), 111
Veidlinger, Jeffrey, 72, 74, 137, 146, 187n10
Veitsblit, I., 36, 66
Veker (newspaper), 78
Vergelis, Aron, 63
Verite, Isaac, 85
Vevyorke, Avrom, 82, 84
village correspondents, 55
Vinnitsa Medical School, 104
Vintshevsky, Moris, 108
Vitebsk, 94
Vitebsker arbeter [Vitebsk worker] (newspaper), 55
Voroshilov, Kliment, 118–19
voting rights, loss of, 100
Vrangel, Baron P. N., 27
VTsIK (All-Russian Central Executive Committee), 118

Warshavsky, Mark, 107, 108, 175
wedding songs, 131, 176–77
Weinryb, Bernard, 158
Weisbeyn, Lazar, 173
Western countries, 2
What Every Militant Godless Should Know (Soviet brochure), 7
White Army (counterrevolutionaries), 28, 35, 91, 163; antisemitism and, 154, 182–83; defeated in civil war, 195n86
women, 7, 90; agricultural labor and, 121; in Bolshevik moral fables, 50–52; love ditties and, 118–19; *mikves* (ritual baths) and, 152–53; personal transformation stories of liberation, 57–58; religious belief among, 37; women's emancipation in songs, 120–21, 124
Wood, Elizabeth, 93, 213n86
worker correspondents movement, 55–64, 191n33
working class, 27, 88; antireligious propaganda and, 11; as heroes in literary works, 101; peasants in relation to, 89; religion and, 5, 150, 156, 157
World War I, 126
World War II, 45, 68, 157, 165; German invasion of Soviet Union, 66; songs about, 180; Yiddish-speaking Jewish communities destroyed in, 182
writers, xx, 46, 69

Yafe, I. I., 85, 90, 92
Yakhin, I., 21
Yakov, M., 24, 26
Yaroslavsky, Emelian, 150
yeshibotniks (yeshiva students), 97–98, 204n74
yeshivas, 93, 97, 120, 204n74
Yiddish language, 144, 183; antireligious propaganda in, 153–54; authorities' knowledge of, 16–17, 36; films in, 166; "Hebraisms" in, 128, 139, 141, 205n2; literacy courses in, xix, 45, 46–54; oral history respondents and, xviii–xix; "purified," 125, 139, 141, 183, 205–206n2; reforms of, xv; Russian and foreign literature in translation, 68; Russian mixed with, 44, 88–89, 124–25, 139–40, 183; school instruction in, xv, 14–20; spoken by post-Soviet Jews, 1; transliteration of, xxiii; Ukrainian dialect, xiii, xxiii, 135. *See also* folk songs; literature, Yiddish; songs; theater, Yiddish
Yiddish-language press: antisemitism as subject of, 165; journals and periodicals, xix, 35–36, *51*, *53*, 54; newspapers, 4, 54–56, 59–61, 63, 65–66, 78; worker correspondents and, 55–56
"Yidishe mame, A" [My Jewish mama] (song), 130
Yom Kippur, xiv, xix, 12, 37, 57; anarchist ceremonies against, 194n74; *kapoyres* custom, 155, 212n51; Russian-language propaganda against, 155–57; theatrical trials against, 93, 94–95, 98–99, 101–102; Yiddish-language propaganda against, 20–21, *22*, *23–24*, *25*, 26–27
Young Pioneers, 11–12, 39, 50, 61, 66, 100
youth culture, xvii, 69
Yudenich, Gen. N. N., 27
Yuditskii, A., 128, 130
Yunge gvardye (periodical), 59
Yunger leninets [The young Leninist] (periodical), 56
Yungvald [Young forest] (periodical), 49, 50, 55–56, 59

Zay greyt! [Be ready!] (newspaper), 56, 66
Zelik, L., 52
Zelikson, Sholem, 58
Zevin, Y. L., 14
Zharkovskiy, Evgenii, 176
Zhitomir, 65
Zindiker, Der [The sinner] (Asch), 71
Zionism, 17, 26, 27, 72, 143; Bolshevik literacy programs and, 47; compared to White gen-

ANNA SHTERNSHIS is Assistant Professor of Yiddish Language and Literature at the University of Toronto.